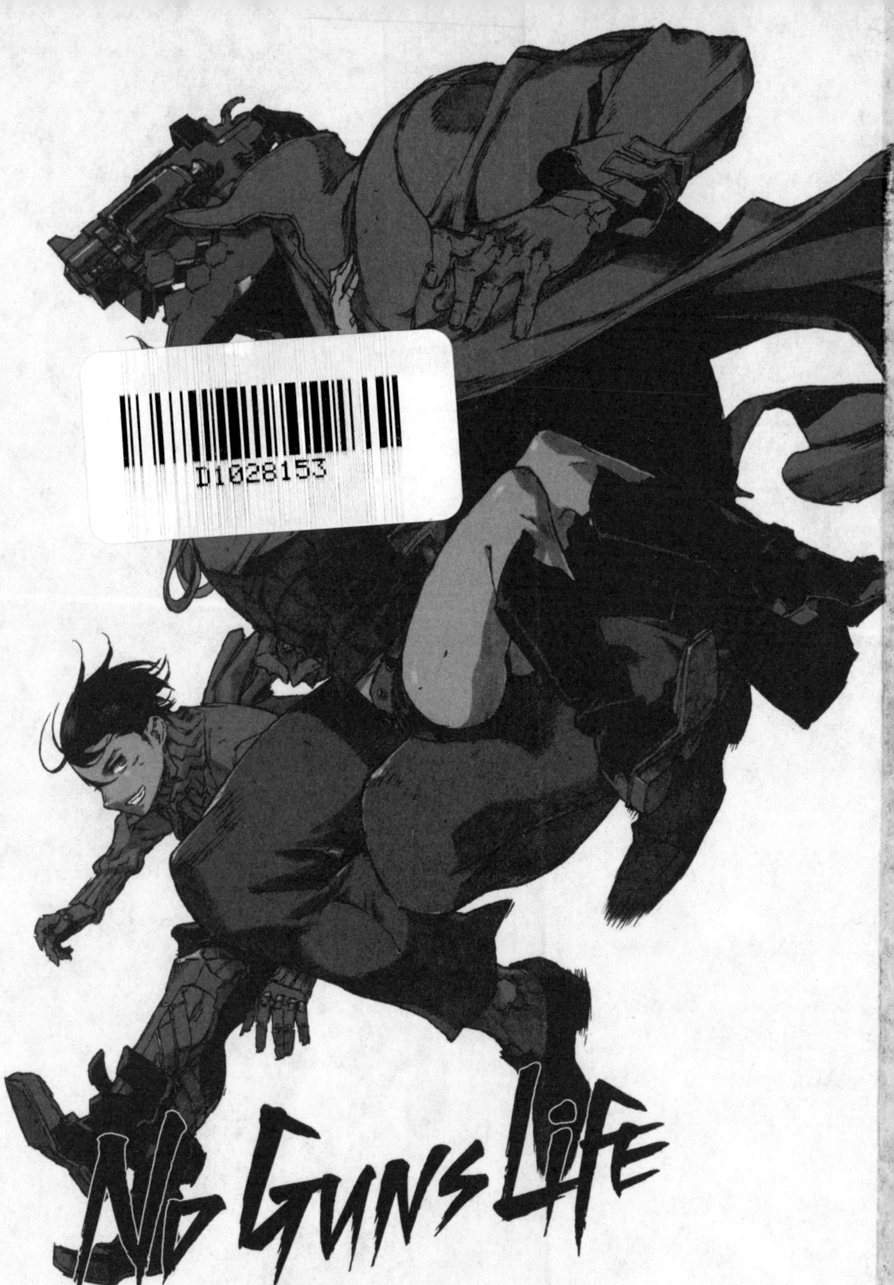

NO GUNS LIFE

10

TASUKU KARASUMA

CONTENTS

57
Essence

003

58
Fabrication

035

59
Relief

067

60
Release

101

61
Rebirth

135

62
Congestion

163

63
Unseal

193

NO GUNS LIFE

Chapter 57
Essence

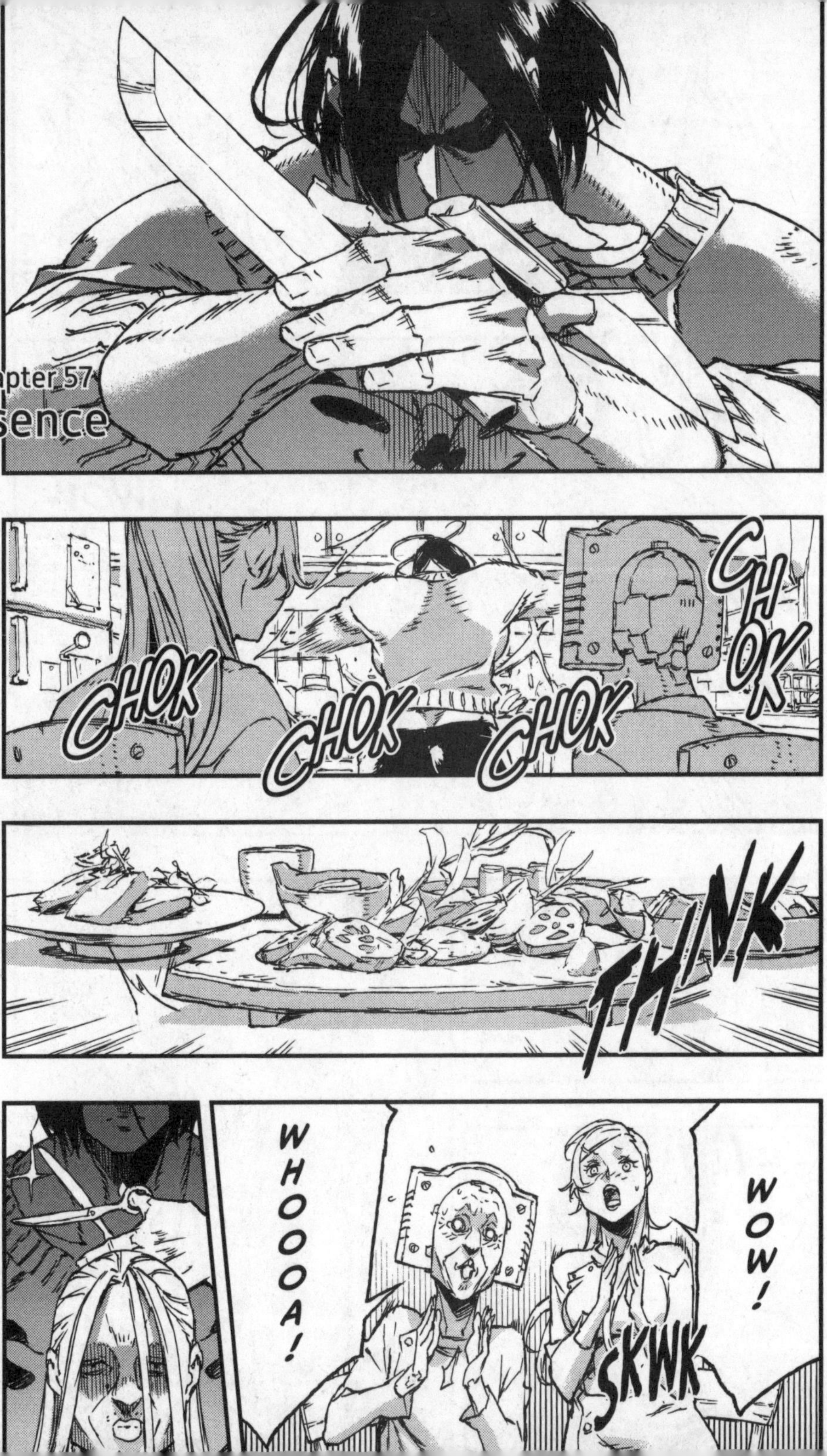
CHOK
CHOK
CHOK
CHOK
THINK
WOW!
SKWK
WHOOOA!

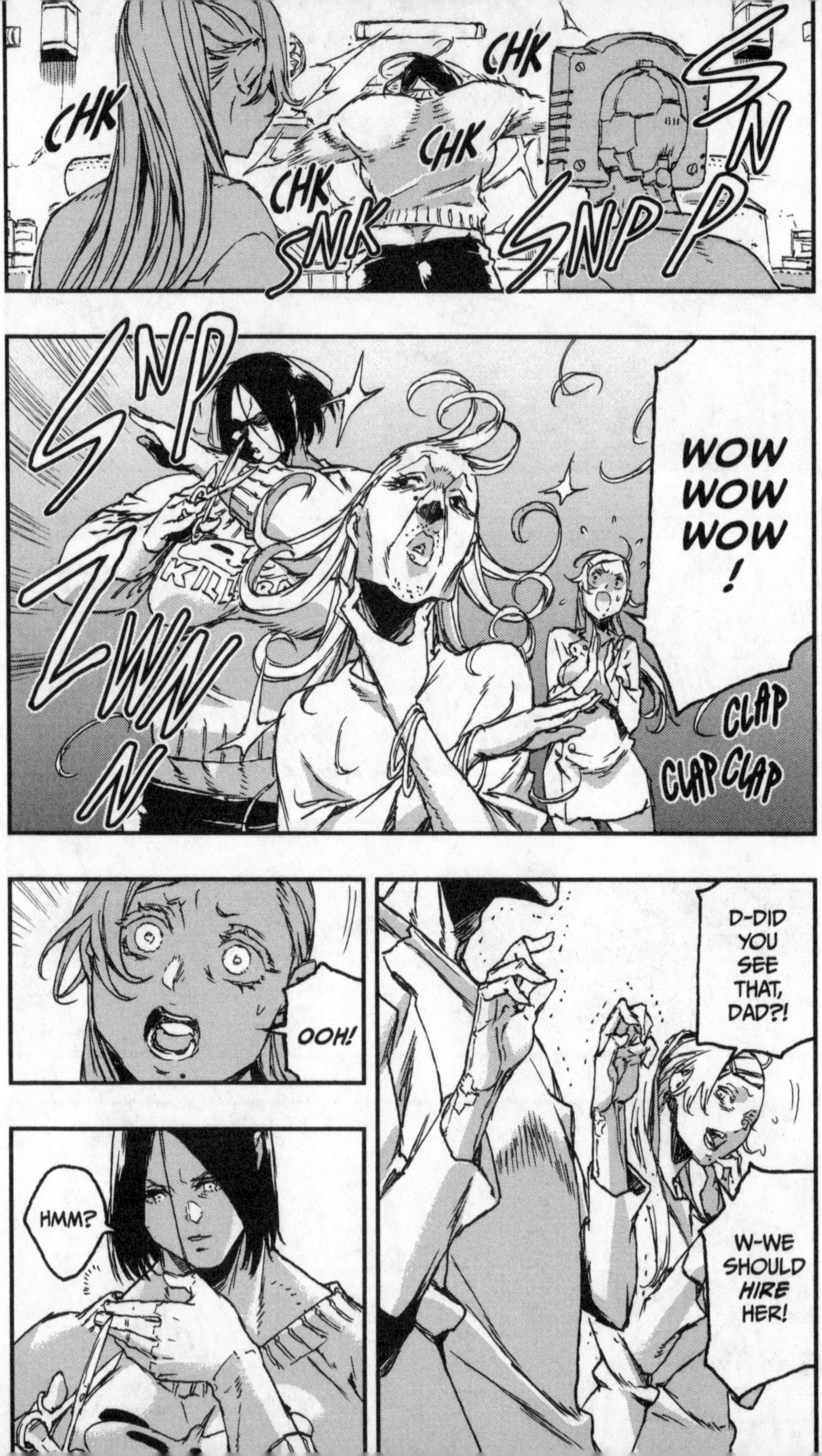
SNP
SNP P
CHK
CHK
CHK
SNK
CHK
WOW WOW WOW!
CLAP
CLAP CLAP
SNP
ZWNN
D-DID YOU SEE THAT, DAD?!
W-WE SHOULD *HIRE* HER!
OOH!
HMM?

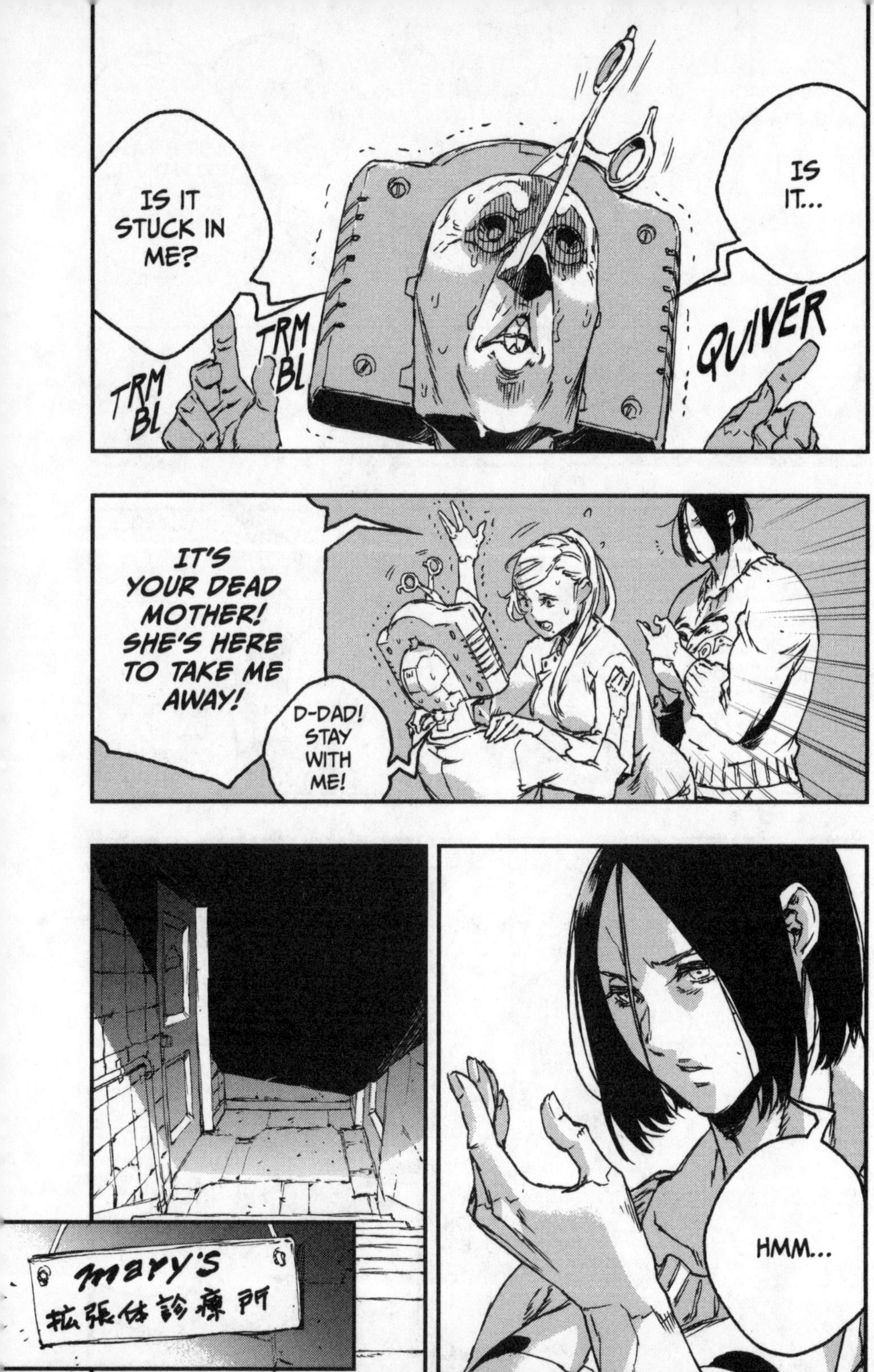
IS IT...
QUIVER
IS IT STUCK IN ME?
TRM BL
TRM BL
IT'S YOUR DEAD MOTHER! SHE'S HERE TO TAKE ME AWAY!
D-DAD! STAY WITH ME!
HMM...
Mary's
拡張体診療所

*Mary's Extension Clinic

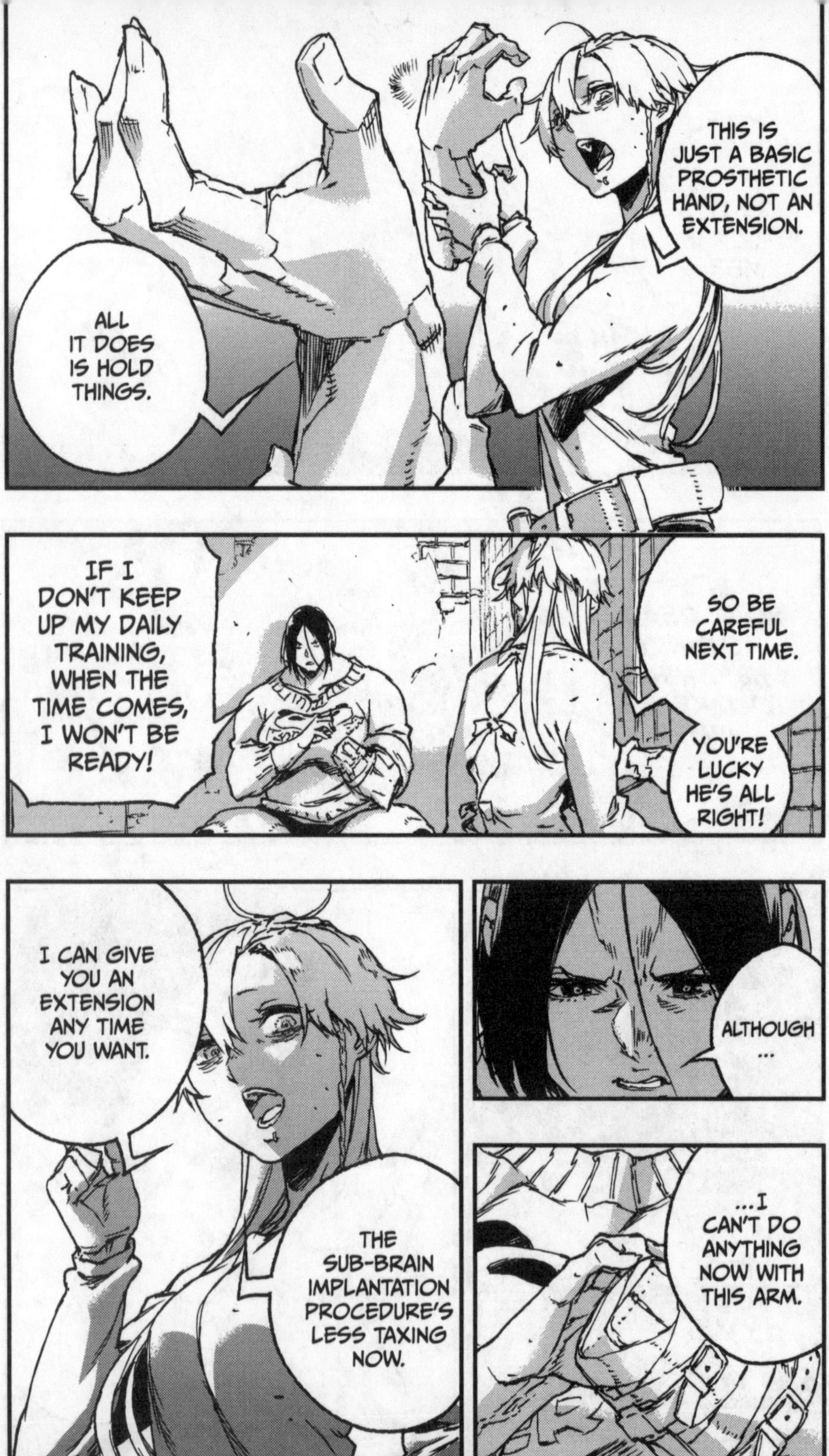
THIS IS JUST A BASIC PROSTHETIC HAND, NOT AN EXTENSION.
ALL IT DOES IS HOLD THINGS.
SO BE CAREFUL NEXT TIME.
YOU'RE LUCKY HE'S ALL RIGHT!
IF I DON'T KEEP UP MY DAILY TRAINING, WHEN THE TIME COMES, I WON'T BE READY!
ALTHOUGH ...
...I CAN'T DO ANYTHING NOW WITH THIS ARM.
I CAN GIVE YOU AN EXTENSION ANY TIME YOU WANT.
THE SUB-BRAIN IMPLANTATION PROCEDURE'S LESS TAXING NOW.

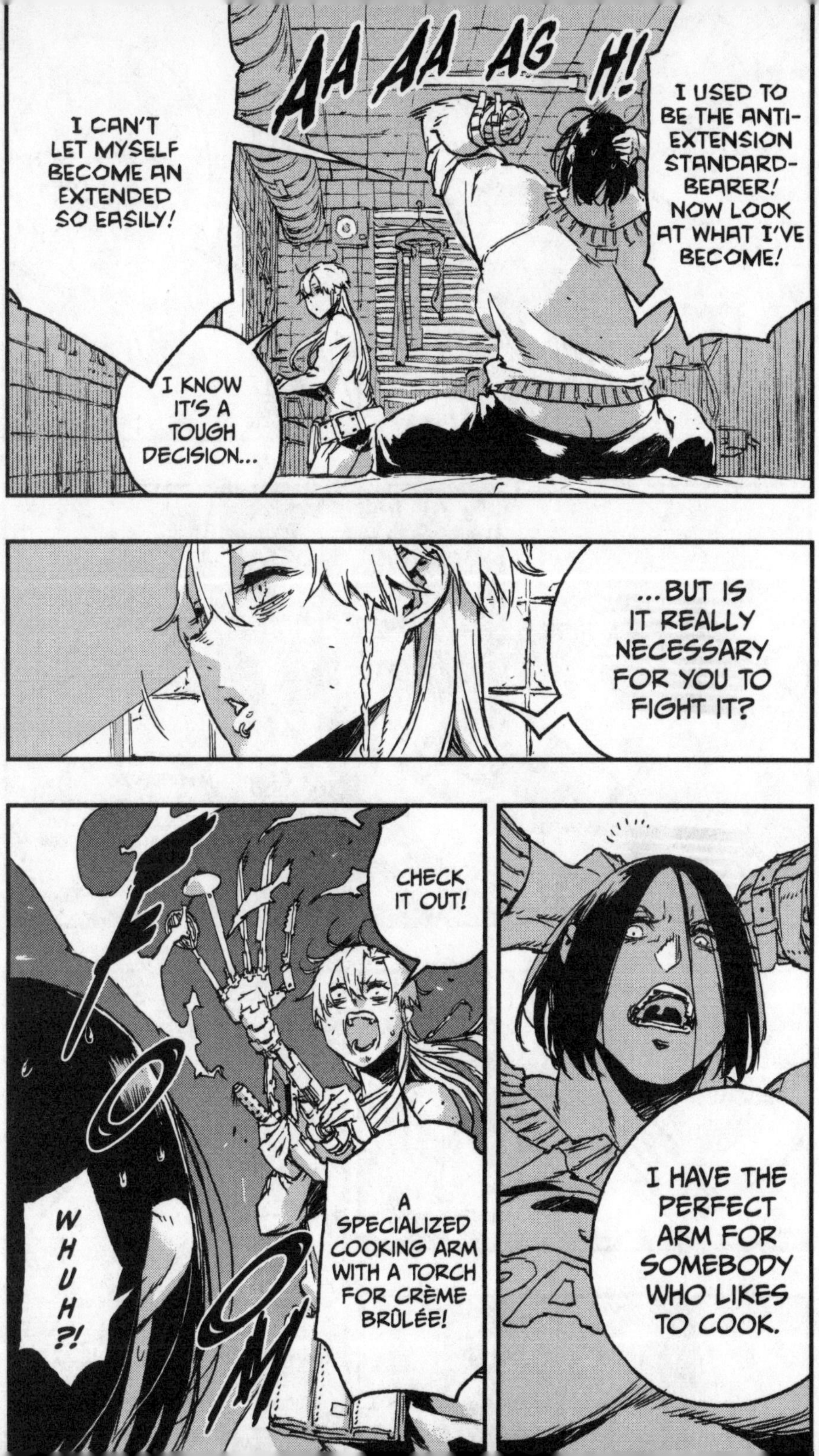
AAAAAGH!
I USED TO BE THE ANTI-EXTENSION STANDARD-BEARER! NOW LOOK AT WHAT I'VE BECOME!
I CAN'T LET MYSELF BECOME AN EXTENDED SO EASILY!
I KNOW IT'S A TOUGH DECISION...
...BUT IS IT REALLY NECESSARY FOR YOU TO FIGHT IT?
I HAVE THE PERFECT ARM FOR SOMEBODY WHO LIKES TO COOK.
CHECK IT OUT!
A SPECIALIZED COOKING ARM WITH A TORCH FOR CRÈME BRÛLÉE!
WHUH?!

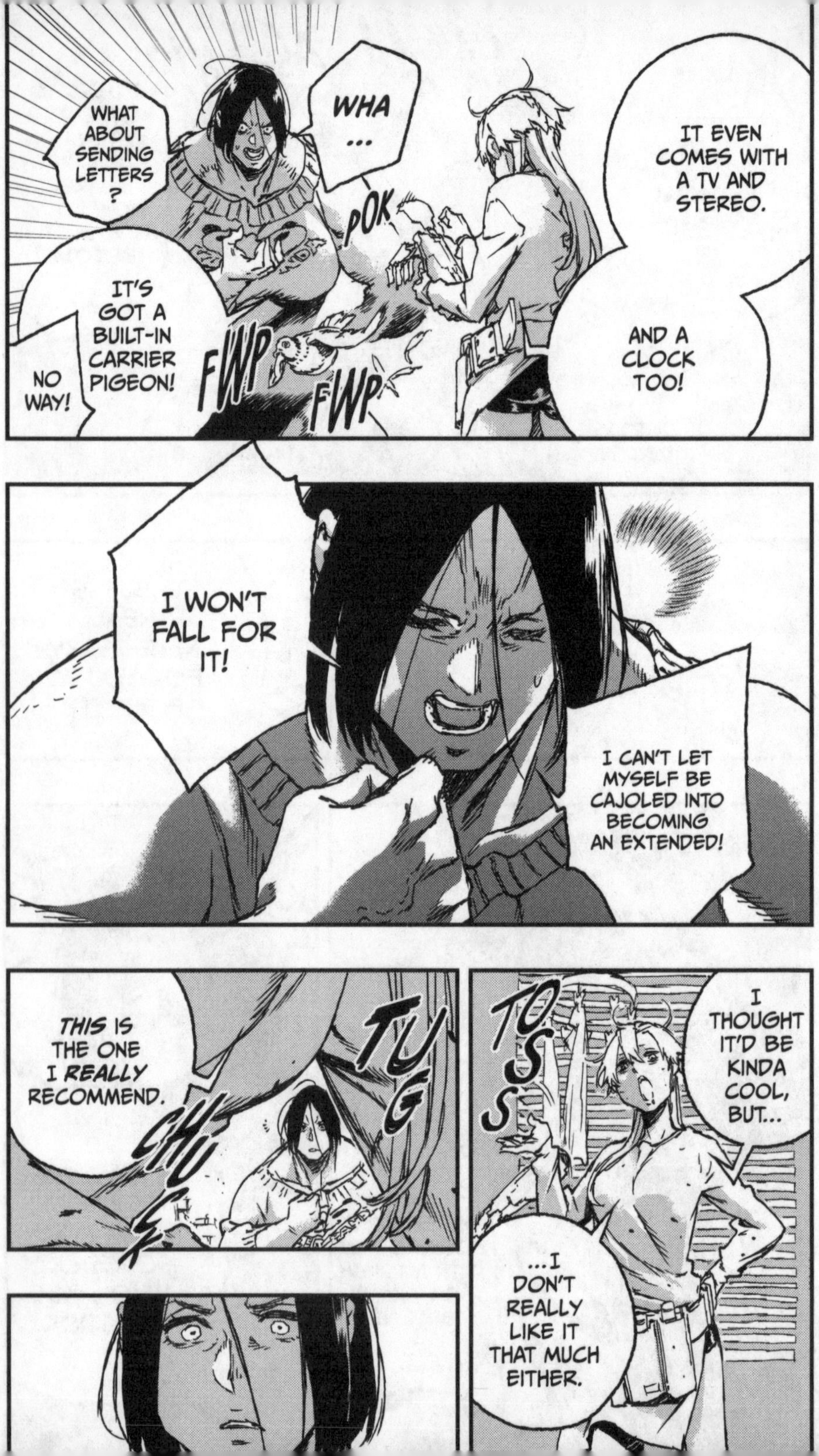
IT EVEN COMES WITH A TV AND STEREO.
AND A CLOCK TOO!
WHA ...
POK
WHAT ABOUT SENDING LETTERS ?
IT'S GOT A BUILT-IN CARRIER PIGEON!
FWP
FWP
NO WAY!
I WON'T FALL FOR IT!
I CAN'T LET MYSELF BE CAJOLED INTO BECOMING AN EXTENDED!
I THOUGHT IT'D BE KINDA COOL, BUT...
TOSS
...I DON'T REALLY LIKE IT THAT MUCH EITHER.
THIS IS THE ONE I *REALLY* RECOMMEND.
TUG
CHUCK

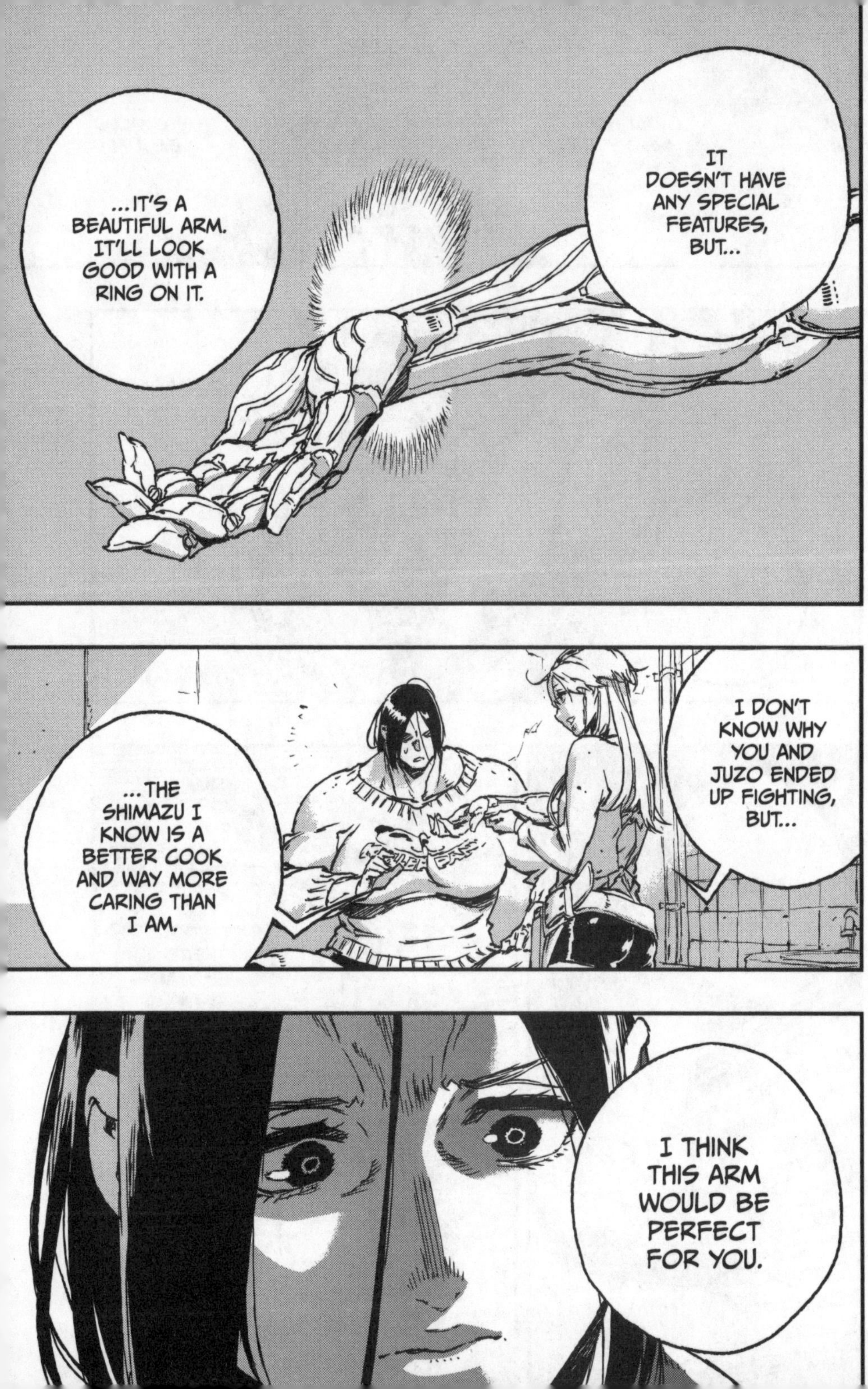
IT DOESN'T HAVE ANY SPECIAL FEATURES, BUT...
...IT'S A BEAUTIFUL ARM. IT'LL LOOK GOOD WITH A RING ON IT.
I DON'T KNOW WHY YOU AND JUZO ENDED UP FIGHTING, BUT...
...THE SHIMAZU I KNOW IS A BETTER COOK AND WAY MORE CARING THAN I AM.
I THINK THIS ARM WOULD BE PERFECT FOR YOU.

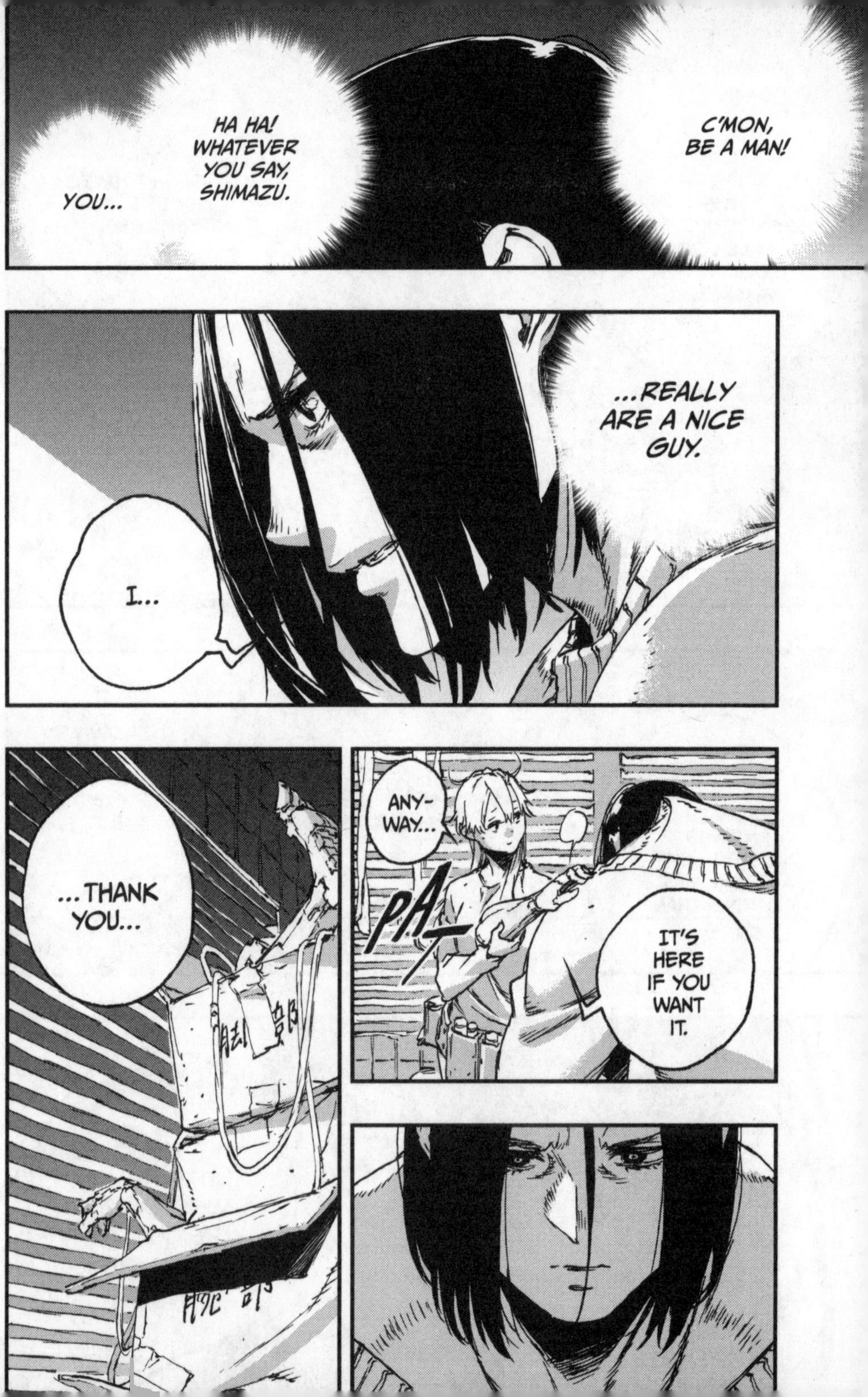
C'MON, BE A MAN!
HA HA! WHATEVER YOU SAY, SHIMAZU.
YOU...
...REALLY ARE A NICE GUY.
I...
ANY-WAY...
PAT
IT'S HERE IF YOU WANT IT.
...THANK YOU...

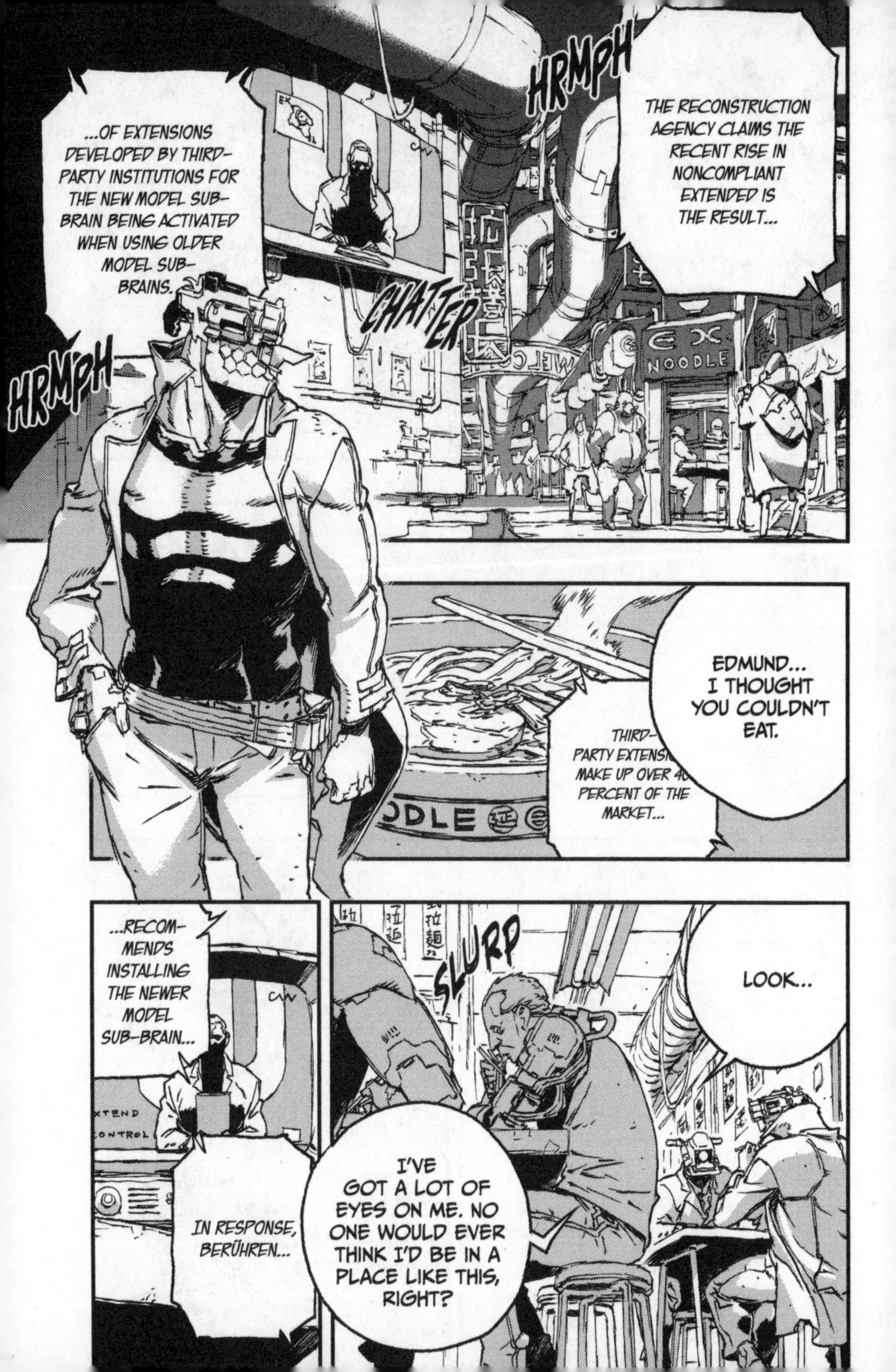
THE RECONSTRUCTION AGENCY CLAIMS THE RECENT RISE IN NONCOMPLIANT EXTENDED IS THE RESULT...
HRMPH
...OF EXTENSIONS DEVELOPED BY THIRD-PARTY INSTITUTIONS FOR THE NEW MODEL SUB-BRAIN BEING ACTIVATED WHEN USING OLDER MODEL SUB-BRAINS.
CHATTER
NOODLE
HRMPH
EDMUND... I THOUGHT YOU COULDN'T EAT.
THIRD-PARTY EXTENSI MAKE UP OVER 40 PERCENT OF THE MARKET...
LOOK...
SLURP
I'VE GOT A LOT OF EYES ON ME. NO ONE WOULD EVER THINK I'D BE IN A PLACE LIKE THIS, RIGHT?
...RECOMMENDS INSTALLING THE NEWER MODEL SUB-BRAIN...
IN RESPONSE, BERÜHREN...

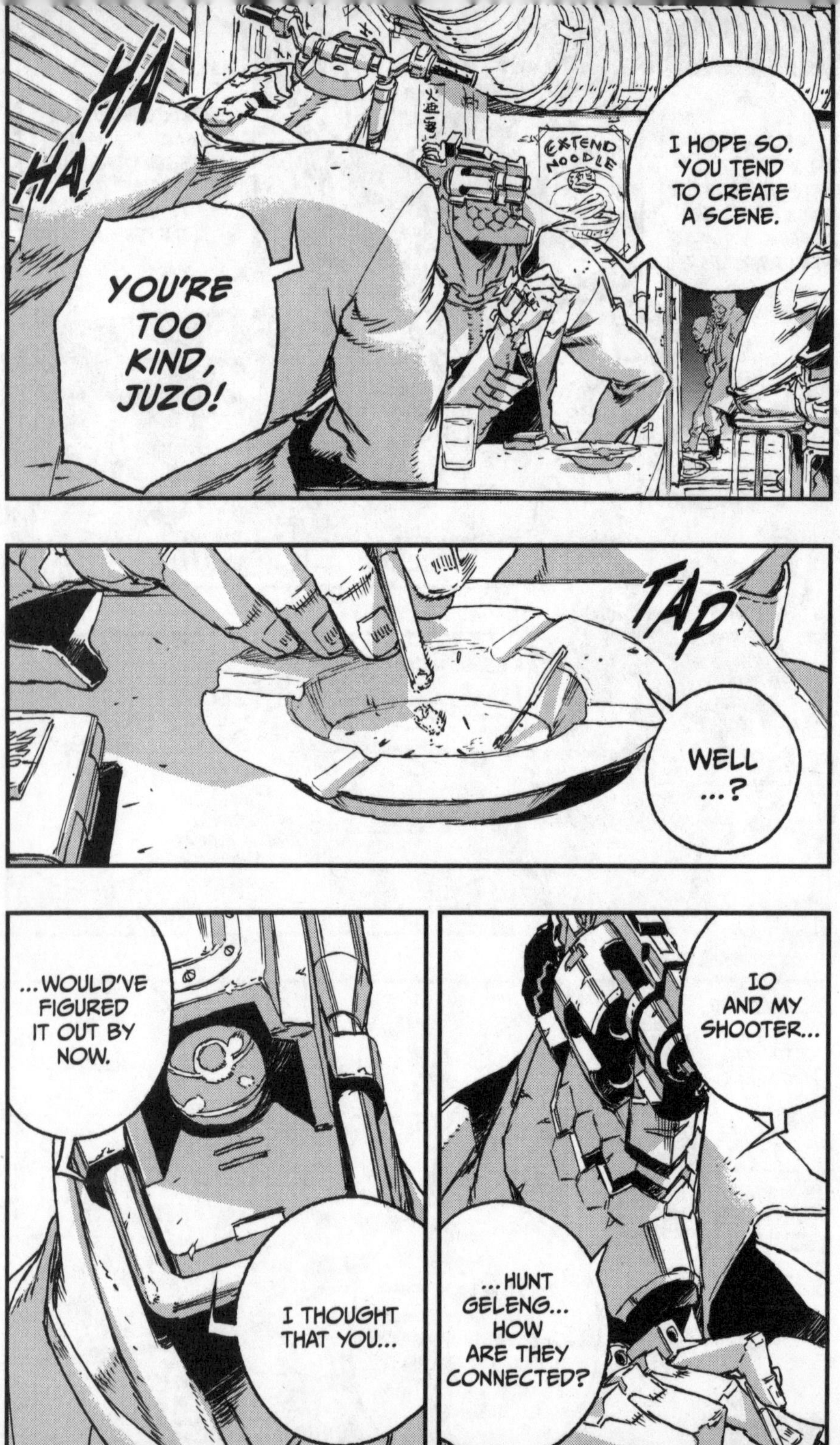
I HOPE SO. YOU TEND TO CREATE A SCENE.
EXTEND NOODLE
HA HA!
YOU'RE TOO KIND, JUZO!
TAP
WELL ...?
IO AND MY SHOOTER...
...HUNT GELENG... HOW ARE THEY CONNECTED?
I THOUGHT THAT YOU...
...WOULD'VE FIGURED IT OUT BY NOW.

THE MAN CLAIMING TO BE YOUR FORMER PARTNER...

...HUNT GELENG—HIS REAL NAME IS SUISO ARAHABAKI.

HE'S LIKE ARAHABAKI AND TETSURO— ONE OF THE GUYS WALKING AROUND...

...WITH THE DNA OF BERÜHREN CEO SOICHIRO ARAHABAKI.

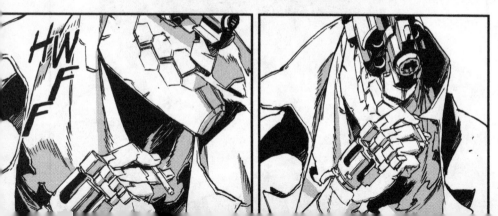

HW F F

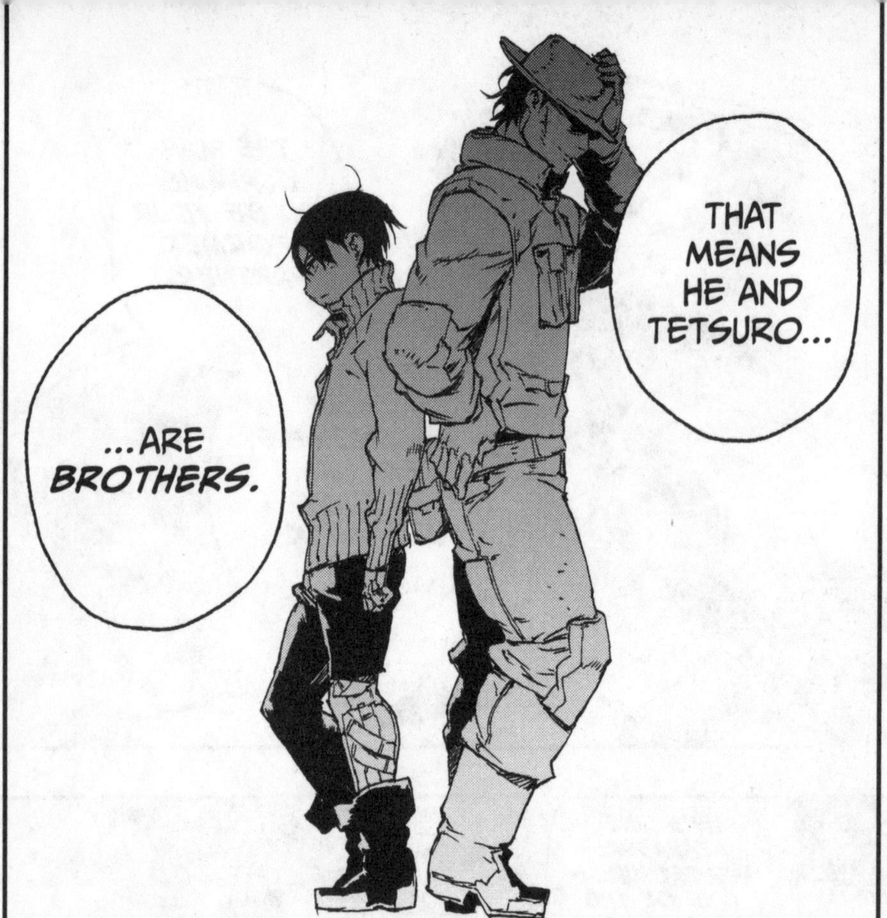
THAT MEANS HE AND TETSURO...
...ARE BROTHERS.

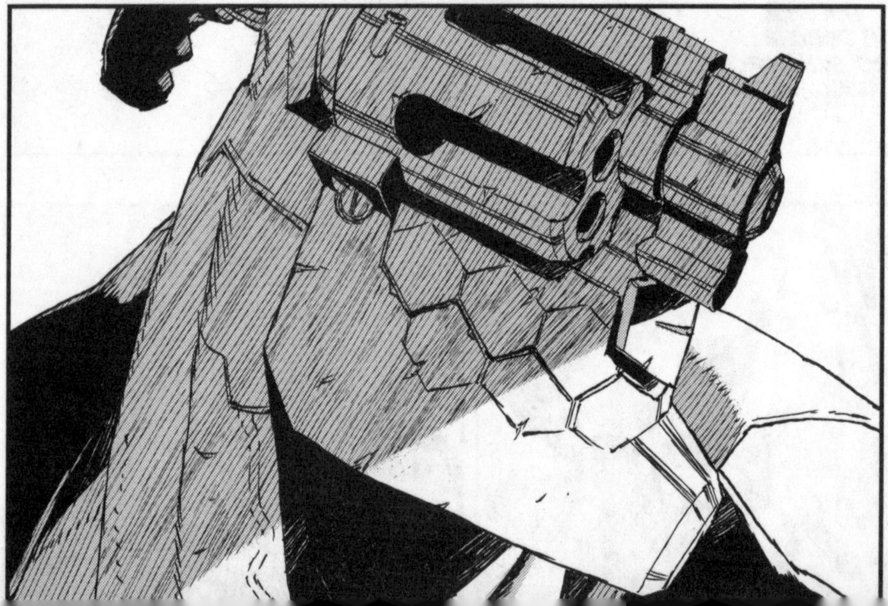

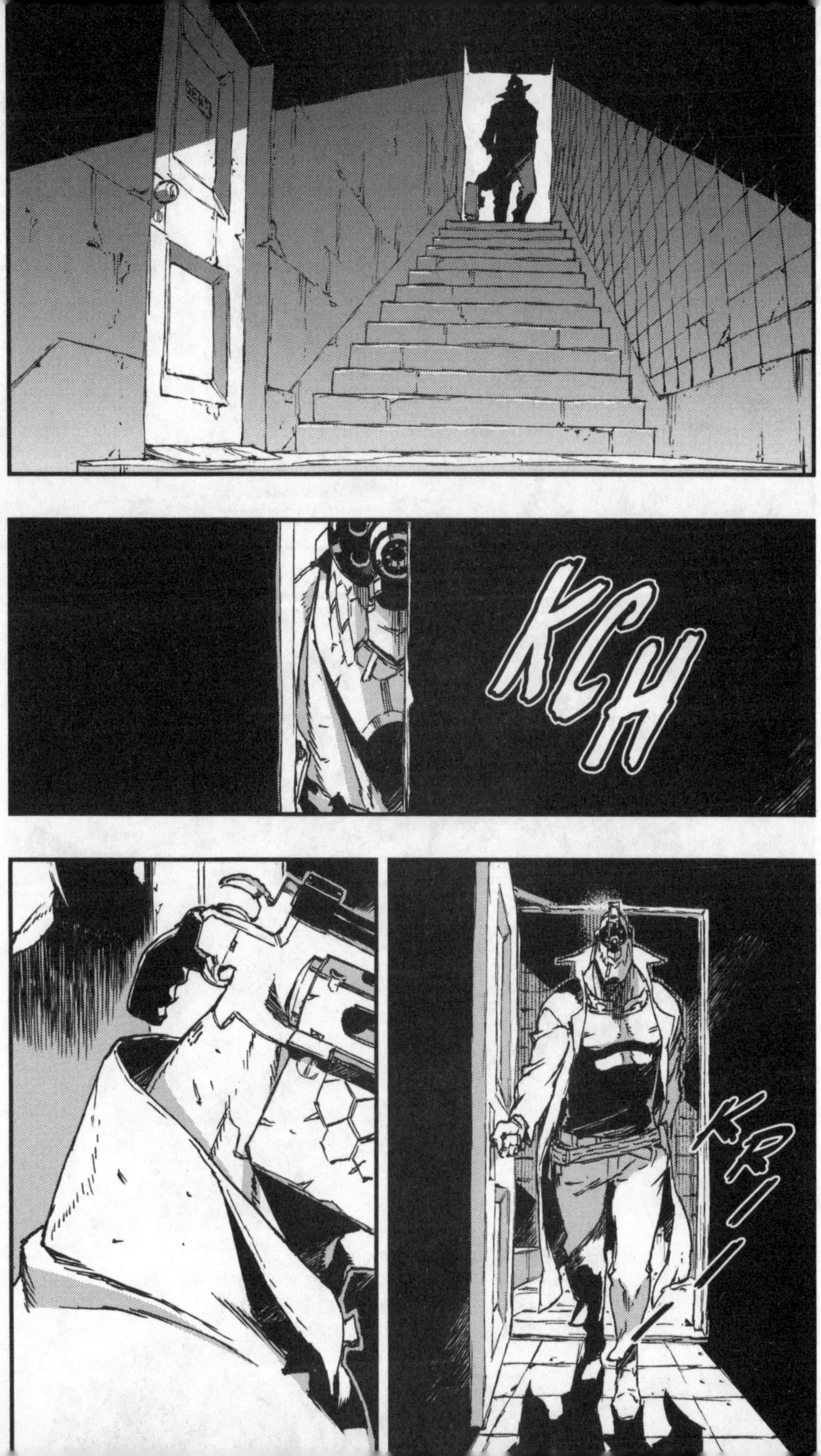
KCH
KRIII

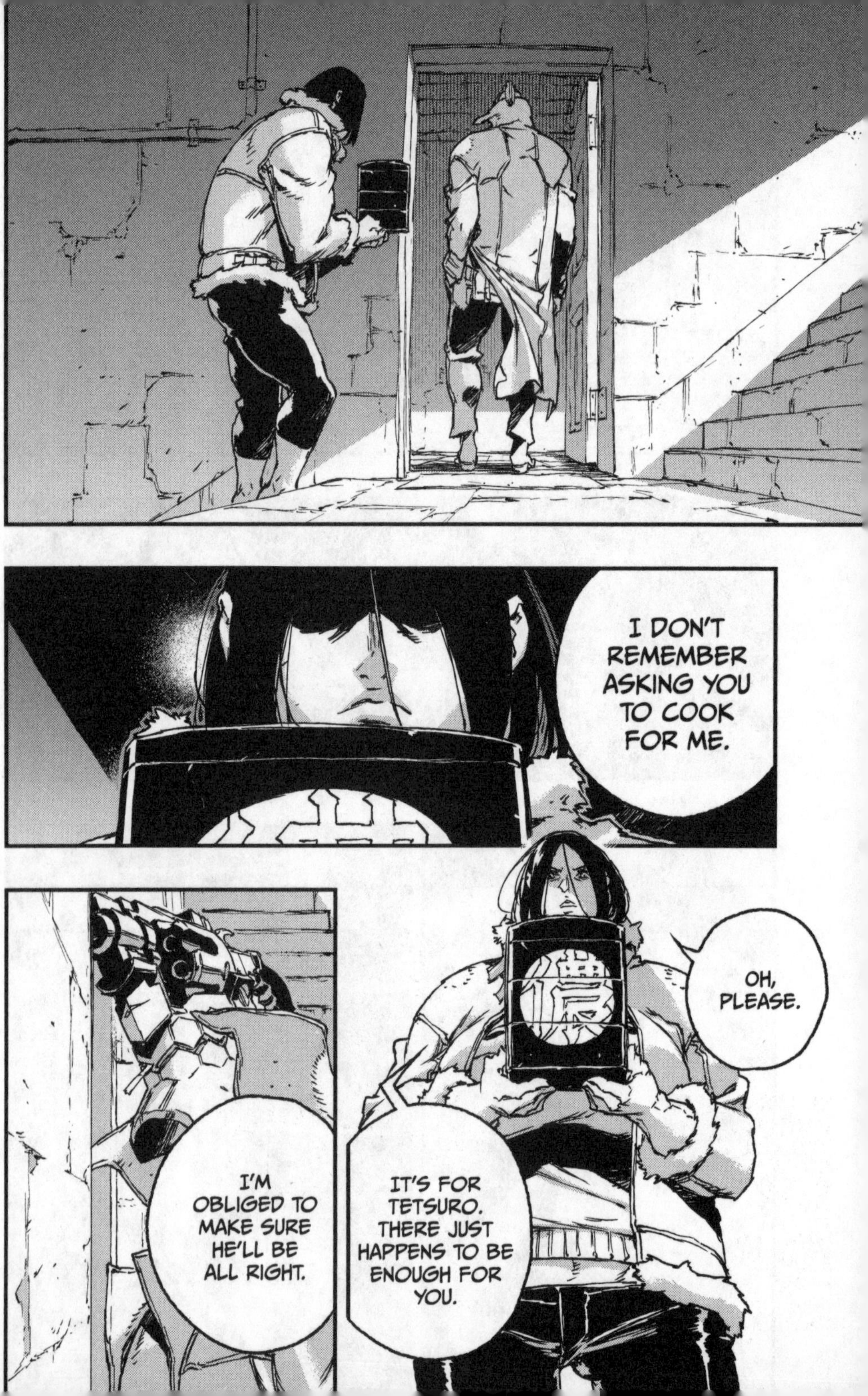
I DON'T REMEMBER ASKING YOU TO COOK FOR ME.
OH, PLEASE.
IT'S FOR TETSURO. THERE JUST HAPPENS TO BE ENOUGH FOR YOU.
I'M OBLIGED TO MAKE SURE HE'LL BE ALL RIGHT.

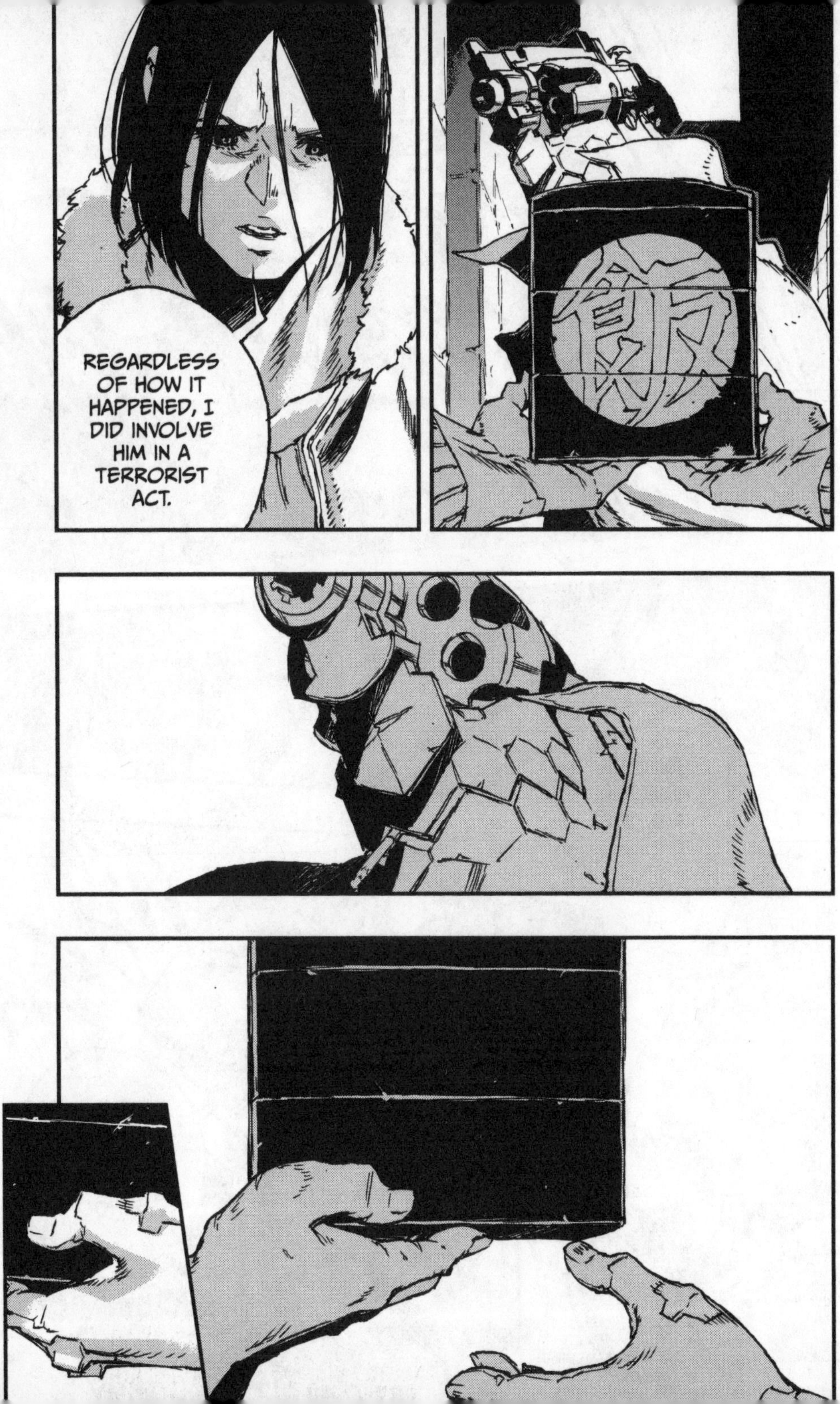
REGARDLESS OF HOW IT HAPPENED, I DID INVOLVE HIM IN A TERRORIST ACT.

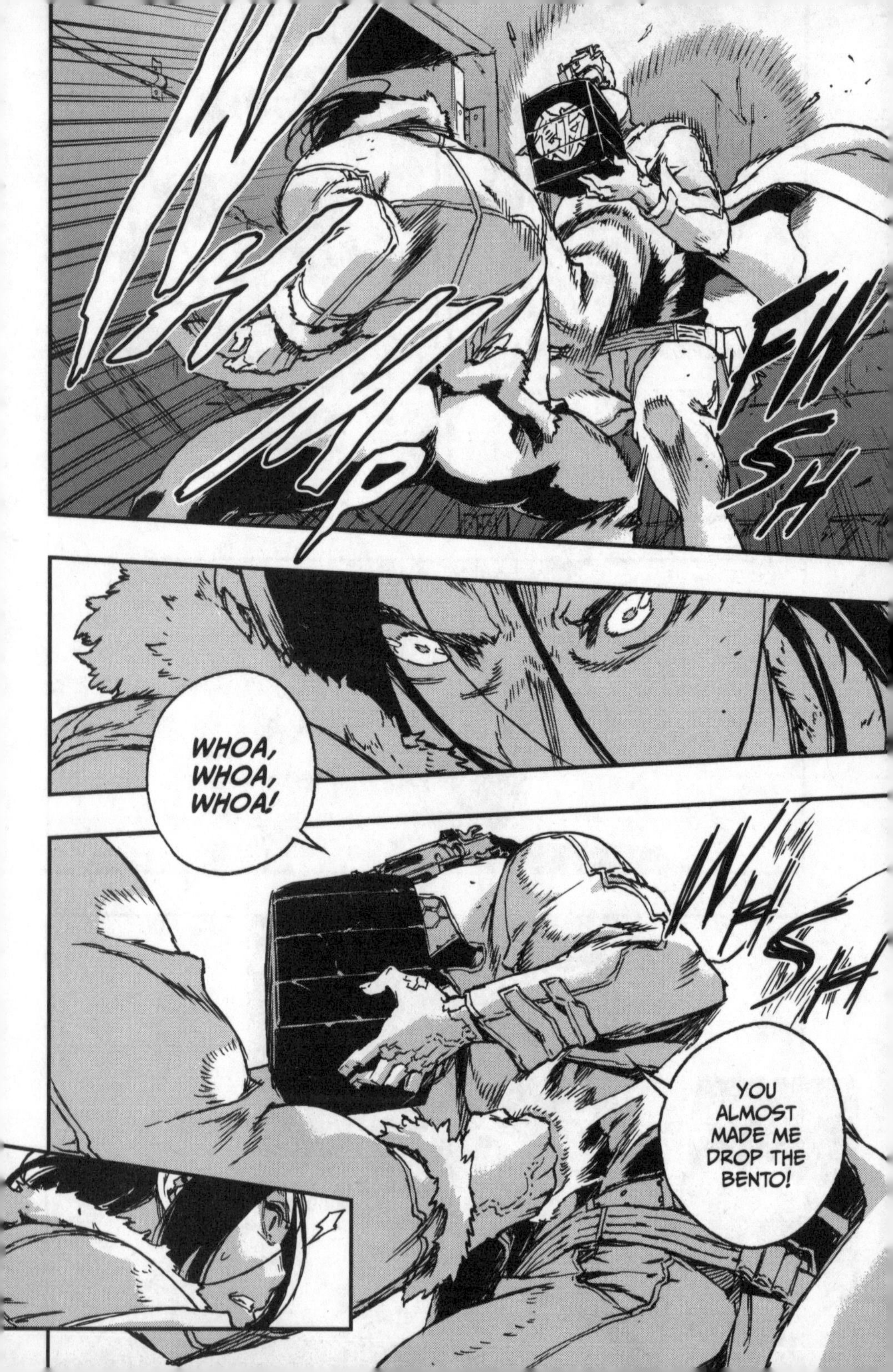
WHMP
FWSH
WHOA, WHOA, WHOA!
WHSH
YOU ALMOST MADE ME DROP THE BENTO!

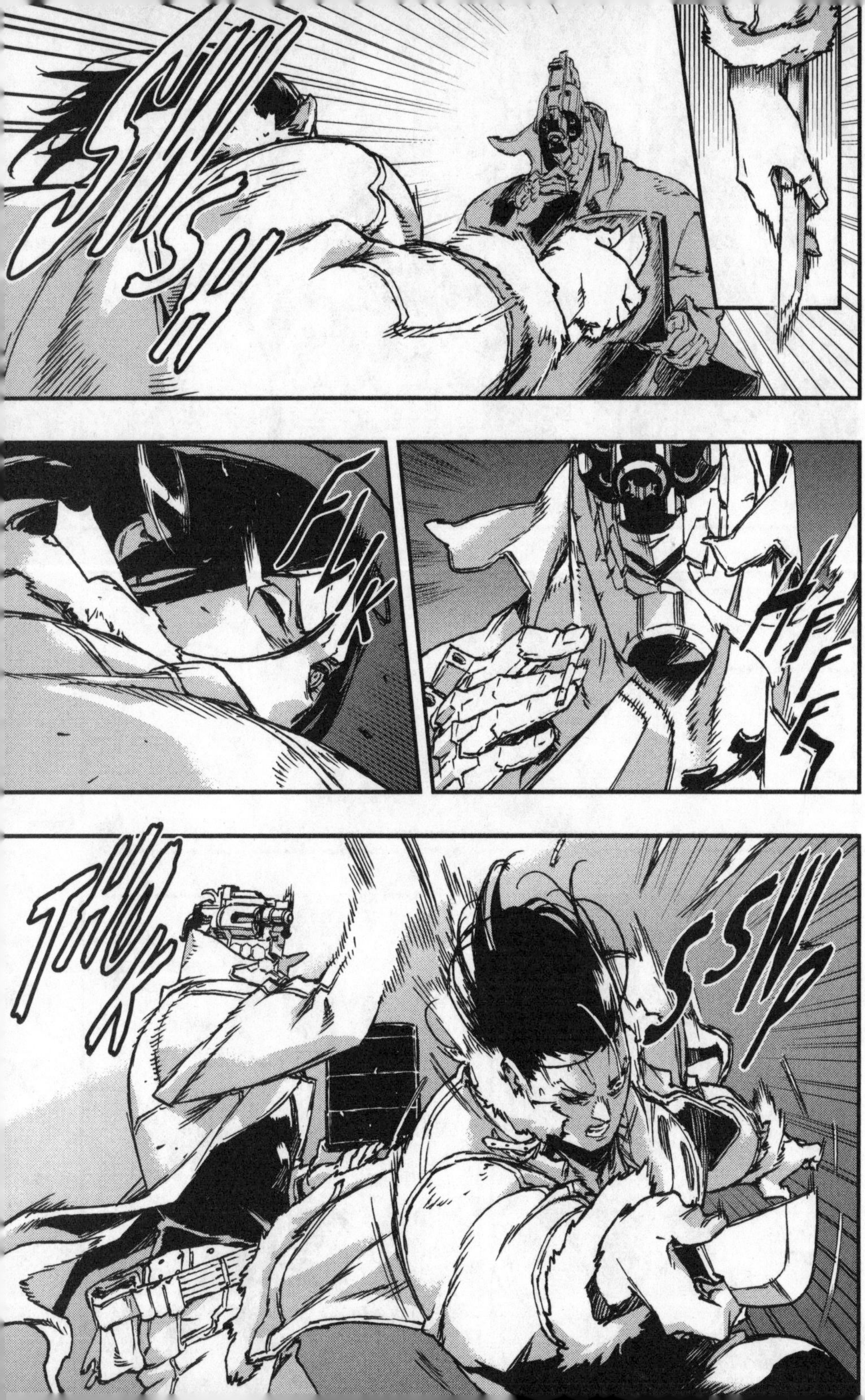
SHSH
HFFF
FLIK
SSHP
THUK

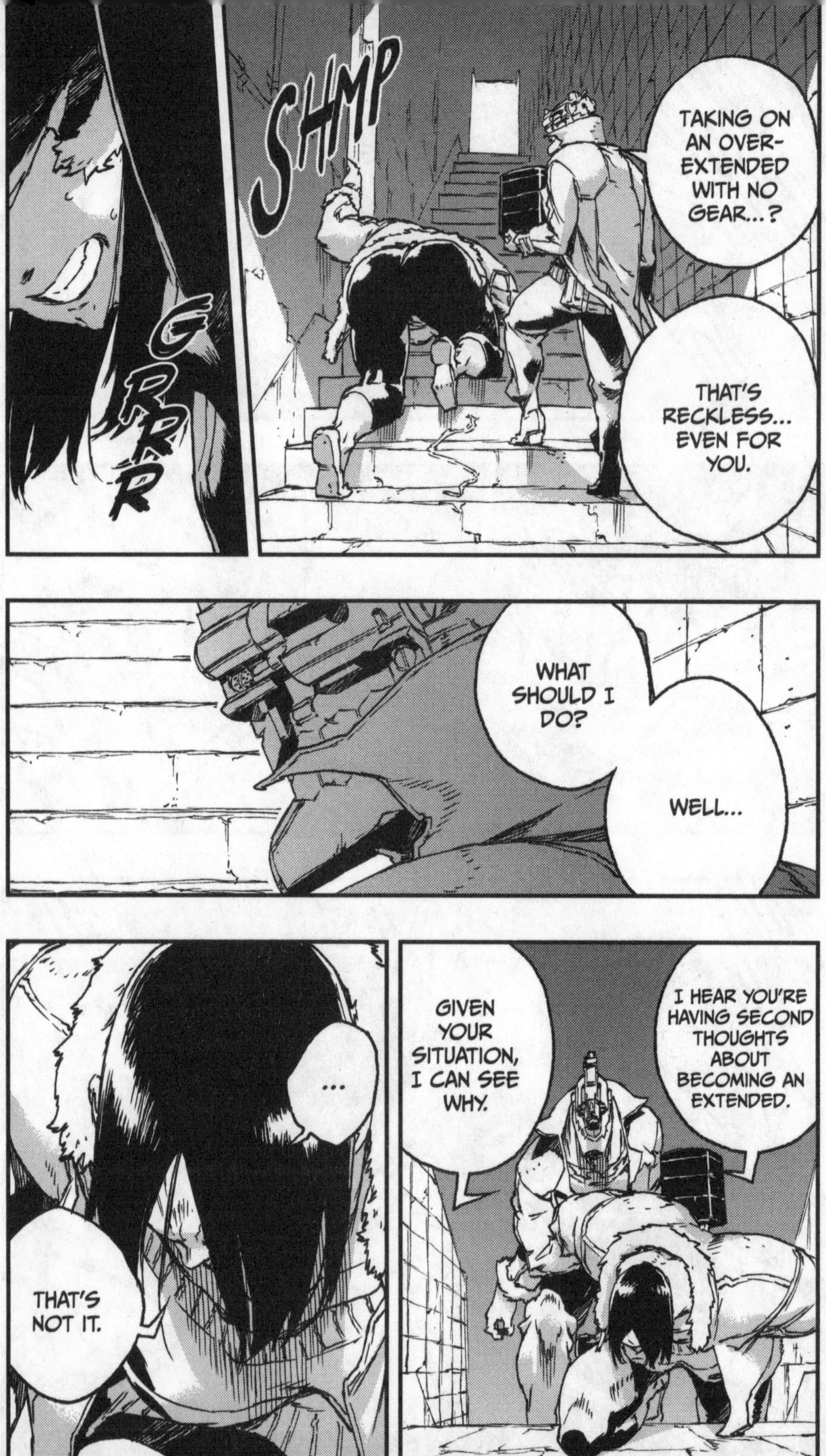
TAKING ON AN OVER-EXTENDED WITH NO GEAR...?
SHMP
THAT'S RECKLESS... EVEN FOR YOU.
GRRRR
WHAT SHOULD I DO?
WELL...
I HEAR YOU'RE HAVING SECOND THOUGHTS ABOUT BECOMING AN EXTENDED.
GIVEN YOUR SITUATION, I CAN SEE WHY.
...
THAT'S NOT IT.

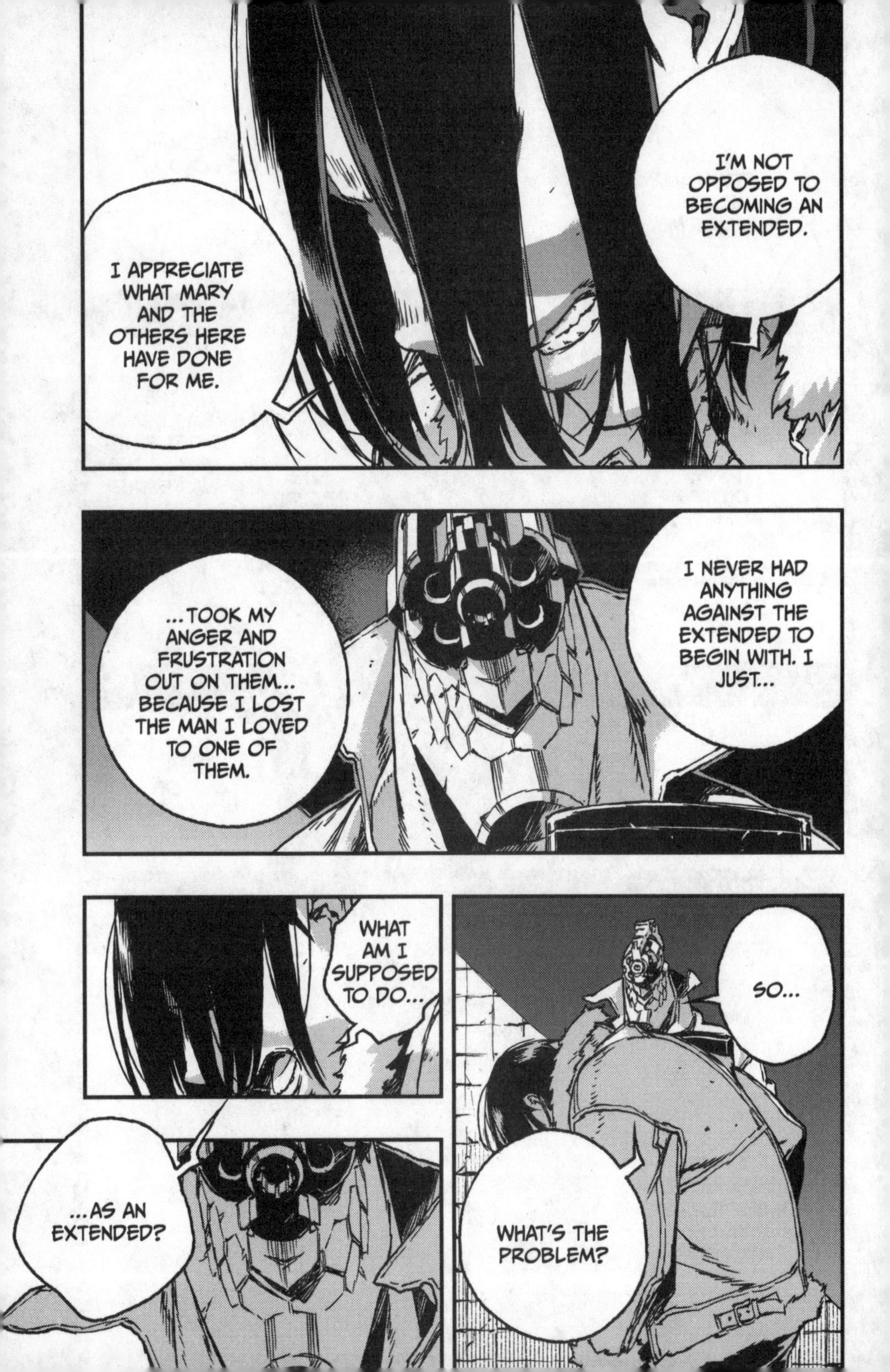
I'M NOT OPPOSED TO BECOMING AN EXTENDED.
I APPRECIATE WHAT MARY AND THE OTHERS HERE HAVE DONE FOR ME.
I NEVER HAD ANYTHING AGAINST THE EXTENDED TO BEGIN WITH. I JUST...
...TOOK MY ANGER AND FRUSTRATION OUT ON THEM... BECAUSE I LOST THE MAN I LOVED TO ONE OF THEM.
SO...
WHAT'S THE PROBLEM?
WHAT AM I SUPPOSED TO DO...
...AS AN EXTENDED?

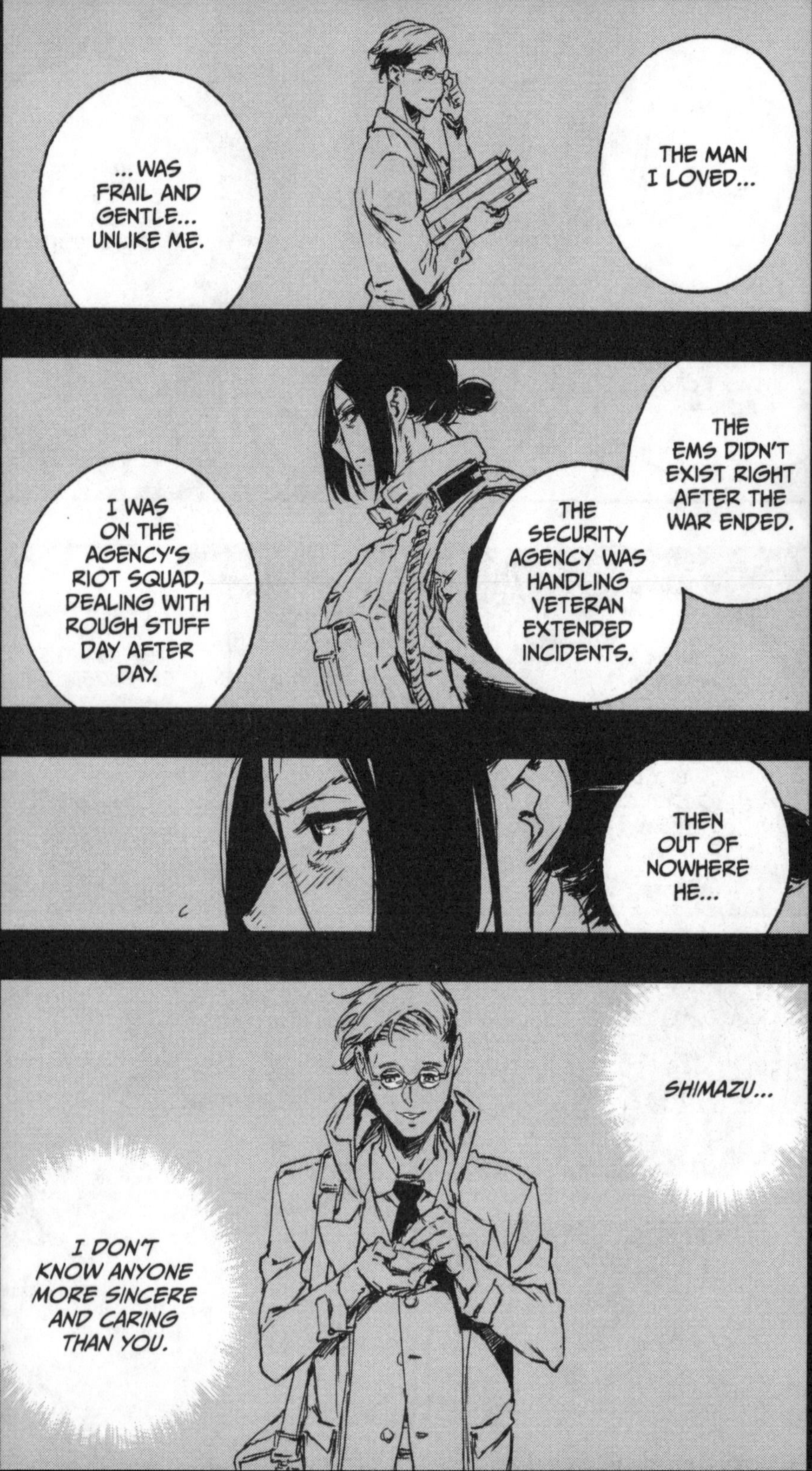
THE MAN I LOVED...
...WAS FRAIL AND GENTLE... UNLIKE ME.
THE EMS DIDN'T EXIST RIGHT AFTER THE WAR ENDED.
THE SECURITY AGENCY WAS HANDLING VETERAN EXTENDED INCIDENTS.
I WAS ON THE AGENCY'S RIOT SQUAD, DEALING WITH ROUGH STUFF DAY AFTER DAY.
THEN OUT OF NOWHERE HE...
SHIMAZU...
I DON'T KNOW ANYONE MORE SINCERE AND CARING THAN YOU.

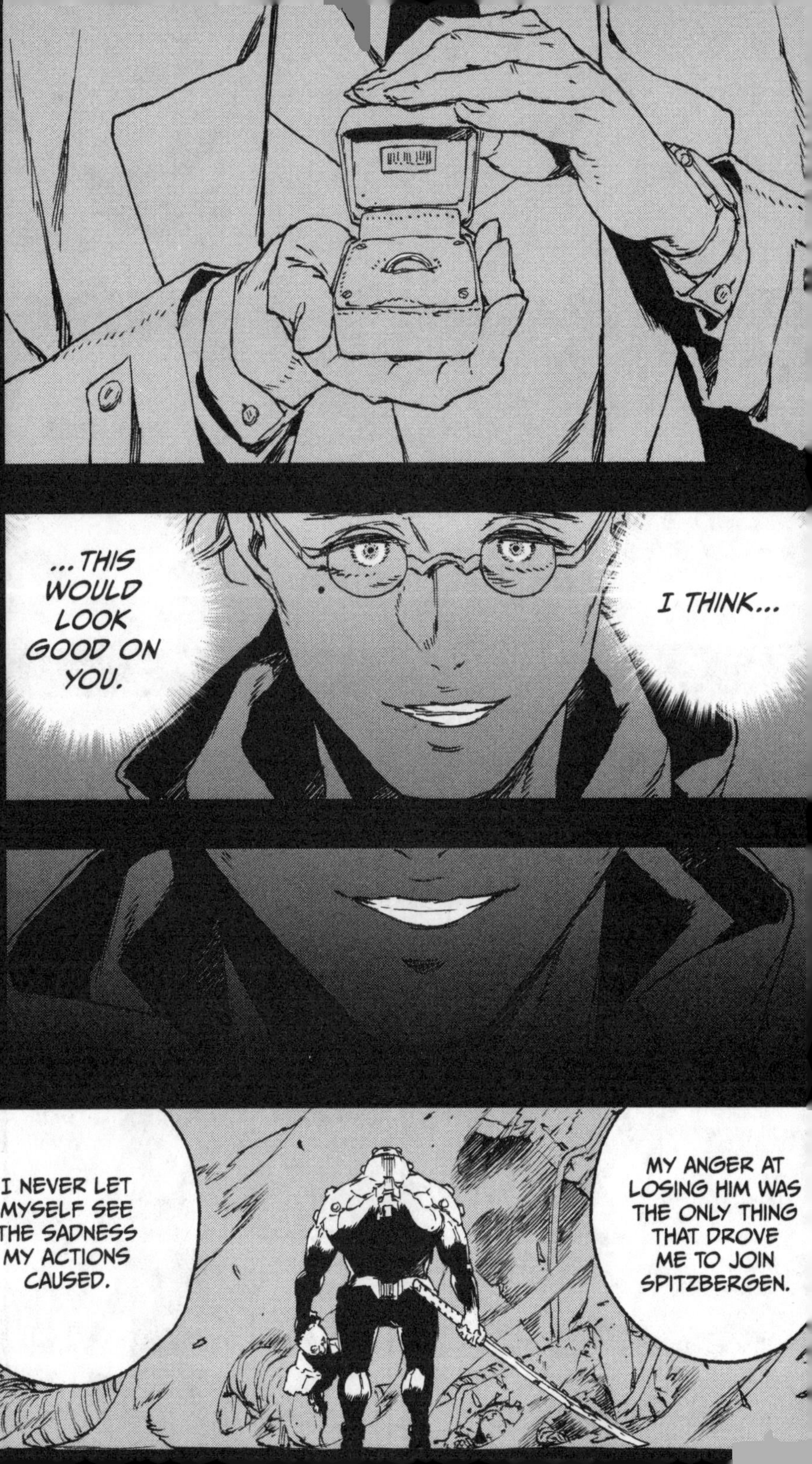
I THINK...
...THIS WOULD LOOK GOOD ON YOU.
MY ANGER AT LOSING HIM WAS THE ONLY THING THAT DROVE ME TO JOIN SPITZBERGEN.
I NEVER LET MYSELF SEE THE SADNESS MY ACTIONS CAUSED.

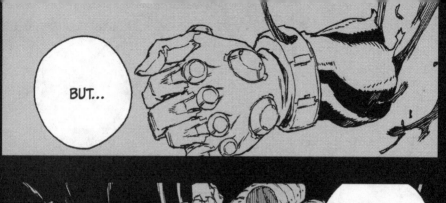

BUT...
...FIGHTING EXTENDED LIKE YOU...
...OPENED MY EYES.
I SAID I WAS FIGHTING FOR THE MAN I LOST, BUT THEN I NOTICED...
...I WASN'T ANYTHING LIKE THE WOMAN HE FELL IN LOVE WITH ANYMORE.
SO, WHAT CAN...
... SOMEONE LIKE ME DO?
WELL, FIRST, YOU NEED AN ARM...
...OR YOU WON'T BE ABLE TO HOLD ANYTHING.

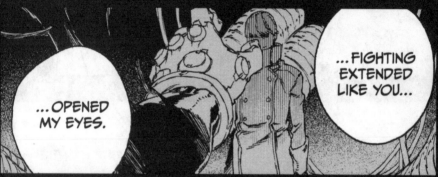

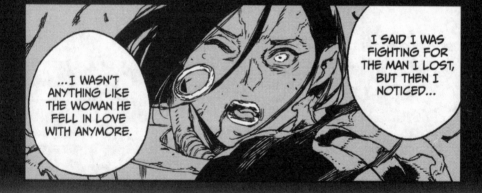

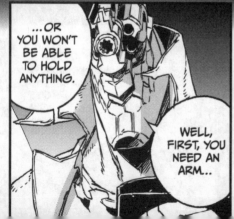

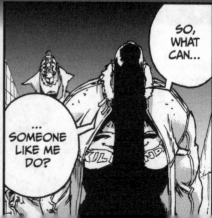

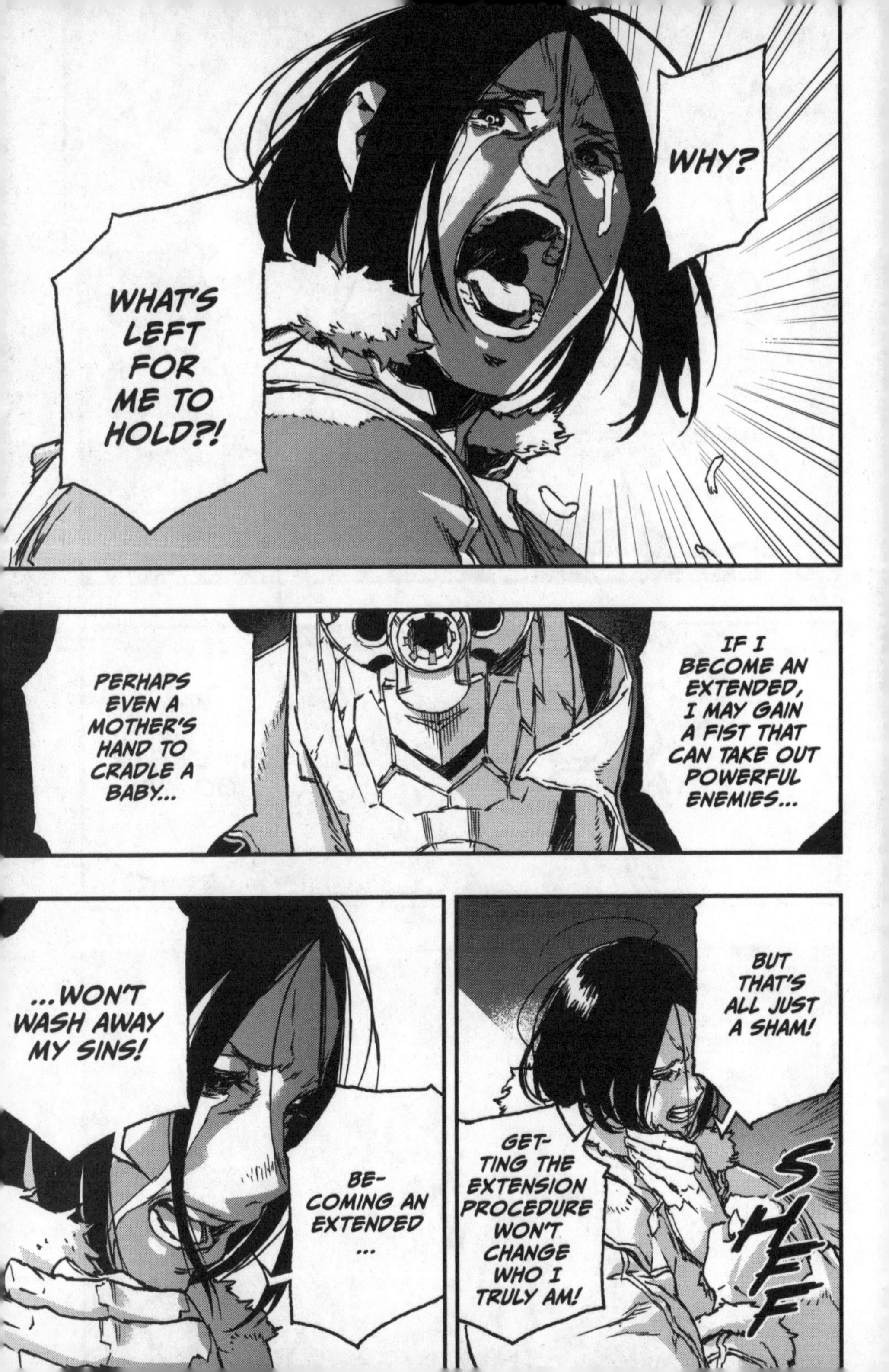
WHY?
WHAT'S LEFT FOR ME TO HOLD?!
IF I BECOME AN EXTENDED, I MAY GAIN A FIST THAT CAN TAKE OUT POWERFUL ENEMIES...
PERHAPS EVEN A MOTHER'S HAND TO CRADLE A BABY...
BUT THAT'S ALL JUST A SHAM!
GET-TING THE EXTENSION PROCEDURE WON'T CHANGE WHO I TRULY AM!
SHFF
BE-COMING AN EXTENDED ...
...WON'T WASH AWAY MY SINS!

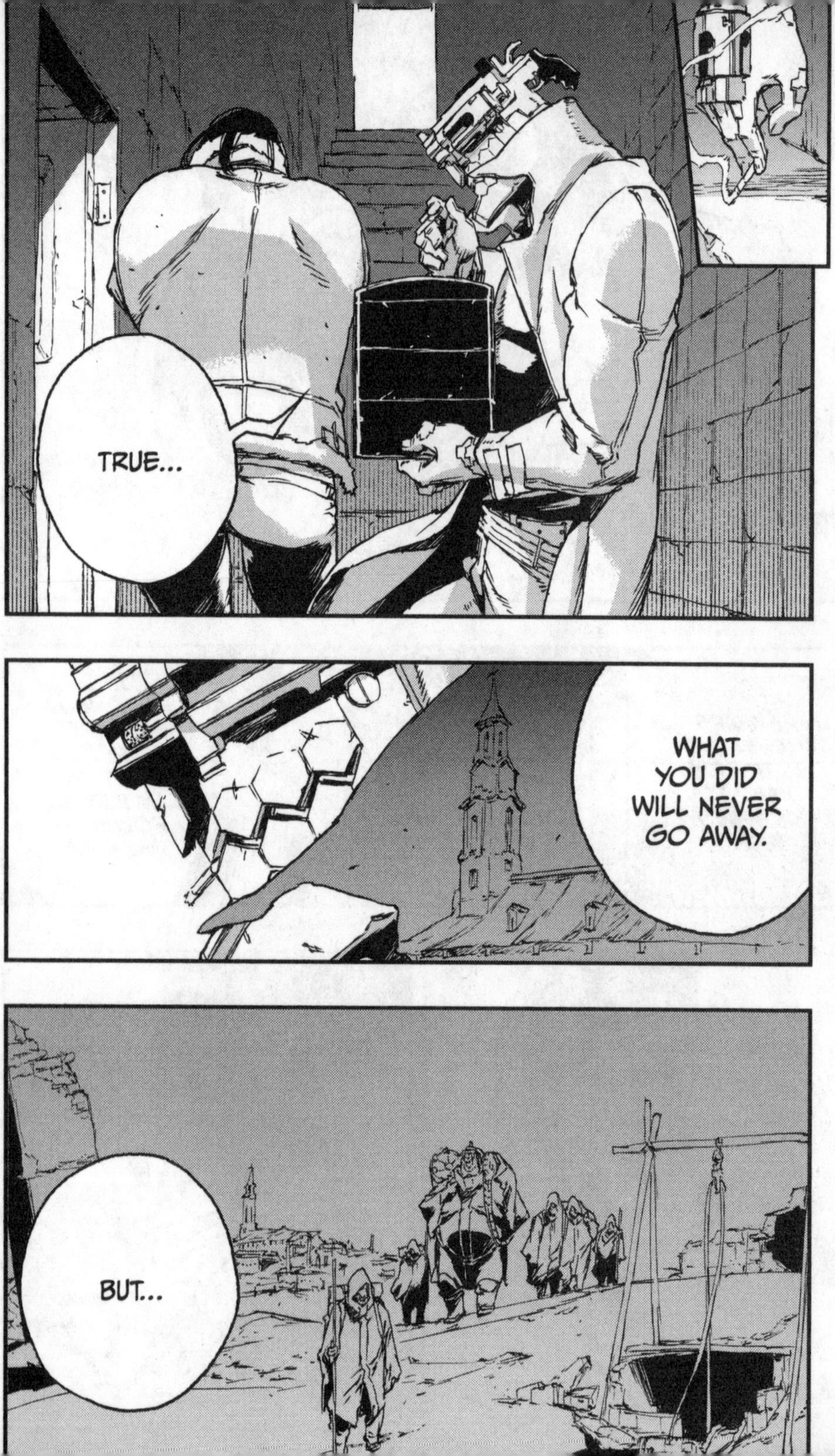
TRUE...
WHAT YOU DID WILL NEVER GO AWAY.
BUT...

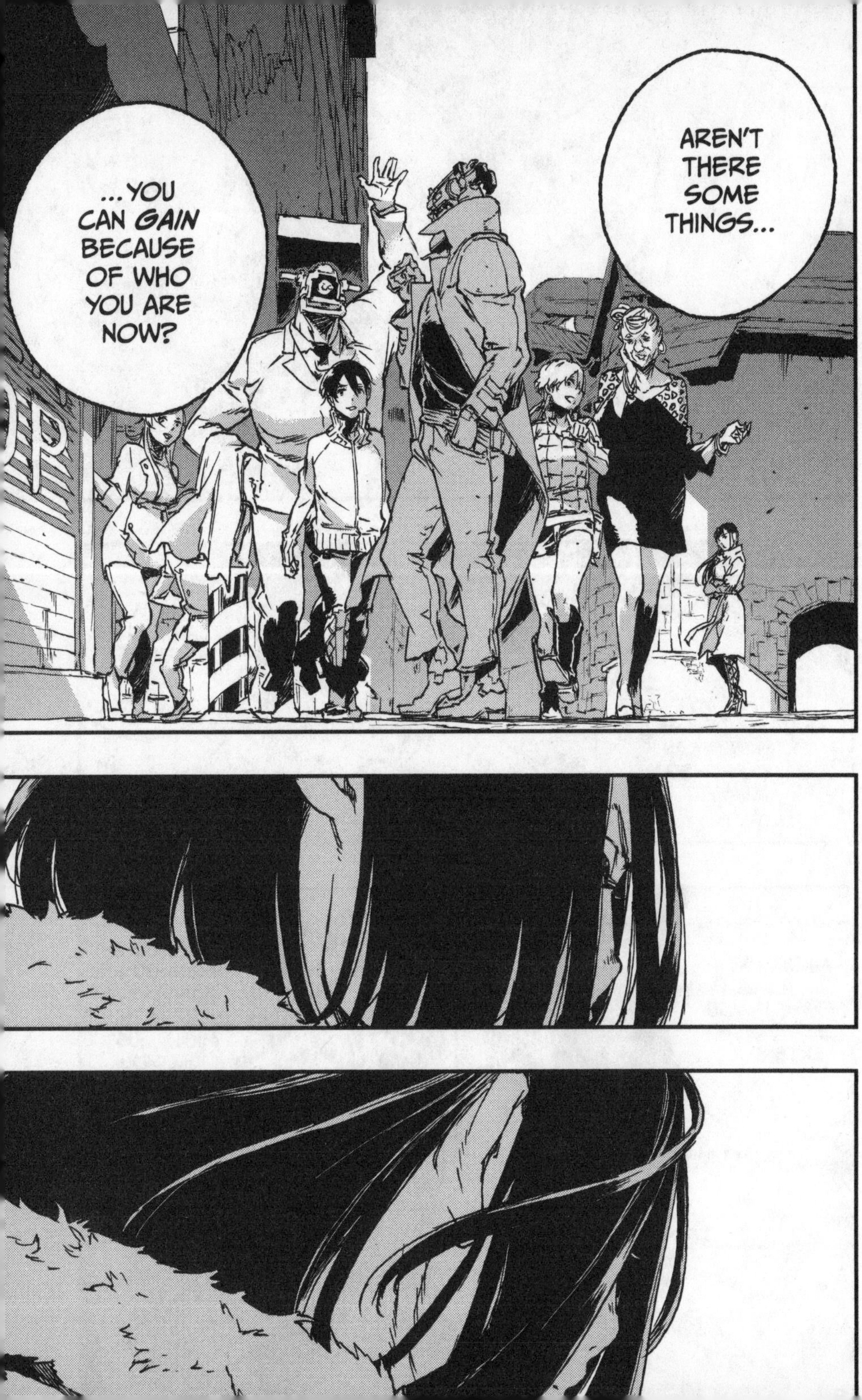
AREN'T THERE SOME THINGS...
...YOU CAN *GAIN* BECAUSE OF WHO YOU ARE NOW?

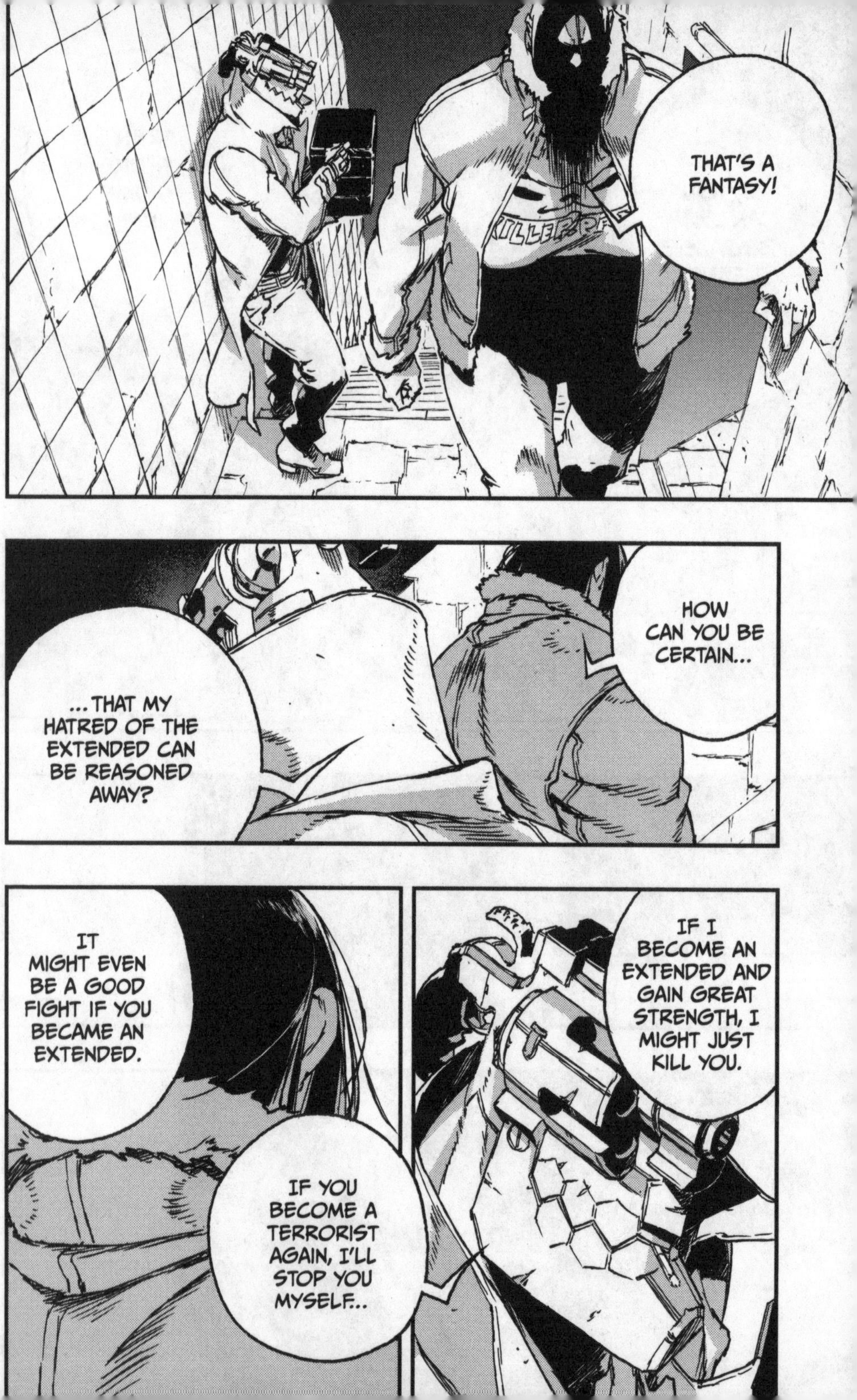
THAT'S A FANTASY!
HOW CAN YOU BE CERTAIN...
...THAT MY HATRED OF THE EXTENDED CAN BE REASONED AWAY?
IF I BECOME AN EXTENDED AND GAIN GREAT STRENGTH, I MIGHT JUST KILL YOU.
IT MIGHT EVEN BE A GOOD FIGHT IF YOU BECAME AN EXTENDED.
IF YOU BECOME A TERRORIST AGAIN, I'LL STOP YOU MYSELF...

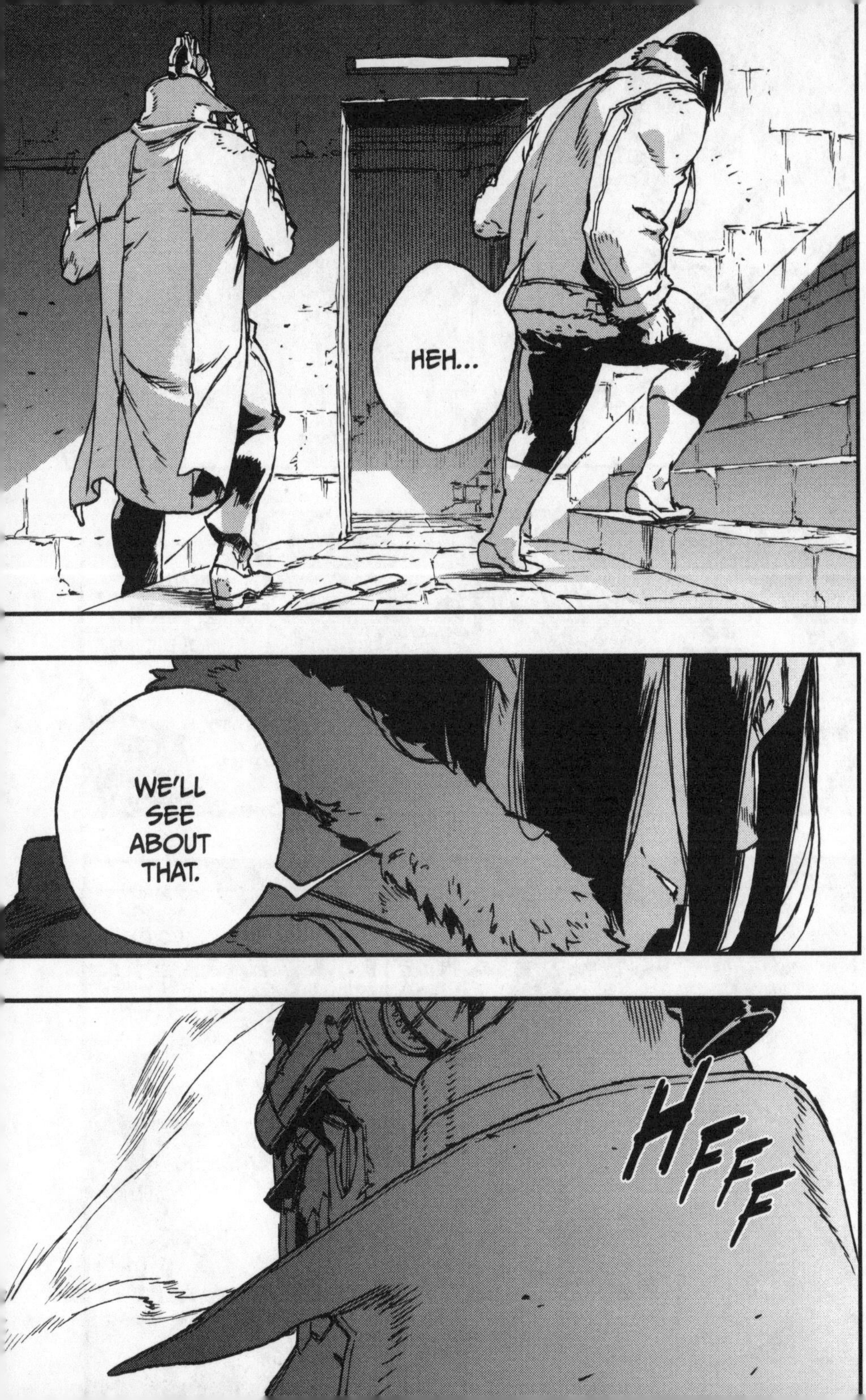
HEH...
WE'LL SEE ABOUT THAT.
HFFF

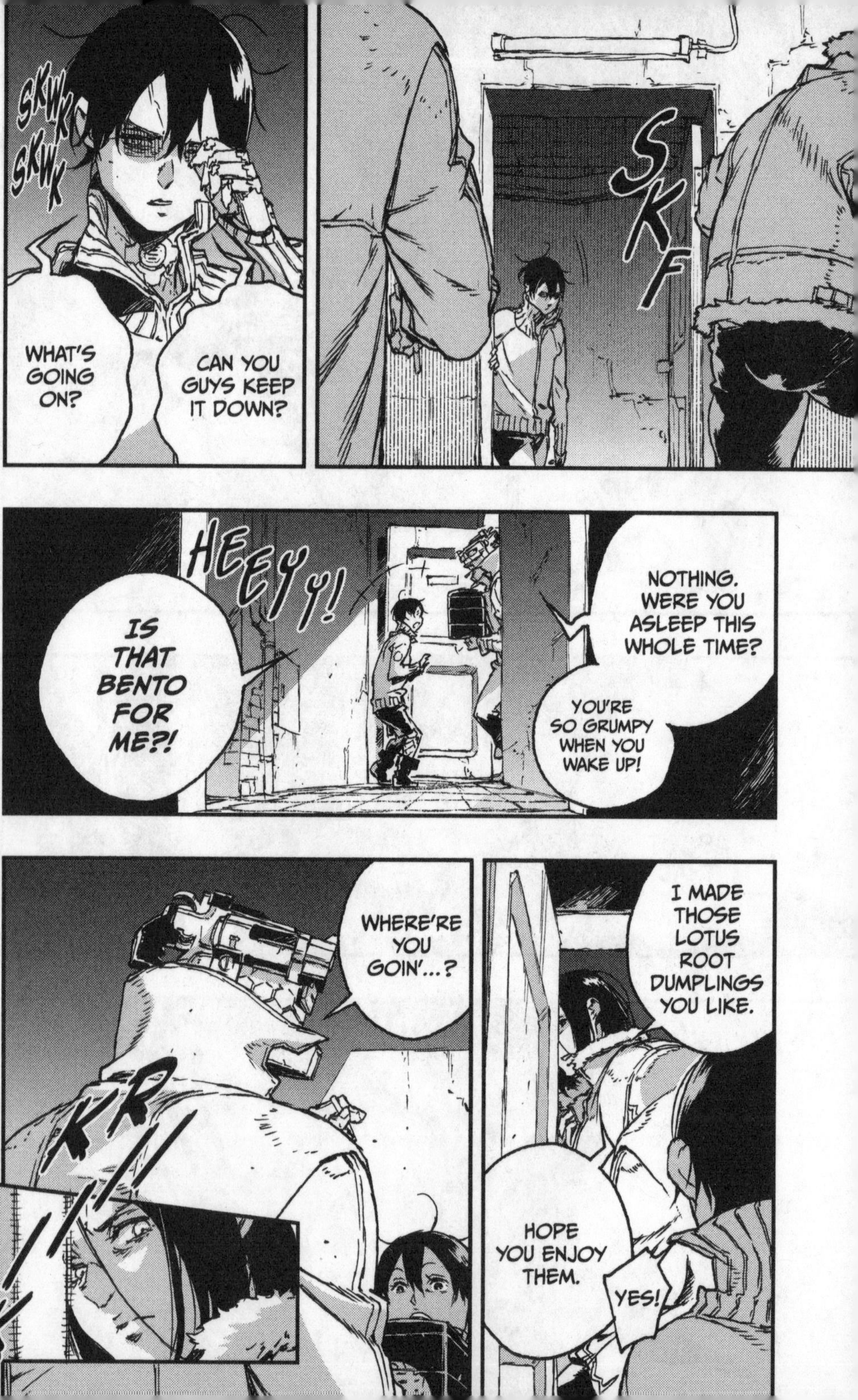
SKF
SKWK SKWK
CAN YOU GUYS KEEP IT DOWN?
WHAT'S GOING ON?
NOTHING. WERE YOU ASLEEP THIS WHOLE TIME?
YOU'RE SO GRUMPY WHEN YOU WAKE UP!
HEEYY!
IS THAT BENTO FOR ME?!
I MADE THOSE LOTUS ROOT DUMPLINGS YOU LIKE.
HOPE YOU ENJOY THEM.
YES!
WHERE'RE YOU GOIN'...?
KRR

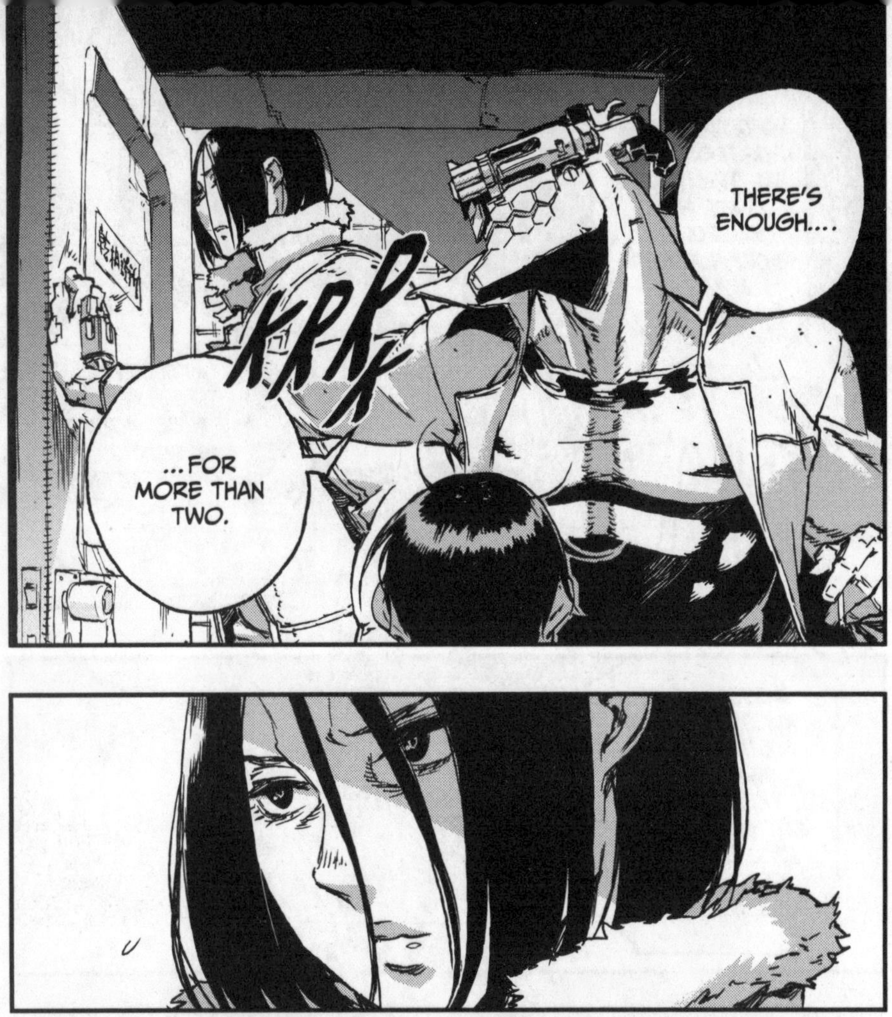
THERE'S ENOUGH....
KRRK
...FOR MORE THAN TWO.

*Inui Consulting

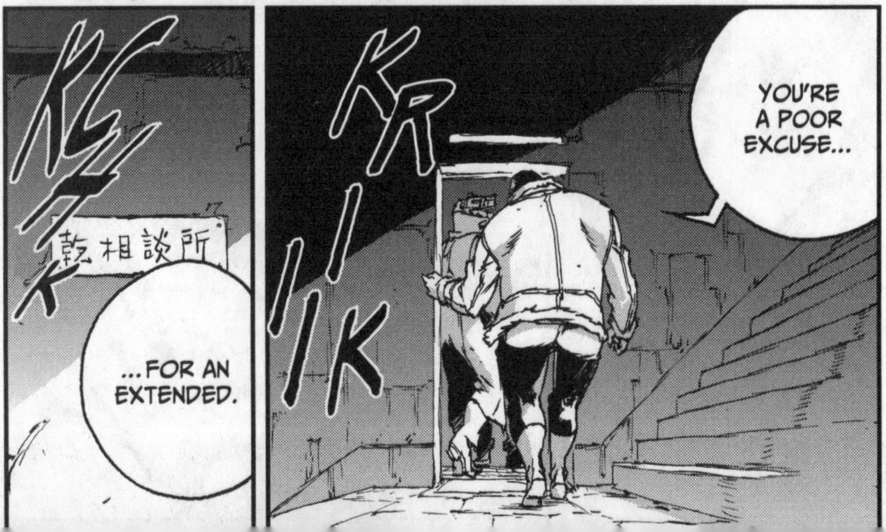
KRIIK
YOU'RE A POOR EXCUSE...
乾相談所
...FOR AN EXTENDED.

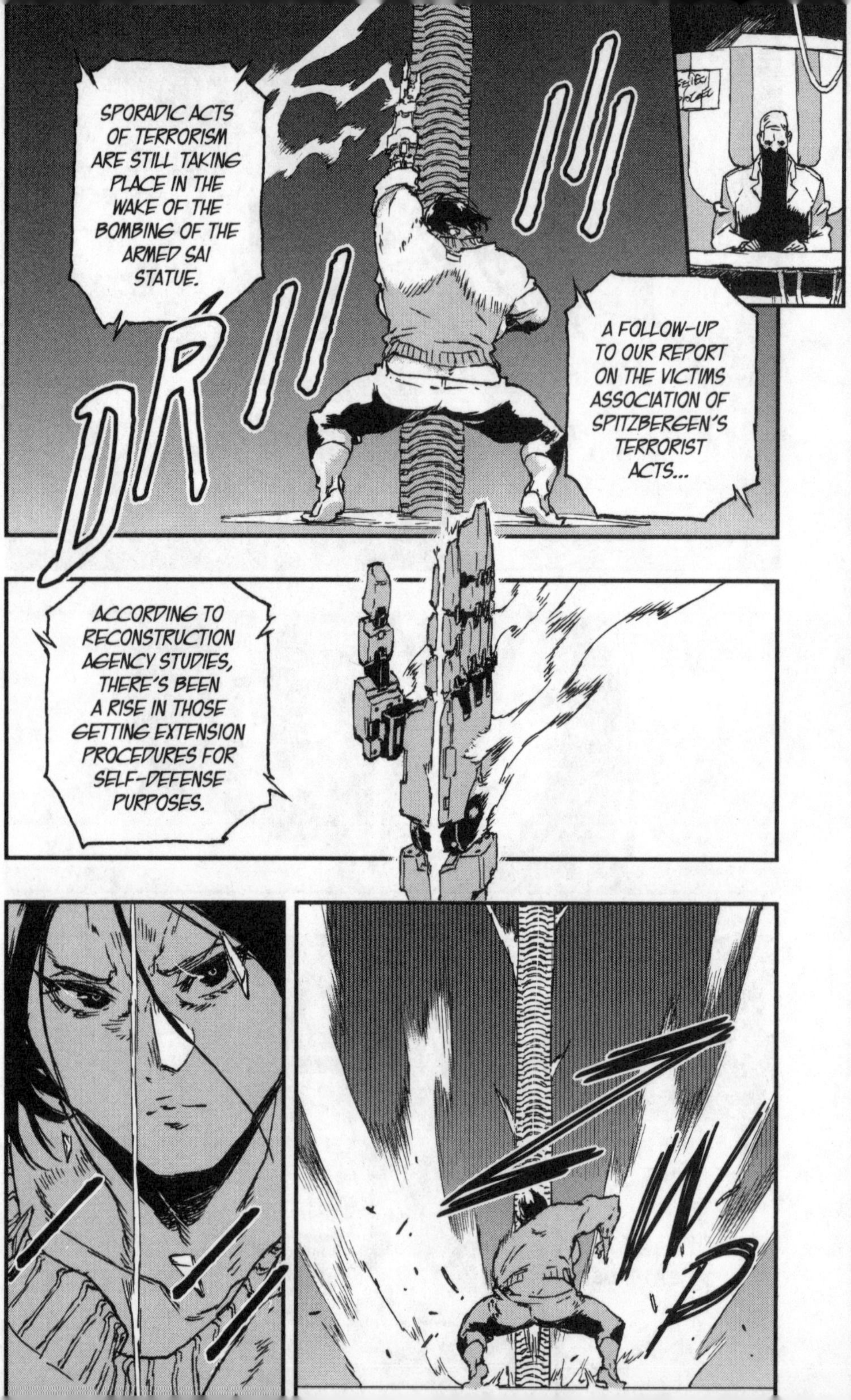
SPORADIC ACTS OF TERRORISM ARE STILL TAKING PLACE IN THE WAKE OF THE BOMBING OF THE ARMED SAI STATUE.
A FOLLOW-UP TO OUR REPORT ON THE VICTIMS ASSOCIATION OF SPITZBERGEN'S TERRORIST ACTS...
DRIII
ACCORDING TO RECONSTRUCTION AGENCY STUDIES, THERE'S BEEN A RISE IN THOSE GETTING EXTENSION PROCEDURES FOR SELF-DEFENSE PURPOSES.

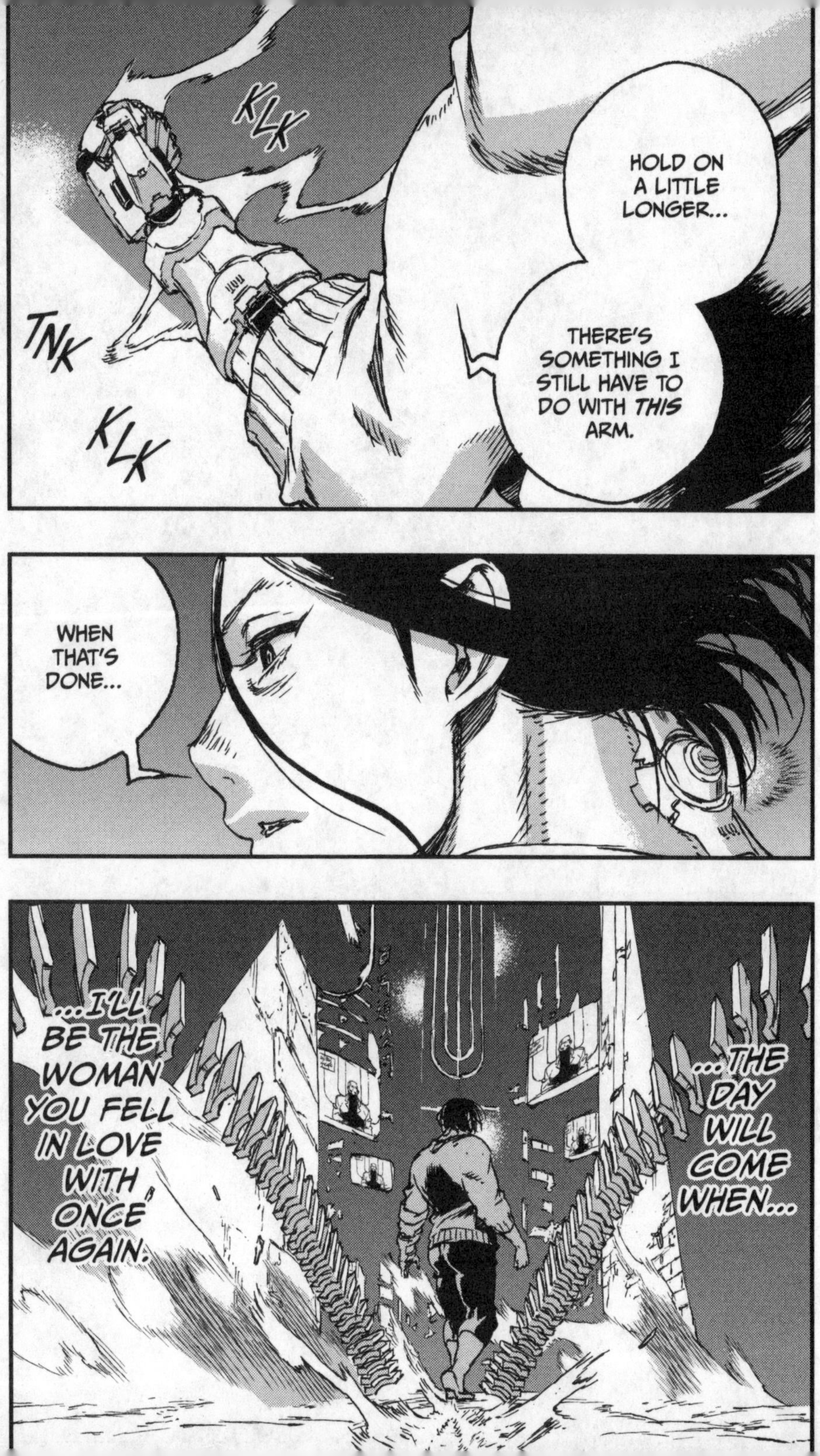
HOLD ON A LITTLE LONGER...
THERE'S SOMETHING I STILL HAVE TO DO WITH *THIS* ARM.
KLK
TNK
KLK
WHEN THAT'S DONE...
...THE DAY WILL COME WHEN...
...I'LL BE THE WOMAN YOU FELL IN LOVE WITH ONCE AGAIN.

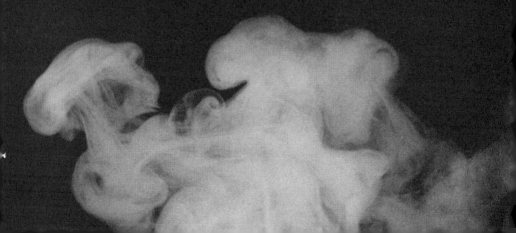

NO
GUNS
LIFE

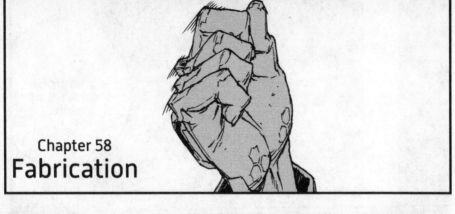

Chapter 58
Fabrication

KNOCK
KNOCK
IT'S INUI.
ARE YOU THE ONE WHO CALLED ME?
KNOCK
KRIIIK

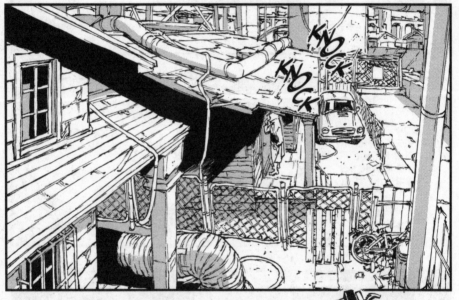

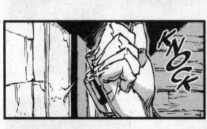

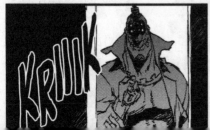

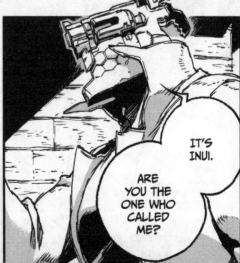

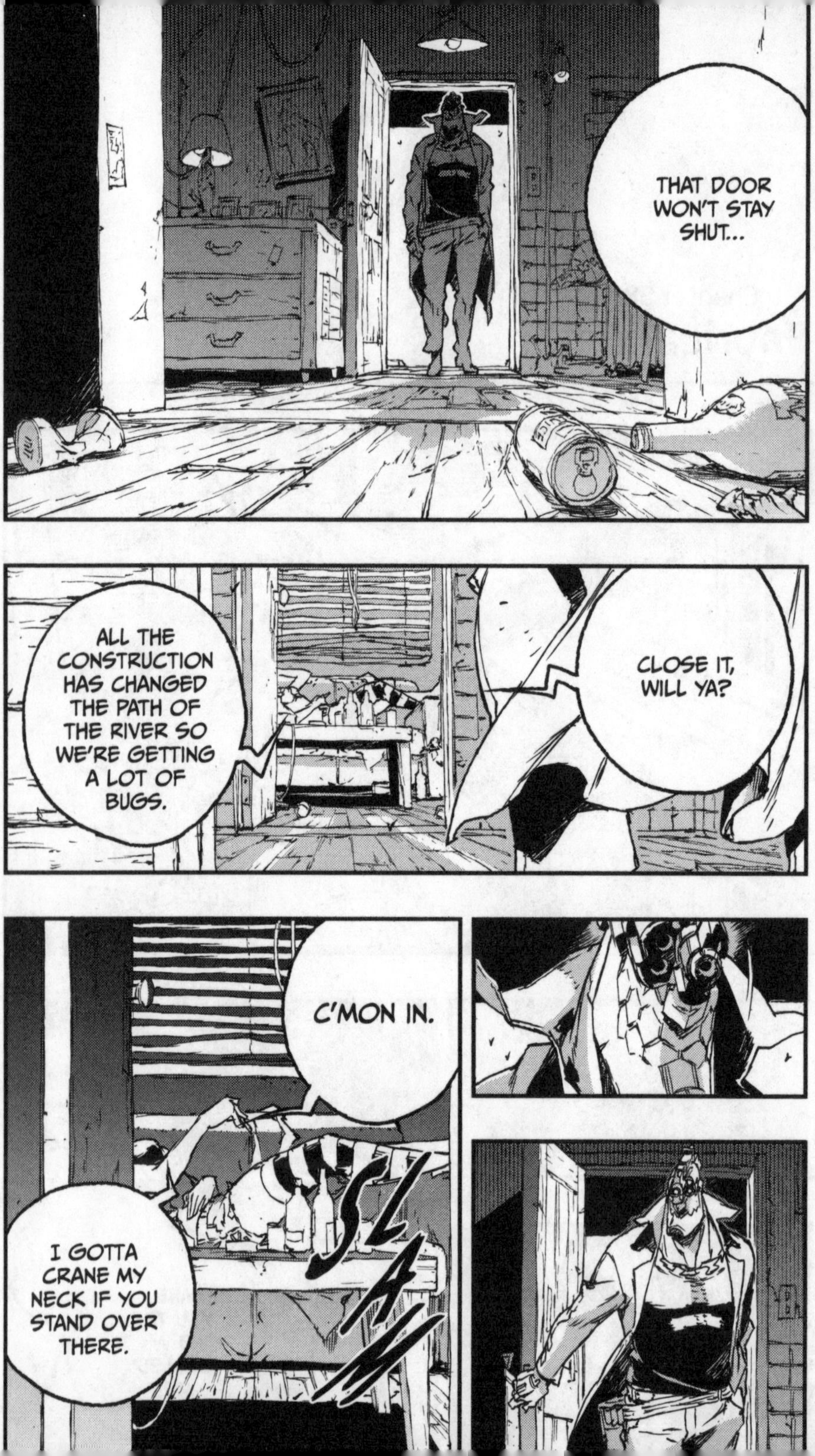
THAT DOOR WON'T STAY SHUT...
CLOSE IT, WILL YA?
ALL THE CONSTRUCTION HAS CHANGED THE PATH OF THE RIVER SO WE'RE GETTING A LOT OF BUGS.
C'MON IN.
SLAM
I GOTTA CRANE MY NECK IF YOU STAND OVER THERE.

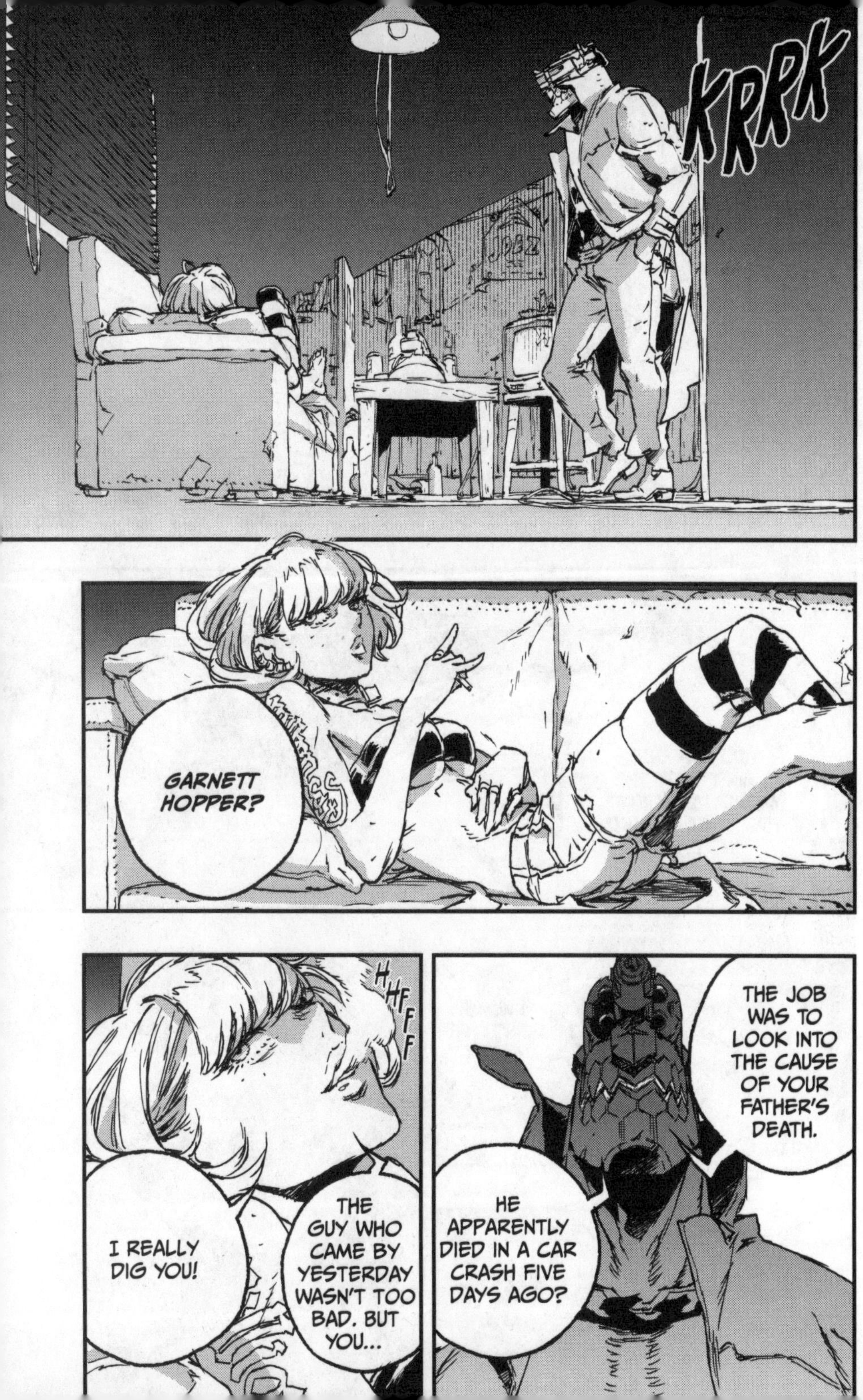
KRRK
GARNETT HOPPER?
THE JOB WAS TO LOOK INTO THE CAUSE OF YOUR FATHER'S DEATH.
HE APPARENTLY DIED IN A CAR CRASH FIVE DAYS AGO?
HHFFF
THE GUY WHO CAME BY YESTERDAY WASN'T TOO BAD. BUT YOU...
I REALLY DIG YOU!

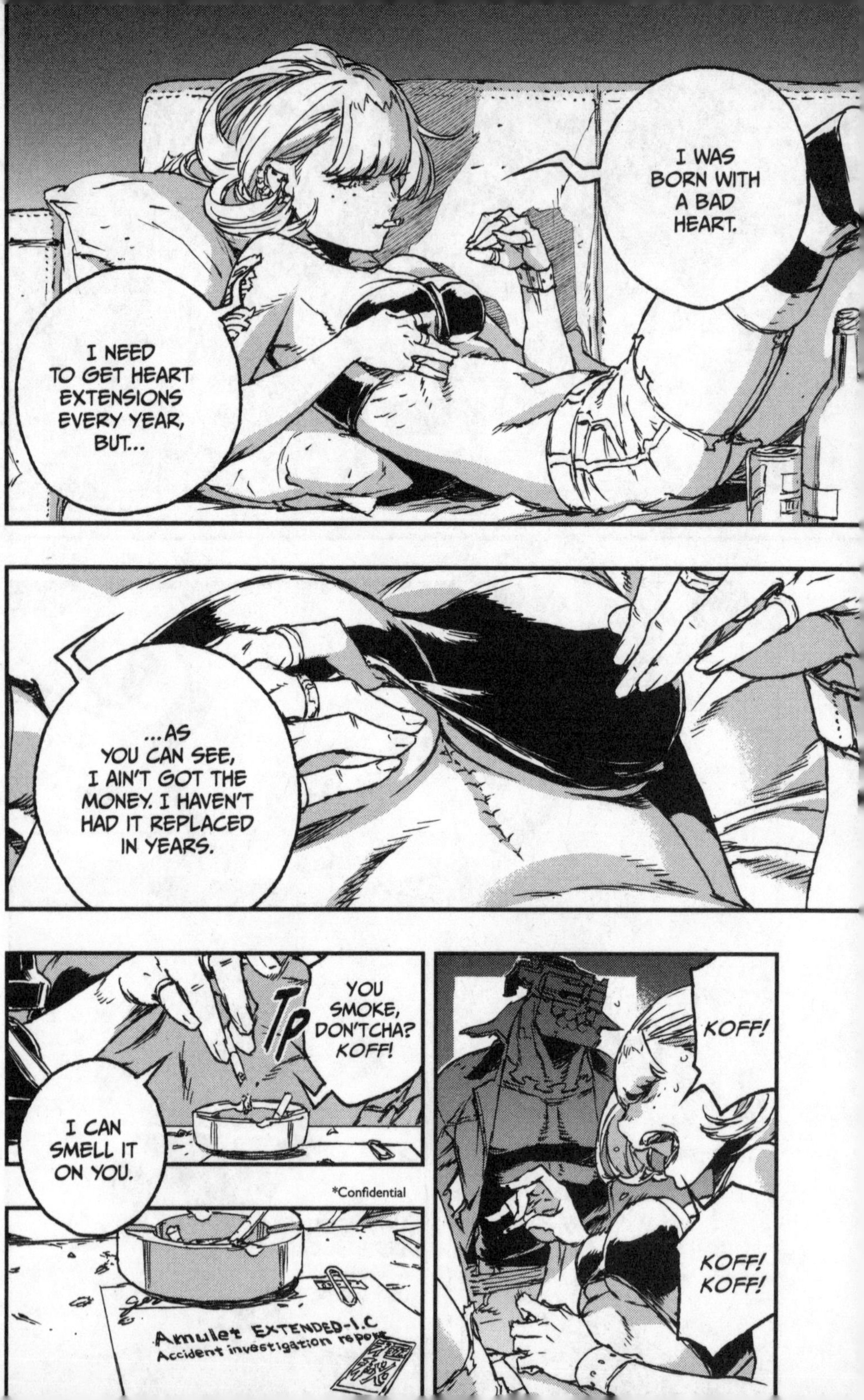
I WAS BORN WITH A BAD HEART.
I NEED TO GET HEART EXTENSIONS EVERY YEAR, BUT...
...AS YOU CAN SEE, I AIN'T GOT THE MONEY. I HAVEN'T HAD IT REPLACED IN YEARS.
KOFF!
KOFF! KOFF!
YOU SMOKE, DON'TCHA? KOFF!
TP
I CAN SMELL IT ON YOU.
*Confidential
Amulet EXTENDED-1.C
Accident investigation

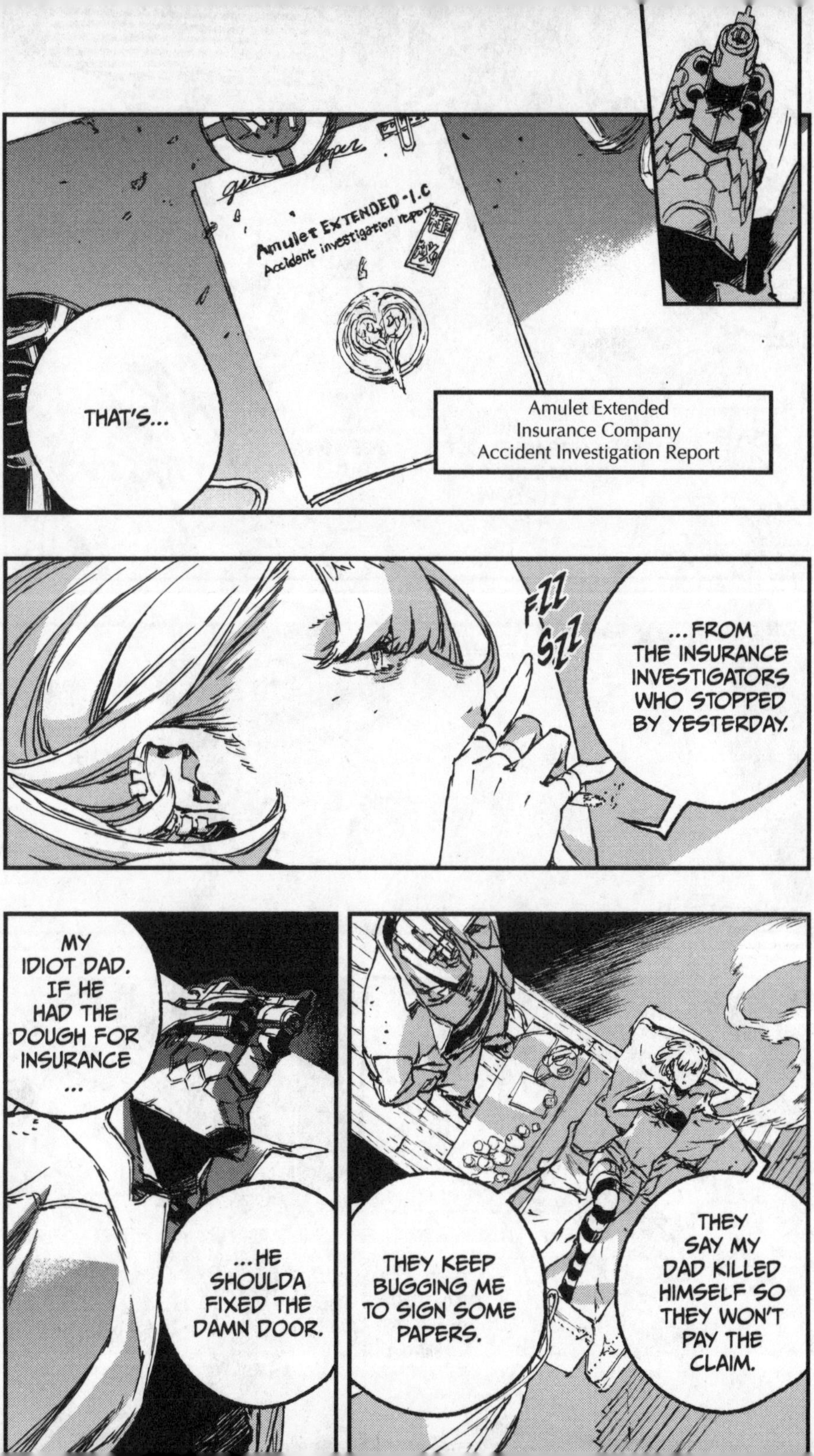
Amulet EXTENDED-1.C
Accident investigation report
Amulet Extended Insurance Company Accident Investigation Report
THAT'S...
FZZ SZZ
...FROM THE INSURANCE INVESTIGATORS WHO STOPPED BY YESTERDAY.
THEY SAY MY DAD KILLED HIMSELF SO THEY WON'T PAY THE CLAIM.
THEY KEEP BUGGING ME TO SIGN SOME PAPERS.
MY IDIOT DAD. IF HE HAD THE DOUGH FOR INSURANCE ...
...HE SHOULDA FIXED THE DAMN DOOR.

IF YOU KNOW THE CAUSE OF DEATH, YOU DON'T NEED ME.

YOU WOULDN'T GUESS IT, BUT...

...HE FREAKED OUT WHENEVER HE SAW A BUG.

KRRK

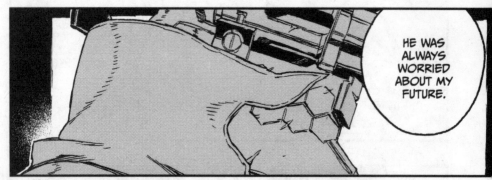

HE WAS ALWAYS WORRIED ABOUT MY FUTURE.

THAT COWARD DIDN'T HAVE THE GUTS TO KILL HIMSELF.

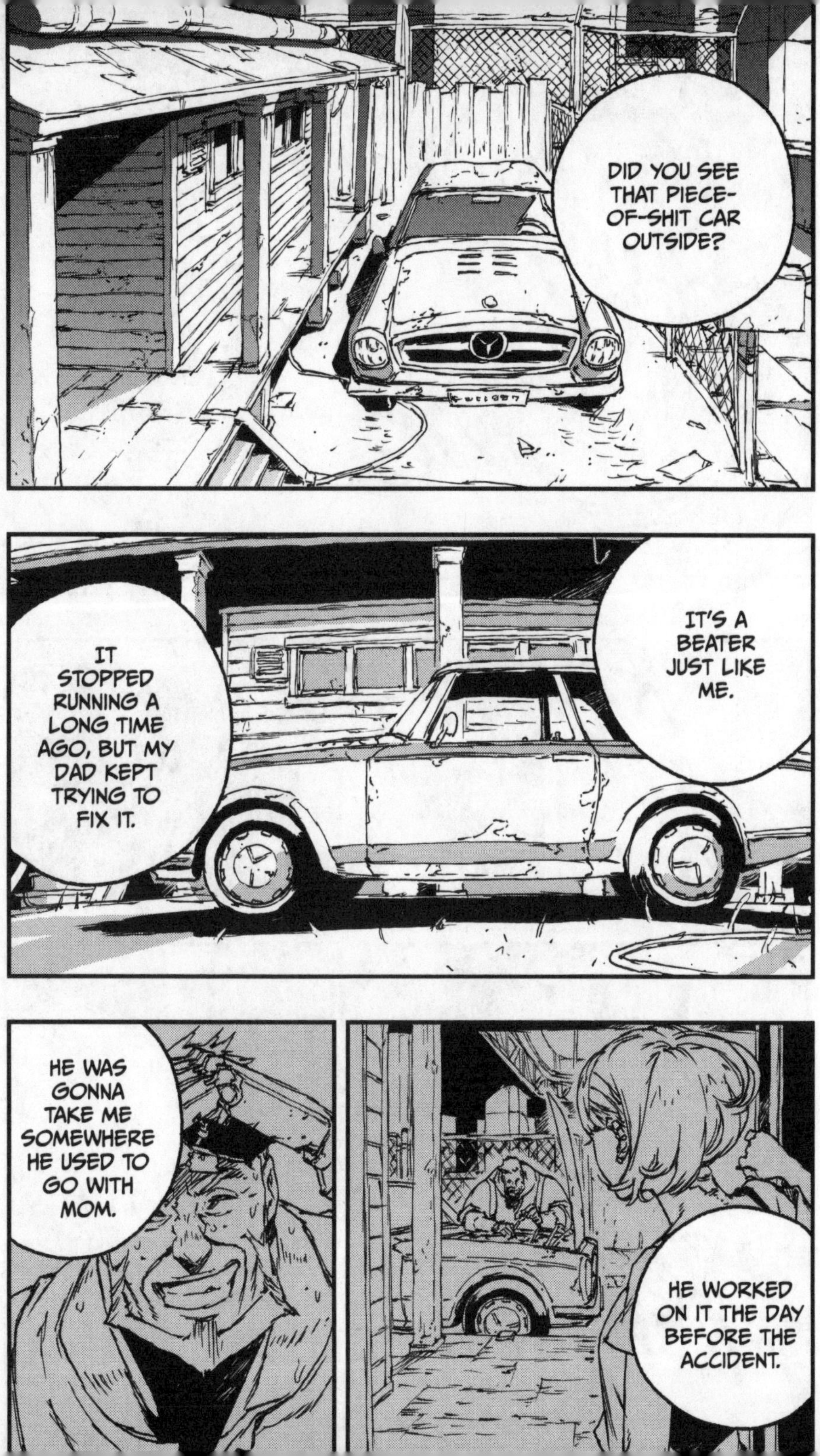
DID YOU SEE THAT PIECE-OF-SHIT CAR OUTSIDE?
IT'S A BEATER JUST LIKE ME.
IT STOPPED RUNNING A LONG TIME AGO, BUT MY DAD KEPT TRYING TO FIX IT.
HE WORKED ON IT THE DAY BEFORE THE ACCIDENT.
HE WAS GONNA TAKE ME SOMEWHERE HE USED TO GO WITH MOM.

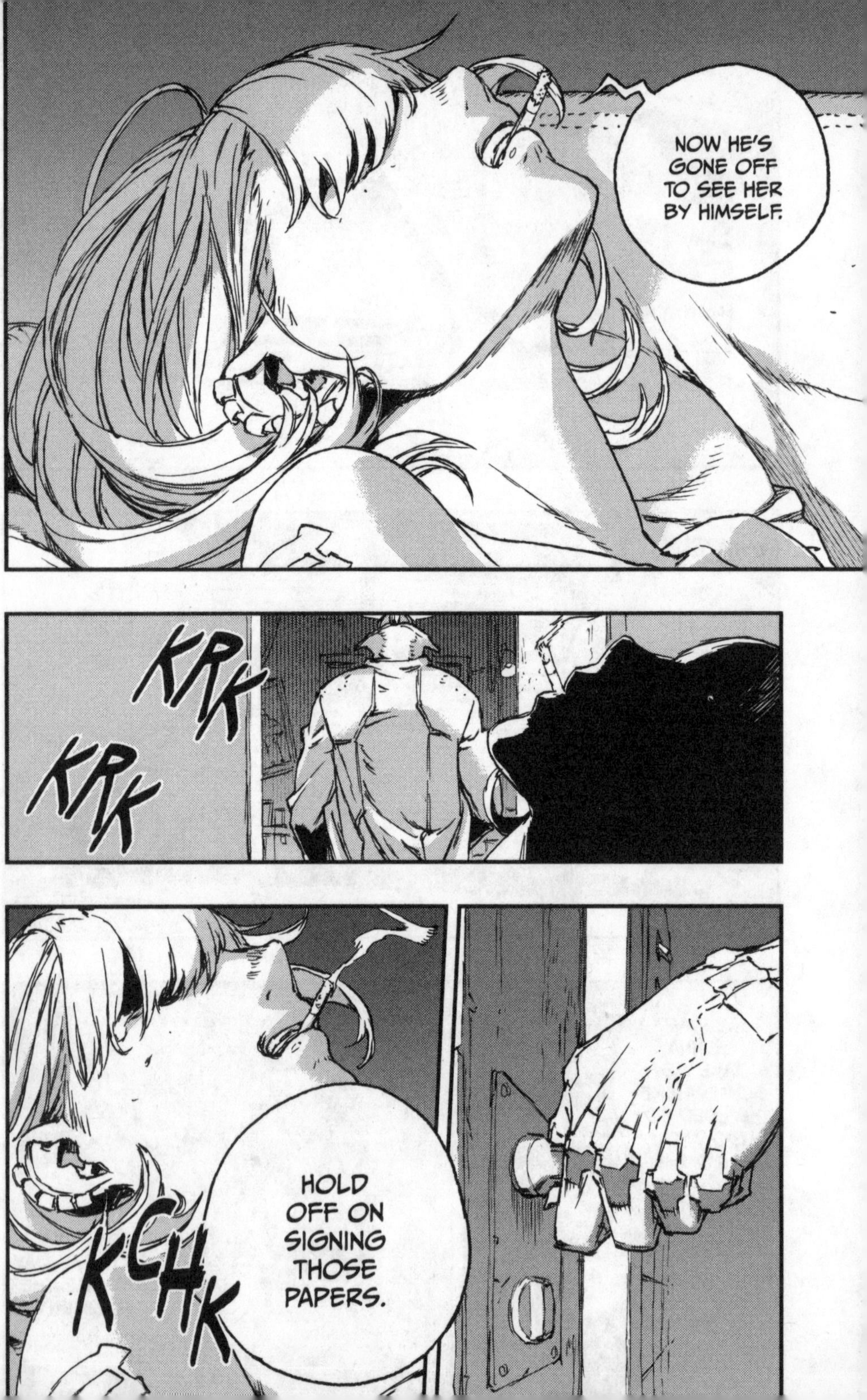
NOW HE'S GONE OFF TO SEE HER BY HIMSELF.
KRK
KRK
HOLD OFF ON SIGNING THOSE PAPERS.
KCHK

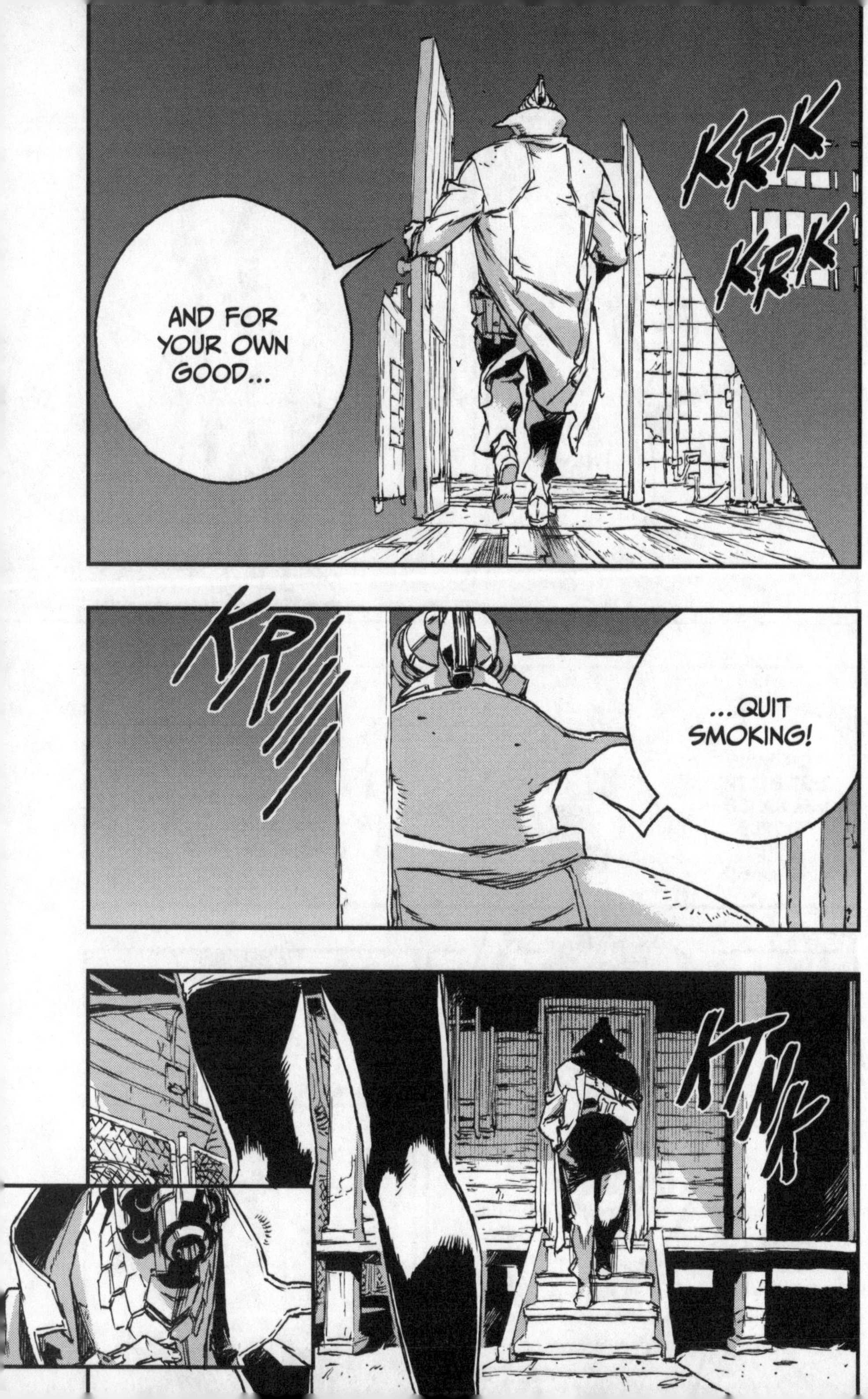
KRK KRK
AND FOR YOUR OWN GOOD...
...QUIT SMOKING!
KRI
KTNK

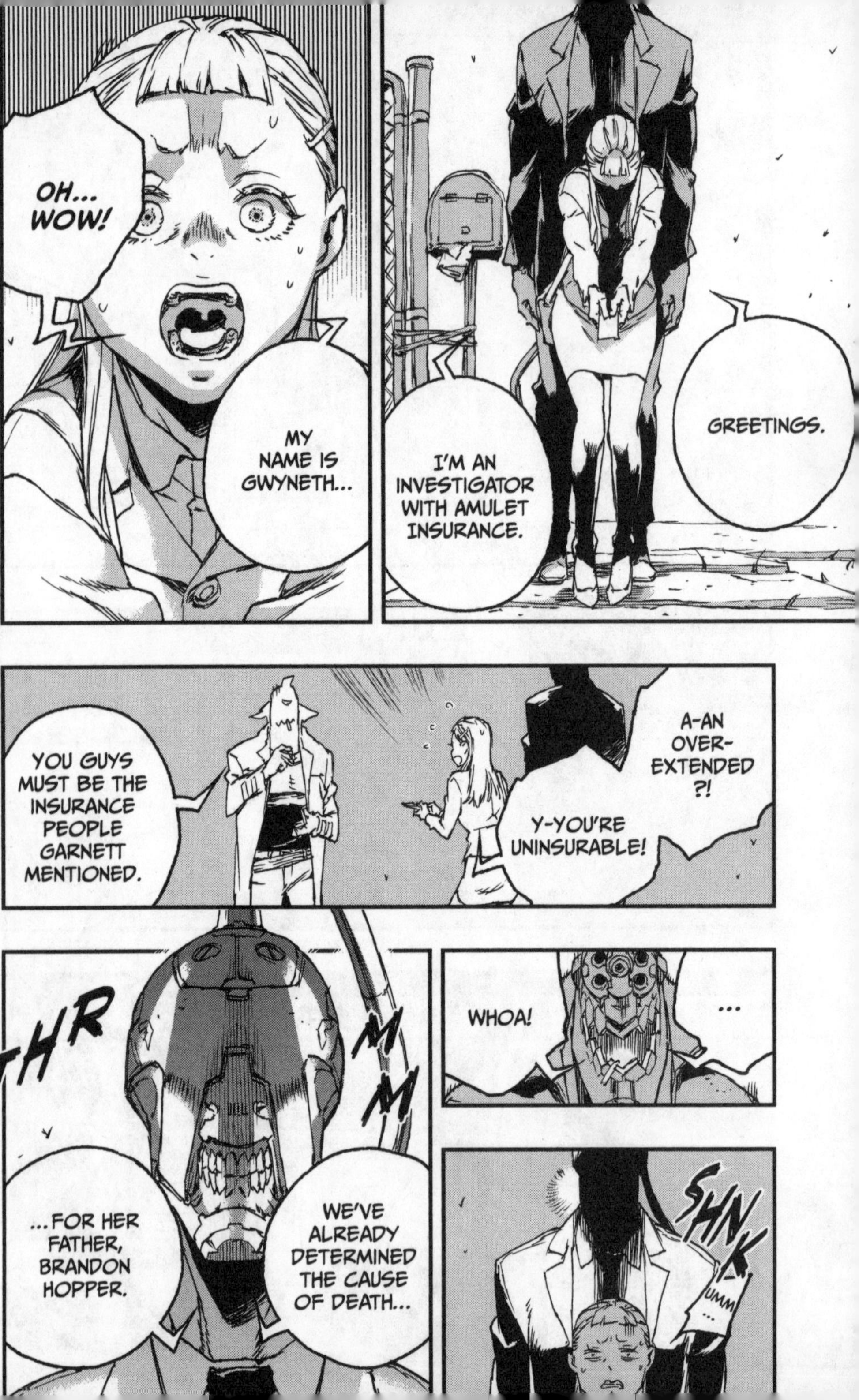
GREETINGS.
I'M AN INVESTIGATOR WITH AMULET INSURANCE.
MY NAME IS GWYNETH...
OH... WOW!
A-AN OVER-EXTENDED ?!
Y-YOU'RE UNINSURABLE!
YOU GUYS MUST BE THE INSURANCE PEOPLE GARNETT MENTIONED.
...
WHOA!
SHNK
UMM...
THRMM
WE'VE ALREADY DETERMINED THE CAUSE OF DEATH...
...FOR HER FATHER, BRANDON HOPPER.

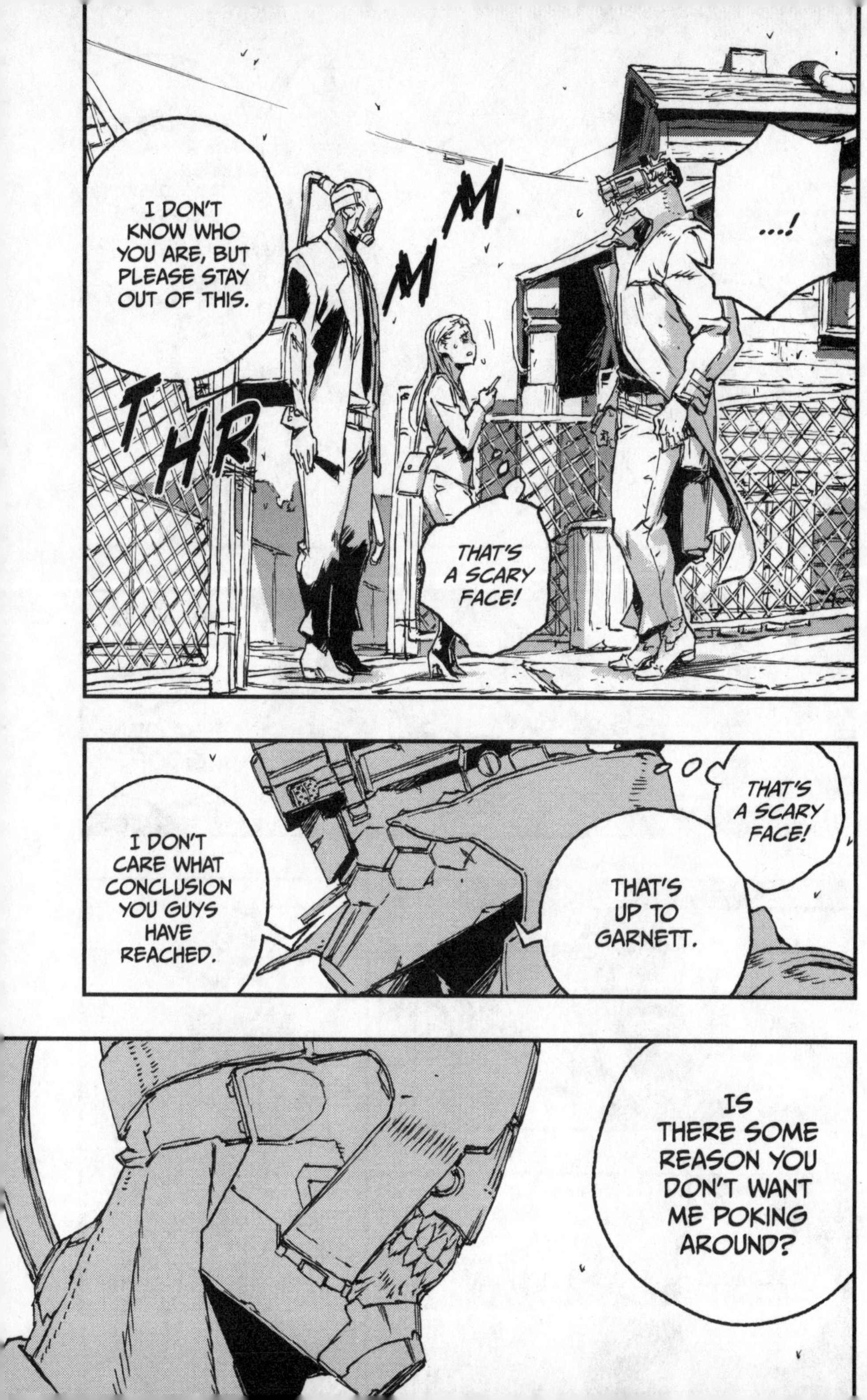
...!
MMM
I DON'T KNOW WHO YOU ARE, BUT PLEASE STAY OUT OF THIS.
THR
THAT'S A SCARY FACE!
THAT'S A SCARY FACE!
THAT'S UP TO GARNETT.
I DON'T CARE WHAT CONCLUSION YOU GUYS HAVE REACHED.
IS THERE SOME REASON YOU DON'T WANT ME POKING AROUND?

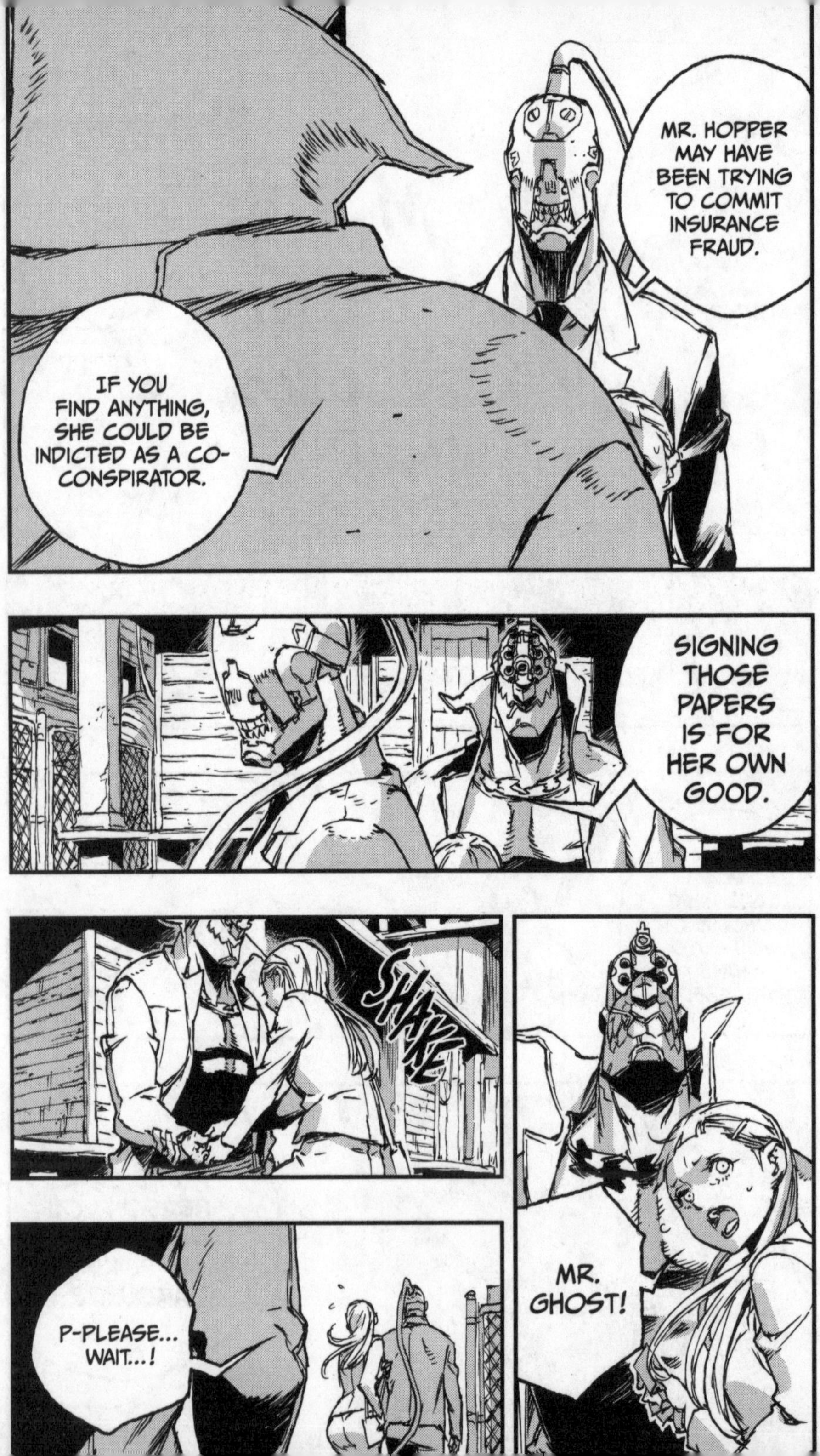
MR. HOPPER MAY HAVE BEEN TRYING TO COMMIT INSURANCE FRAUD.
IF YOU FIND ANYTHING, SHE COULD BE INDICTED AS A CO-CONSPIRATOR.
SIGNING THOSE PAPERS IS FOR HER OWN GOOD.
MR. GHOST!
SHAKE
P-PLEASE... WAIT...!

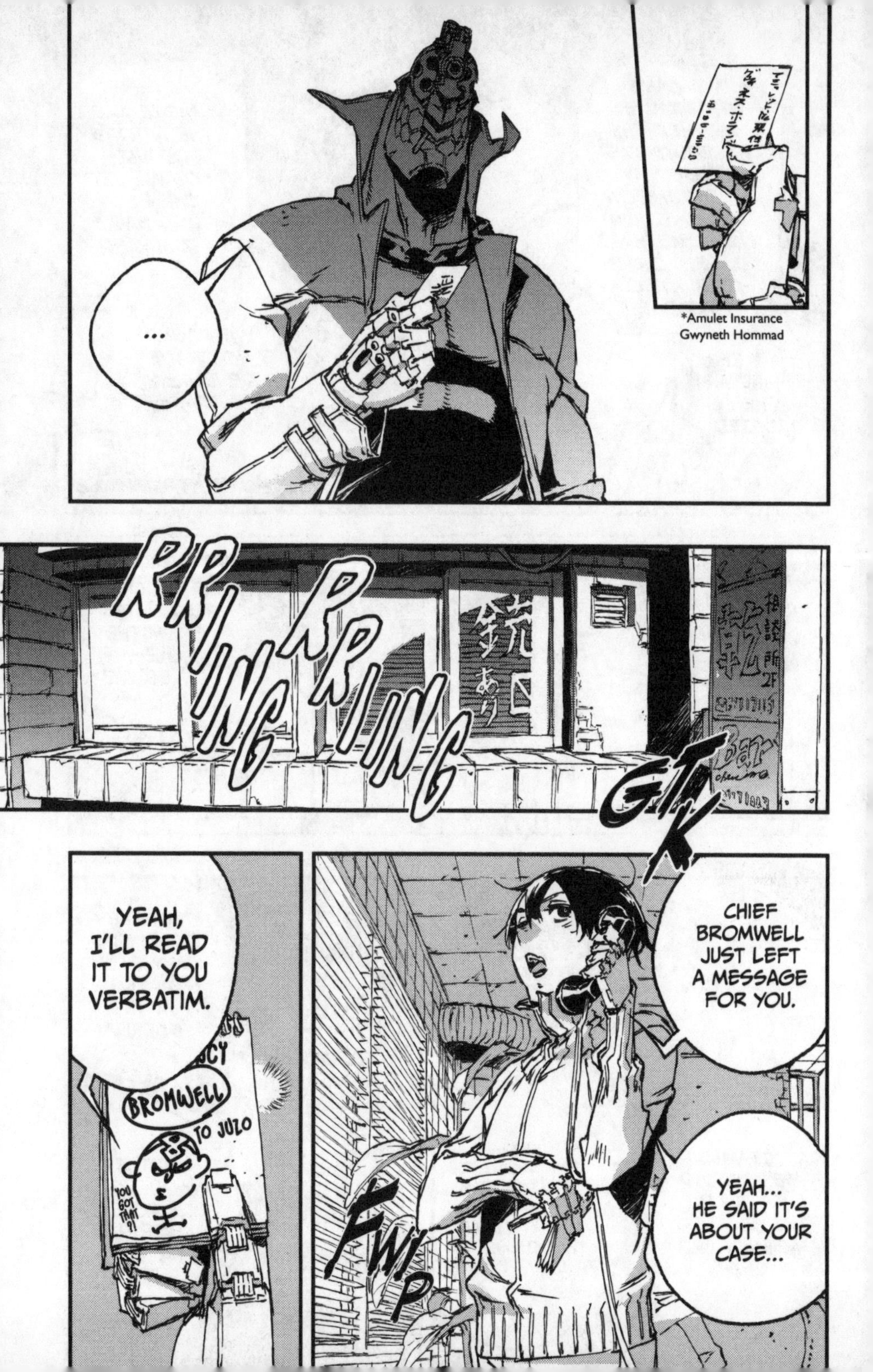
*Amulet Insurance
Gwyneth Hommad
...
RRING
RRING
GTK
CHIEF BROMWELL JUST LEFT A MESSAGE FOR YOU.
YEAH... HE SAID IT'S ABOUT YOUR CASE...
FWIP
YEAH, I'LL READ IT TO YOU VERBATIM.
BROMWELL
TO JUZO
YOU GOT THAT?!

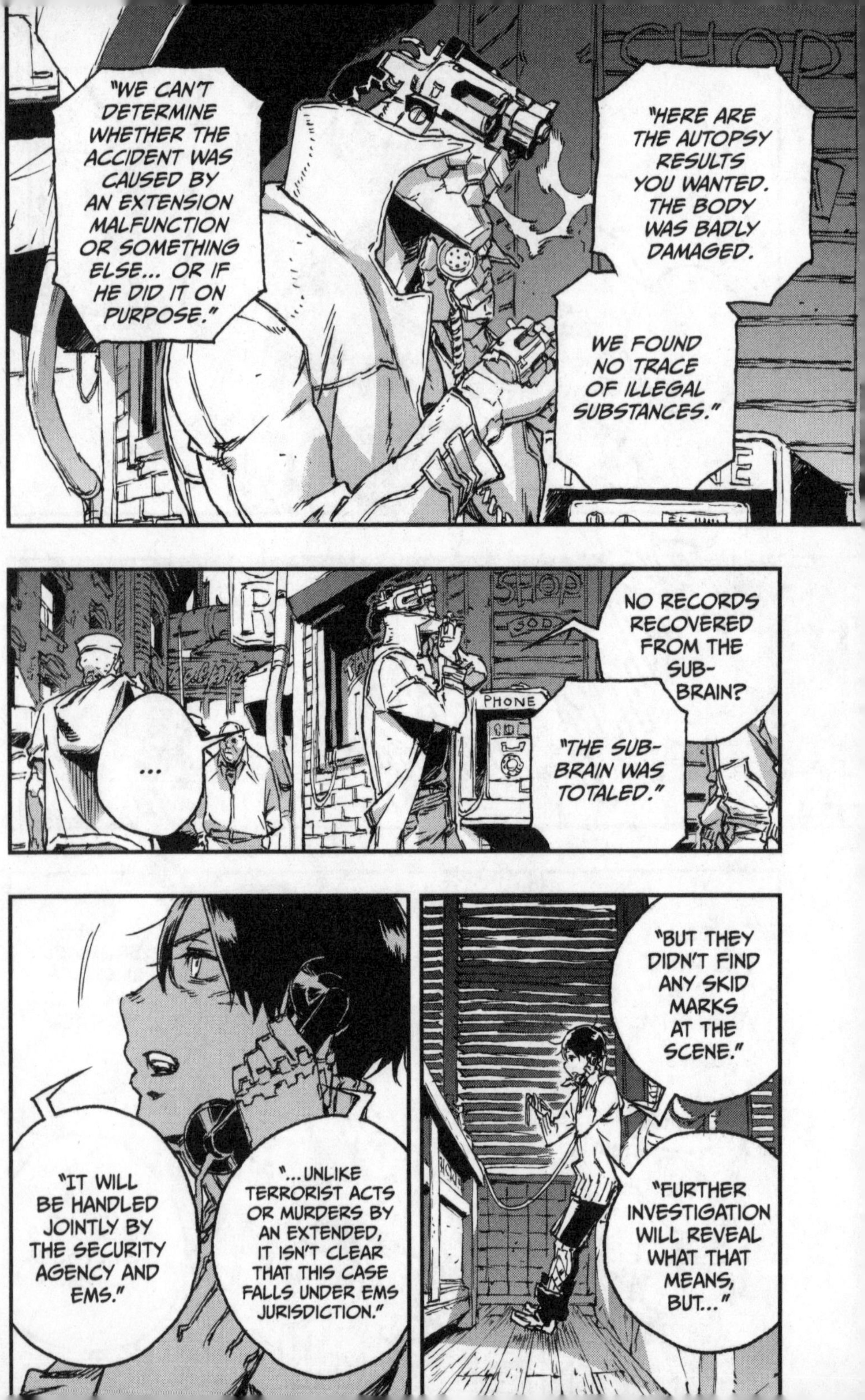
"HERE ARE THE AUTOPSY RESULTS YOU WANTED. THE BODY WAS BADLY DAMAGED.
WE FOUND NO TRACE OF ILLEGAL SUBSTANCES."
"WE CAN'T DETERMINE WHETHER THE ACCIDENT WAS CAUSED BY AN EXTENSION MALFUNCTION OR SOMETHING ELSE... OR IF HE DID IT ON PURPOSE."
SHOP
NO RECORDS RECOVERED FROM THE SUB-BRAIN?
PHONE
"THE SUB-BRAIN WAS TOTALED."
...
"BUT THEY DIDN'T FIND ANY SKID MARKS AT THE SCENE."
"FURTHER INVESTIGATION WILL REVEAL WHAT THAT MEANS, BUT..."
"...UNLIKE TERRORIST ACTS OR MURDERS BY AN EXTENDED, IT ISN'T CLEAR THAT THIS CASE FALLS UNDER EMS JURISDICTION."
"IT WILL BE HANDLED JOINTLY BY THE SECURITY AGENCY AND EMS."

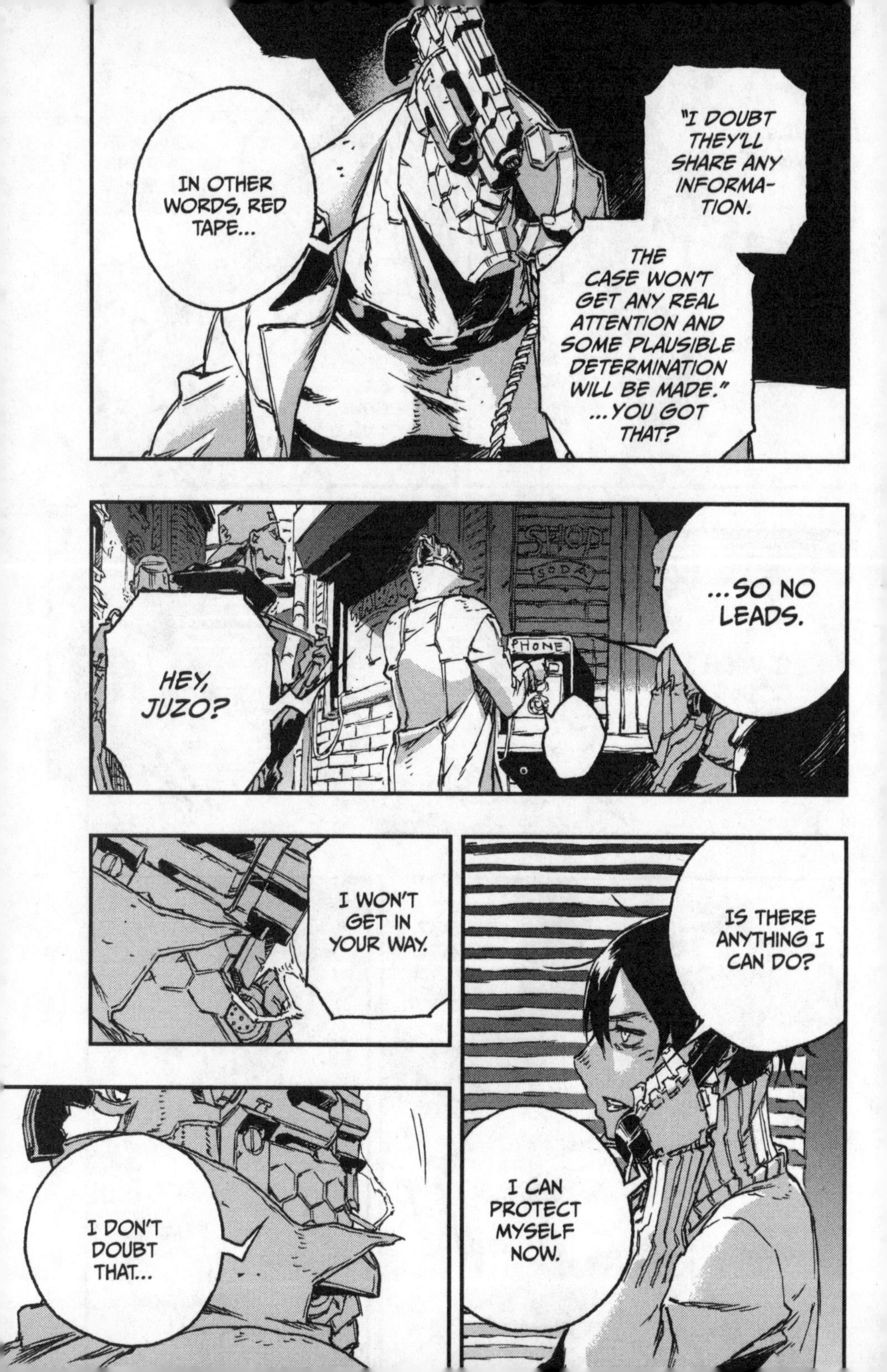
"I DOUBT THEY'LL SHARE ANY INFORMATION.
THE CASE WON'T GET ANY REAL ATTENTION AND SOME PLAUSIBLE DETERMINATION WILL BE MADE." ...YOU GOT THAT?
IN OTHER WORDS, RED TAPE...
...SO NO LEADS.
SHOP
SODA
PHONE
HEY, JUZO?
IS THERE ANYTHING I CAN DO?
I CAN PROTECT MYSELF NOW.
I WON'T GET IN YOUR WAY.
I DON'T DOUBT THAT...

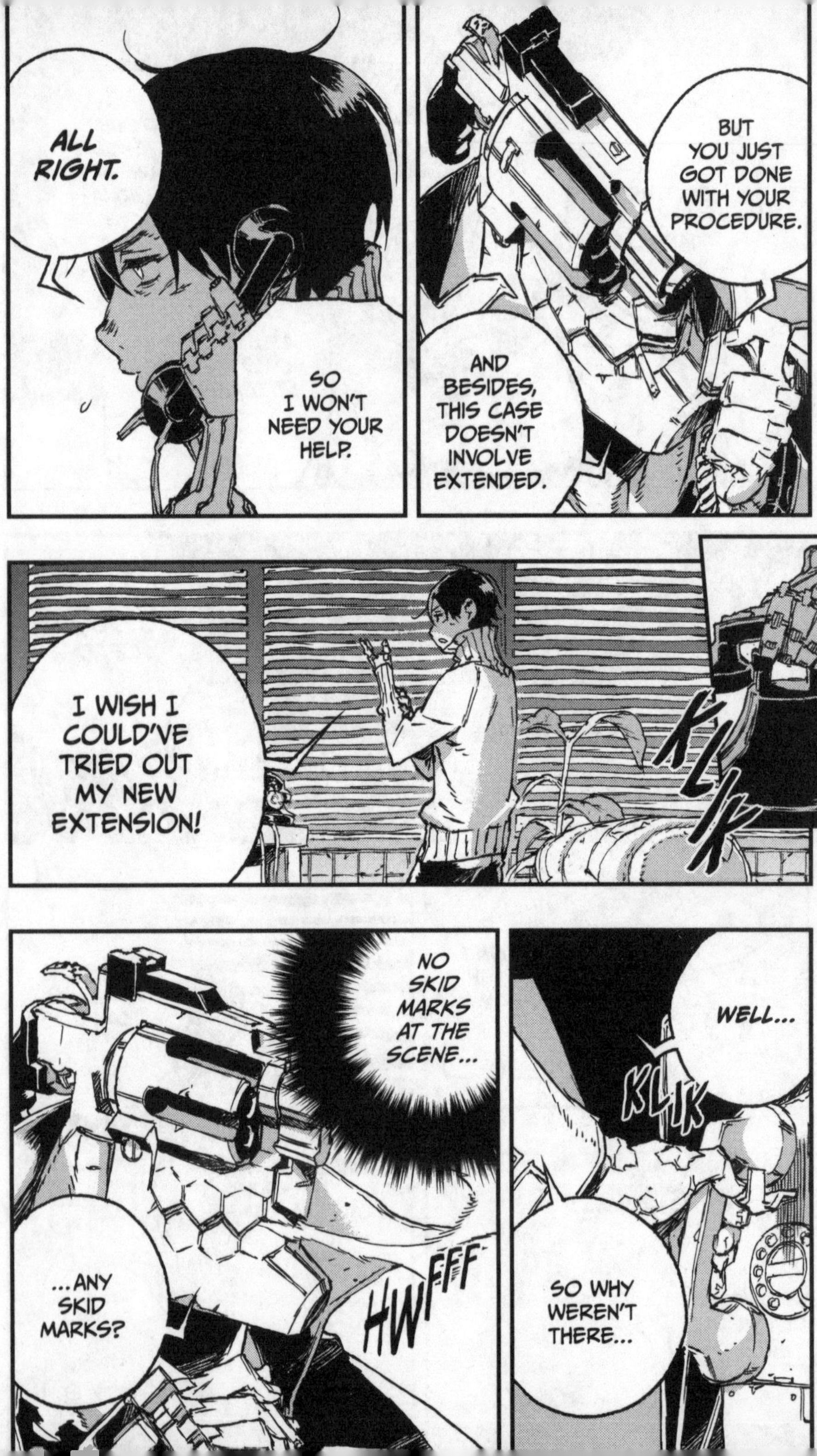
BUT YOU JUST GOT DONE WITH YOUR PROCEDURE.
AND BESIDES, THIS CASE DOESN'T INVOLVE EXTENDED.
ALL RIGHT.
SO I WON'T NEED YOUR HELP.
KLIK
I WISH I COULD'VE TRIED OUT MY NEW EXTENSION!
WELL...
KLIK
SO WHY WEREN'T THERE...
NO SKID MARKS AT THE SCENE...
...ANY SKID MARKS?
HWFFF

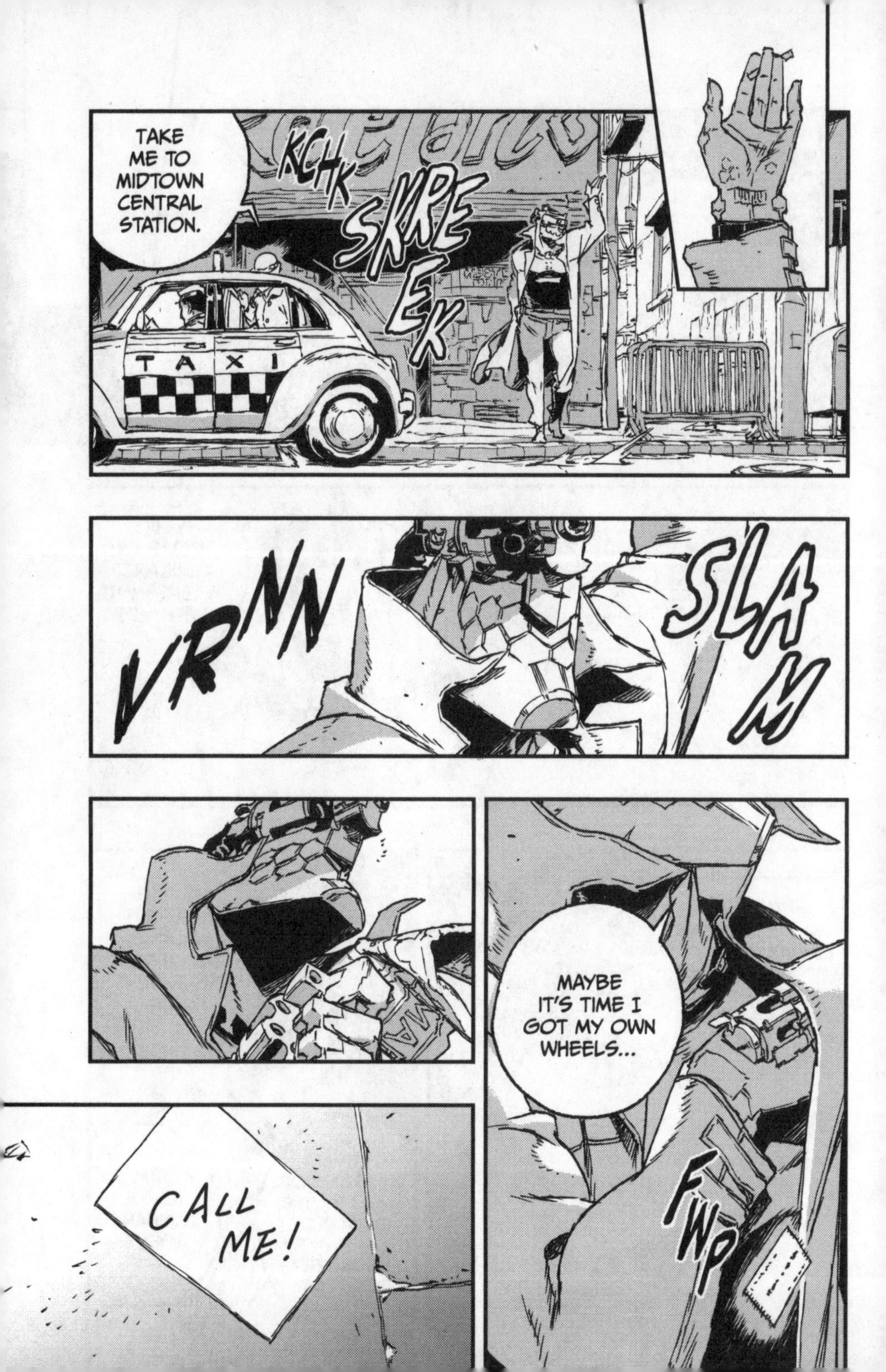
TAKE ME TO MIDTOWN CENTRAL STATION.
KCHK
SKREEK
SLAM
VRNNN
MAYBE IT'S TIME I GOT MY OWN WHEELS...
FWP
CALL ME!

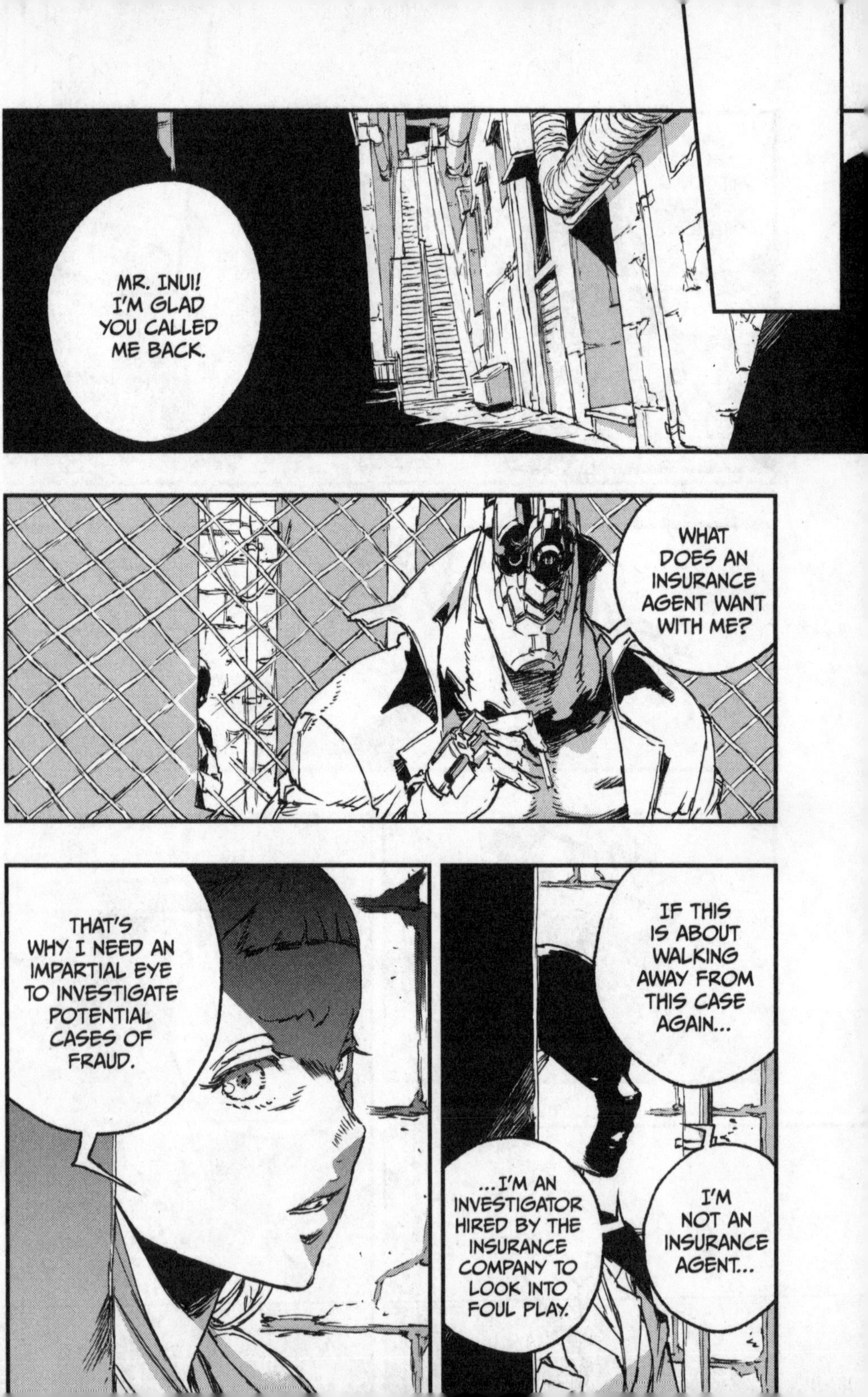
MR. INUI! I'M GLAD YOU CALLED ME BACK.
WHAT DOES AN INSURANCE AGENT WANT WITH ME?
IF THIS IS ABOUT WALKING AWAY FROM THIS CASE AGAIN...
I'M NOT AN INSURANCE AGENT...
...I'M AN INVESTIGATOR HIRED BY THE INSURANCE COMPANY TO LOOK INTO FOUL PLAY.
THAT'S WHY I NEED AN IMPARTIAL EYE TO INVESTIGATE POTENTIAL CASES OF FRAUD.

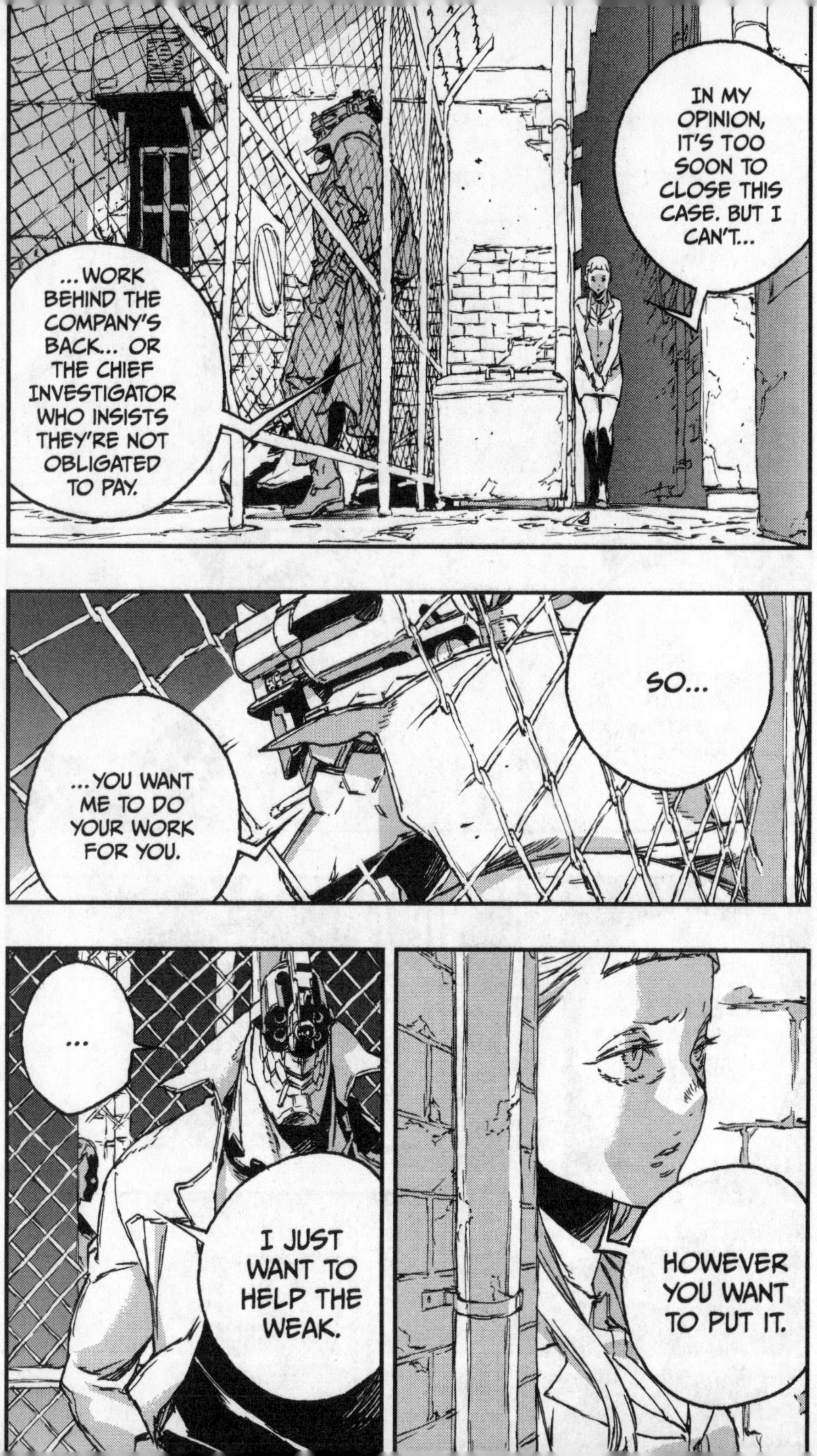
IN MY OPINION, IT'S TOO SOON TO CLOSE THIS CASE. BUT I CAN'T...
...WORK BEHIND THE COMPANY'S BACK... OR THE CHIEF INVESTIGATOR WHO INSISTS THEY'RE NOT OBLIGATED TO PAY.
SO...
...YOU WANT ME TO DO YOUR WORK FOR YOU.
HOWEVER YOU WANT TO PUT IT.
...
I JUST WANT TO HELP THE WEAK.

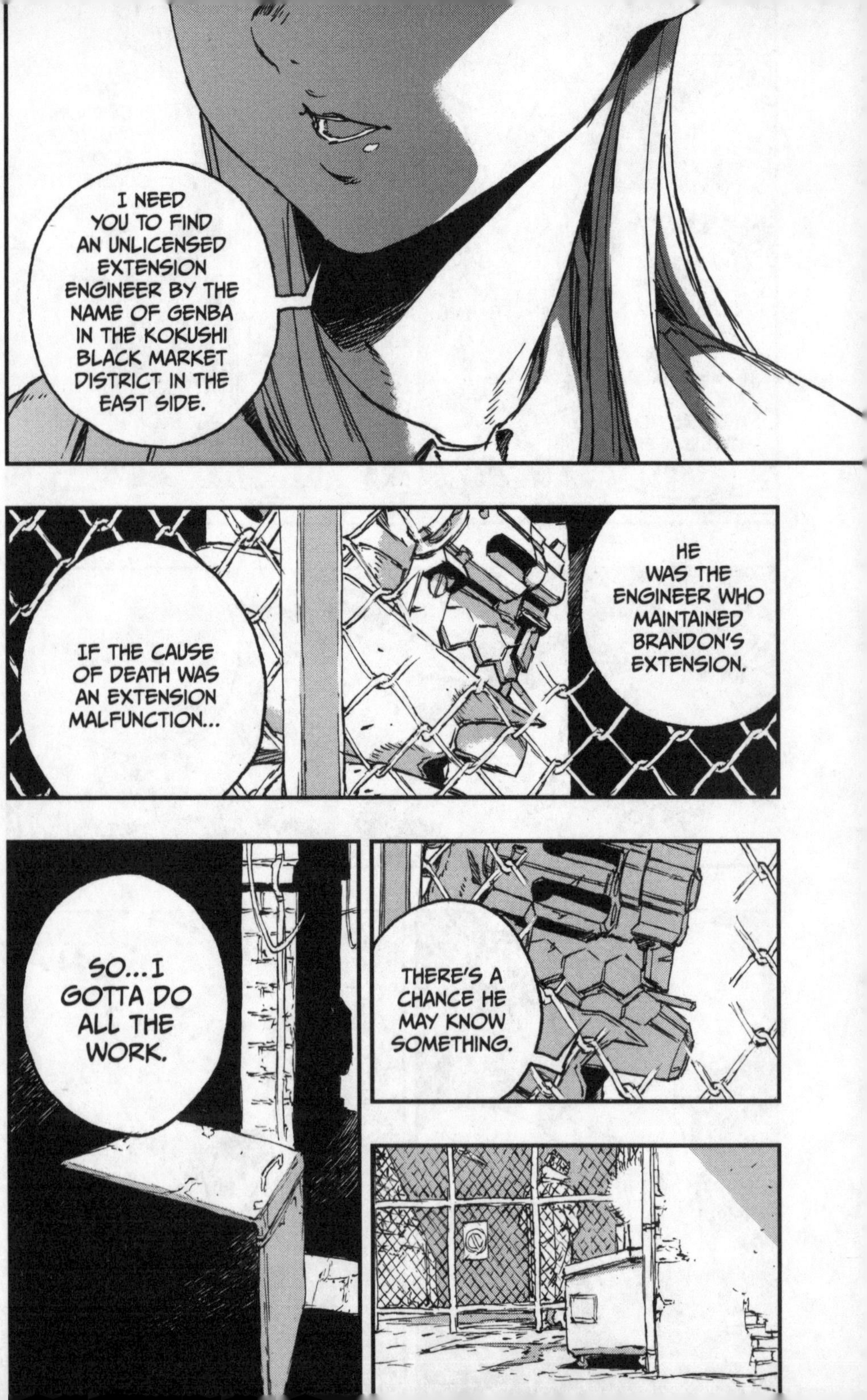
I NEED YOU TO FIND AN UNLICENSED EXTENSION ENGINEER BY THE NAME OF GENBA IN THE KOKUSHI BLACK MARKET DISTRICT IN THE EAST SIDE.
HE WAS THE ENGINEER WHO MAINTAINED BRANDON'S EXTENSION.
IF THE CAUSE OF DEATH WAS AN EXTENSION MALFUNCTION...
THERE'S A CHANCE HE MAY KNOW SOMETHING.
SO...I GOTTA DO ALL THE WORK.

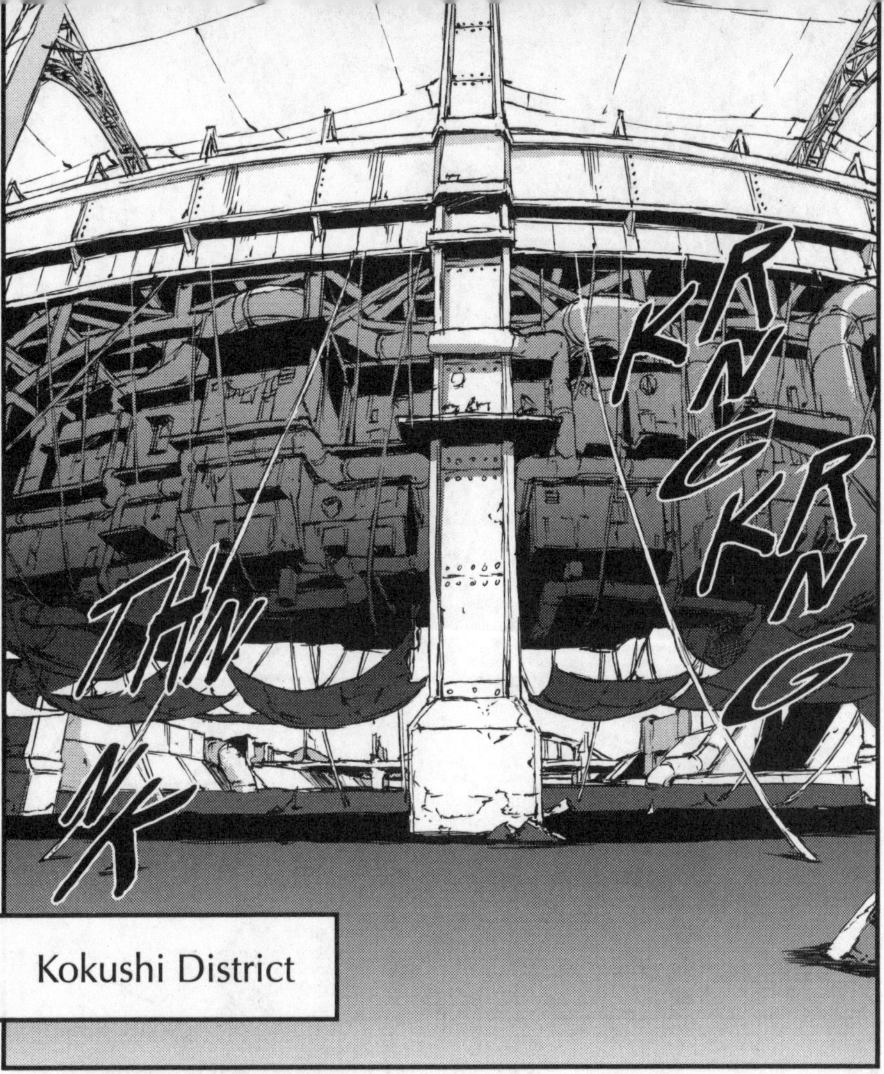
KRNG KRNG
THNK
Kokushi District

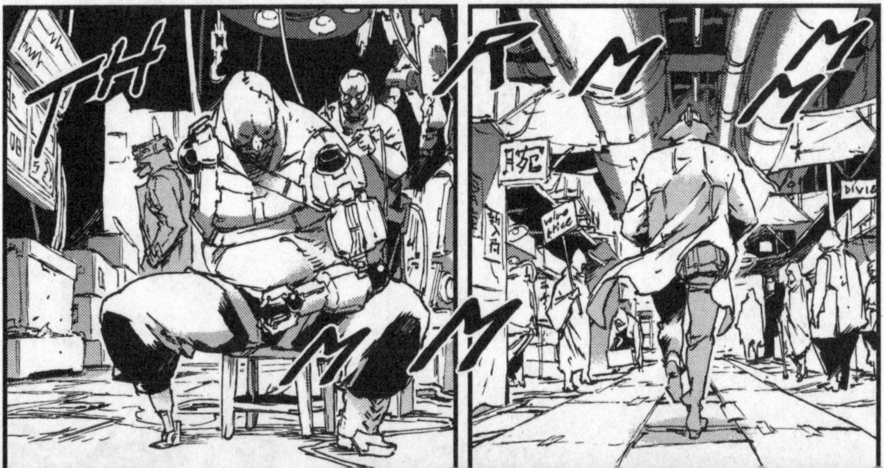
THRMMM
MMM

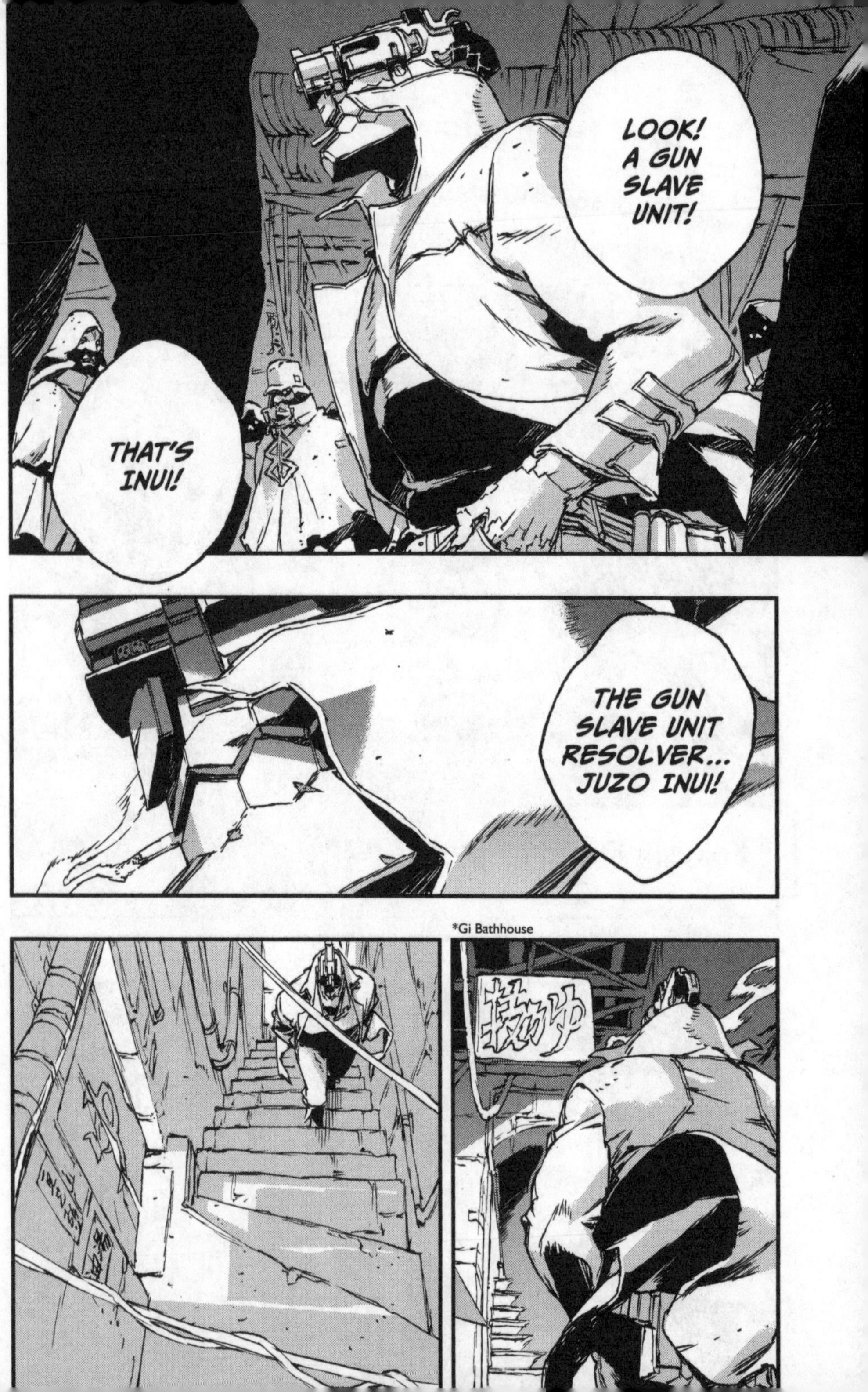
LOOK! A GUN SLAVE UNIT!
THAT'S INUI!
THE GUN SLAVE UNIT RESOLVER... JUZO INUI!
*Gi Bathhouse

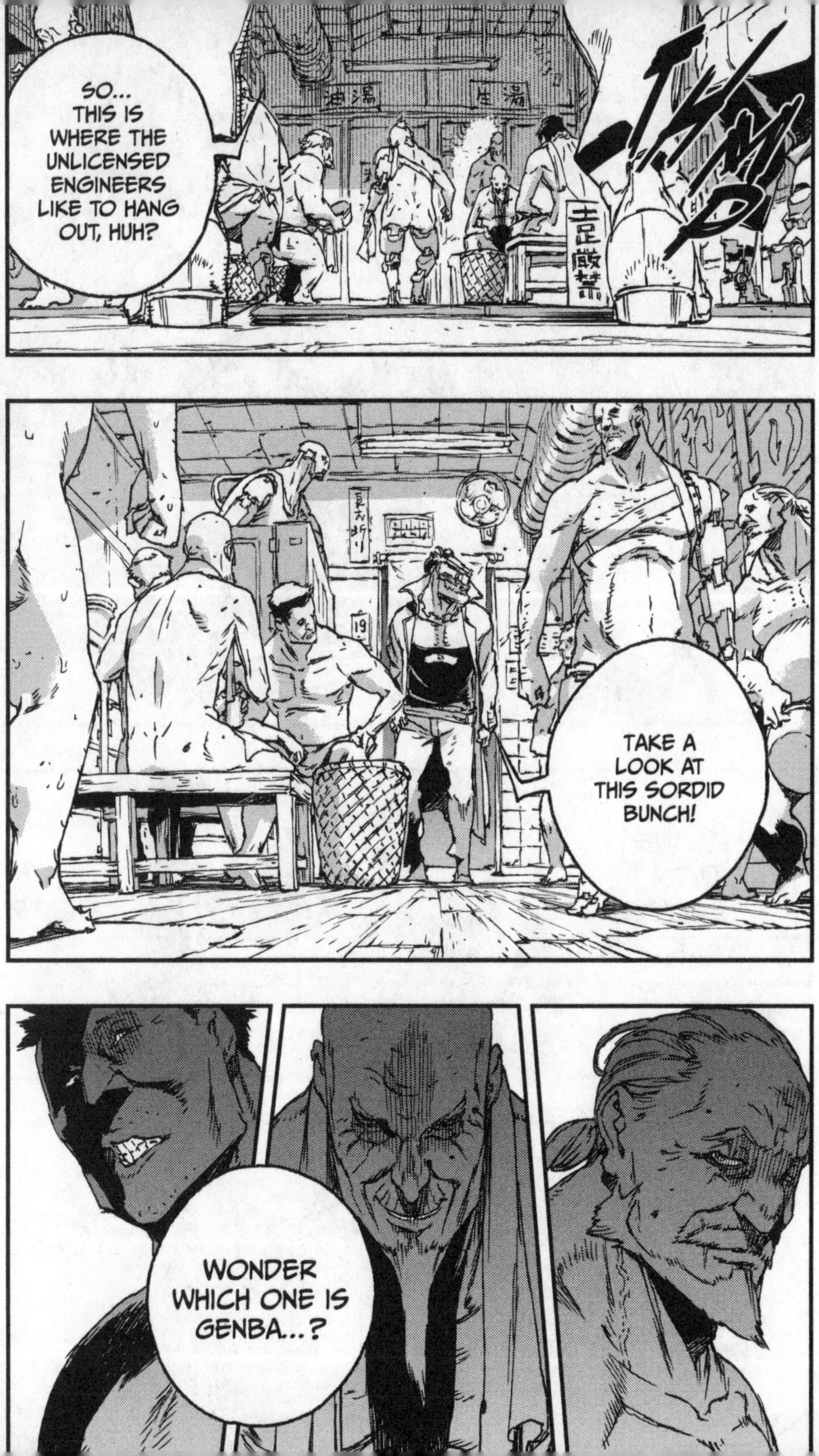
SO... THIS IS WHERE THE UNLICENSED ENGINEERS LIKE TO HANG OUT, HUH?
TAKE A LOOK AT THIS SORDID BUNCH!
WONDER WHICH ONE IS GENBA...?

...WE DON'T ALLOW WALK-INS.

I'M SORRY...

...SHE SENT ME HERE.

SO *THAT'S* WHY...

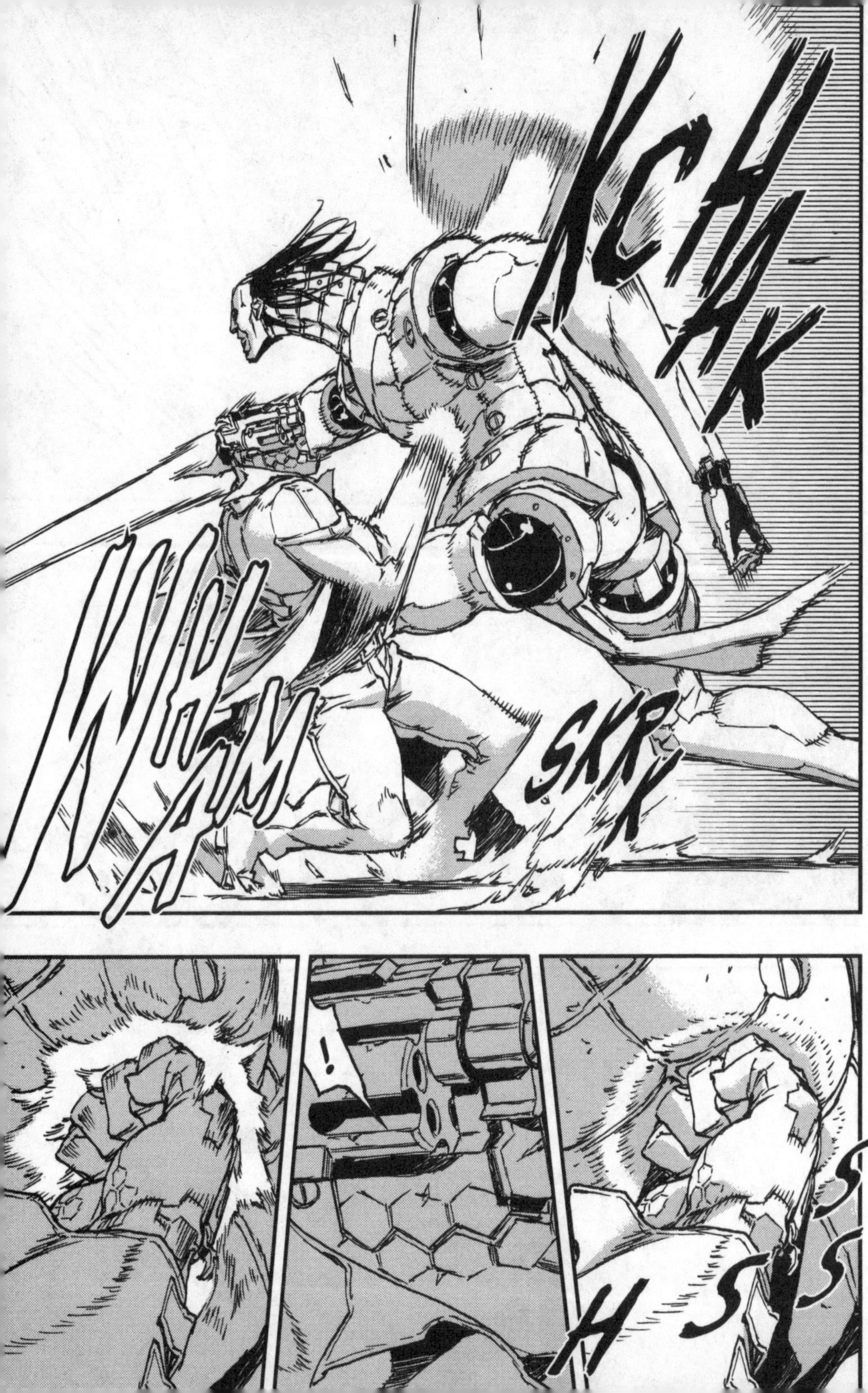
KCH-AK
WHAM
SKRK
HSSS
!

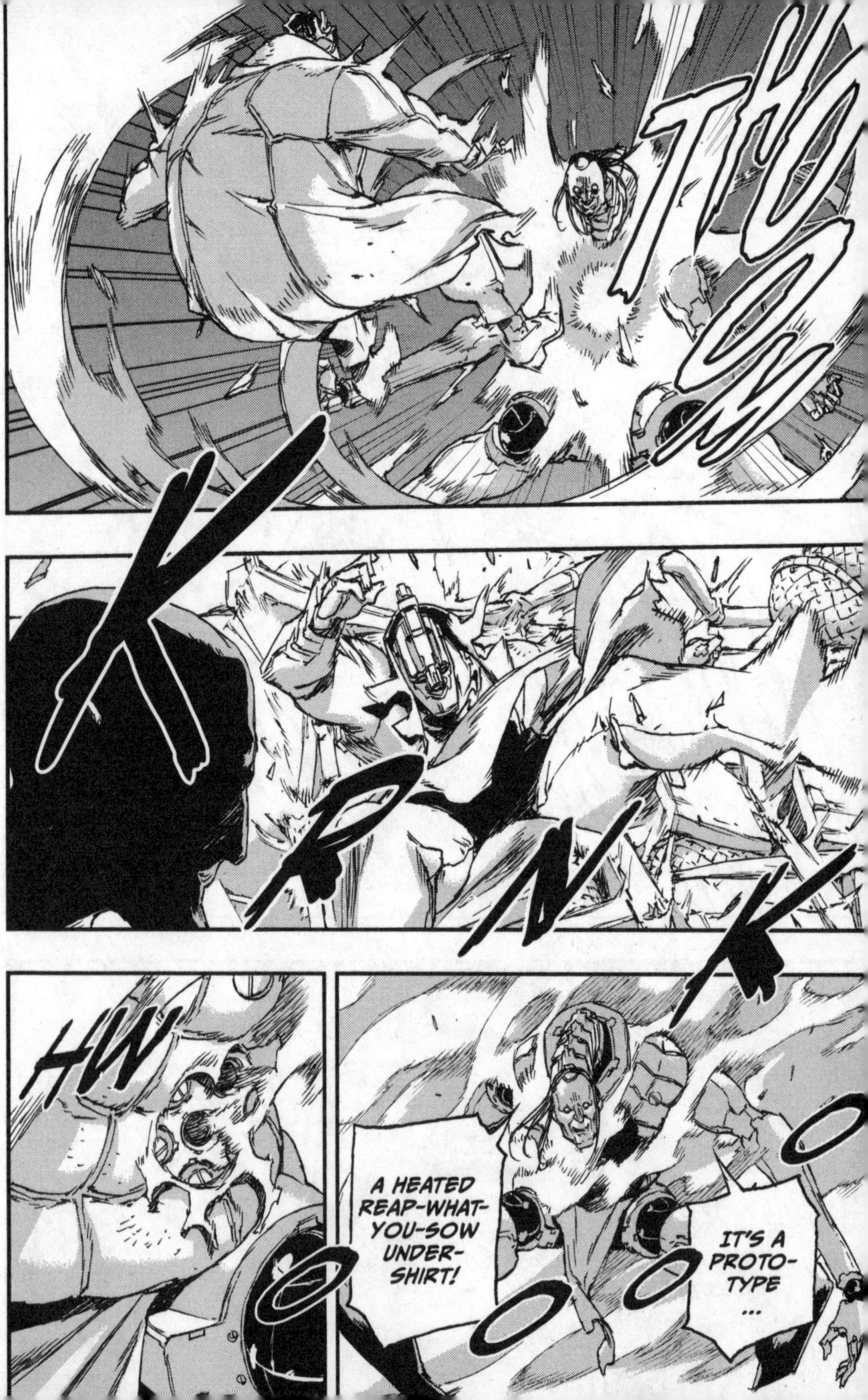
KRNK
IT'S A PROTO-TYPE ...
A HEATED REAP-WHAT-YOU-SOW UNDER-SHIRT!
HW

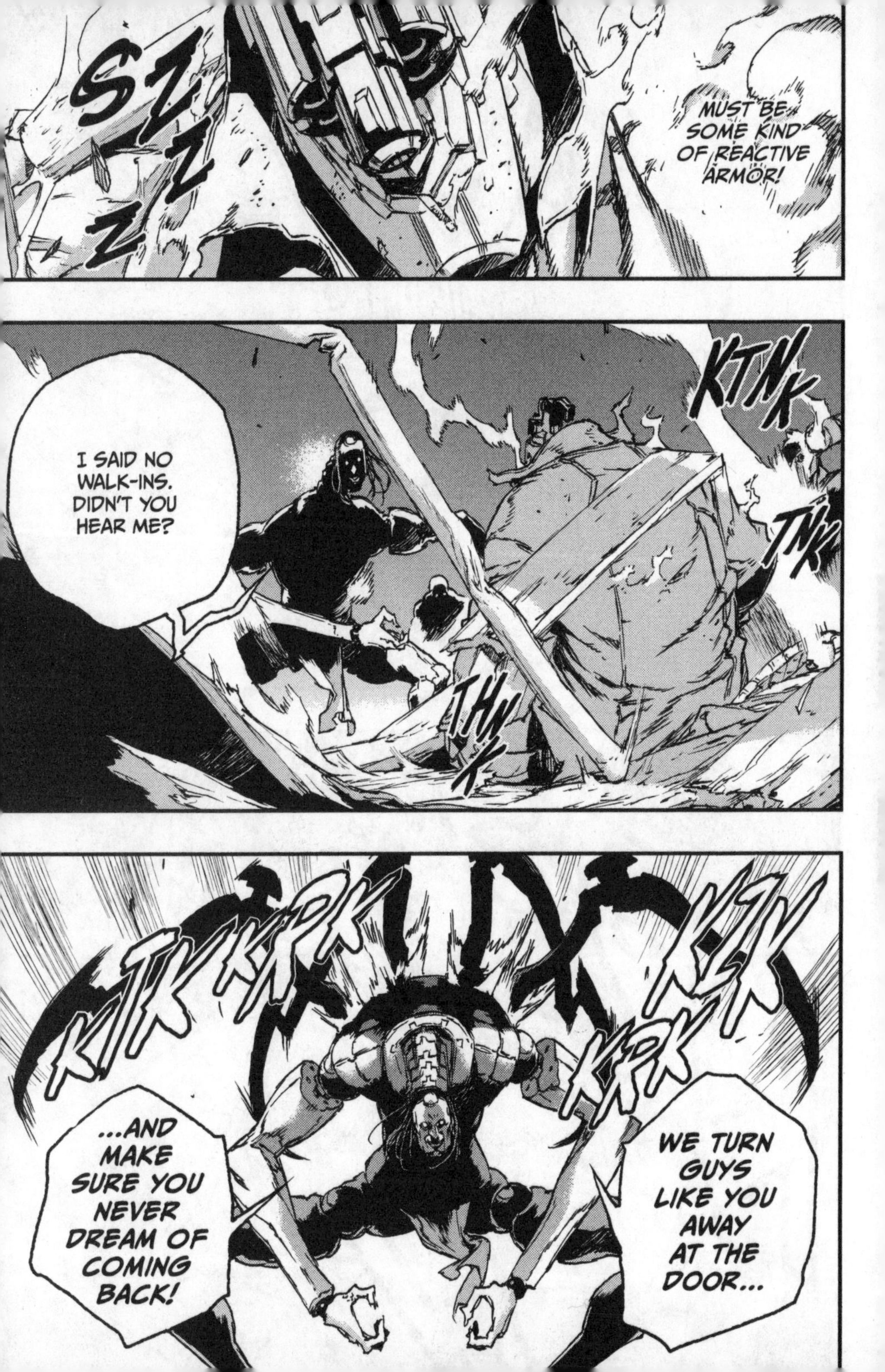
MUST BE SOME KIND OF REACTIVE ARMOR!
SZZZZ
KTNK
TNK
I SAID NO WALK-INS. DIDN'T YOU HEAR ME?
THNK
KRK
WE TURN GUYS LIKE YOU AWAY AT THE DOOR...
...AND MAKE SURE YOU NEVER DREAM OF COMING BACK!

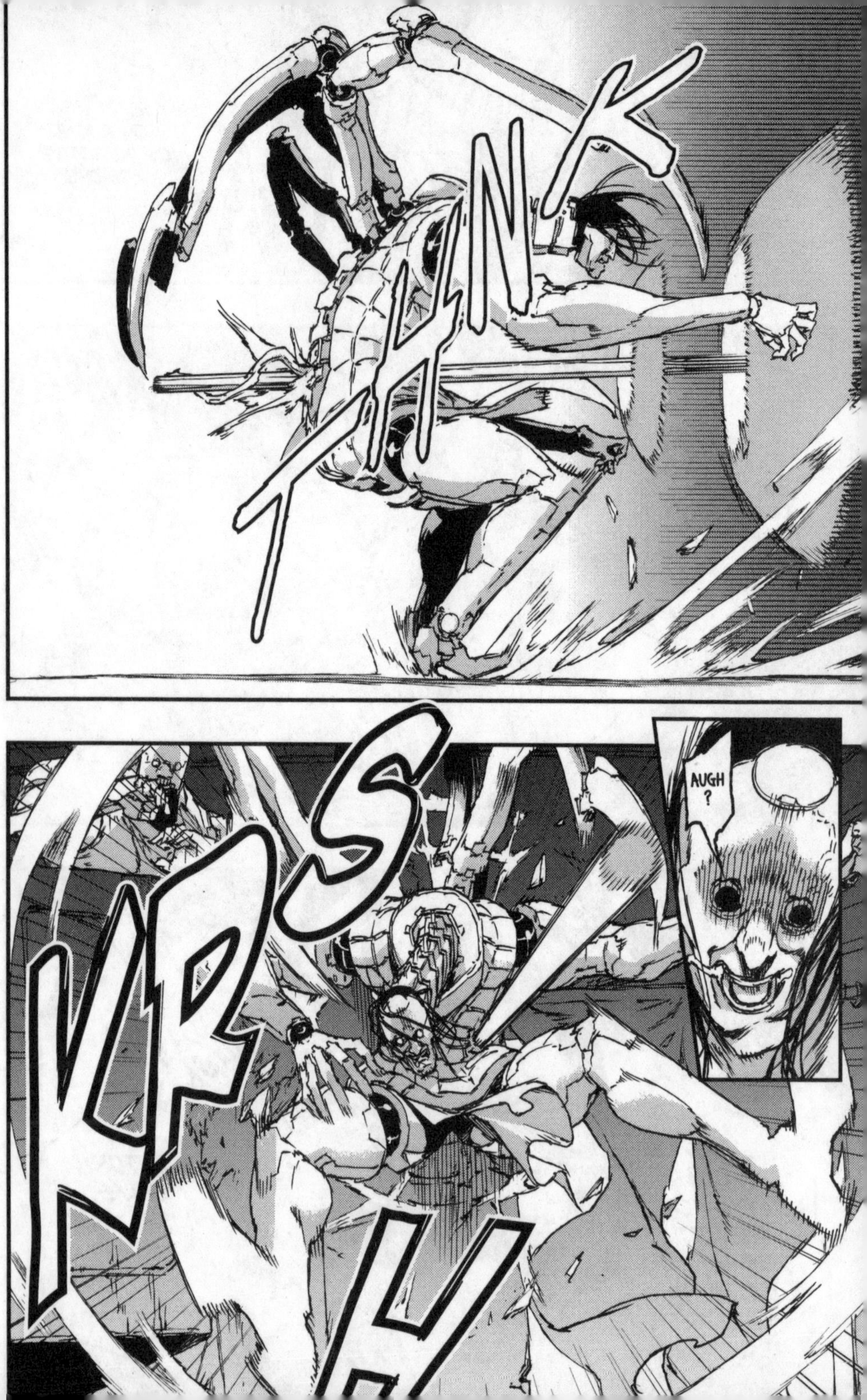
AUGH
?

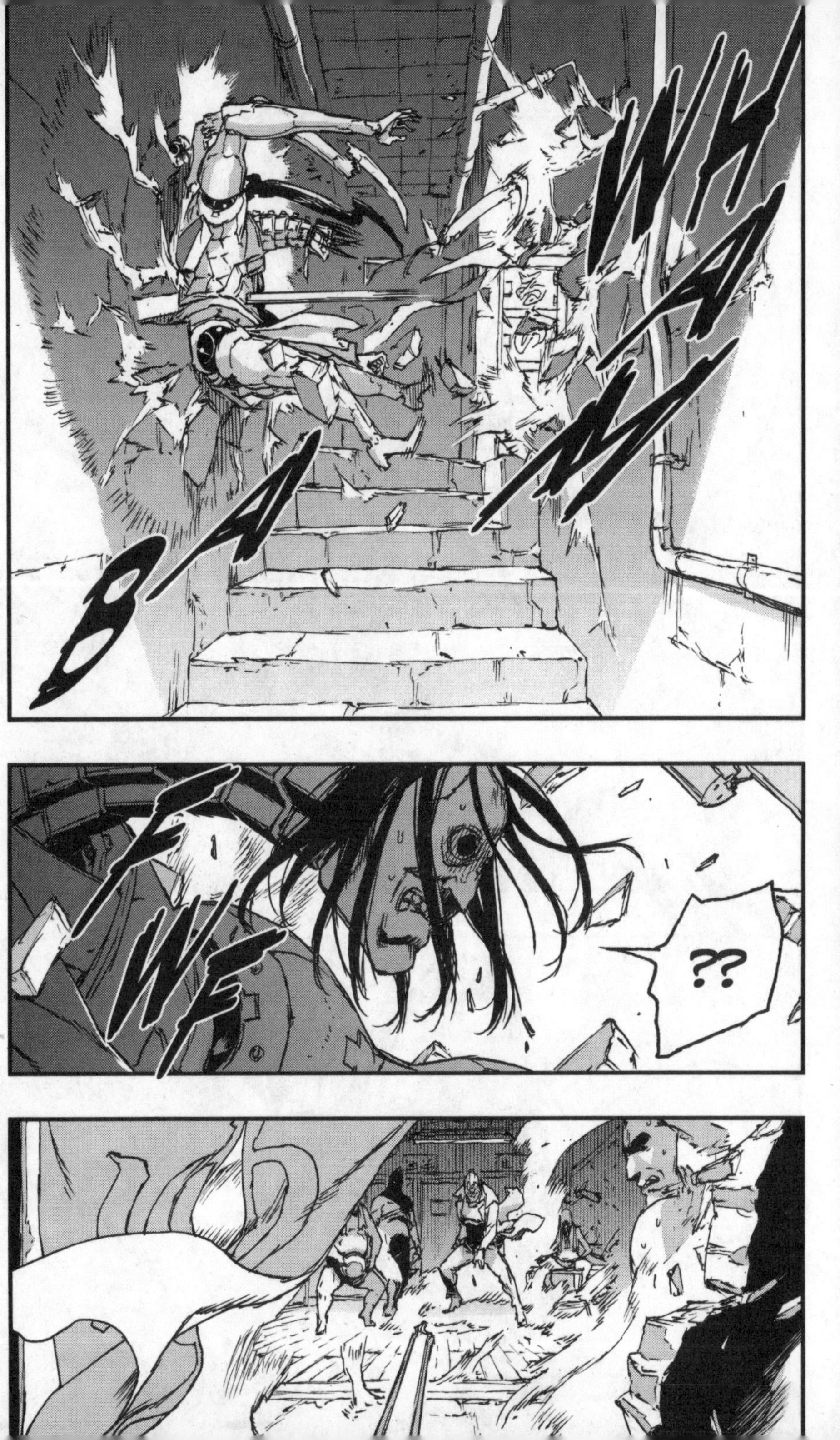
FWF
??

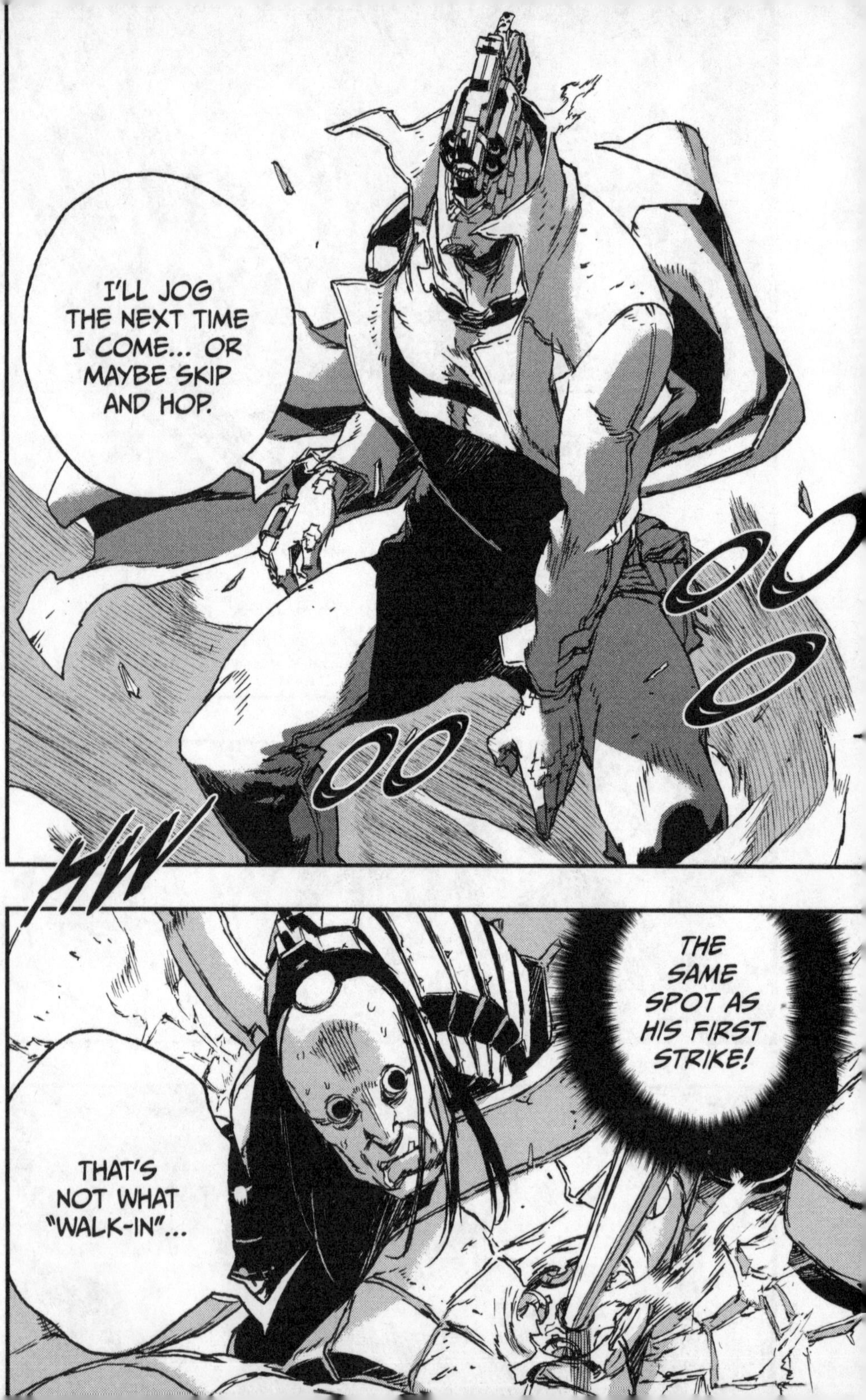
I'LL JOG THE NEXT TIME I COME... OR MAYBE SKIP AND HOP.
HW
THE SAME SPOT AS HIS FIRST STRIKE!
THAT'S NOT WHAT "WALK-IN"...

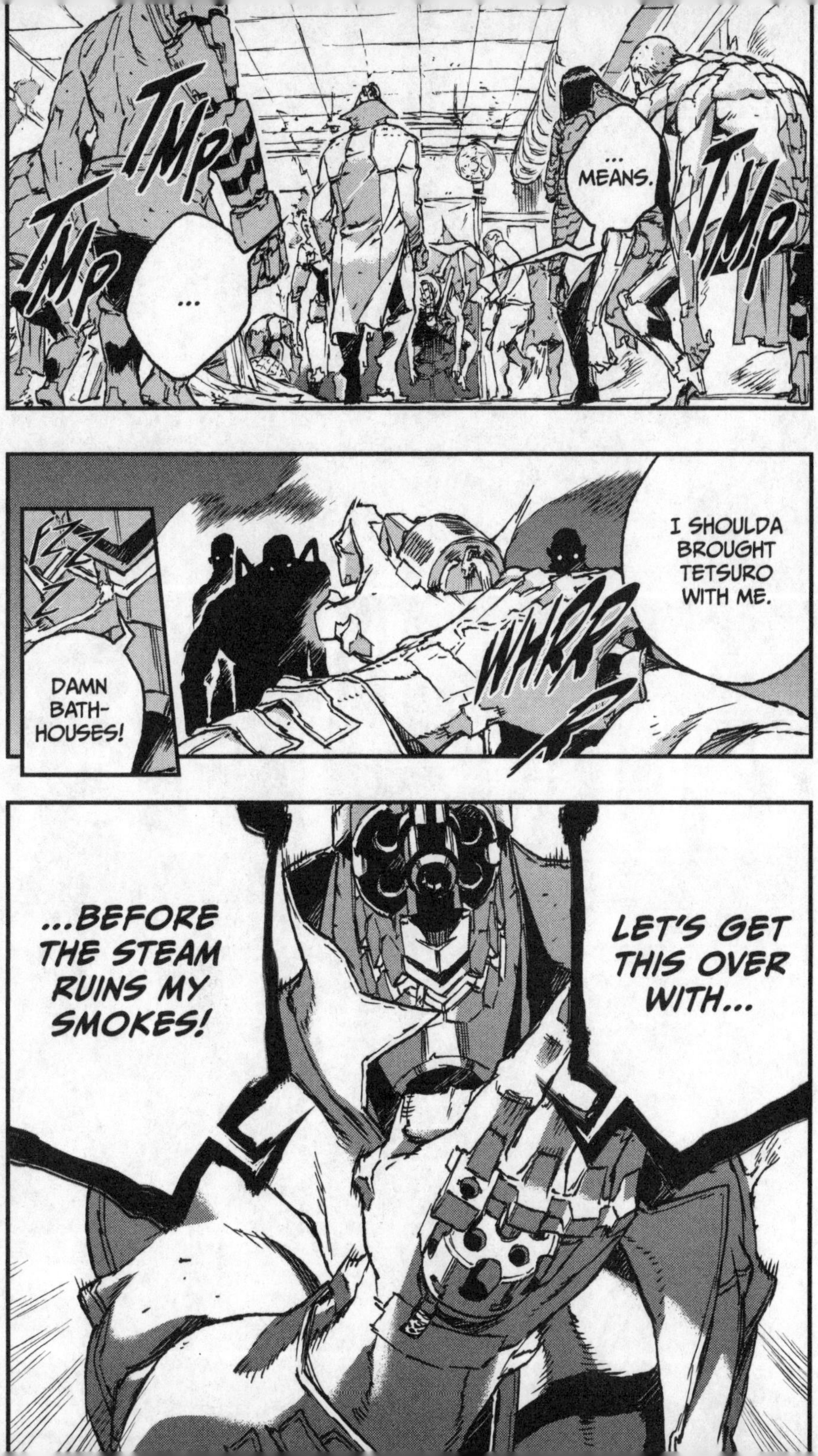
... MEANS.
TMP
TMP
TMP
...
I SHOULDA BROUGHT TETSURO WITH ME.
WHRRR
DAMN BATH-HOUSES!
LET'S GET THIS OVER WITH...
...BEFORE THE STEAM RUINS MY SMOKES!

NO GU
GUNS LIFE

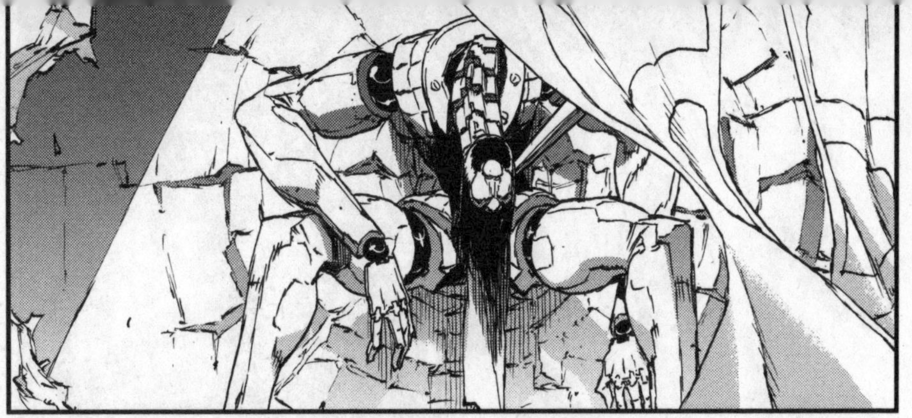

Chapter 59
Relief

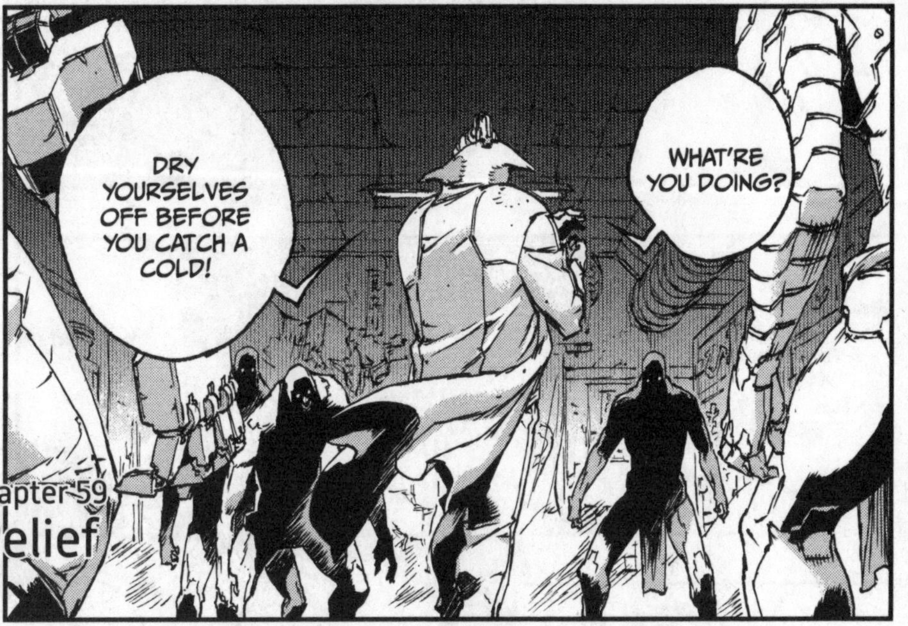
WHAT'RE YOU DOING?
DRY YOURSELVES OFF BEFORE YOU CATCH A COLD!

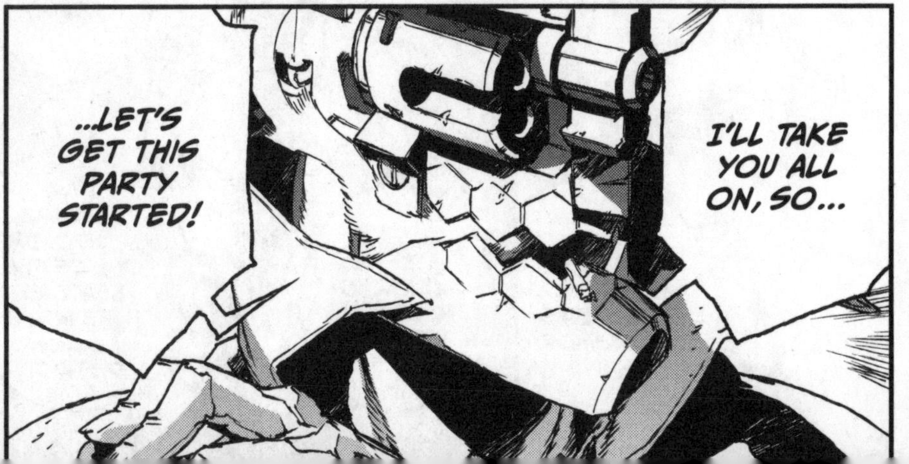
I'LL TAKE YOU ALL ON, SO...
...LET'S GET THIS PARTY STARTED!

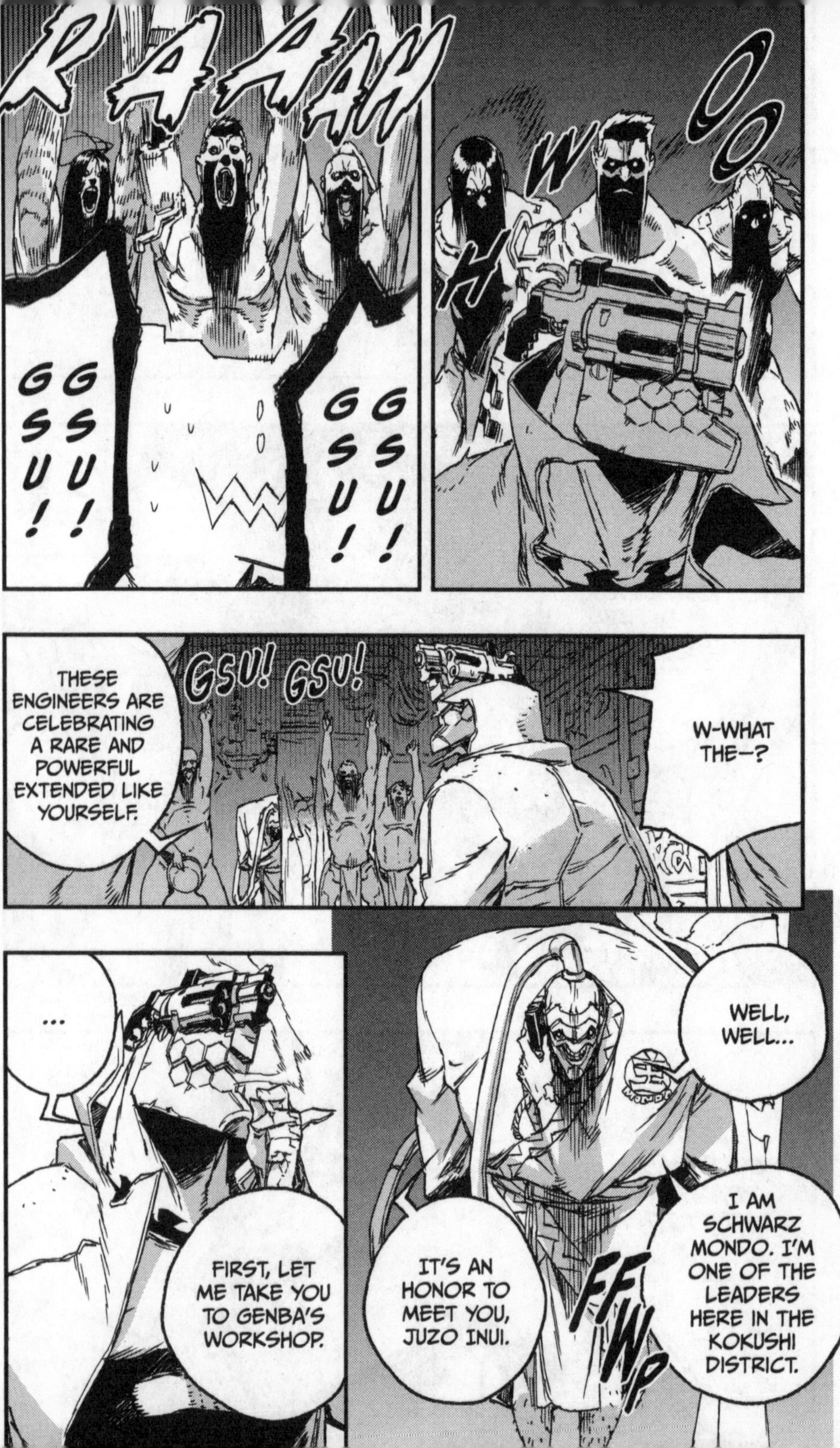
WHOO
RAAAH
GSU! GSU!
GSU! GSU!
W-WHAT THE—?
THESE ENGINEERS ARE CELEBRATING A RARE AND POWERFUL EXTENDED LIKE YOURSELF.
GSU! GSU!
WELL, WELL...
I AM SCHWARZ MONDO. I'M ONE OF THE LEADERS HERE IN THE KOKUSHI DISTRICT.
FFWP
IT'S AN HONOR TO MEET YOU, JUZO INUI.
...
FIRST, LET ME TAKE YOU TO GENBA'S WORKSHOP.

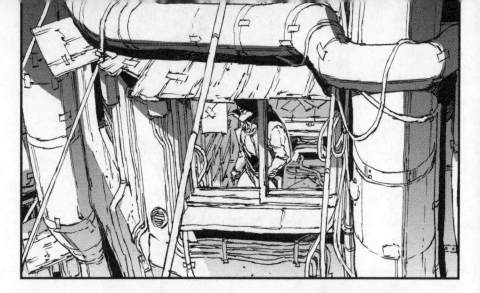

A CELL?

GENBA HAS BROKEN OUR RULES AND IS BEING HELD IN A CELL BELOW THE NO. 3 BRIDGE PIER.

WELL...?

WHERE IS HE?

UH... THANKS.

*Policy Guide

DON'T WORRY. I'VE ARRANGED FOR HIM TO BE BROUGHT HERE.

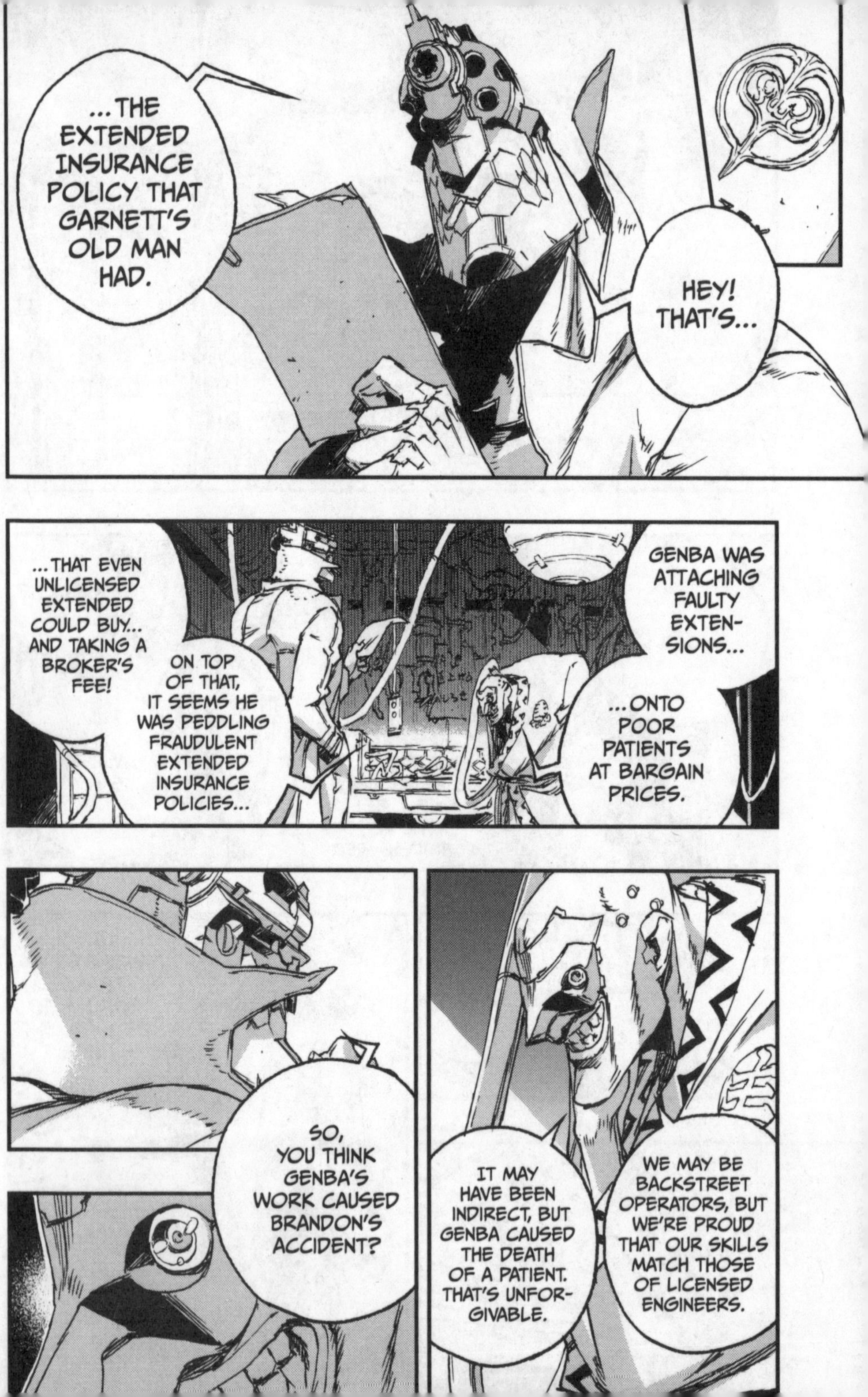
HEY! THAT'S...
...THE EXTENDED INSURANCE POLICY THAT GARNETT'S OLD MAN HAD.
GENBA WAS ATTACHING FAULTY EXTEN- SIONS...
...ONTO POOR PATIENTS AT BARGAIN PRICES.
ON TOP OF THAT, IT SEEMS HE WAS PEDDLING FRAUDULENT EXTENDED INSURANCE POLICIES...
...THAT EVEN UNLICENSED EXTENDED COULD BUY... AND TAKING A BROKER'S FEE!
WE MAY BE BACKSTREET OPERATORS, BUT WE'RE PROUD THAT OUR SKILLS MATCH THOSE OF LICENSED ENGINEERS.
IT MAY HAVE BEEN INDIRECT, BUT GENBA CAUSED THE DEATH OF A PATIENT. THAT'S UNFORGIVABLE.
SO, YOU THINK GENBA'S WORK CAUSED BRANDON'S ACCIDENT?

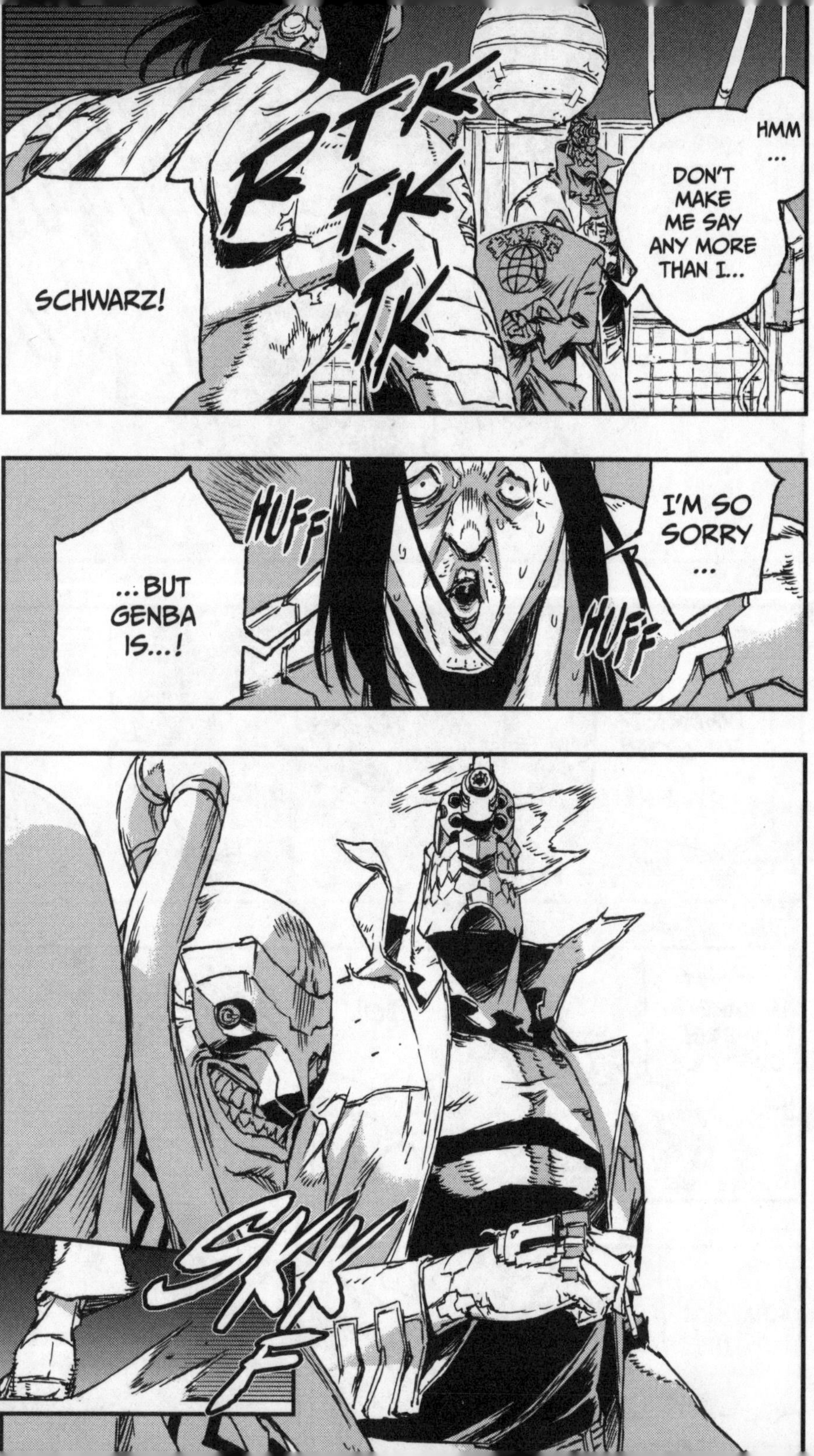
HMM ... DON'T MAKE ME SAY ANY MORE THAN I...
BTK TK TK
SCHWARZ!
I'M SO SORRY ...
HUFF
HUFF
...BUT GENBA IS...!
SKKF

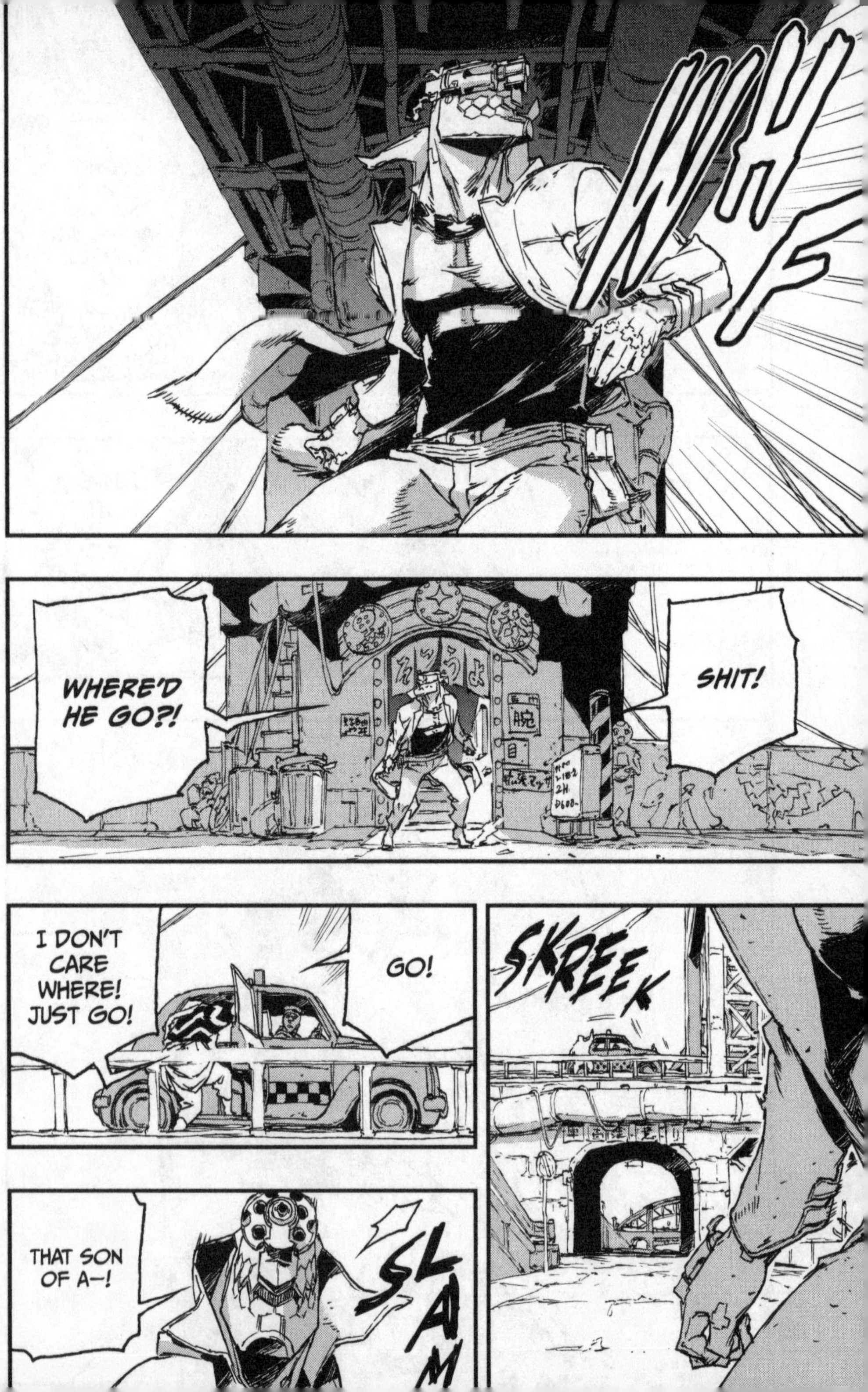
SHIT!
WHERE'D HE GO?!
SKREEK
GO!
I DON'T CARE WHERE! JUST GO!
SLAM
THAT SON OF A—!

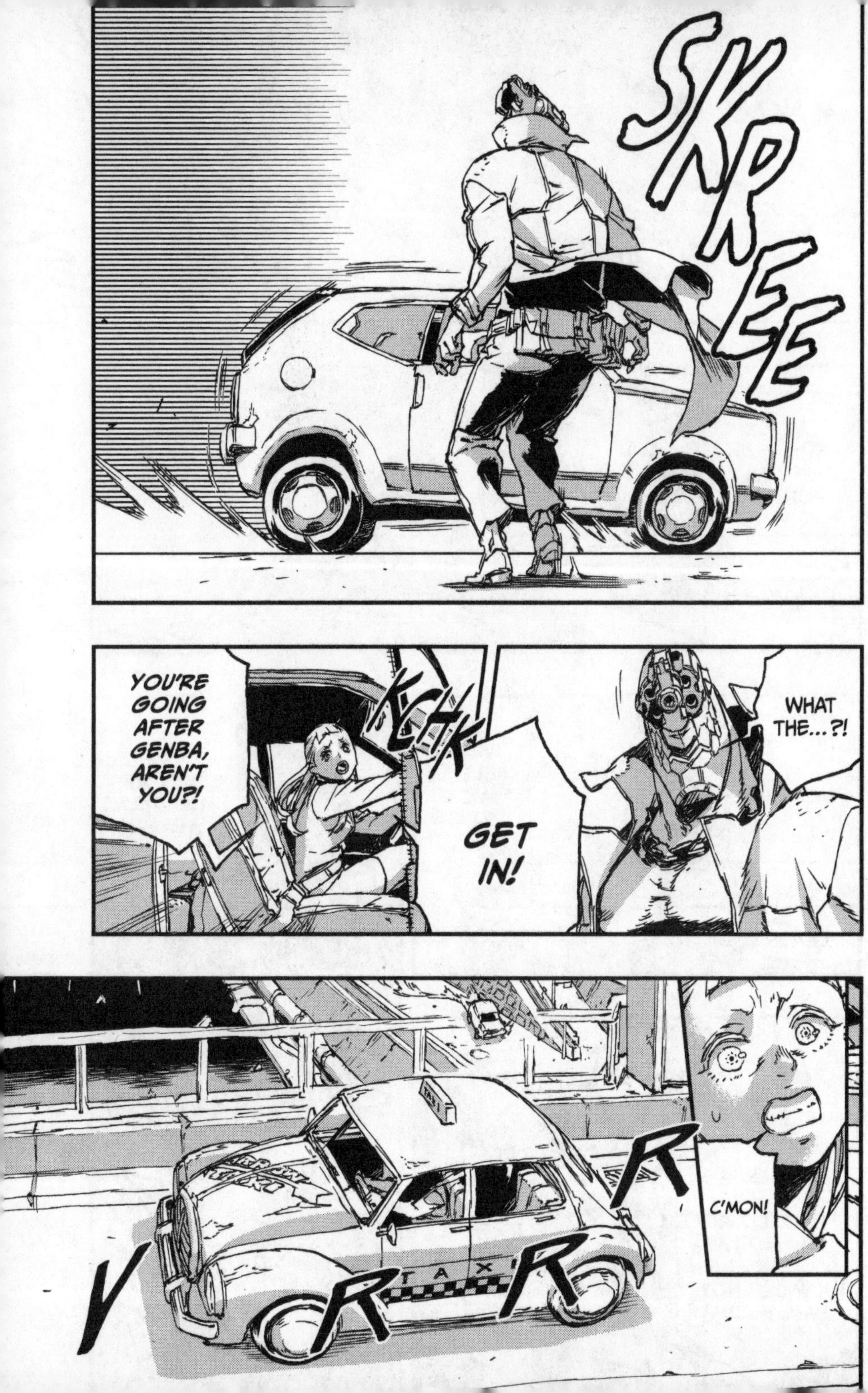
SKREEE
WHAT THE...?!
YOU'RE GOING AFTER GENBA, AREN'T YOU?!
KCHK
GET IN!
C'MON!
VRRRR

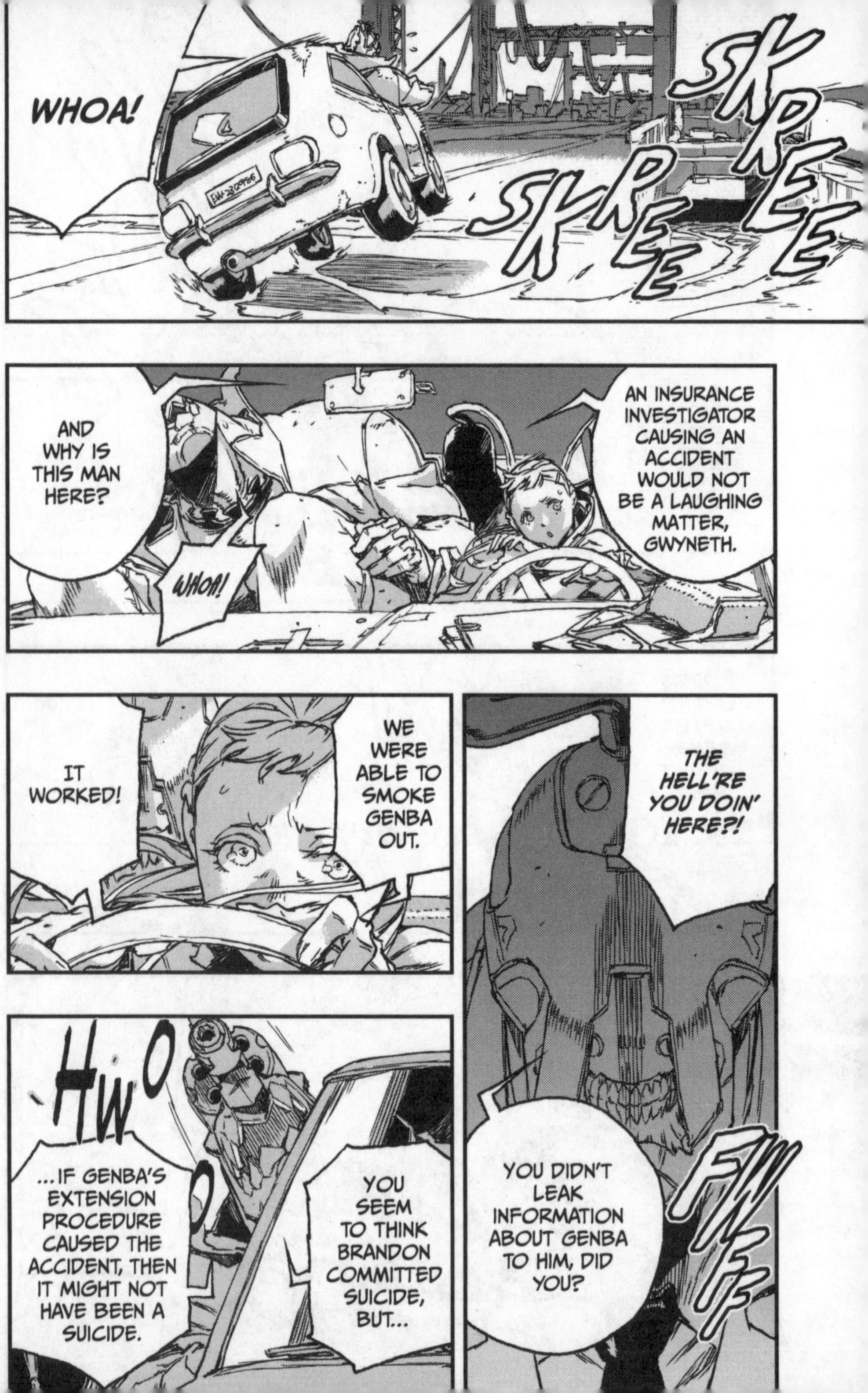
WHOA!
SKREEE
SKREEE
AN INSURANCE INVESTIGATOR CAUSING AN ACCIDENT WOULD NOT BE A LAUGHING MATTER, GWYNETH.
AND WHY IS THIS MAN HERE?
WHOA!
THE HELL'RE YOU DOIN' HERE?!
FWFF
YOU DIDN'T LEAK INFORMATION ABOUT GENBA TO HIM, DID YOU?
WE WERE ABLE TO SMOKE GENBA OUT.
IT WORKED!
HWOO
YOU SEEM TO THINK BRANDON COMMITTED SUICIDE, BUT...
...IF GENBA'S EXTENSION PROCEDURE CAUSED THE ACCIDENT, THEN IT MIGHT NOT HAVE BEEN A SUICIDE.

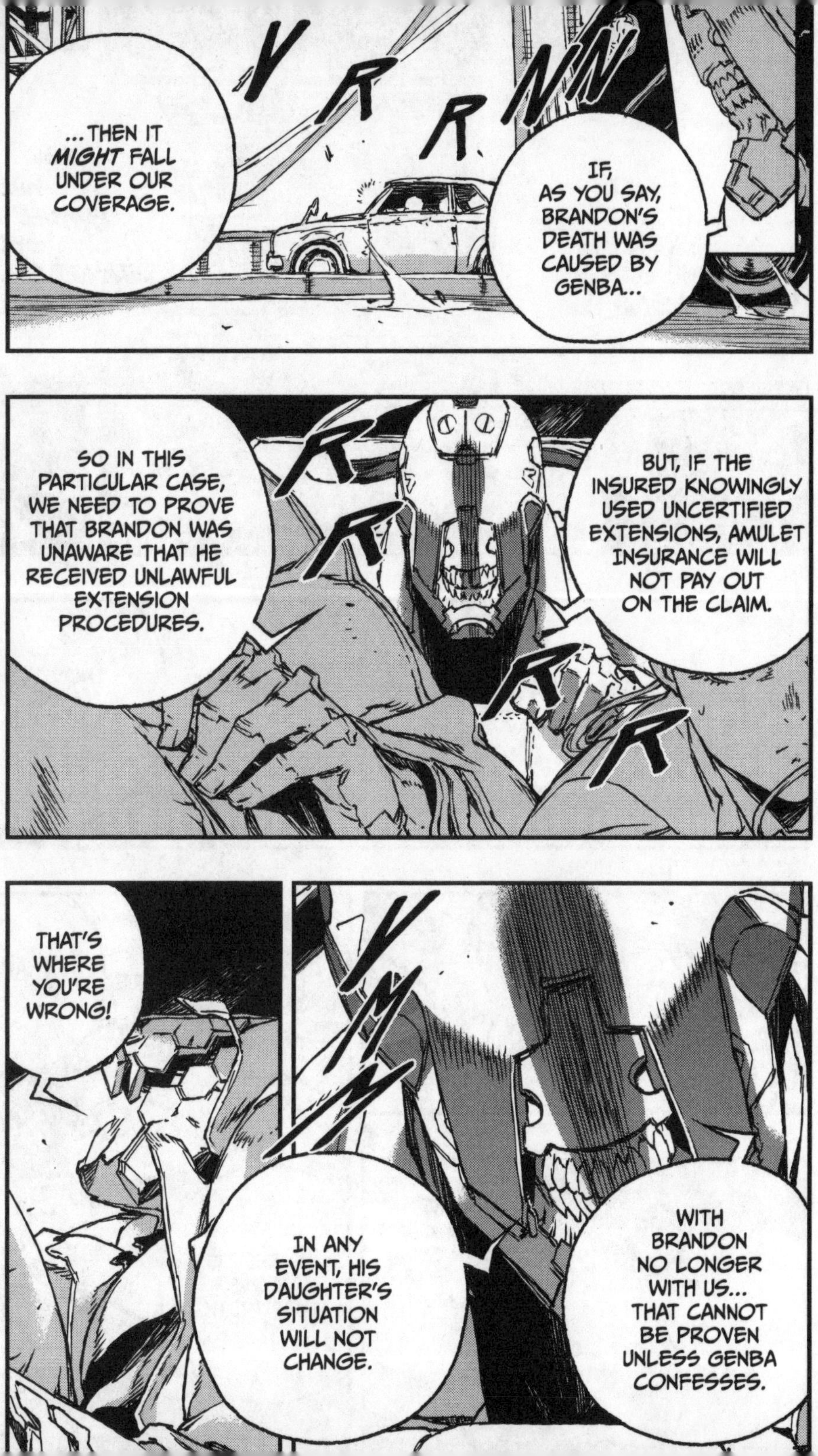
VRRNN
IF, AS YOU SAY, BRANDON'S DEATH WAS CAUSED BY GENBA...
...THEN IT *MIGHT* FALL UNDER OUR COVERAGE.
RRRR
BUT, IF THE INSURED KNOWINGLY USED UNCERTIFIED EXTENSIONS, AMULET INSURANCE WILL NOT PAY OUT ON THE CLAIM.
SO IN THIS PARTICULAR CASE, WE NEED TO PROVE THAT BRANDON WAS UNAWARE THAT HE RECEIVED UNLAWFUL EXTENSION PROCEDURES.
VMM
WITH BRANDON NO LONGER WITH US... THAT CANNOT BE PROVEN UNLESS GENBA CONFESSES.
IN ANY EVENT, HIS DAUGHTER'S SITUATION WILL NOT CHANGE.
THAT'S WHERE YOU'RE WRONG!

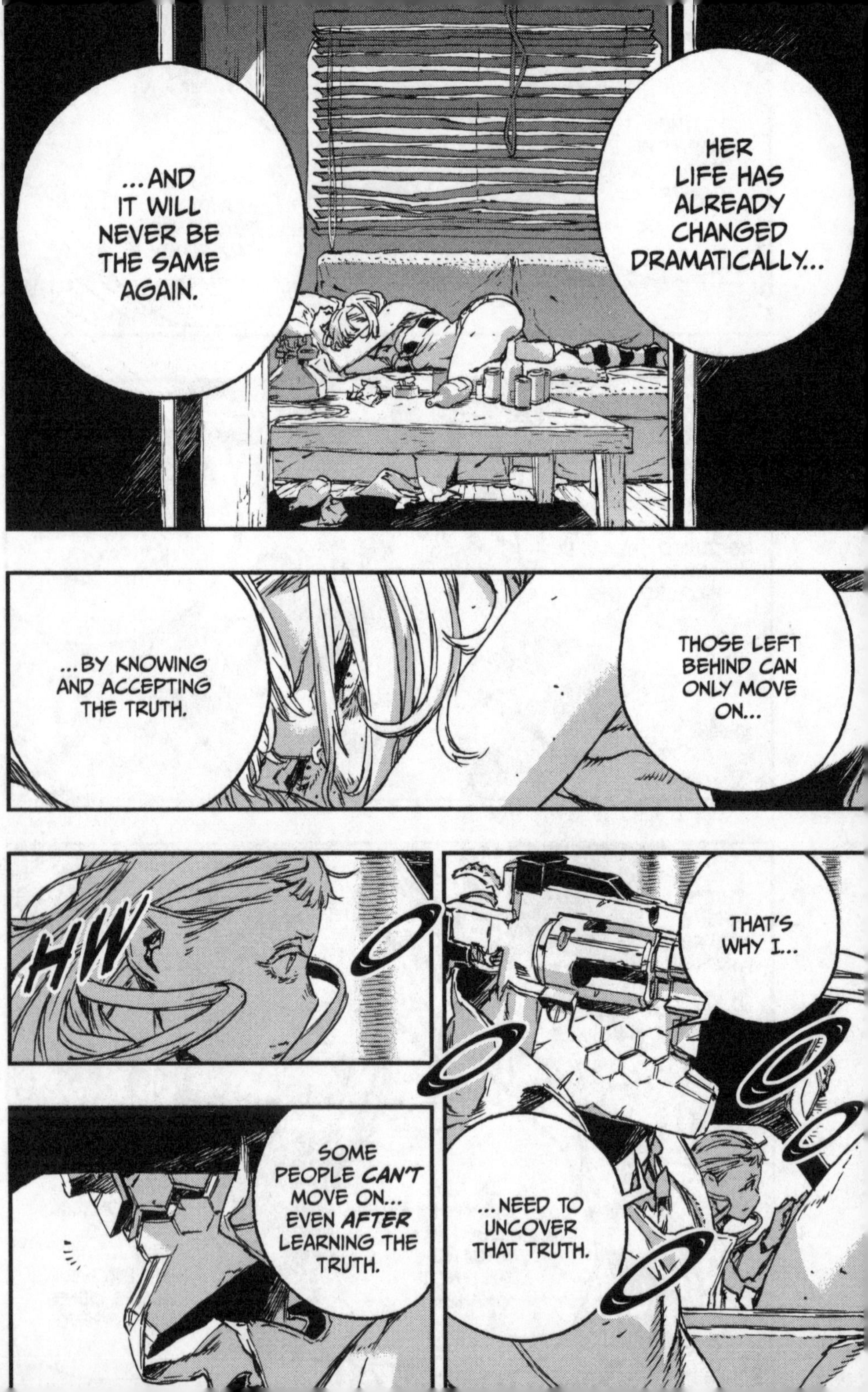
HER LIFE HAS ALREADY CHANGED DRAMATICALLY...
...AND IT WILL NEVER BE THE SAME AGAIN.
THOSE LEFT BEHIND CAN ONLY MOVE ON...
...BY KNOWING AND ACCEPTING THE TRUTH.
THAT'S WHY I...
...NEED TO UNCOVER THAT TRUTH.
HW
SOME PEOPLE *CAN'T* MOVE ON... EVEN *AFTER* LEARNING THE TRUTH.

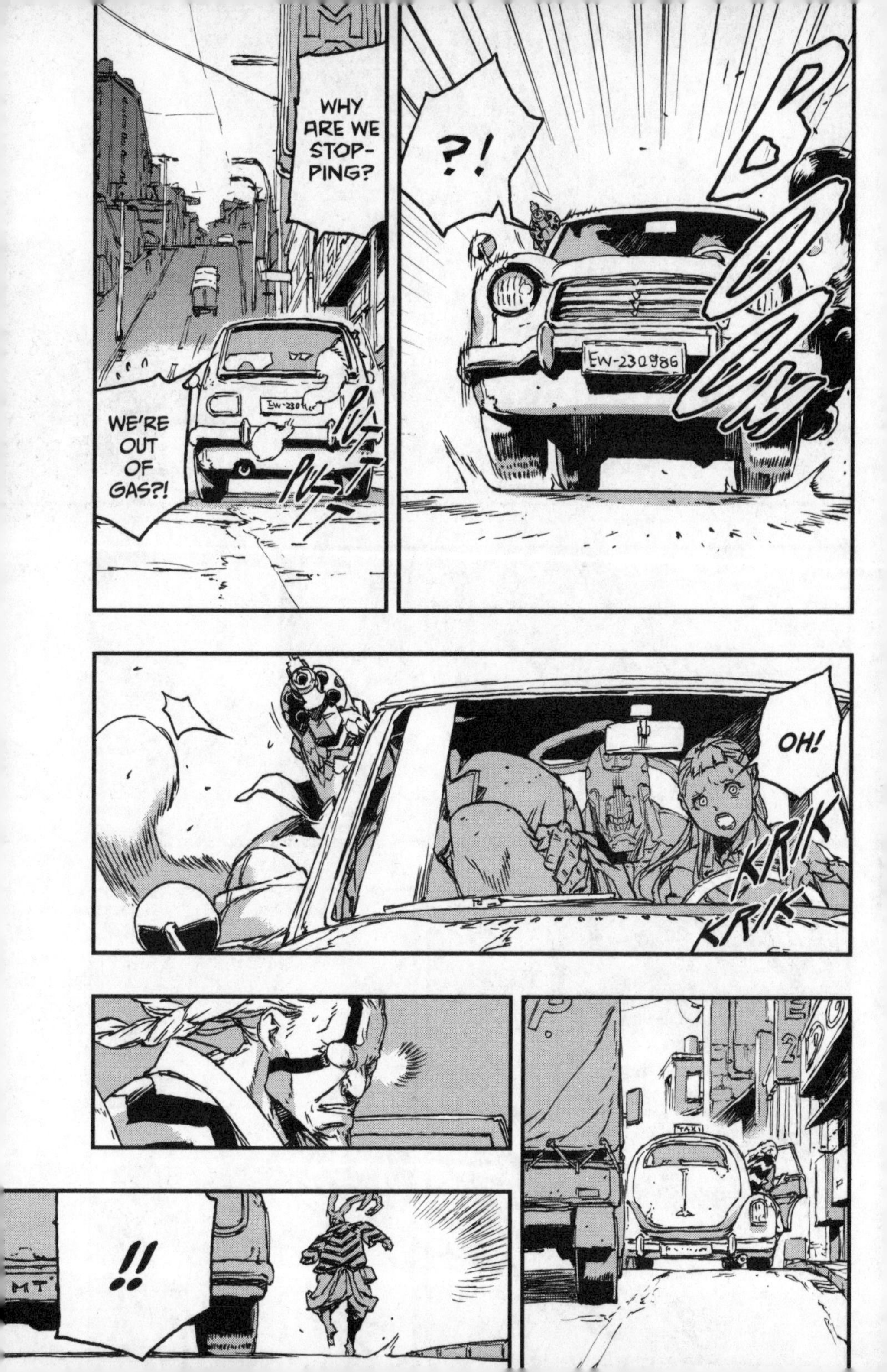

?!
BOOOM
EW-230986
WHY ARE WE STOP-PING?
WE'RE OUT OF GAS?!
PUT
PUT
OH!
KRIK
KRIK
TAXI
!!

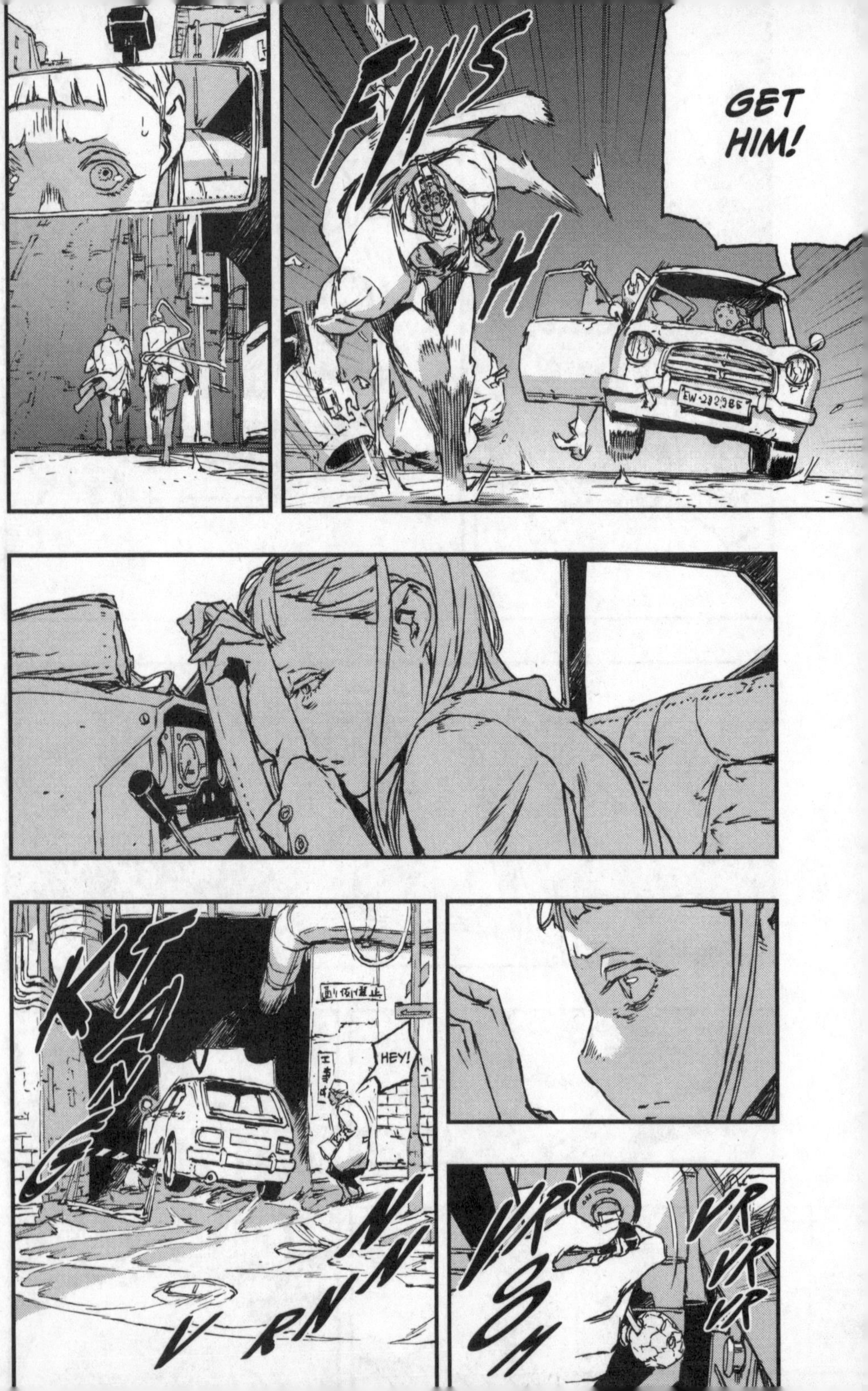
GET HIM!
FWSH
HEY!
KYANNG...
VRNNN
VROOM
VRVRVR

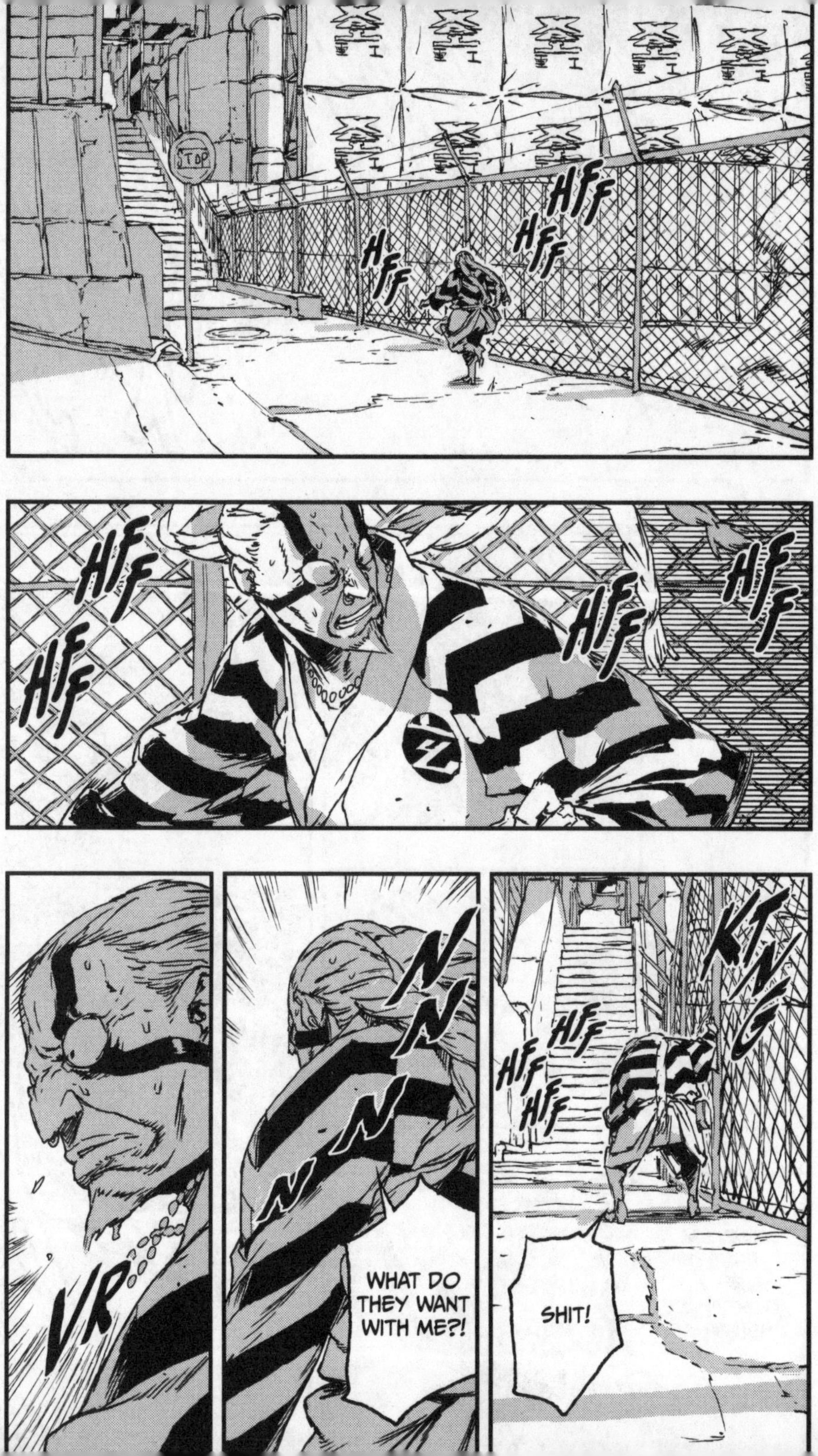
HFF
HFF
HFF
HFF
HFF
HFF
HFF
KTNG
HFF
HFF
HFF
SHIT!
NNN
NNN
WHAT DO THEY WANT WITH ME?!
VR

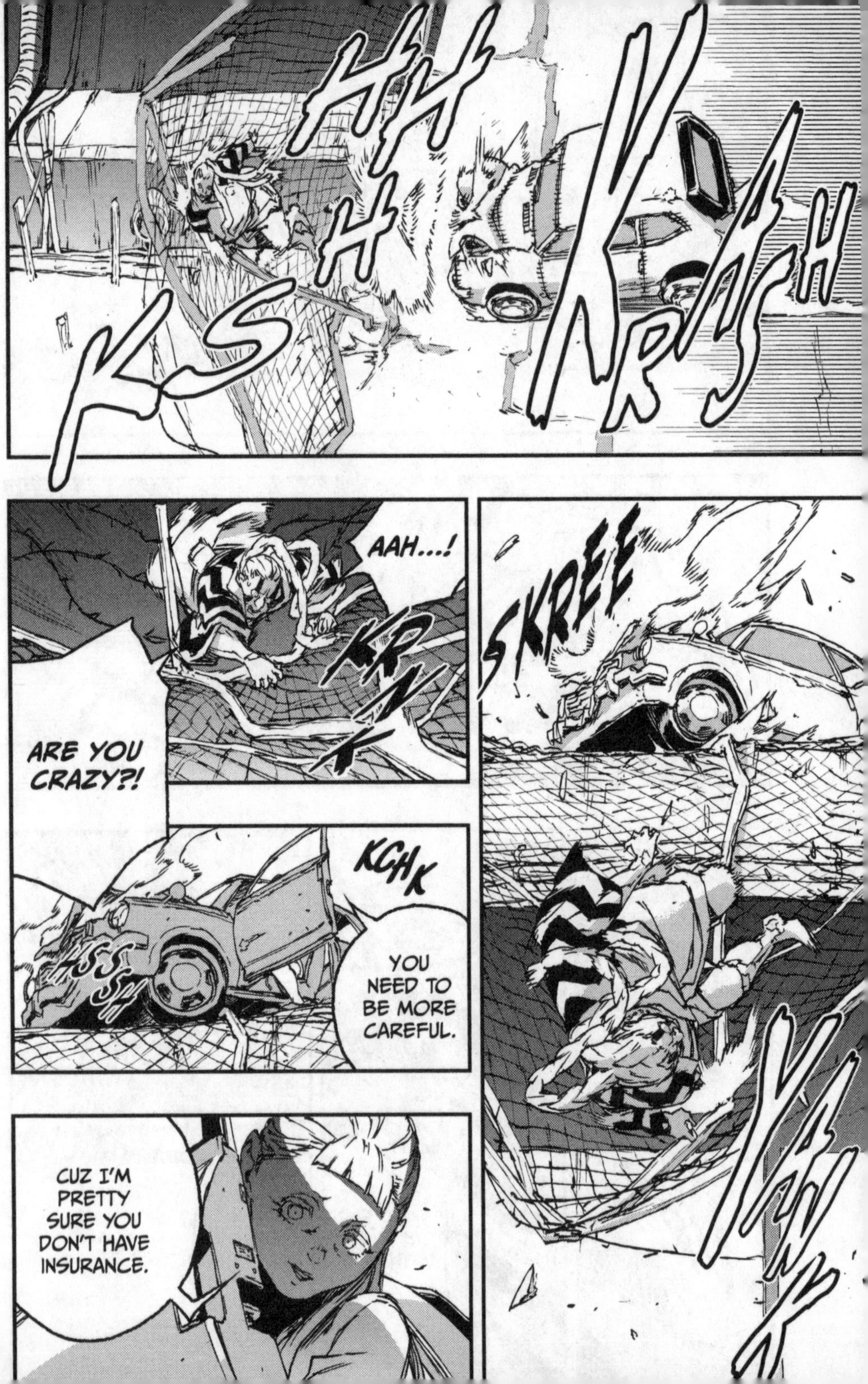
SKREE
AAH...!
KRNK
ARE YOU CRAZY?!
KCHK
YOU NEED TO BE MORE CAREFUL.
CUZ I'M PRETTY SURE YOU DON'T HAVE INSURANCE.

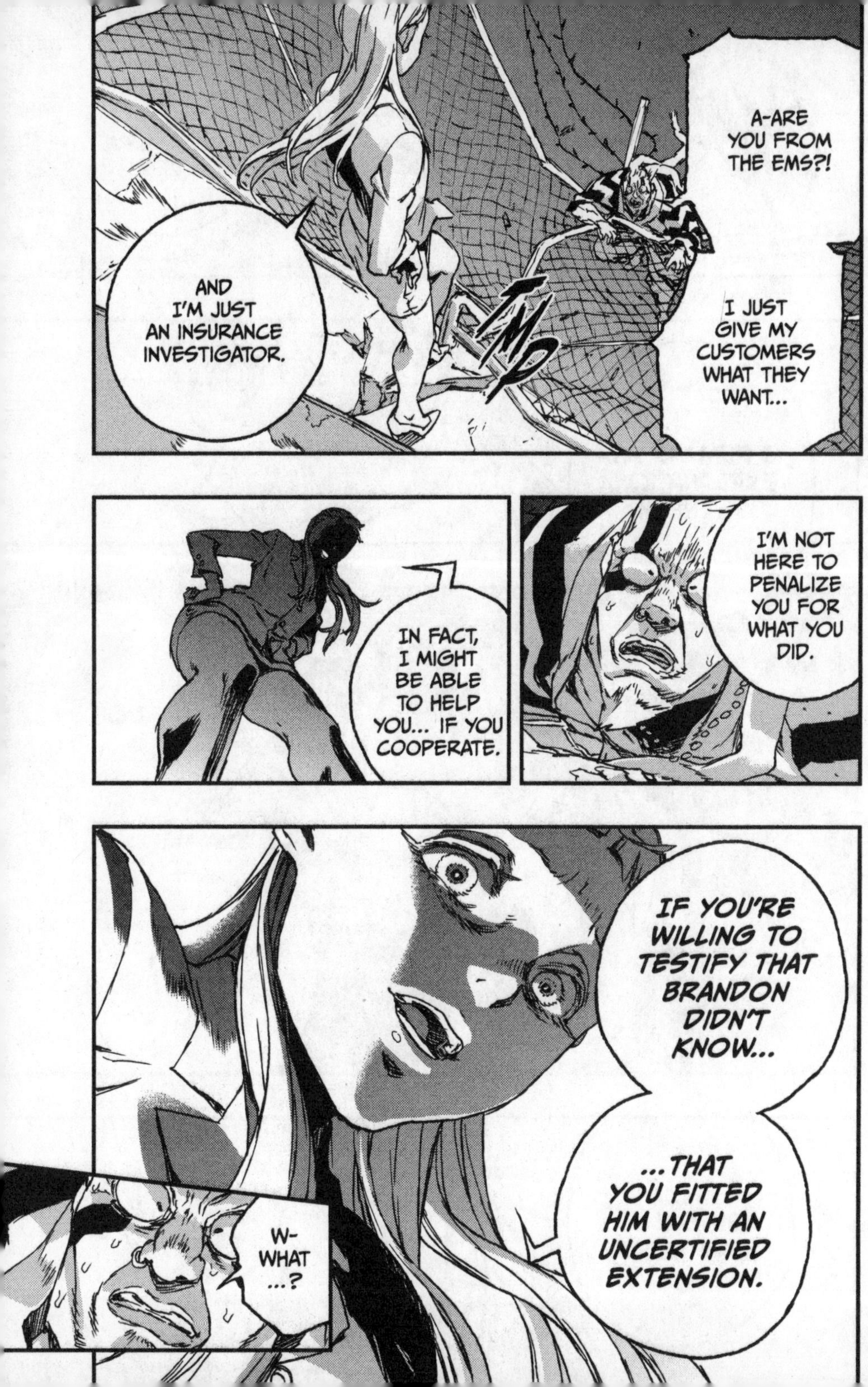
A-ARE YOU FROM THE EMS?!
I JUST GIVE MY CUSTOMERS WHAT THEY WANT...
TMP
AND I'M JUST AN INSURANCE INVESTIGATOR.
I'M NOT HERE TO PENALIZE YOU FOR WHAT YOU DID.
IN FACT, I MIGHT BE ABLE TO HELP YOU... IF YOU COOPERATE.
IF YOU'RE WILLING TO TESTIFY THAT BRANDON DIDN'T KNOW...
...THAT YOU FITTED HIM WITH AN UNCERTIFIED EXTENSION.
W-WHAT...?

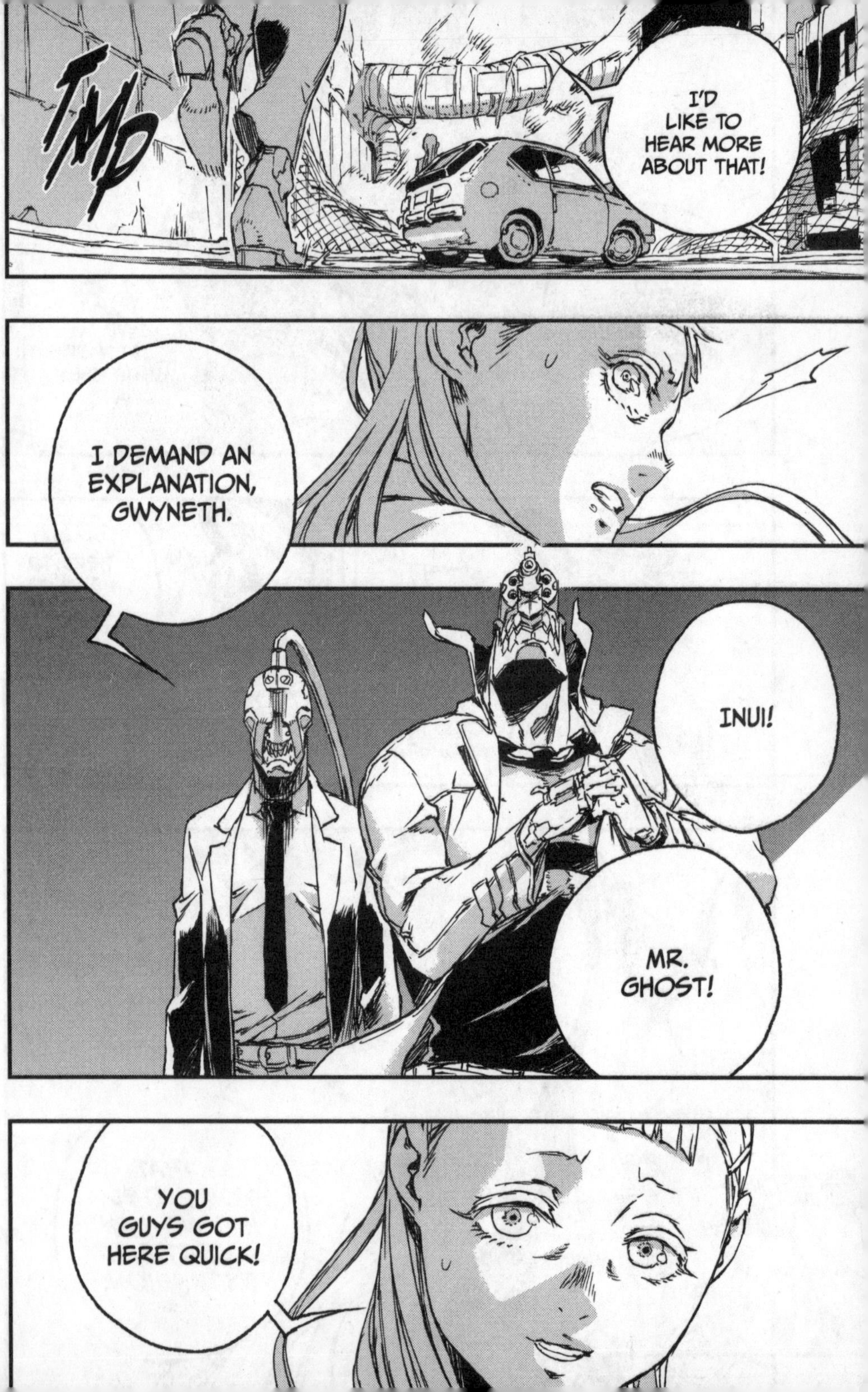
I'D LIKE TO HEAR MORE ABOUT THAT!
TMP
I DEMAND AN EXPLANATION, GWYNETH.
INUI!
MR. GHOST!
YOU GUYS GOT HERE QUICK!

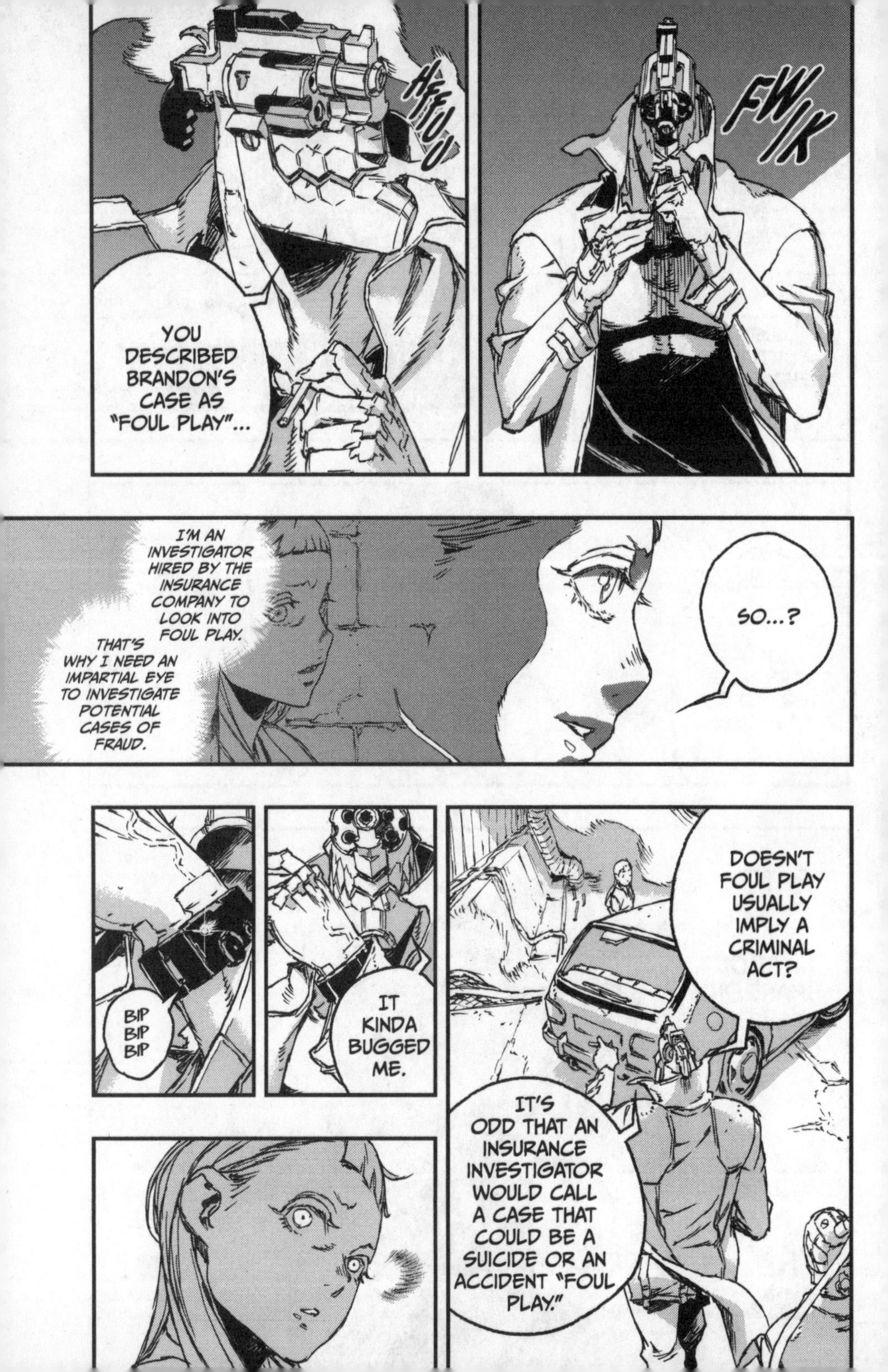
FWIK
HFFUU
YOU DESCRIBED BRANDON'S CASE AS "FOUL PLAY"...
I'M AN INVESTIGATOR HIRED BY THE INSURANCE COMPANY TO LOOK INTO FOUL PLAY.
THAT'S WHY I NEED AN IMPARTIAL EYE TO INVESTIGATE POTENTIAL CASES OF FRAUD.
SO...?
DOESN'T FOUL PLAY USUALLY IMPLY A CRIMINAL ACT?
IT'S ODD THAT AN INSURANCE INVESTIGATOR WOULD CALL A CASE THAT COULD BE A SUICIDE OR AN ACCIDENT "FOUL PLAY."
IT KINDA BUGGED ME.
BIP BIP BIP

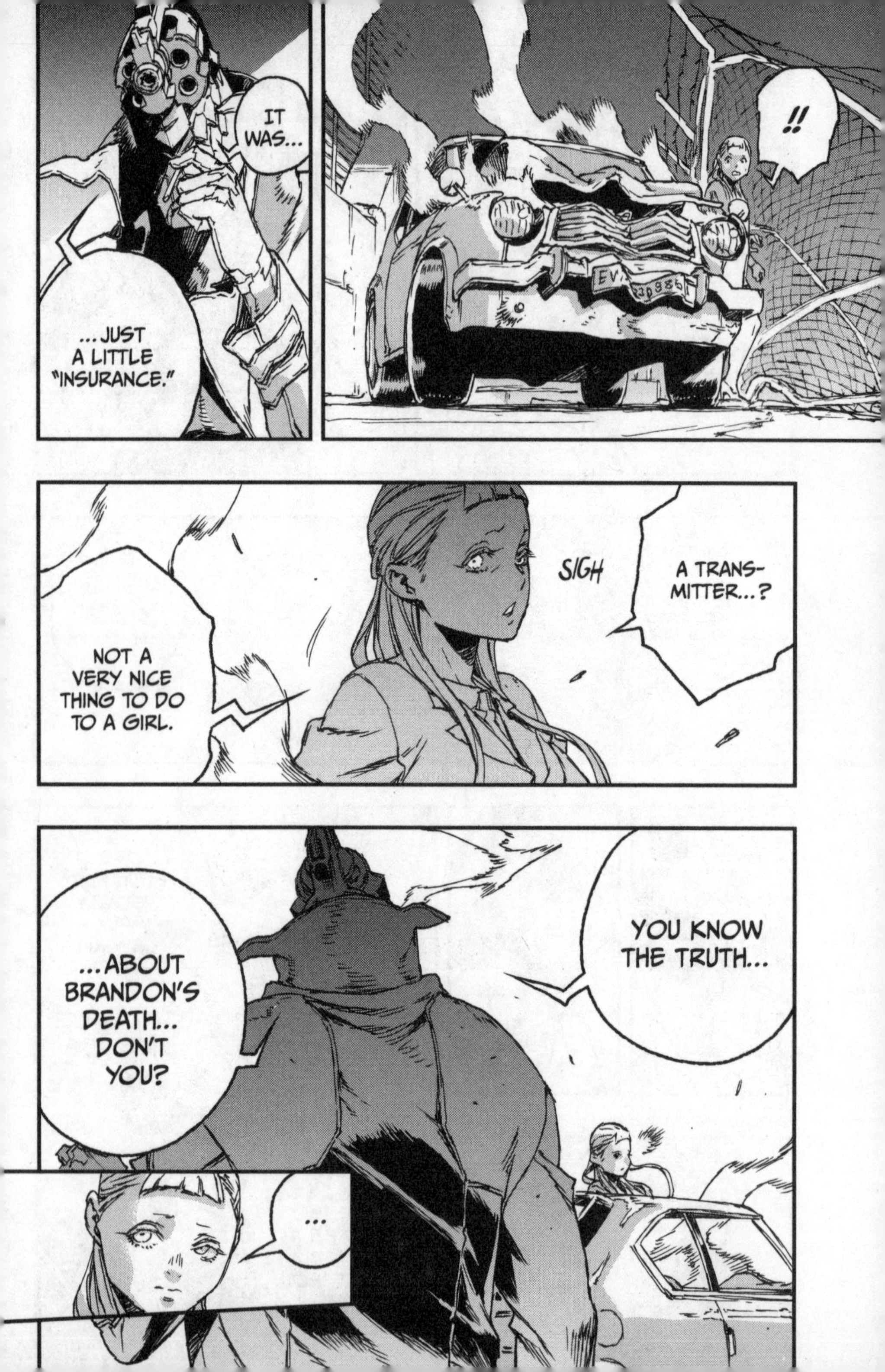
!!
IT WAS...
...JUST A LITTLE "INSURANCE."
A TRANS-MITTER...?
SIGH
NOT A VERY NICE THING TO DO TO A GIRL.
YOU KNOW THE TRUTH...
...ABOUT BRANDON'S DEATH... DON'T YOU?
...

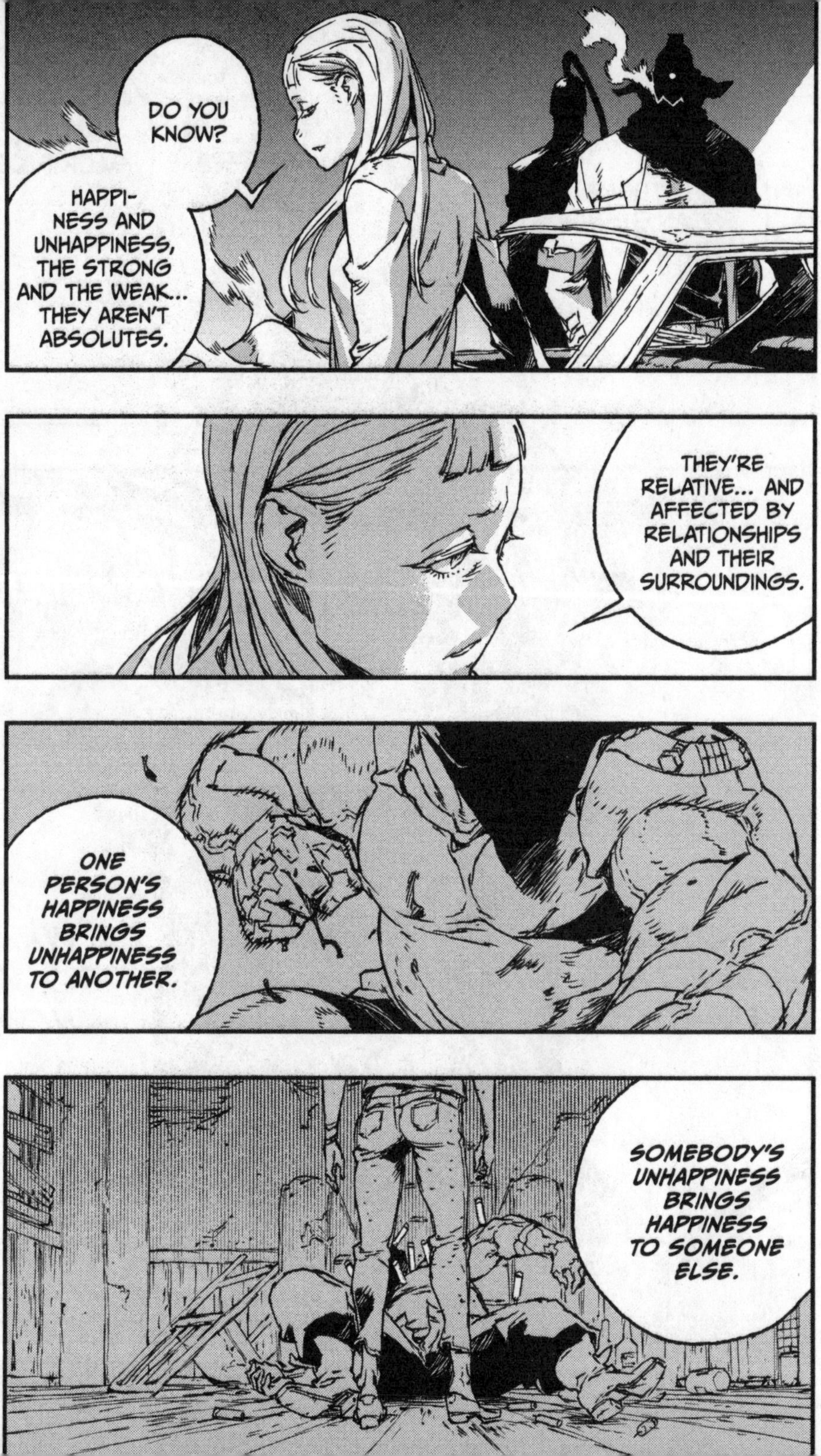
DO YOU KNOW?
HAPPINESS AND UNHAPPINESS, THE STRONG AND THE WEAK... THEY AREN'T ABSOLUTES.
THEY'RE RELATIVE... AND AFFECTED BY RELATIONSHIPS AND THEIR SURROUNDINGS.
ONE PERSON'S HAPPINESS BRINGS UNHAPPINESS TO ANOTHER.
SOMEBODY'S UNHAPPINESS BRINGS HAPPINESS TO SOMEONE ELSE.

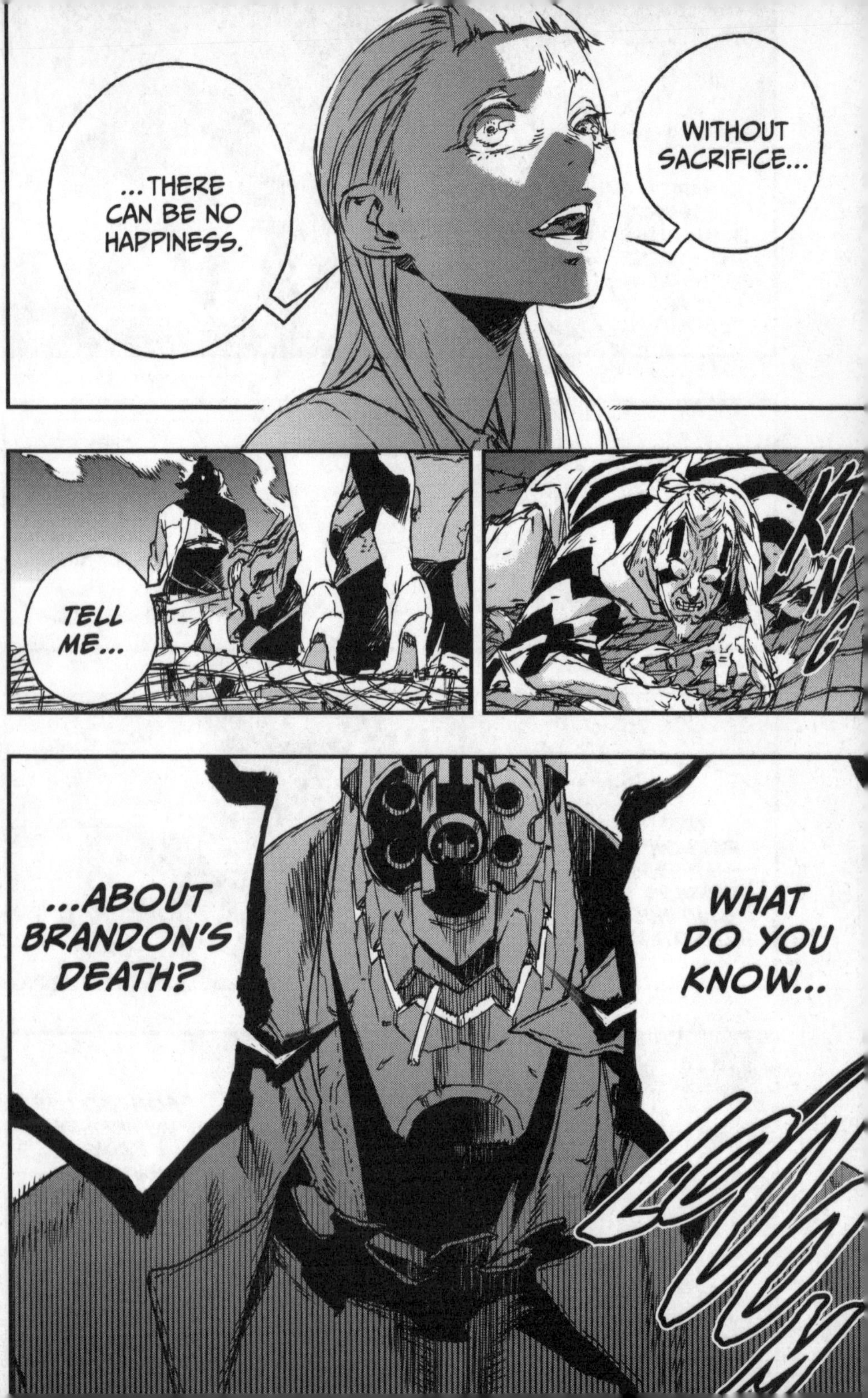
WITHOUT SACRIFICE...
...THERE CAN BE NO HAPPINESS.
TELL ME...
WHAT DO YOU KNOW...
...ABOUT BRANDON'S DEATH?

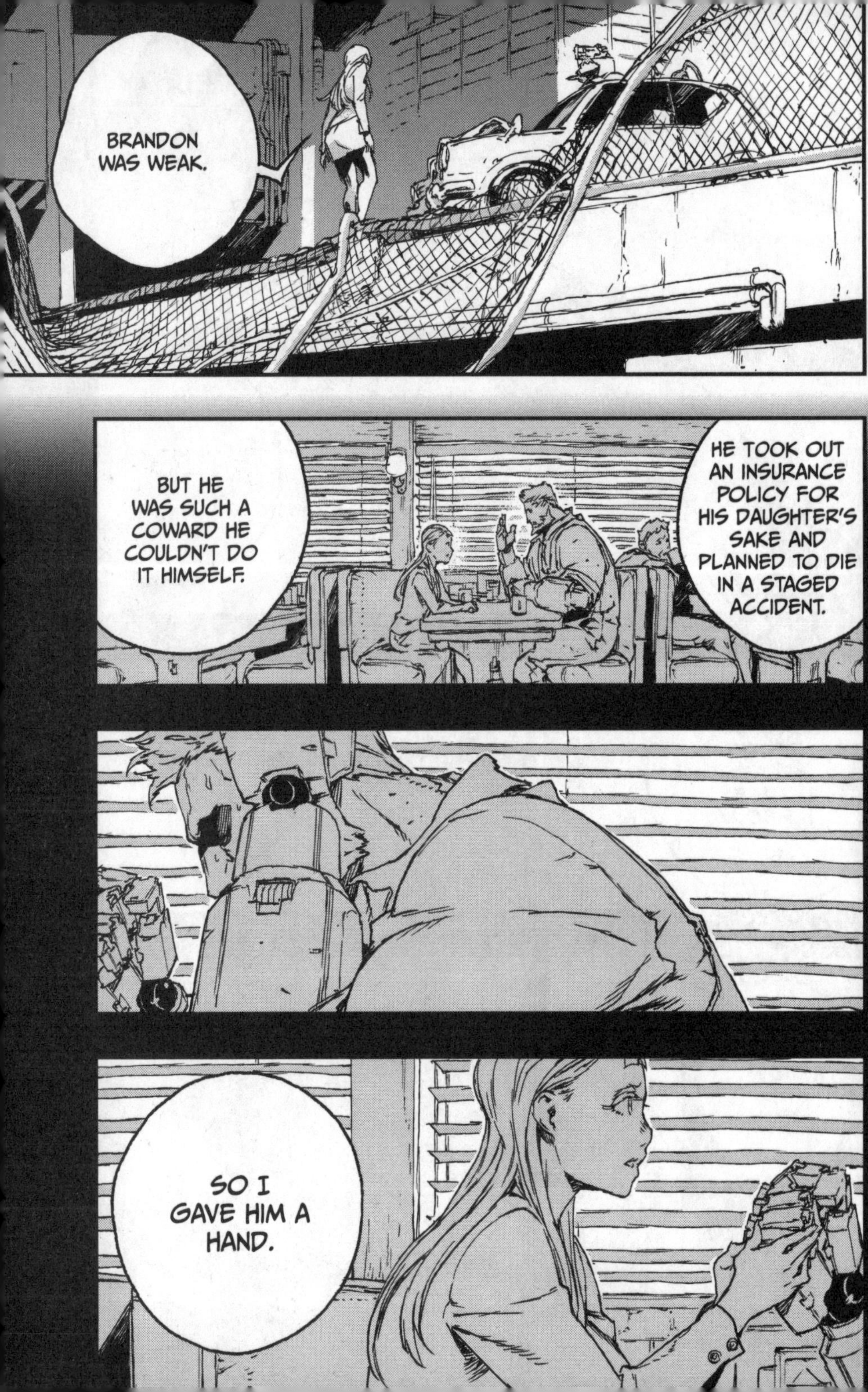
BRANDON WAS WEAK.
HE TOOK OUT AN INSURANCE POLICY FOR HIS DAUGHTER'S SAKE AND PLANNED TO DIE IN A STAGED ACCIDENT.
BUT HE WAS SUCH A COWARD HE COULDN'T DO IT HIMSELF.
SO I GAVE HIM A HAND.

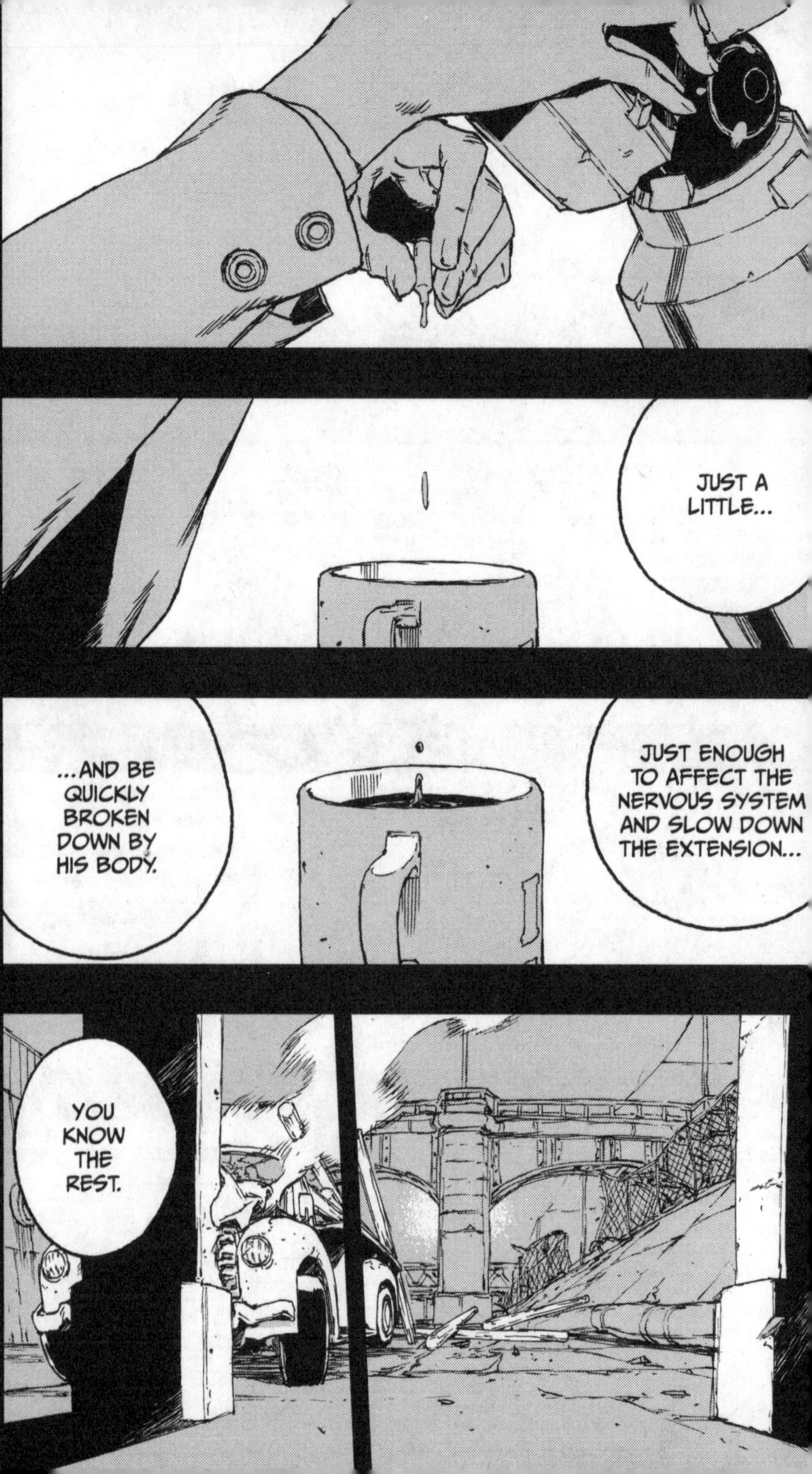
JUST A LITTLE...
JUST ENOUGH TO AFFECT THE NERVOUS SYSTEM AND SLOW DOWN THE EXTENSION...
...AND BE QUICKLY BROKEN DOWN BY HIS BODY.
YOU KNOW THE REST.

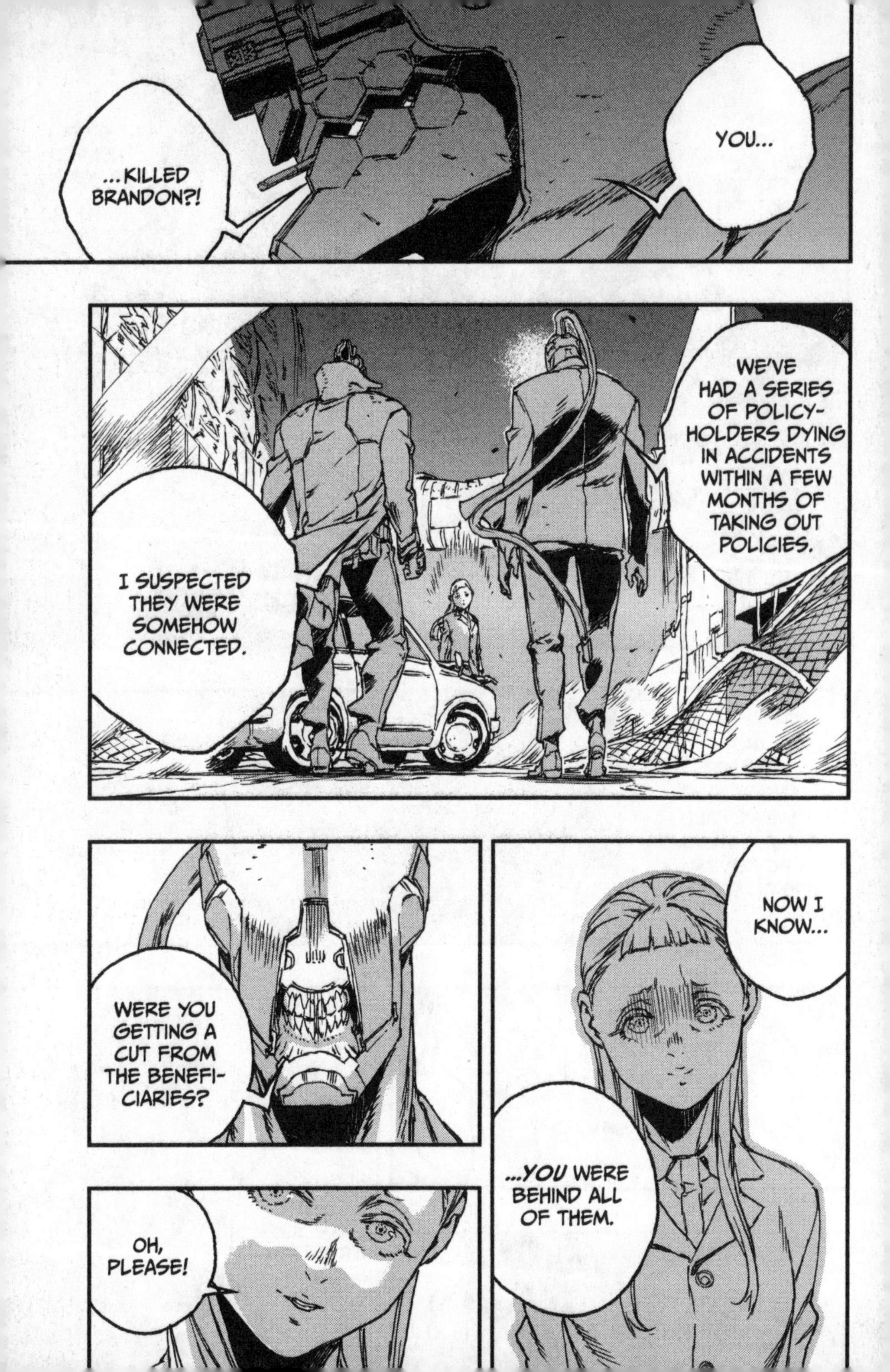
YOU...
...KILLED BRANDON?!
WE'VE HAD A SERIES OF POLICY-HOLDERS DYING IN ACCIDENTS WITHIN A FEW MONTHS OF TAKING OUT POLICIES.
I SUSPECTED THEY WERE SOMEHOW CONNECTED.
NOW I KNOW...
...*YOU* WERE BEHIND ALL OF THEM.
WERE YOU GETTING A CUT FROM THE BENEFI-CIARIES?
OH, PLEASE!

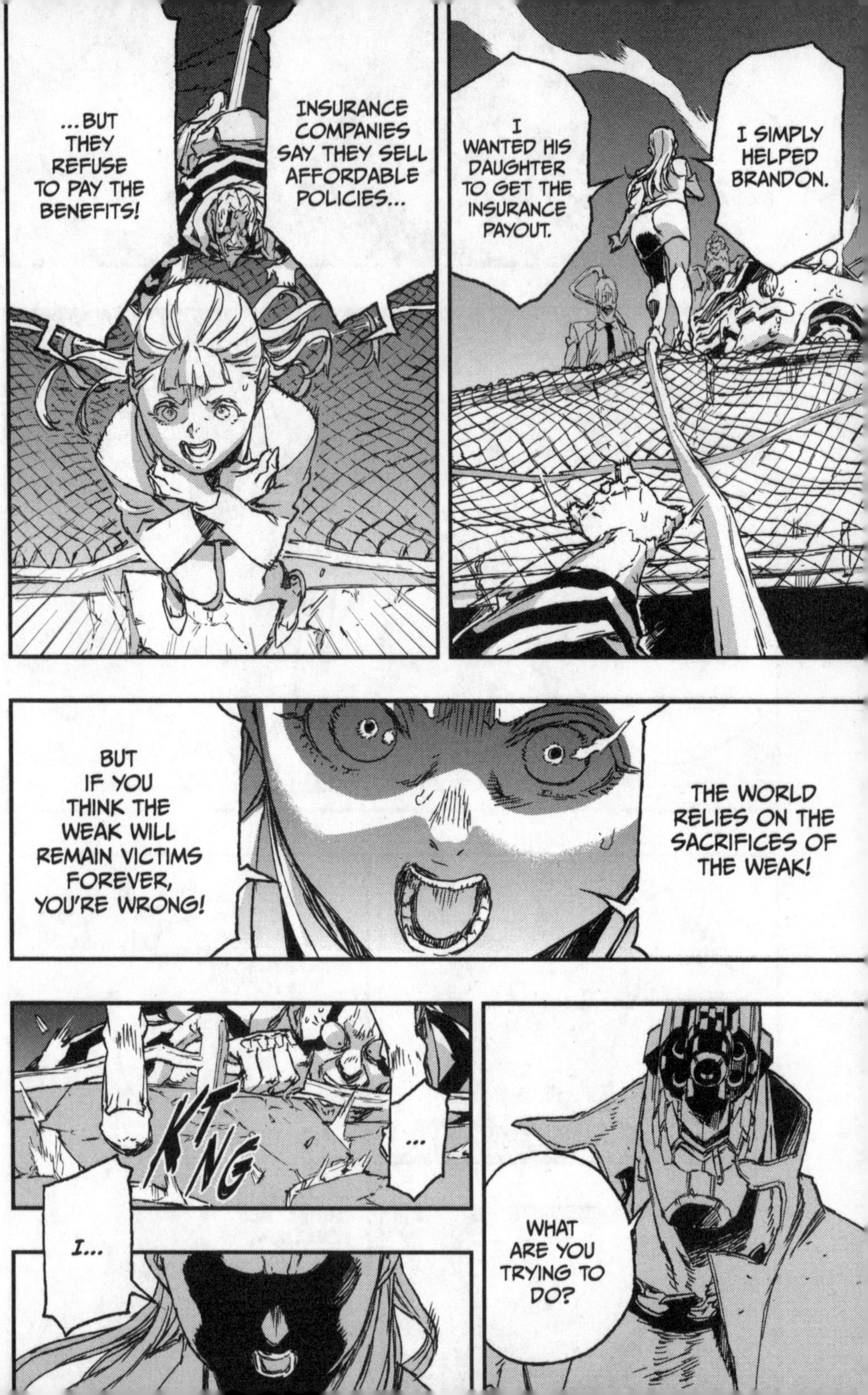
I SIMPLY HELPED BRANDON.
I WANTED HIS DAUGHTER TO GET THE INSURANCE PAYOUT.
INSURANCE COMPANIES SAY THEY SELL AFFORDABLE POLICIES...
...BUT THEY REFUSE TO PAY THE BENEFITS!
THE WORLD RELIES ON THE SACRIFICES OF THE WEAK!
BUT IF YOU THINK THE WEAK WILL REMAIN VICTIMS FOREVER, YOU'RE WRONG!
WHAT ARE YOU TRYING TO DO?
...
KTNG
I...

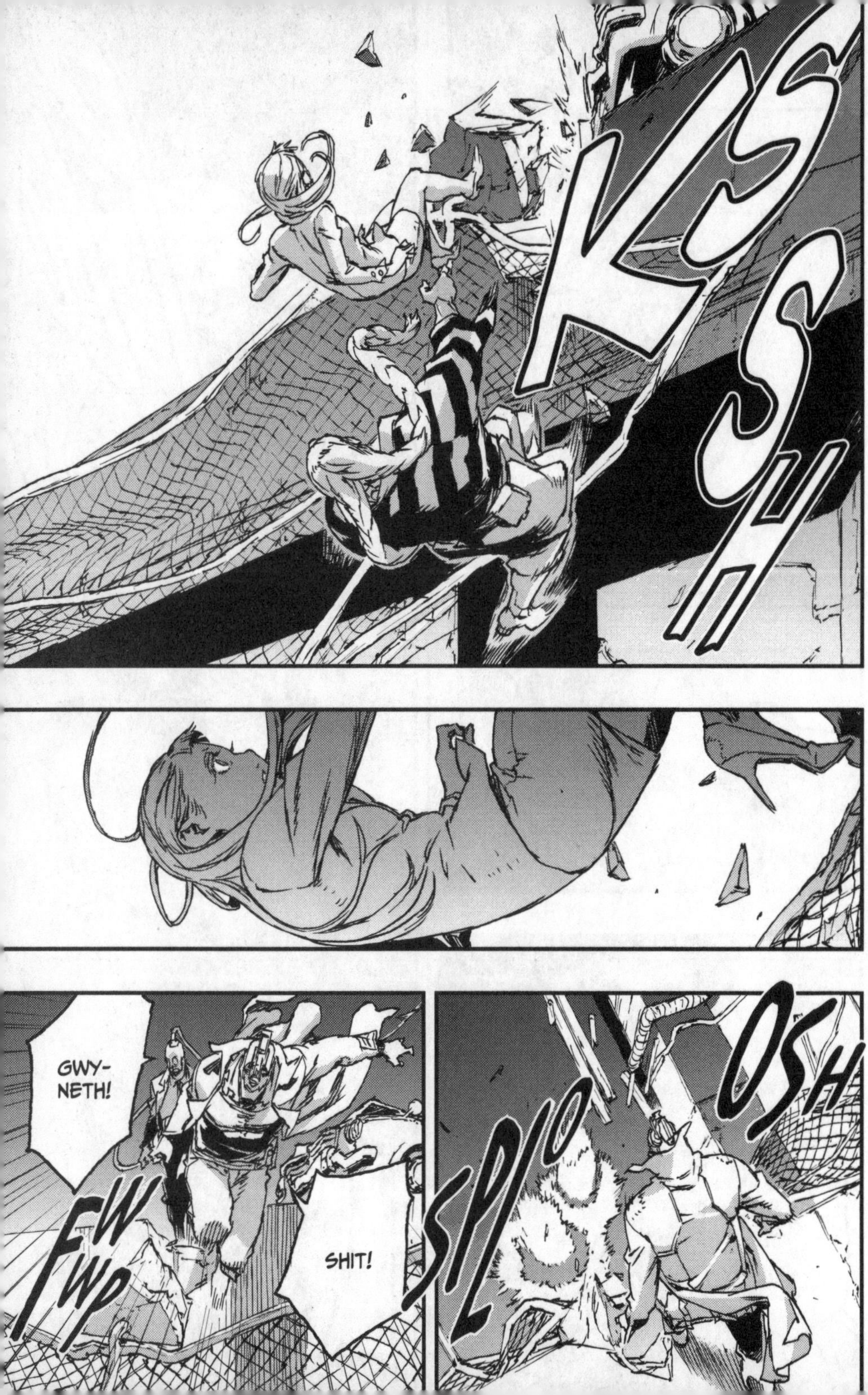
KSSH
SPLOOSH
GWY-NETH!
SHIT!
FWWP

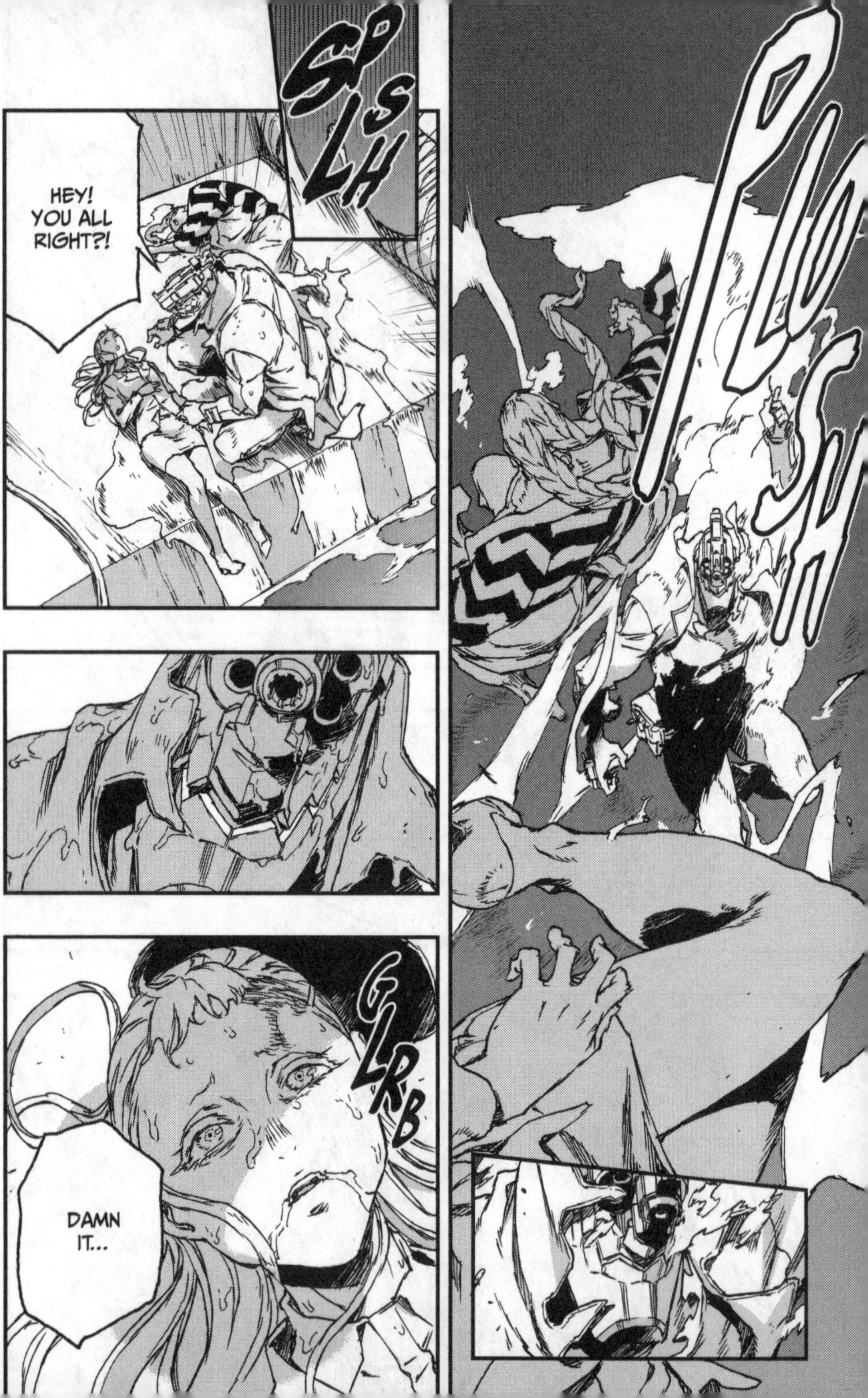
PLOOSH
SPLSH
HEY! YOU ALL RIGHT?!
GLRB
DAMN IT...

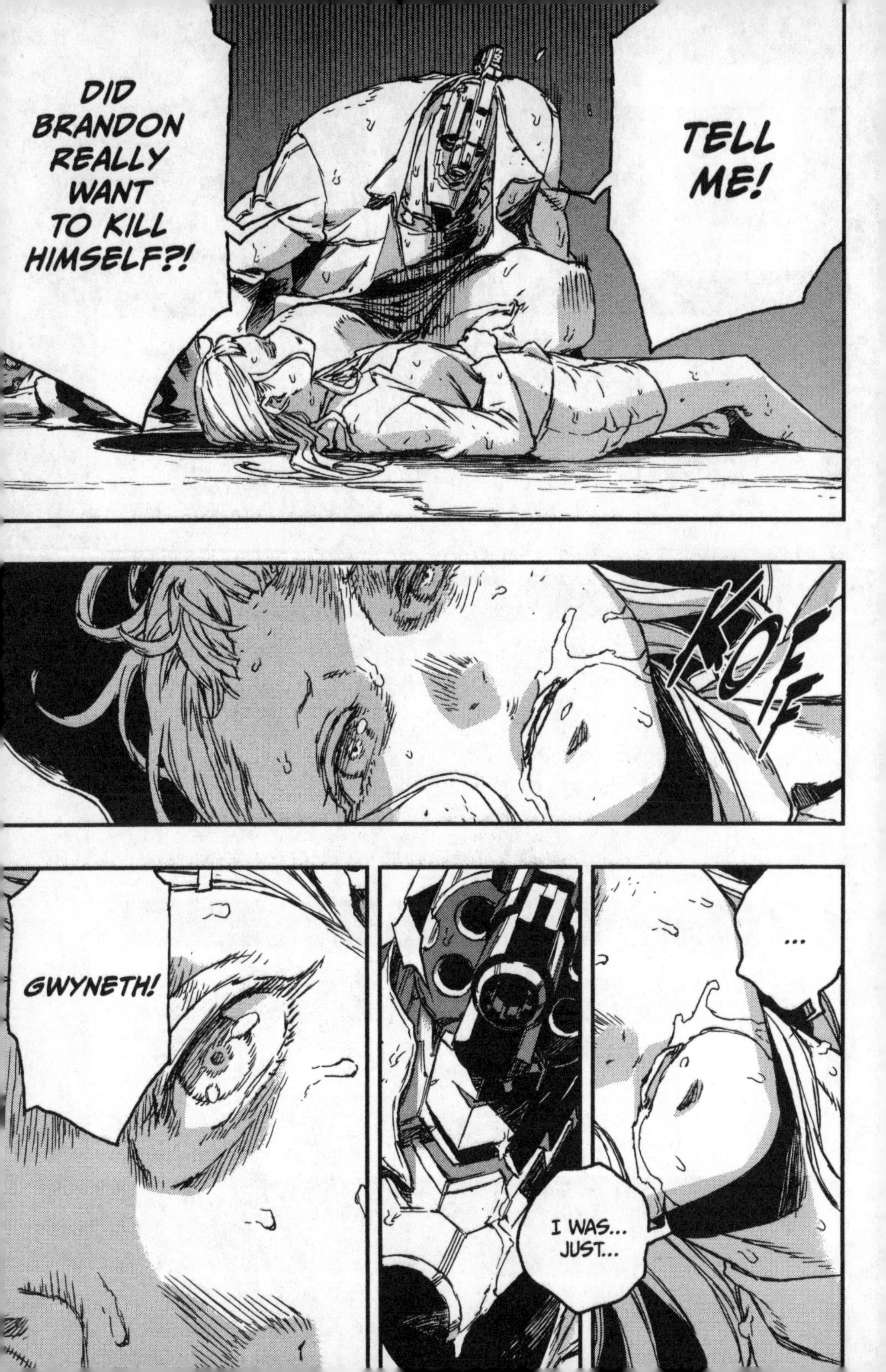
DID BRANDON REALLY WANT TO KILL HIMSELF?!
TELL ME!
KOFF
...
I WAS... JUST...
GWYNETH!

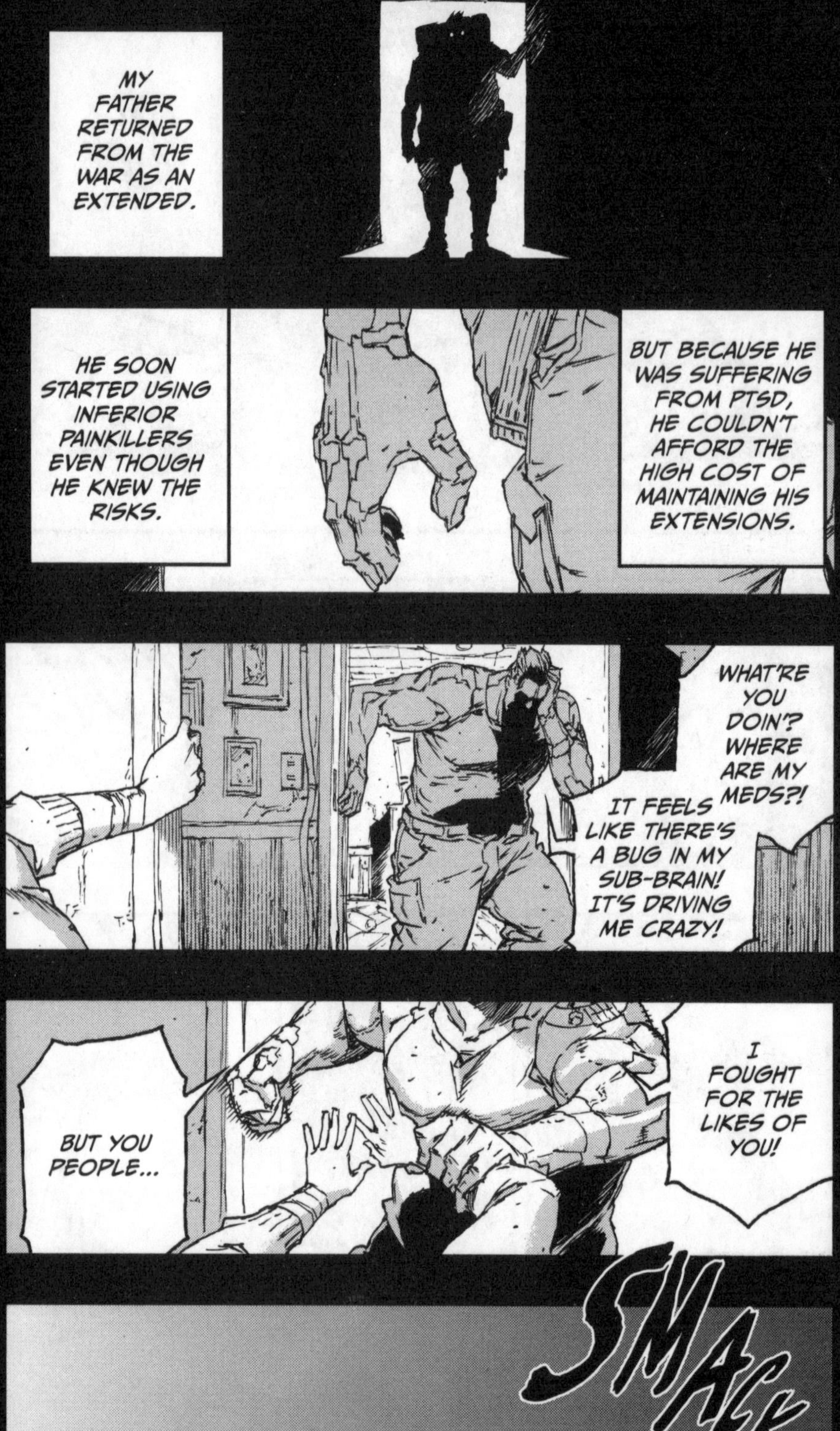
MY FATHER RETURNED FROM THE WAR AS AN EXTENDED.
BUT BECAUSE HE WAS SUFFERING FROM PTSD, HE COULDN'T AFFORD THE HIGH COST OF MAINTAINING HIS EXTENSIONS.
HE SOON STARTED USING INFERIOR PAINKILLERS EVEN THOUGH HE KNEW THE RISKS.
WHAT'RE YOU DOIN'? WHERE ARE MY MEDS?!
IT FEELS LIKE THERE'S A BUG IN MY SUB-BRAIN! IT'S DRIVING ME CRAZY!
I FOUGHT FOR THE LIKES OF YOU!
BUT YOU PEOPLE...
SMACK

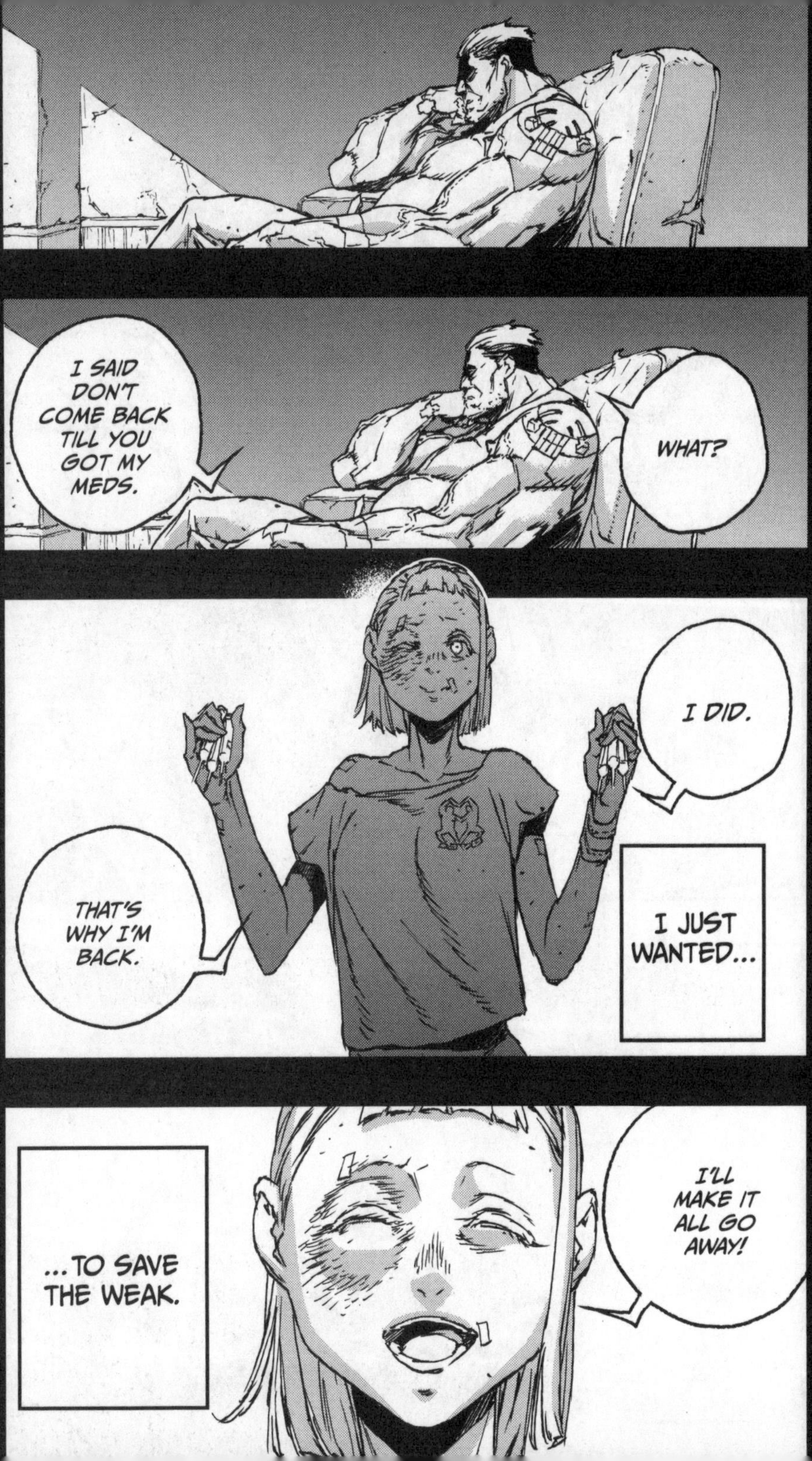
WHAT?
I SAID DON'T COME BACK TILL YOU GOT MY MEDS.
I DID.
THAT'S WHY I'M BACK.
I JUST WANTED...
I'LL MAKE IT ALL GO AWAY!
...TO SAVE THE WEAK.

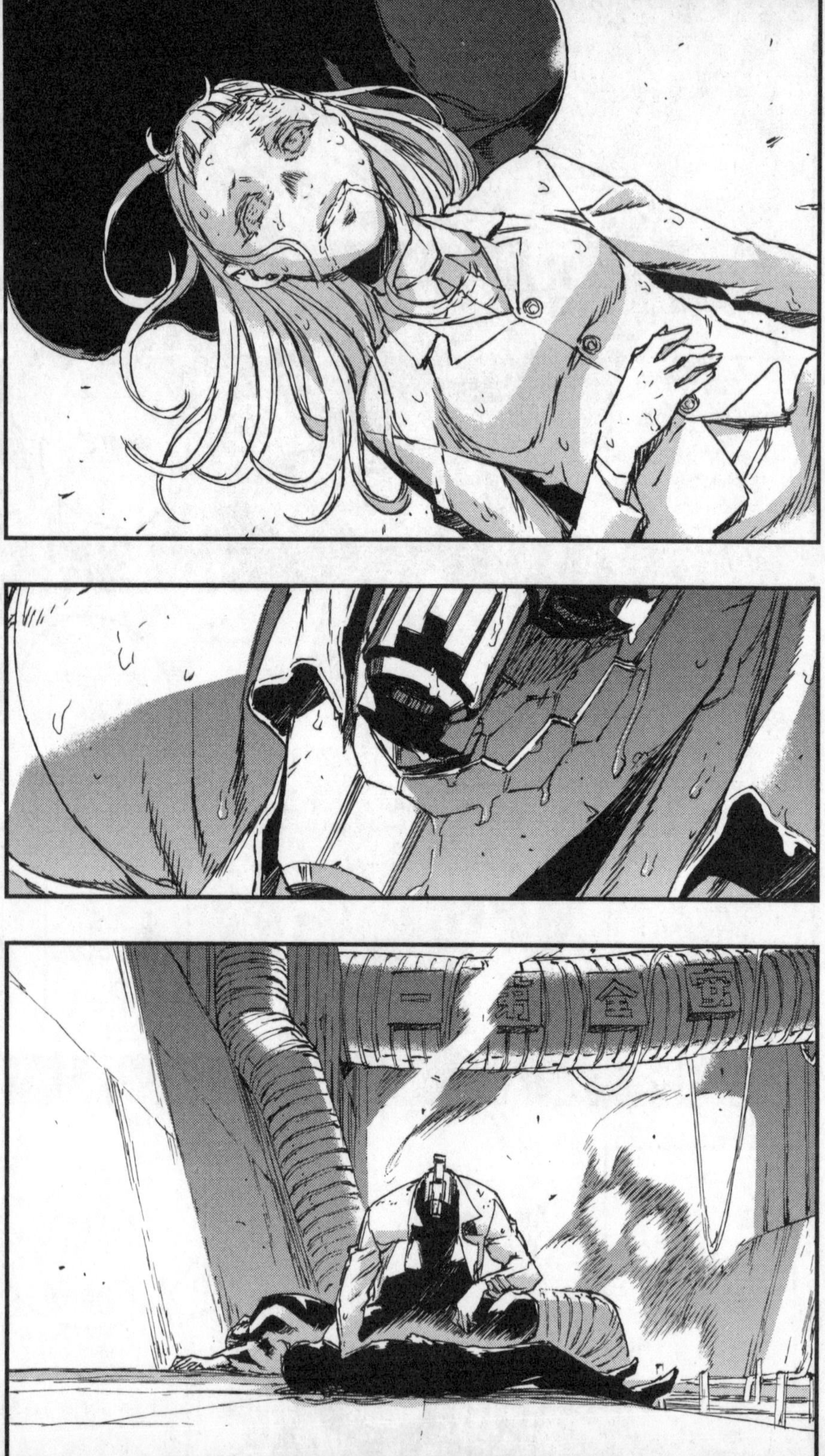

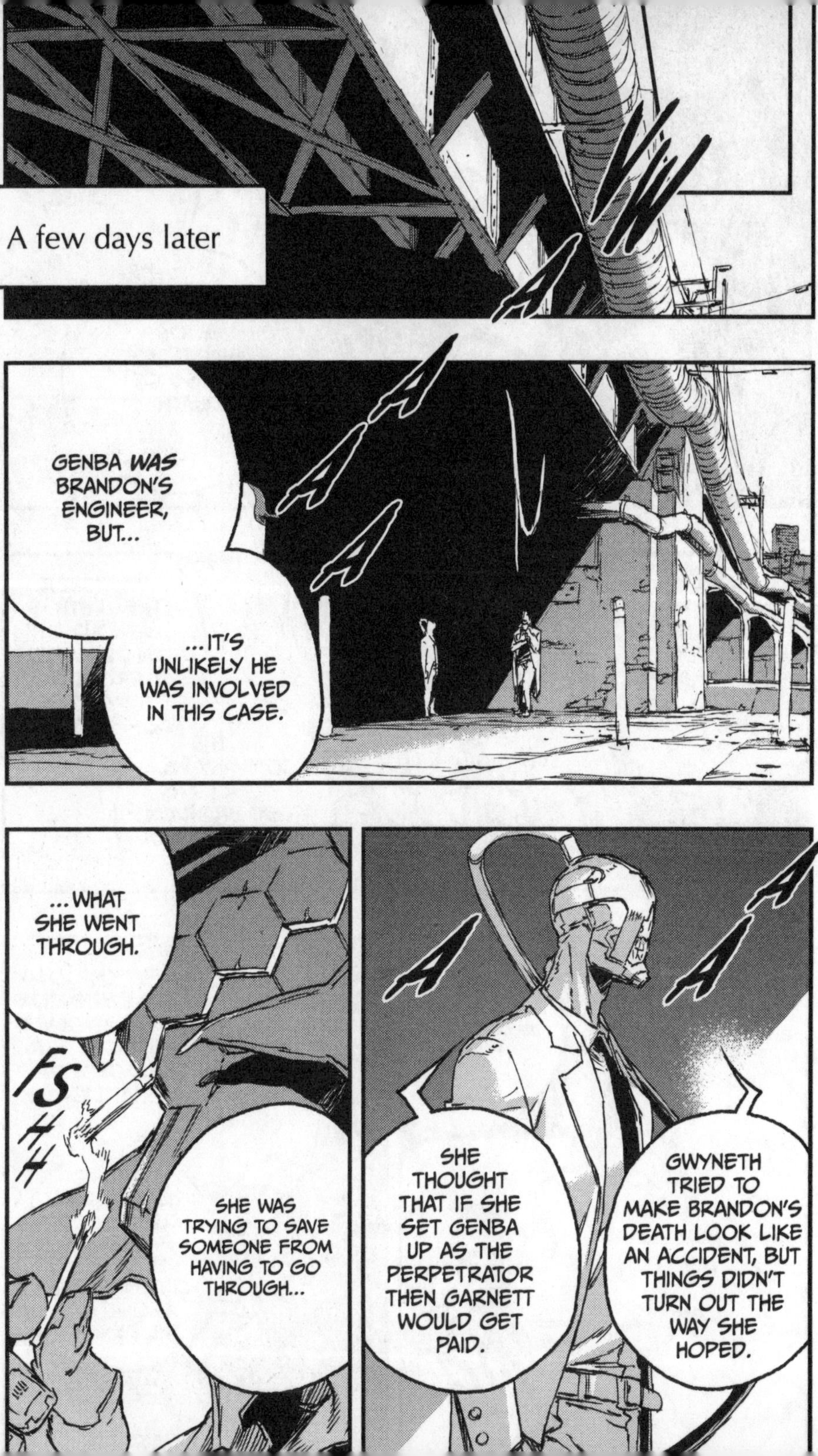
A few days later
GENBA WAS BRANDON'S ENGINEER, BUT...
...IT'S UNLIKELY HE WAS INVOLVED IN THIS CASE.
GWYNETH TRIED TO MAKE BRANDON'S DEATH LOOK LIKE AN ACCIDENT, BUT THINGS DIDN'T TURN OUT THE WAY SHE HOPED.
SHE THOUGHT THAT IF SHE SET GENBA UP AS THE PERPETRATOR THEN GARNETT WOULD GET PAID.
SHE WAS TRYING TO SAVE SOMEONE FROM HAVING TO GO THROUGH...
...WHAT SHE WENT THROUGH.
FSHH

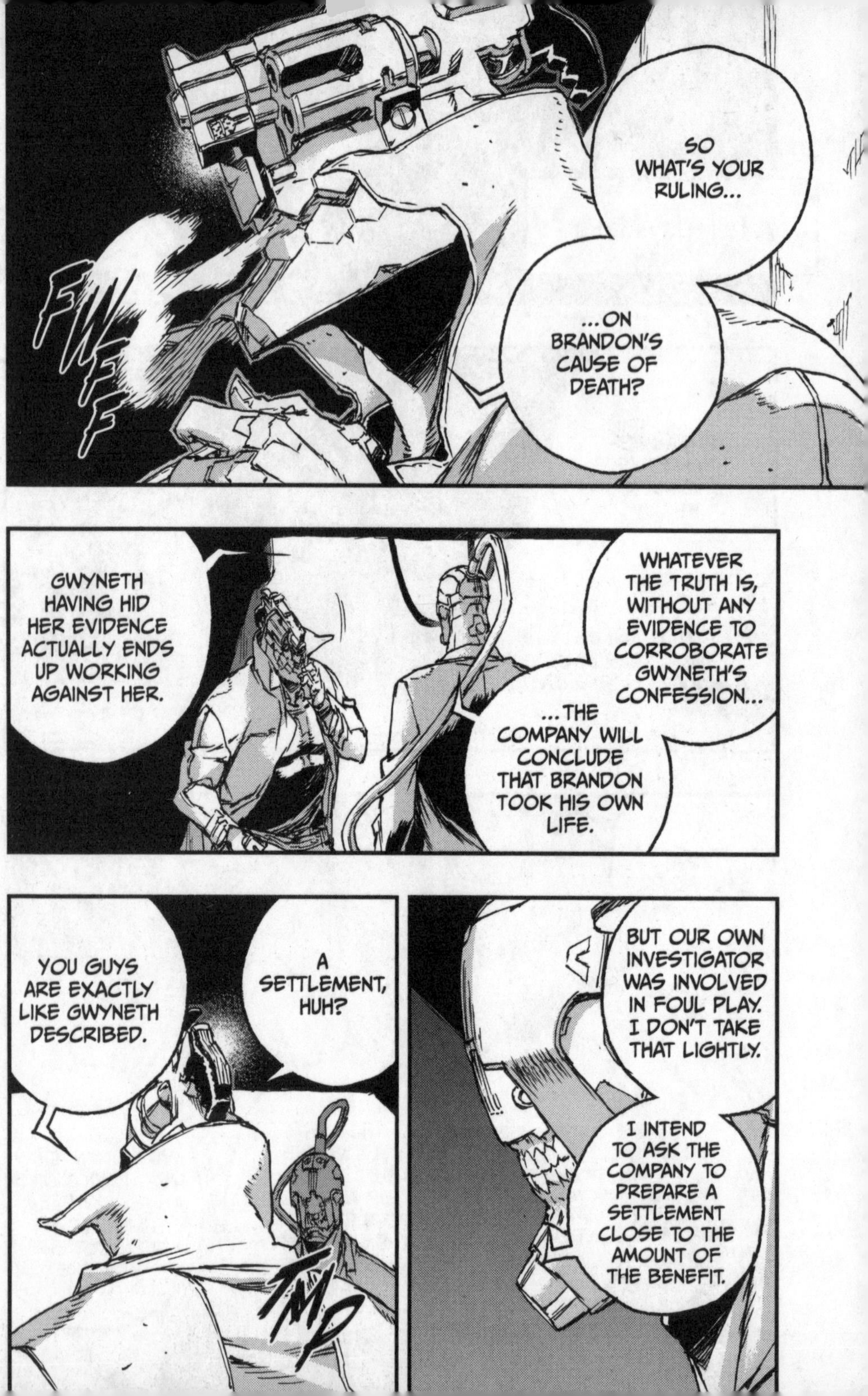
SO WHAT'S YOUR RULING...
...ON BRANDON'S CAUSE OF DEATH?
FWFF
WHATEVER THE TRUTH IS, WITHOUT ANY EVIDENCE TO CORROBORATE GWYNETH'S CONFESSION...
...THE COMPANY WILL CONCLUDE THAT BRANDON TOOK HIS OWN LIFE.
GWYNETH HAVING HID HER EVIDENCE ACTUALLY ENDS UP WORKING AGAINST HER.
BUT OUR OWN INVESTIGATOR WAS INVOLVED IN FOUL PLAY. I DON'T TAKE THAT LIGHTLY.
I INTEND TO ASK THE COMPANY TO PREPARE A SETTLEMENT CLOSE TO THE AMOUNT OF THE BENEFIT.
A SETTLEMENT, HUH?
YOU GUYS ARE EXACTLY LIKE GWYNETH DESCRIBED.

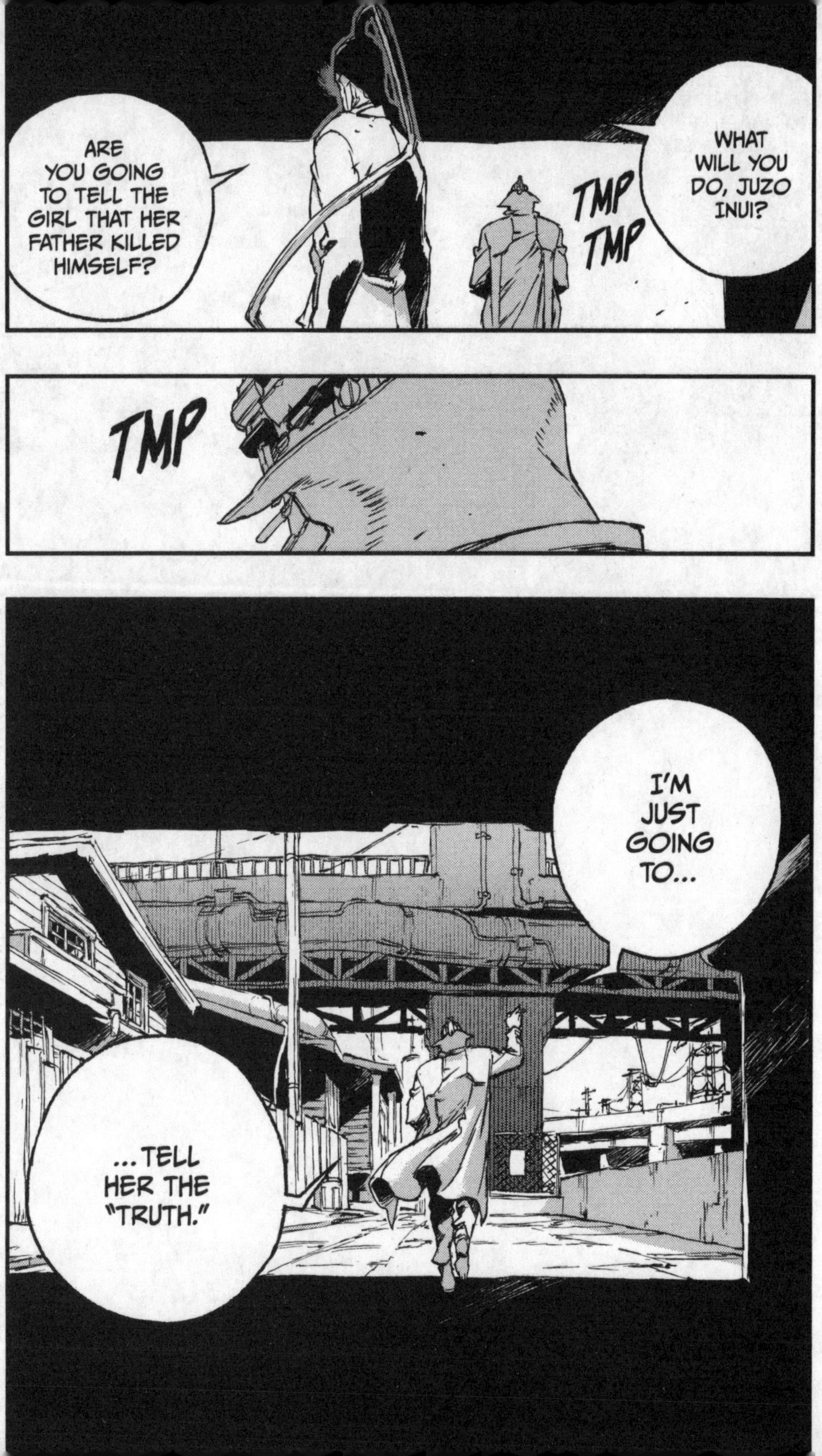
WHAT WILL YOU DO, JUZO INUI?
TMP TMP
ARE YOU GOING TO TELL THE GIRL THAT HER FATHER KILLED HIMSELF?
TMP
I'M JUST GOING TO...
...TELL HER THE "TRUTH."

NO
GUNS
LIFE

The gunsmoke drifts, the muzzle talks

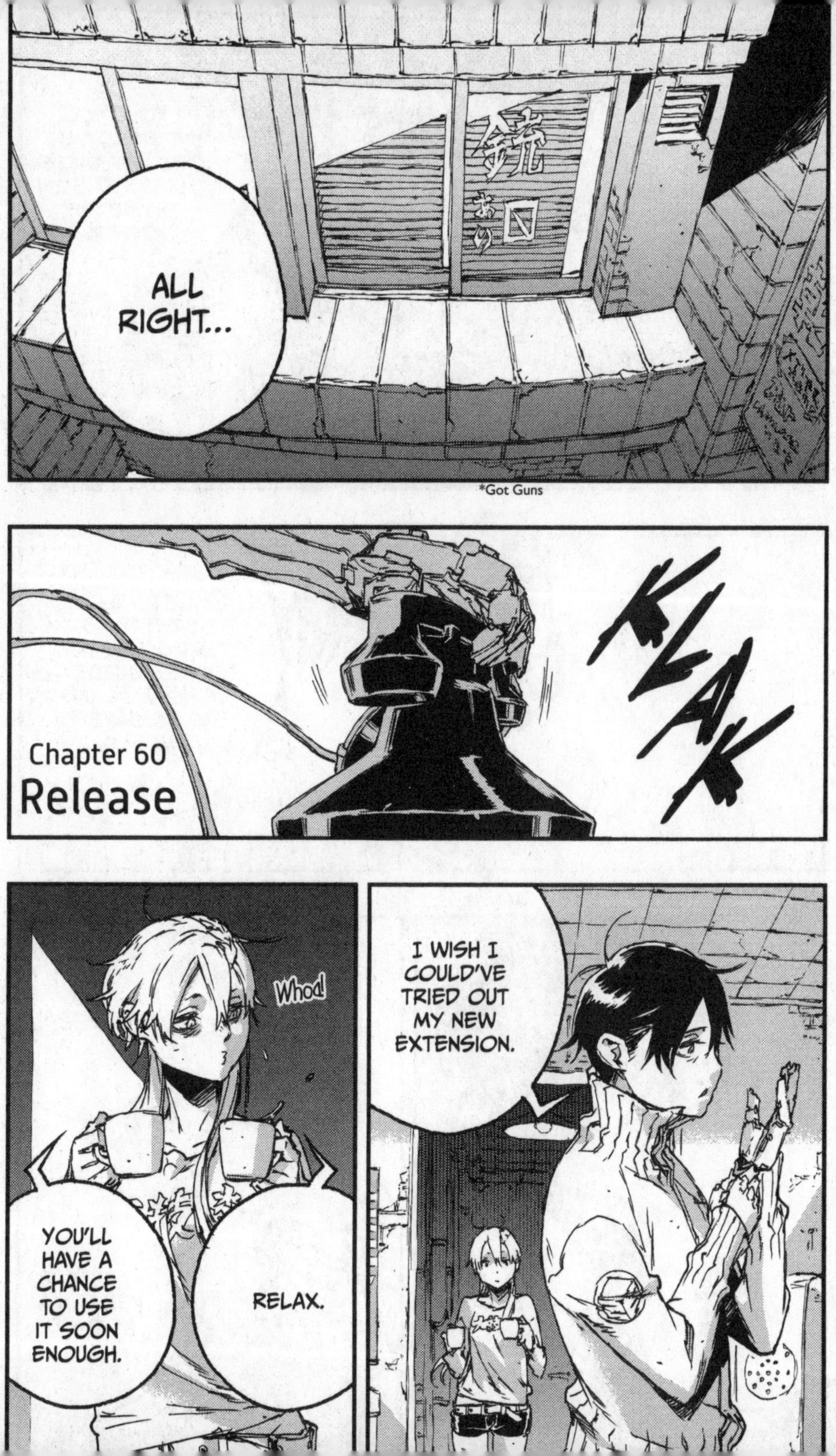
ALL RIGHT...
*Got Guns
KLAK
Chapter 60
Release
I WISH I COULD'VE TRIED OUT MY NEW EXTENSION.
Whoa!
RELAX.
YOU'LL HAVE A CHANCE TO USE IT SOON ENOUGH.

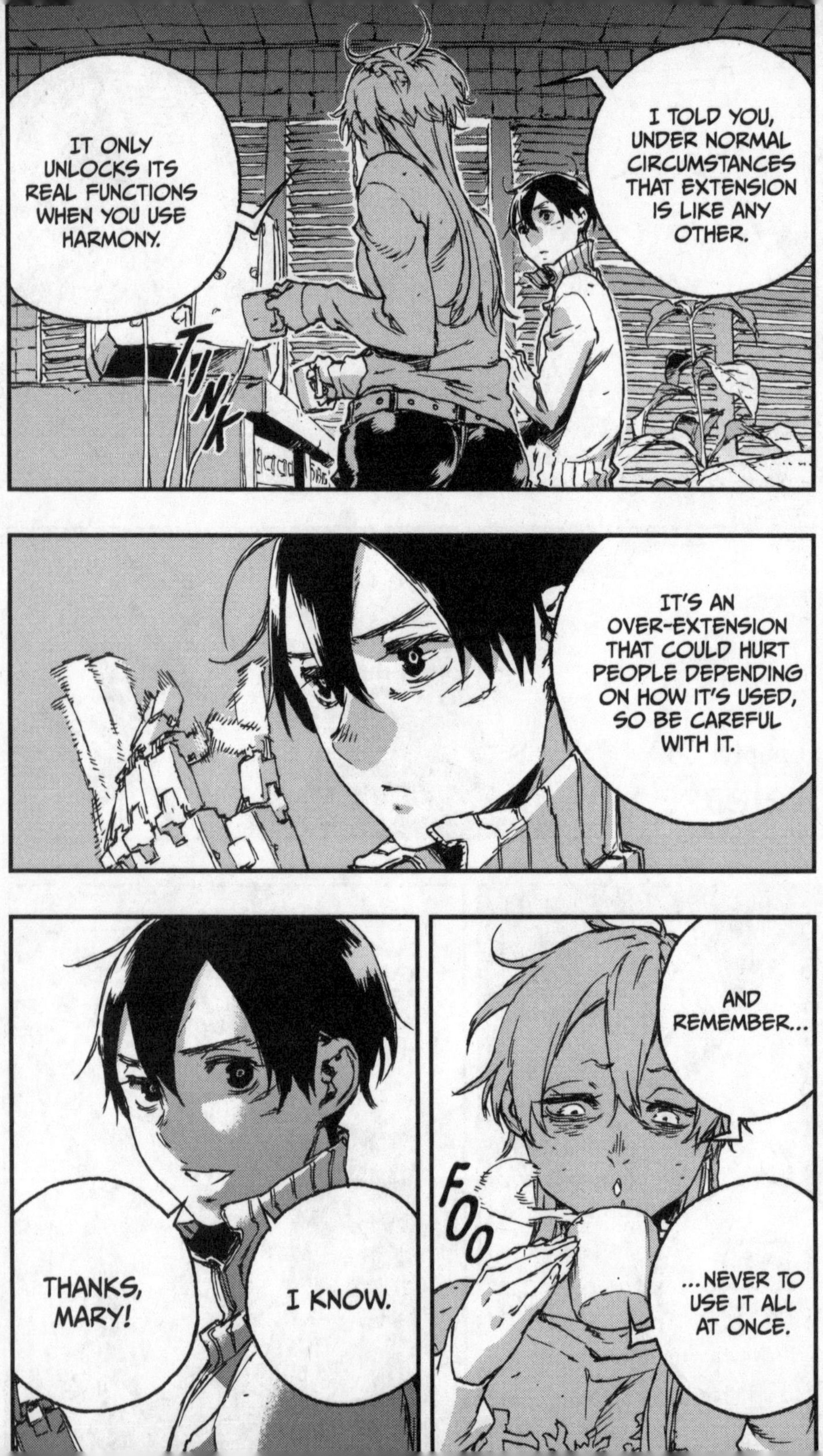
I TOLD YOU, UNDER NORMAL CIRCUMSTANCES THAT EXTENSION IS LIKE ANY OTHER.
IT ONLY UNLOCKS ITS REAL FUNCTIONS WHEN YOU USE HARMONY.
TINK
IT'S AN OVER-EXTENSION THAT COULD HURT PEOPLE DEPENDING ON HOW IT'S USED, SO BE CAREFUL WITH IT.
AND REMEMBER...
FOO
...NEVER TO USE IT ALL AT ONCE.
I KNOW.
THANKS, MARY!

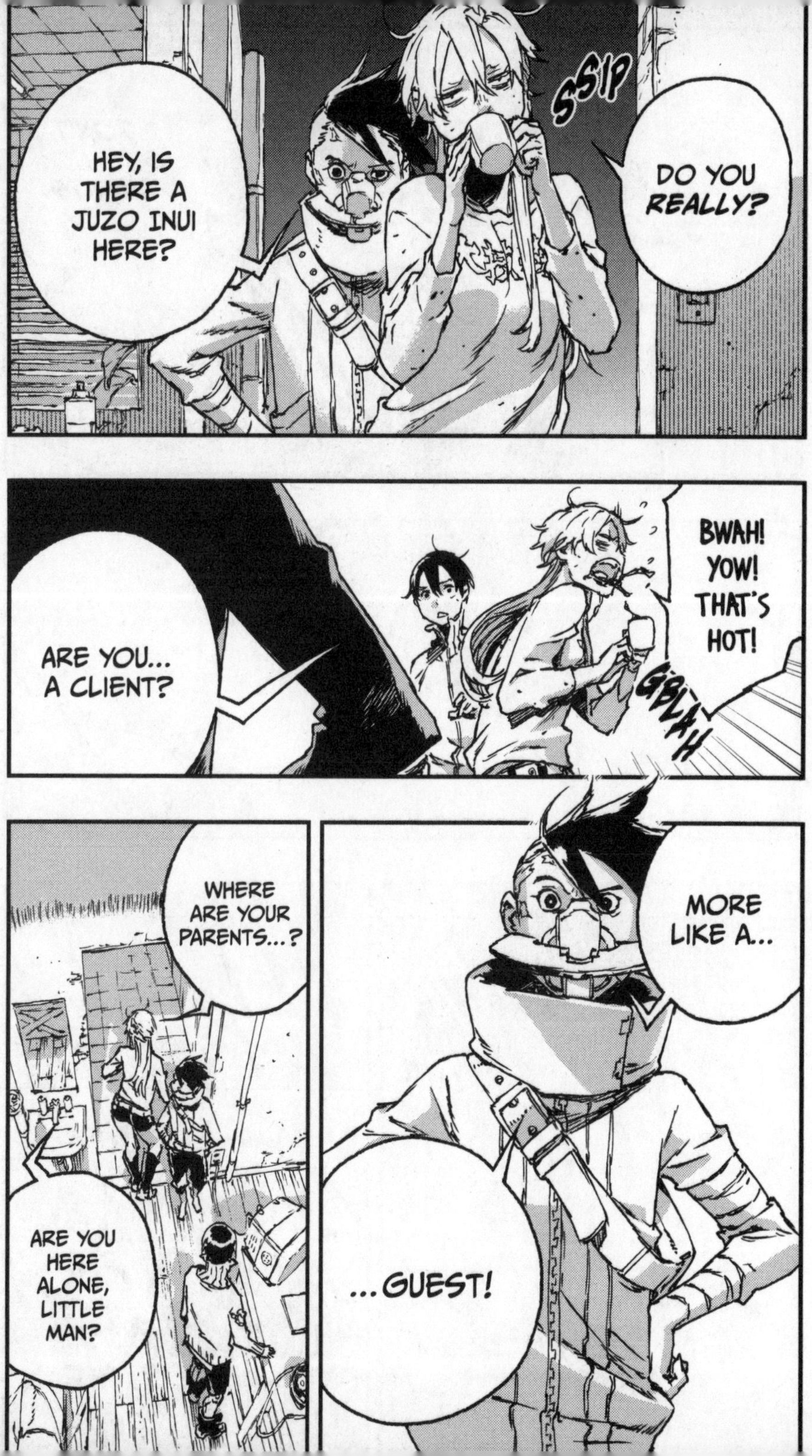
SSIP
DO YOU REALLY?
HEY, IS THERE A JUZO INUI HERE?
BWAH! YOW! THAT'S HOT!
GBLAH
ARE YOU... A CLIENT?
MORE LIKE A...
...GUEST!
WHERE ARE YOUR PARENTS...?
ARE YOU HERE ALONE, LITTLE MAN?

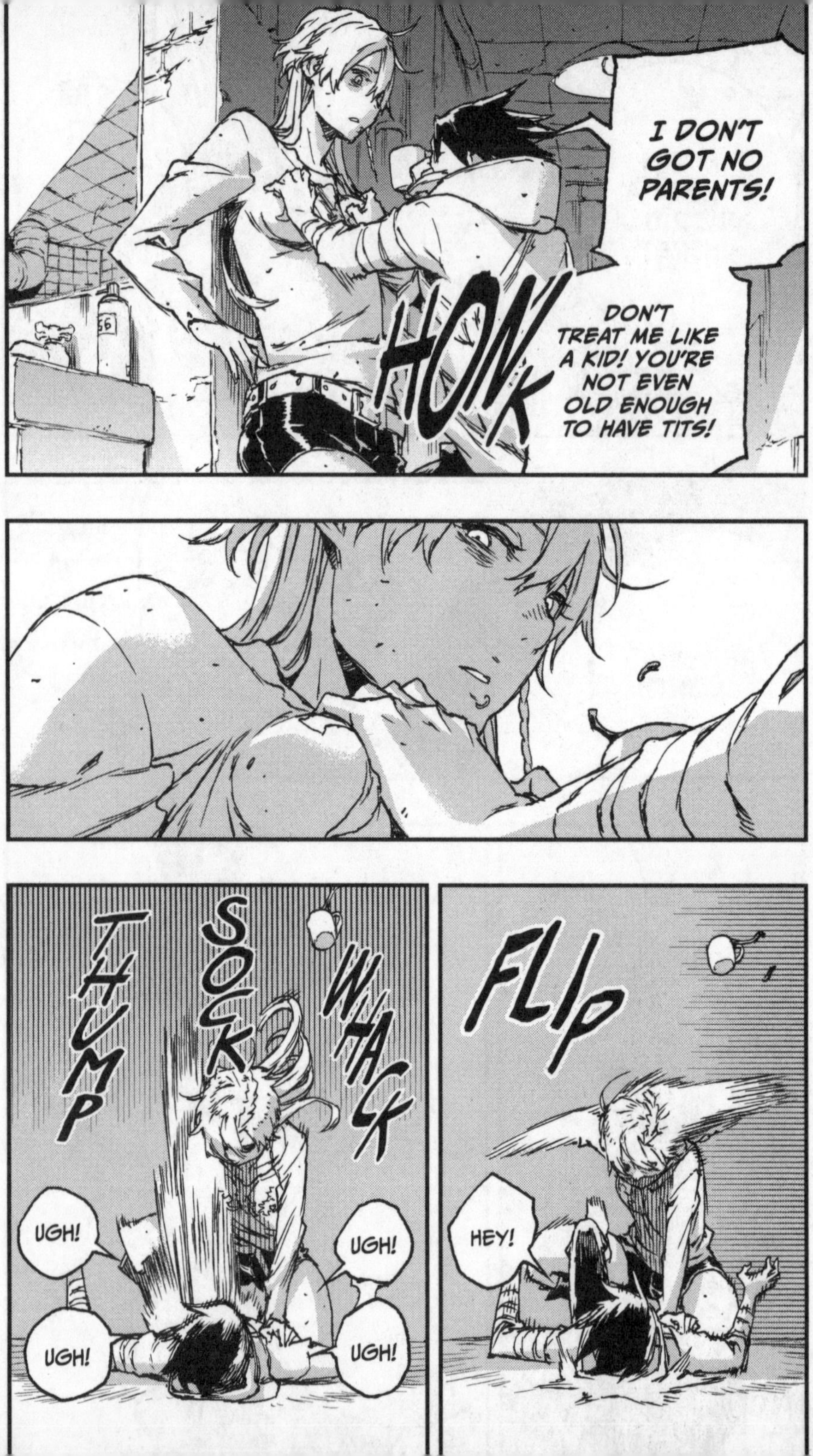
I DON'T GOT NO PARENTS!
DON'T TREAT ME LIKE A KID! YOU'RE NOT EVEN OLD ENOUGH TO HAVE TITS!
HONK
FLIP
HEY!
WHACK
SOCK
THUMP
UGH!
UGH!
UGH!
UGH!

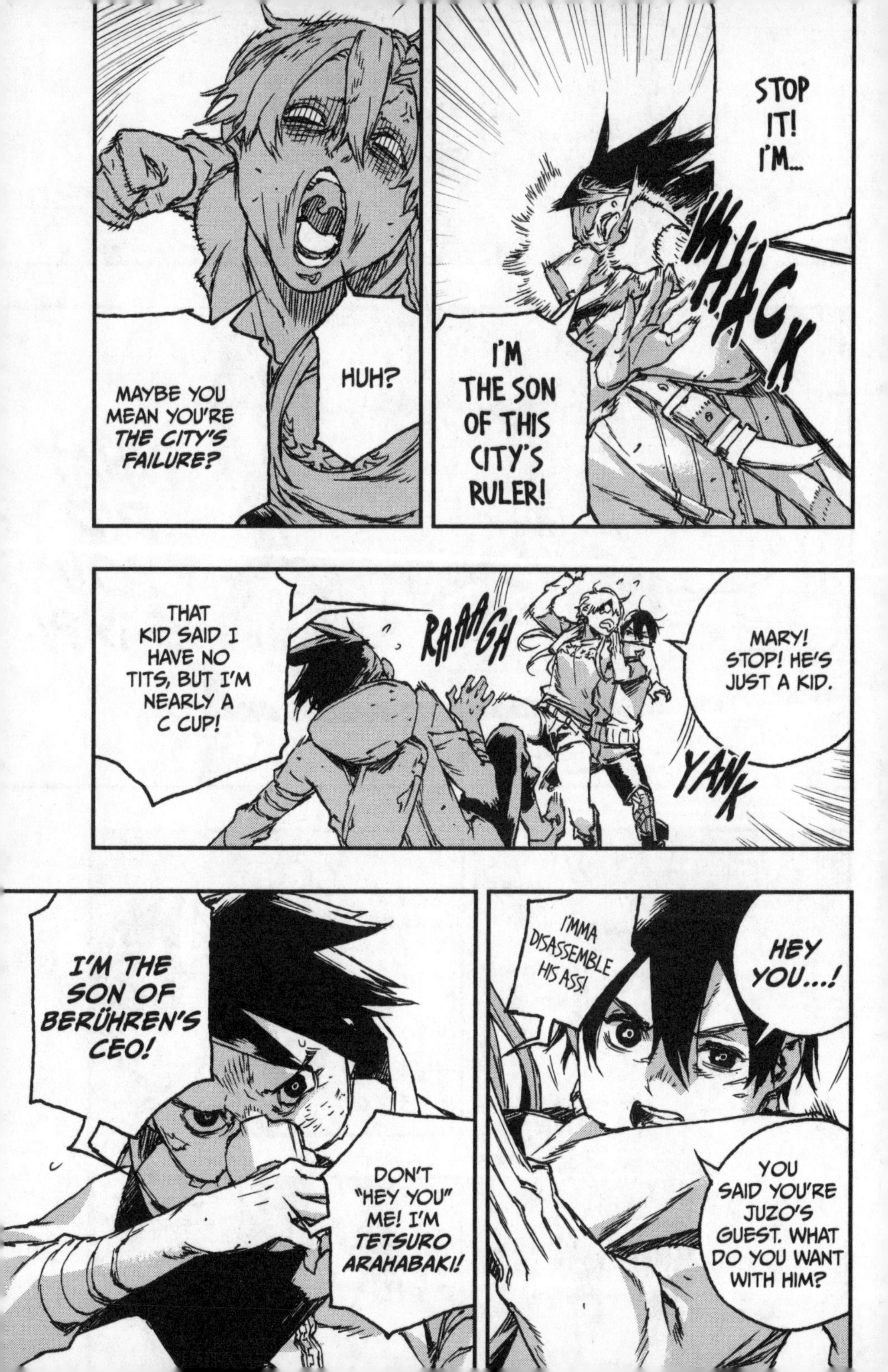
STOP IT! I'M...
WHACK
I'M THE SON OF THIS CITY'S RULER!
HUH?
MAYBE YOU MEAN YOU'RE THE CITY'S FAILURE?
MARY! STOP! HE'S JUST A KID.
YANK
RAAAGH
THAT KID SAID I HAVE NO TITS, BUT I'M NEARLY A C CUP!
HEY YOU...!
I'MMA DISASSEMBLE HIS ASS!
YOU SAID YOU'RE JUZO'S GUEST. WHAT DO YOU WANT WITH HIM?
DON'T "HEY YOU" ME! I'M TETSURO ARAHABAKI!
I'M THE SON OF BERÜHREN'S CEO!

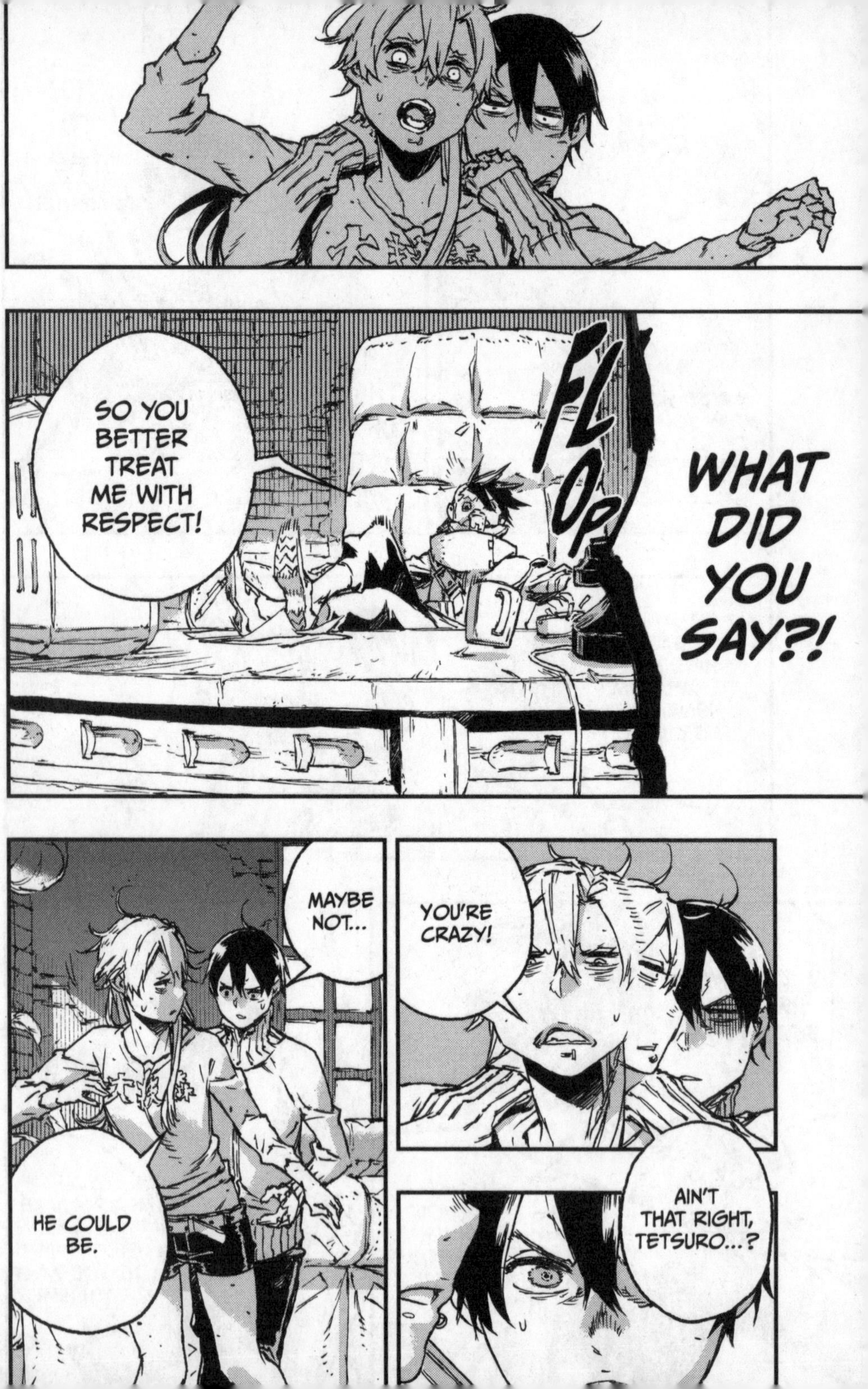
WHAT DID YOU SAY?!
FLOP
SO YOU BETTER TREAT ME WITH RESPECT!
YOU'RE CRAZY!
AIN'T THAT RIGHT, TETSURO...?
MAYBE NOT...
HE COULD BE.

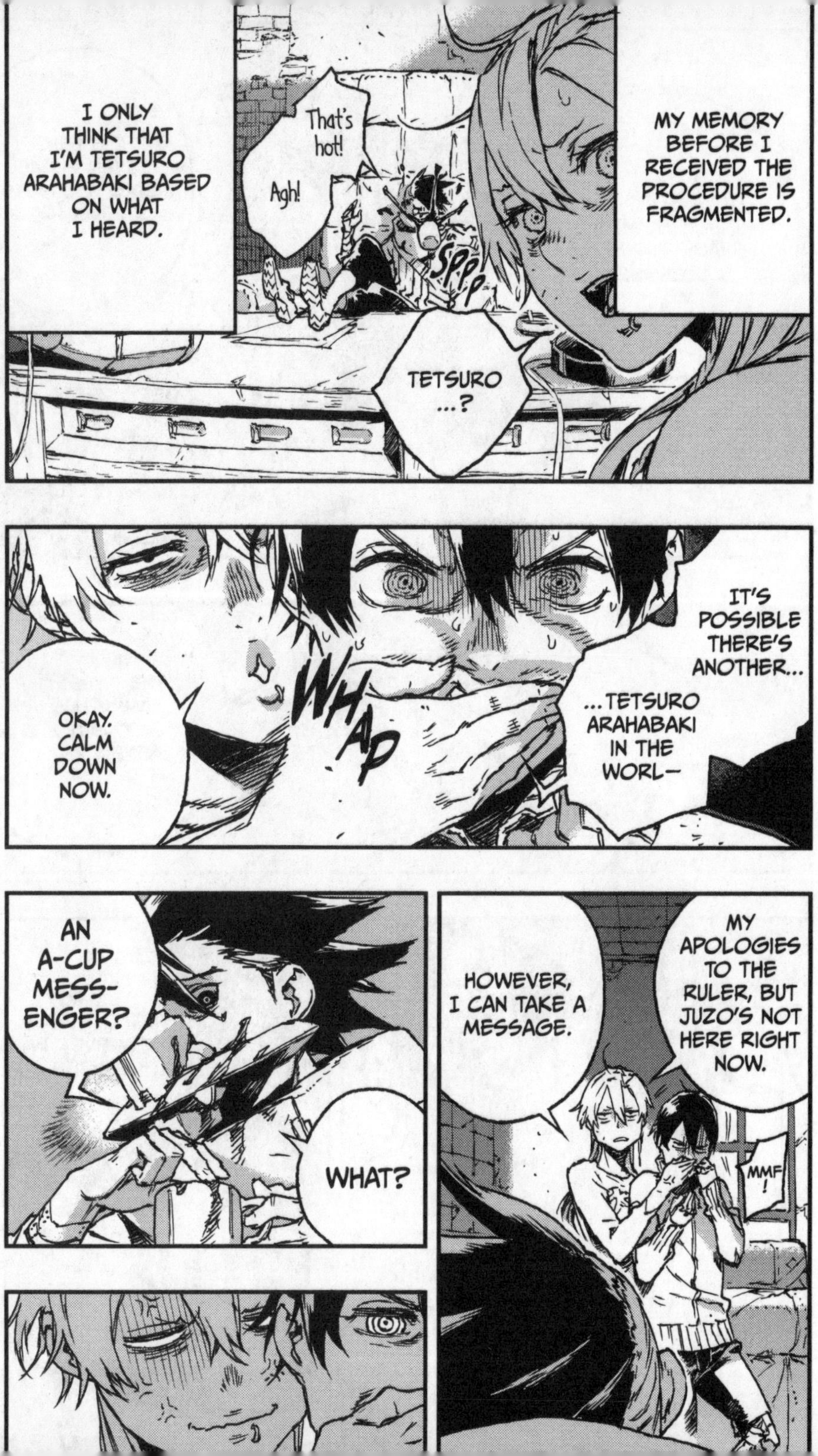
MY MEMORY BEFORE I RECEIVED THE PROCEDURE IS FRAGMENTED.
That's hot!
Agh!
SPPP
I ONLY THINK THAT I'M TETSURO ARAHABAKI BASED ON WHAT I HEARD.
TETSURO ...?
IT'S POSSIBLE THERE'S ANOTHER...
...TETSURO ARAHABAKI IN THE WORL—
WHAP
OKAY. CALM DOWN NOW.
MY APOLOGIES TO THE RULER, BUT JUZO'S NOT HERE RIGHT NOW.
HOWEVER, I CAN TAKE A MESSAGE.
MMF!
AN A-CUP MESS-ENGER?
WHAT?

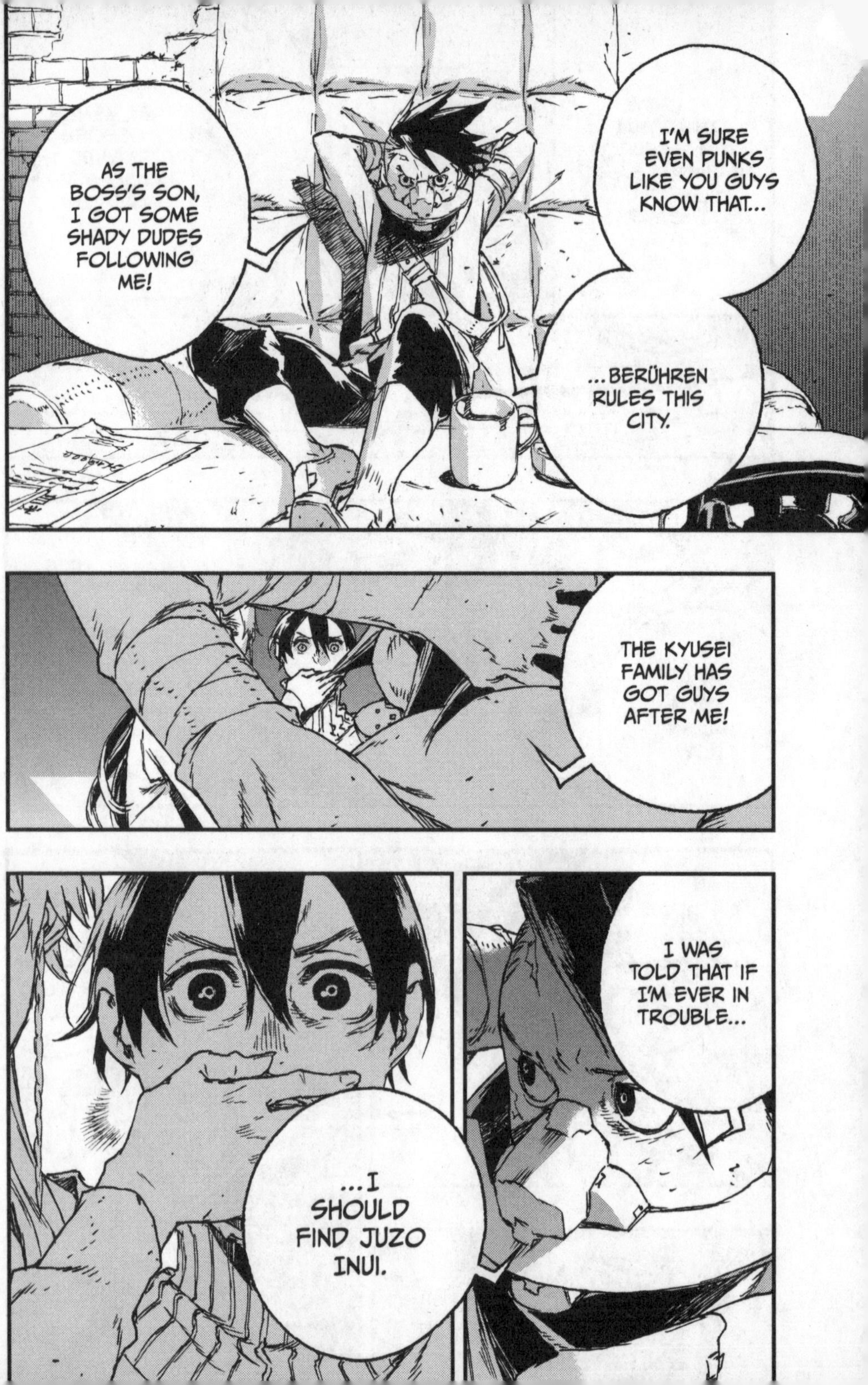
I'M SURE EVEN PUNKS LIKE YOU GUYS KNOW THAT...
...BERÜHREN RULES THIS CITY.
AS THE BOSS'S SON, I GOT SOME SHADY DUDES FOLLOWING ME!
THE KYUSEI FAMILY HAS GOT GUYS AFTER ME!
I WAS TOLD THAT IF I'M EVER IN TROUBLE...
...I SHOULD FIND JUZO INUI.

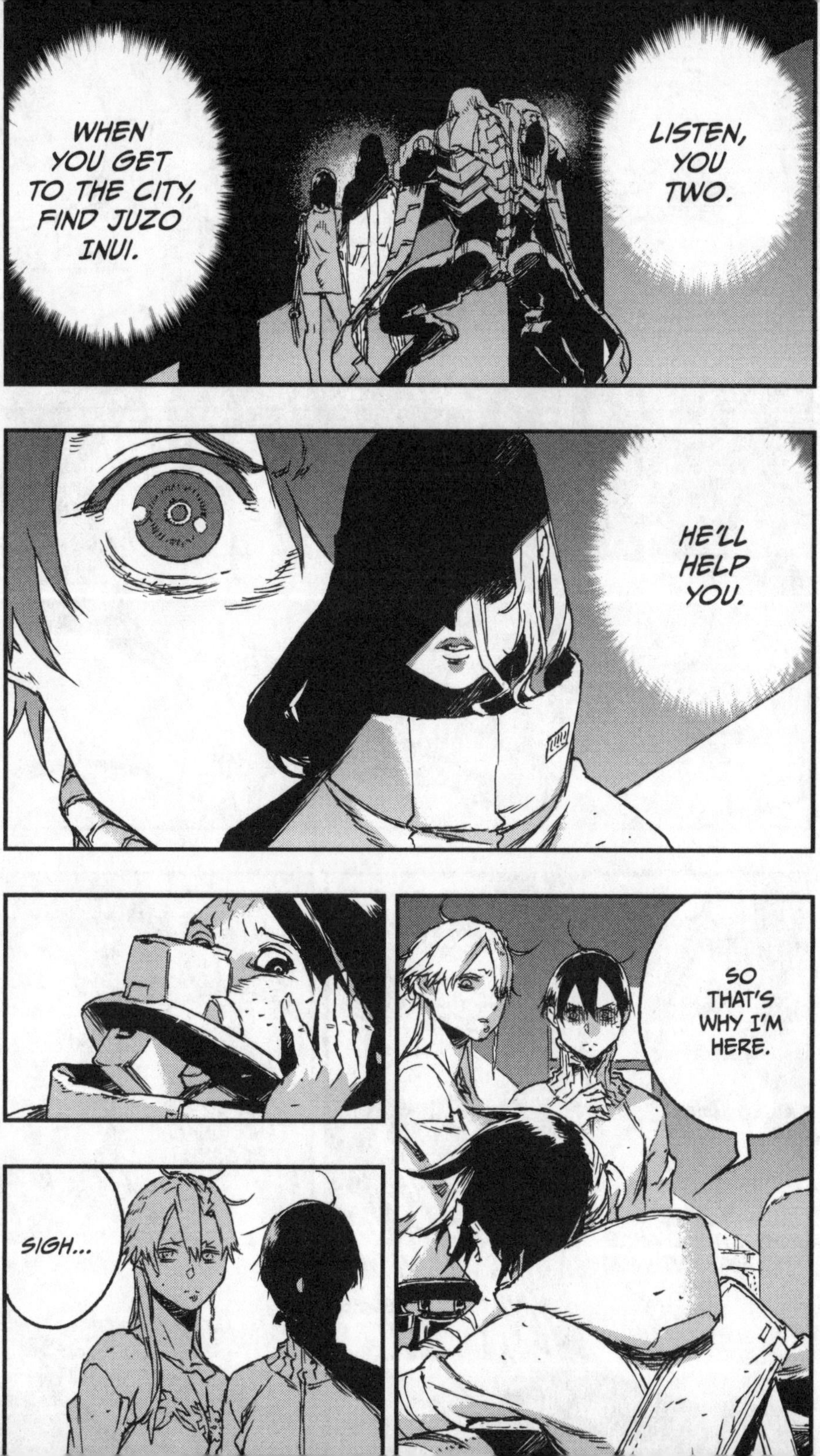
LISTEN, YOU TWO.
WHEN YOU GET TO THE CITY, FIND JUZO INUI.
HE'LL HELP YOU.
SO THAT'S WHY I'M HERE.
SIGH...

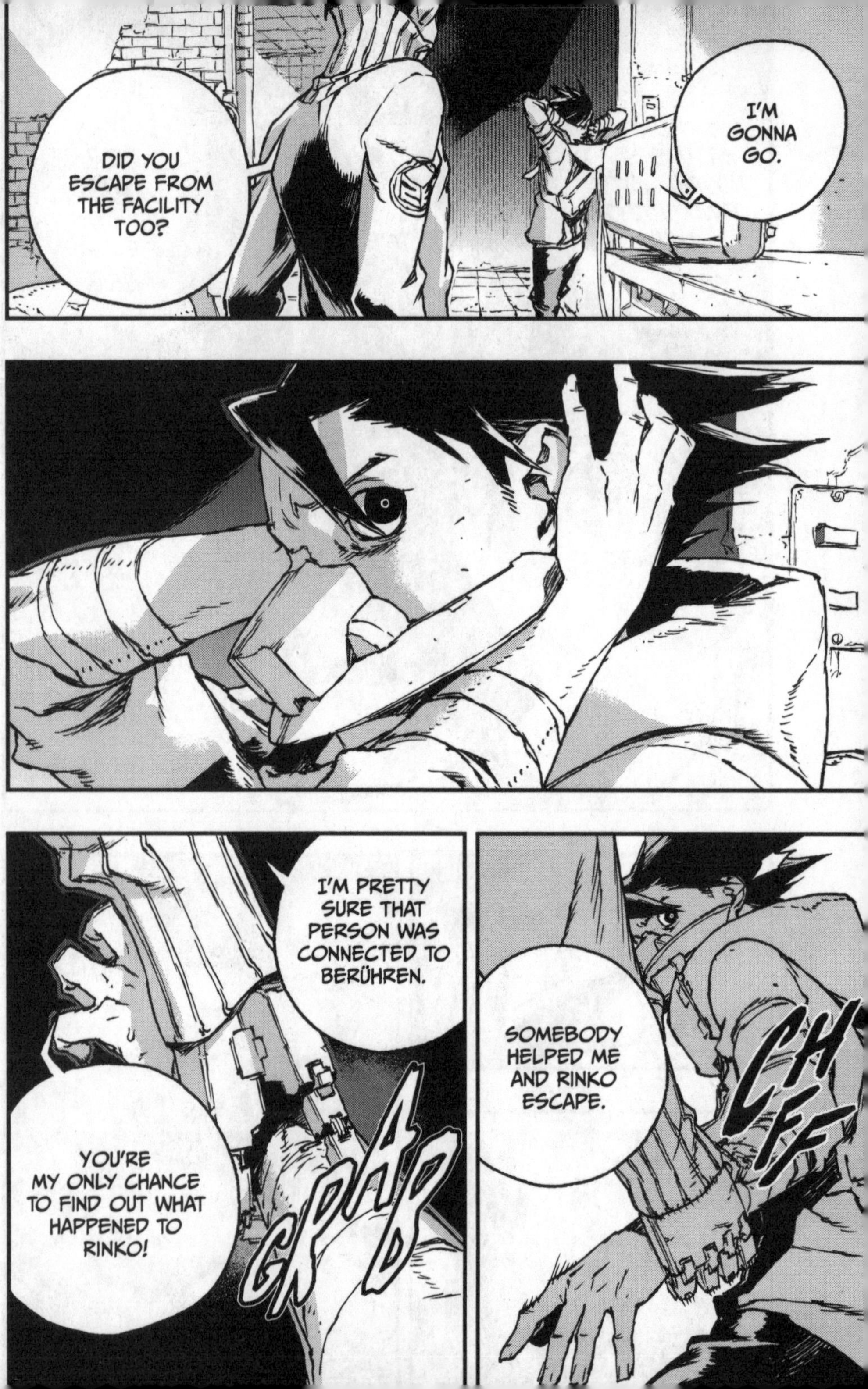
I'M GONNA GO.
DID YOU ESCAPE FROM THE FACILITY TOO?
SOMEBODY HELPED ME AND RINKO ESCAPE.
CHFF
I'M PRETTY SURE THAT PERSON WAS CONNECTED TO BERÜHREN.
GRAB
YOU'RE MY ONLY CHANCE TO FIND OUT WHAT HAPPENED TO RINKO!

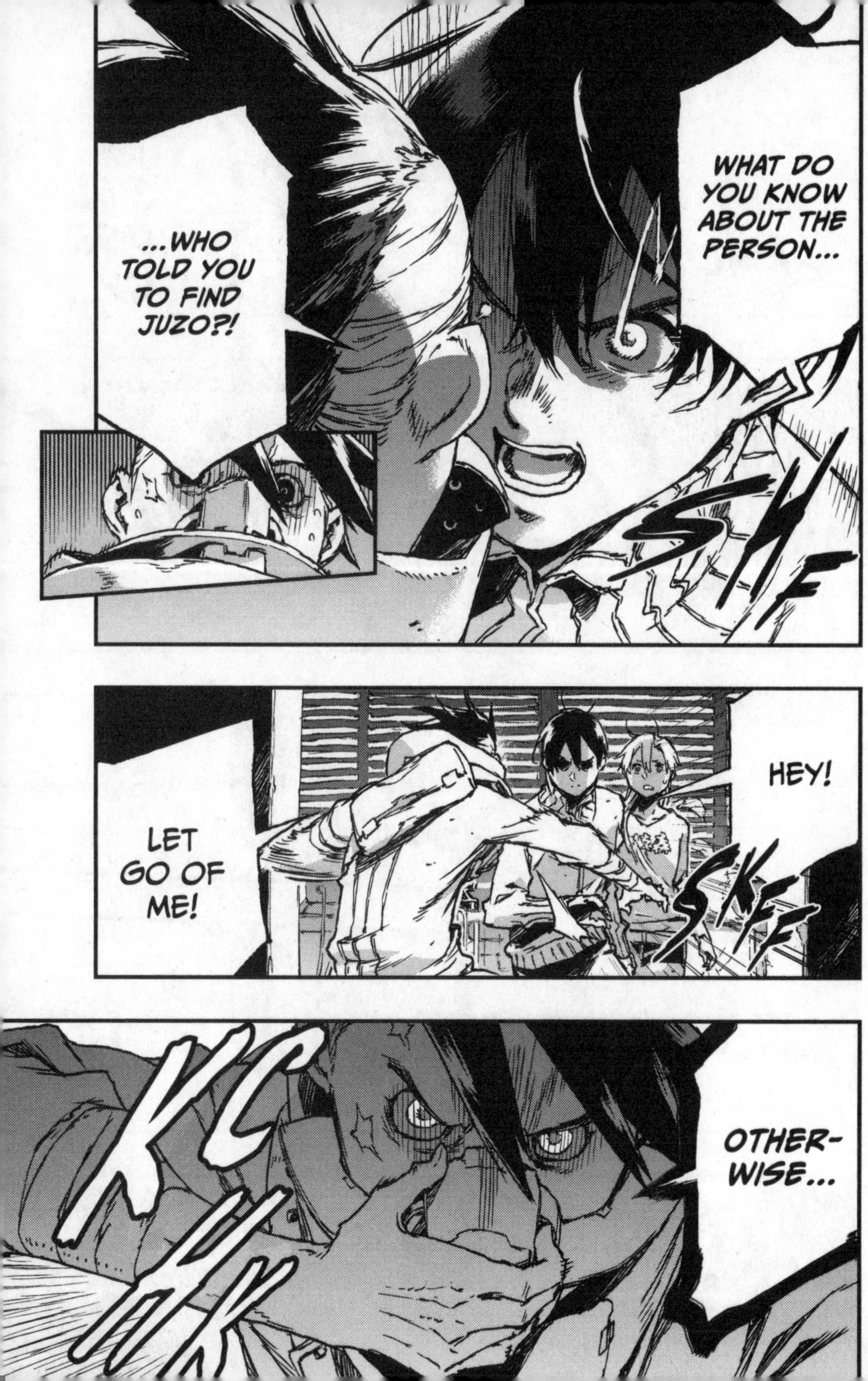
WHAT DO YOU KNOW ABOUT THE PERSON...
...WHO TOLD YOU TO FIND JUZO?!
SHF
HEY!
SKFF
LET GO OF ME!
OTHER-WISE...

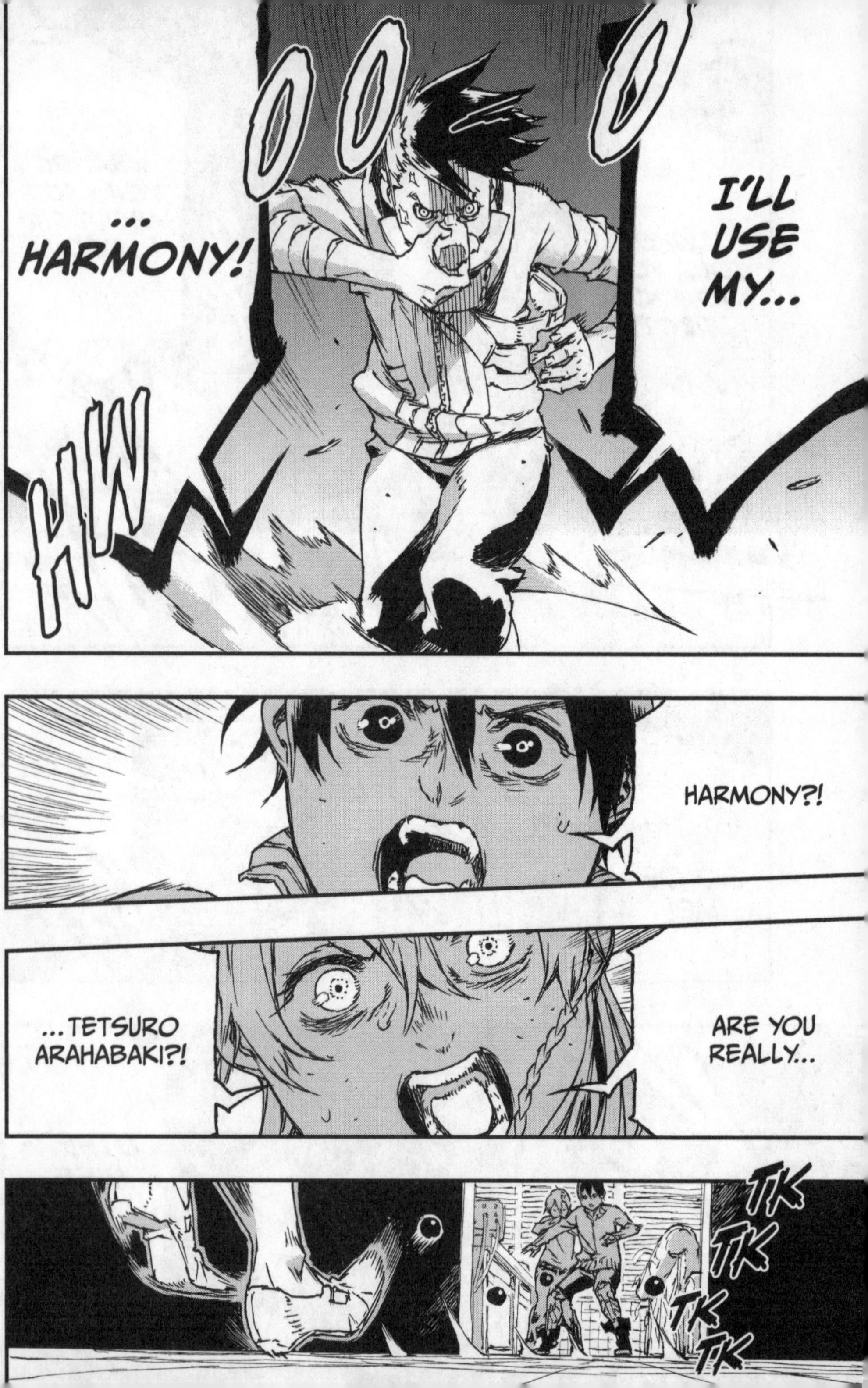
OOOO
I'LL USE MY...
...HARMONY!
HW
HARMONY?!
ARE YOU REALLY...
...TETSURO ARAHABAKI?!
TK TK TK TK

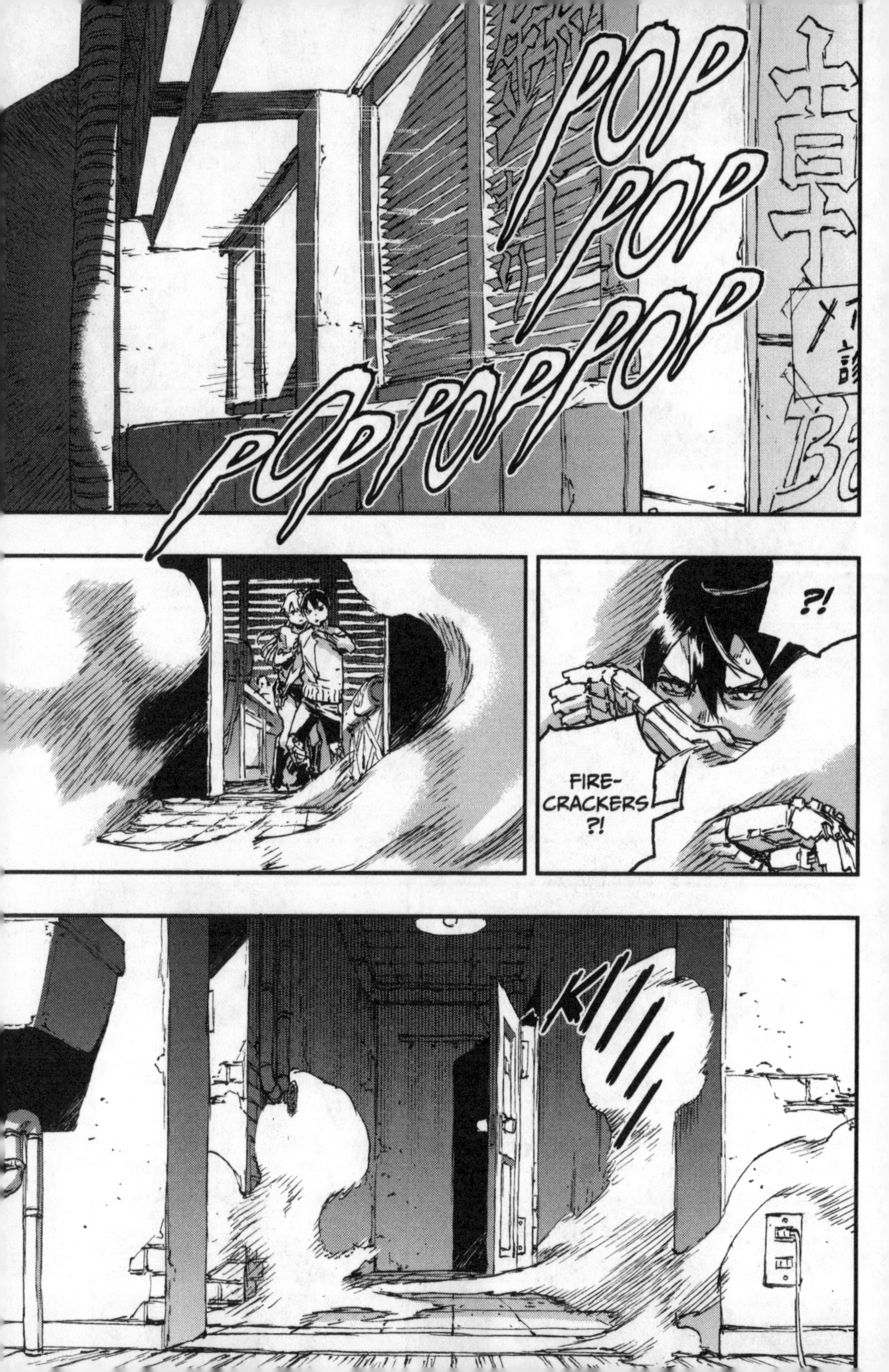
POP POP POPPOPPOP
?!
FIRE-CRACKERS ?!
KI

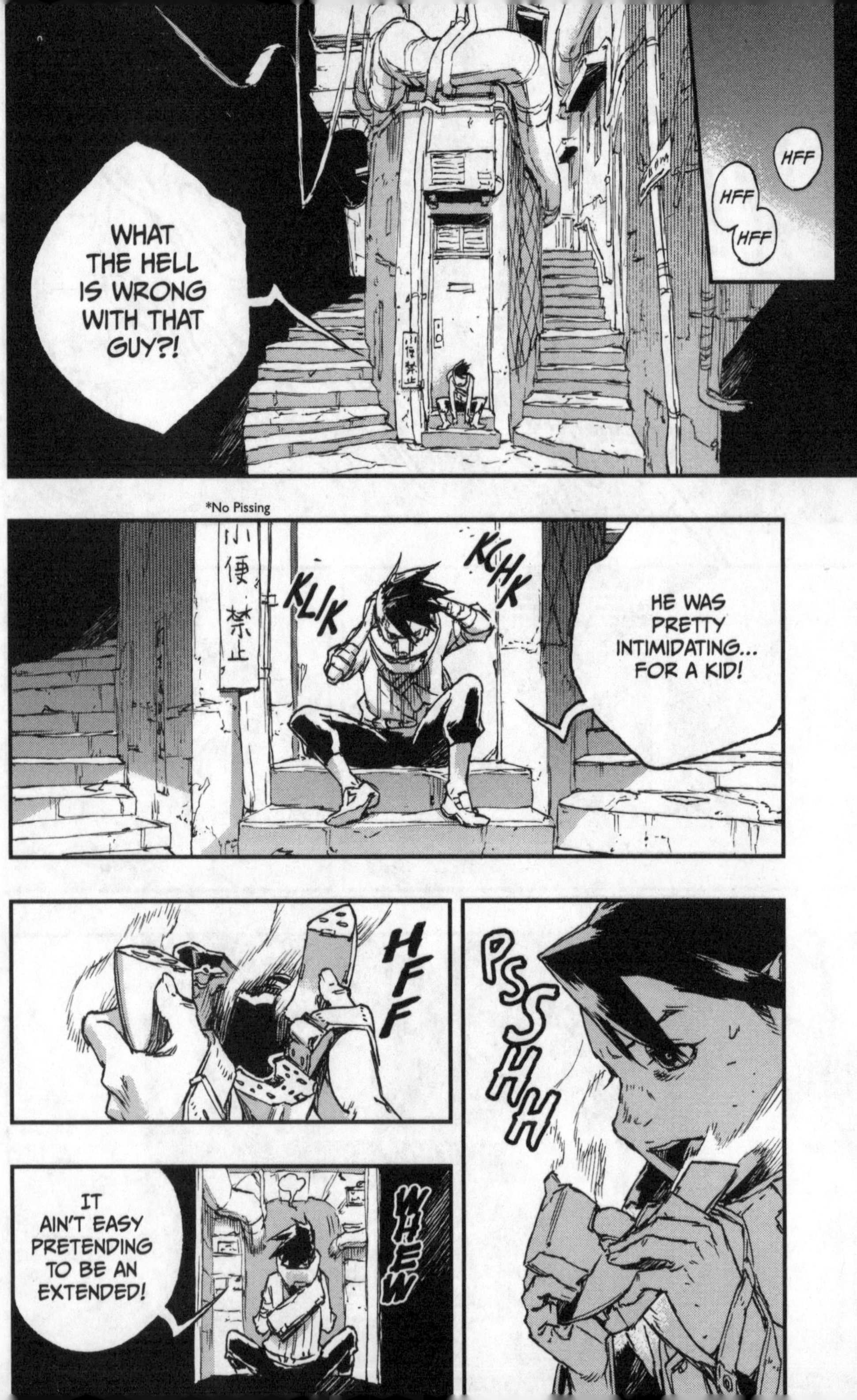
HFF
HFF
HFF
WHAT THE HELL IS WRONG WITH THAT GUY?!
*No Pissing
小便禁止
KCHK
KLIK
HE WAS PRETTY INTIMIDATING... FOR A KID!
PSSHHH
HFF
WHEW
IT AIN'T EASY PRETENDING TO BE AN EXTENDED!

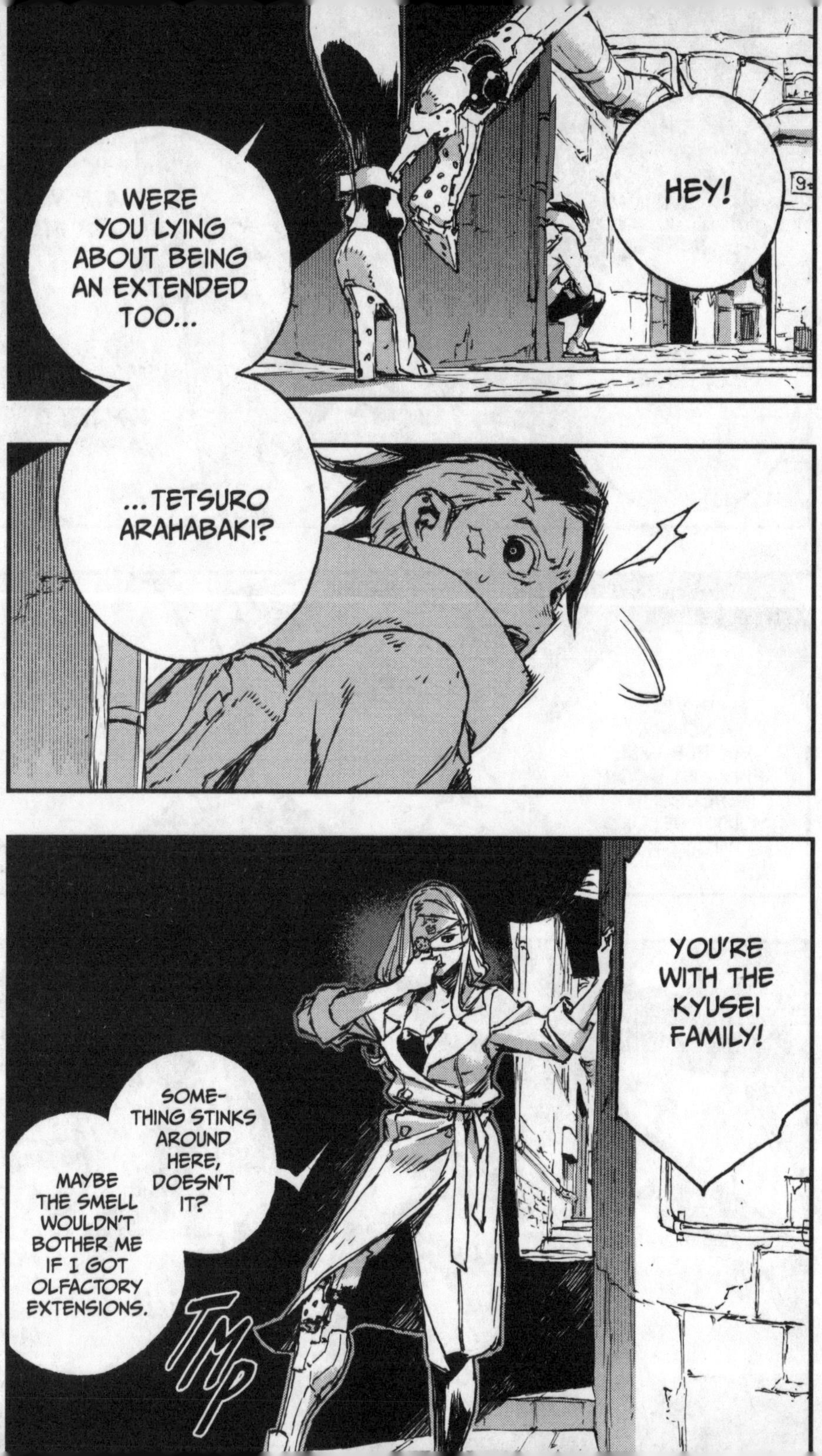
HEY!
WERE YOU LYING ABOUT BEING AN EXTENDED TOO...
...TETSURO ARAHABAKI?
YOU'RE WITH THE KYUSEI FAMILY!
SOME-THING STINKS AROUND HERE, DOESN'T IT?
MAYBE THE SMELL WOULDN'T BOTHER ME IF I GOT OLFACTORY EXTENSIONS.
TMP

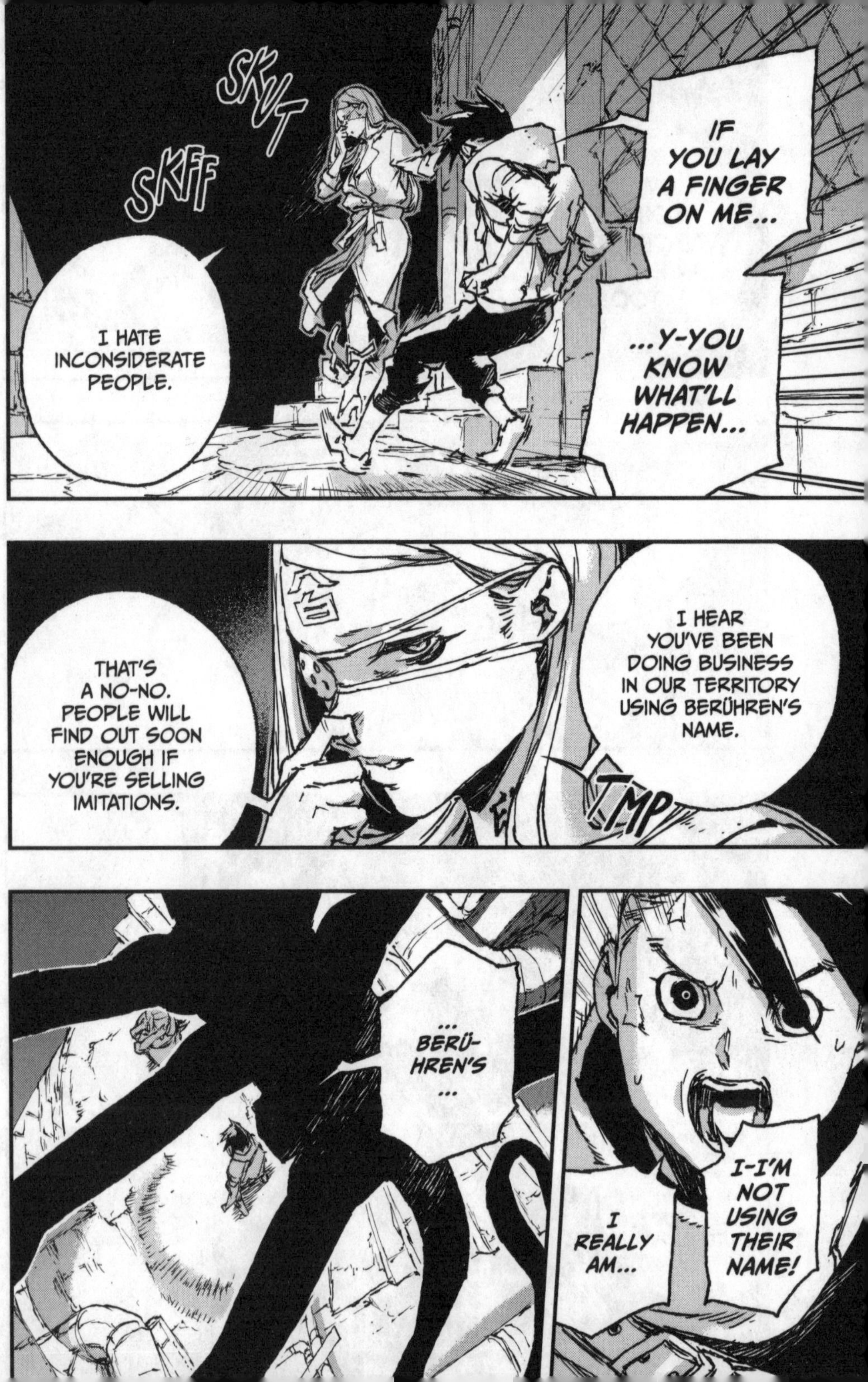
IF YOU LAY A FINGER ON ME...
...Y-YOU KNOW WHAT'LL HAPPEN...
SKVT
SKFF
I HATE INCONSIDERATE PEOPLE.
I HEAR YOU'VE BEEN DOING BUSINESS IN OUR TERRITORY USING BERÜHREN'S NAME.
TMP
THAT'S A NO-NO. PEOPLE WILL FIND OUT SOON ENOUGH IF YOU'RE SELLING IMITATIONS.
I-I'M NOT USING THEIR NAME!
I REALLY AM...
...BERÜ-HREN'S...

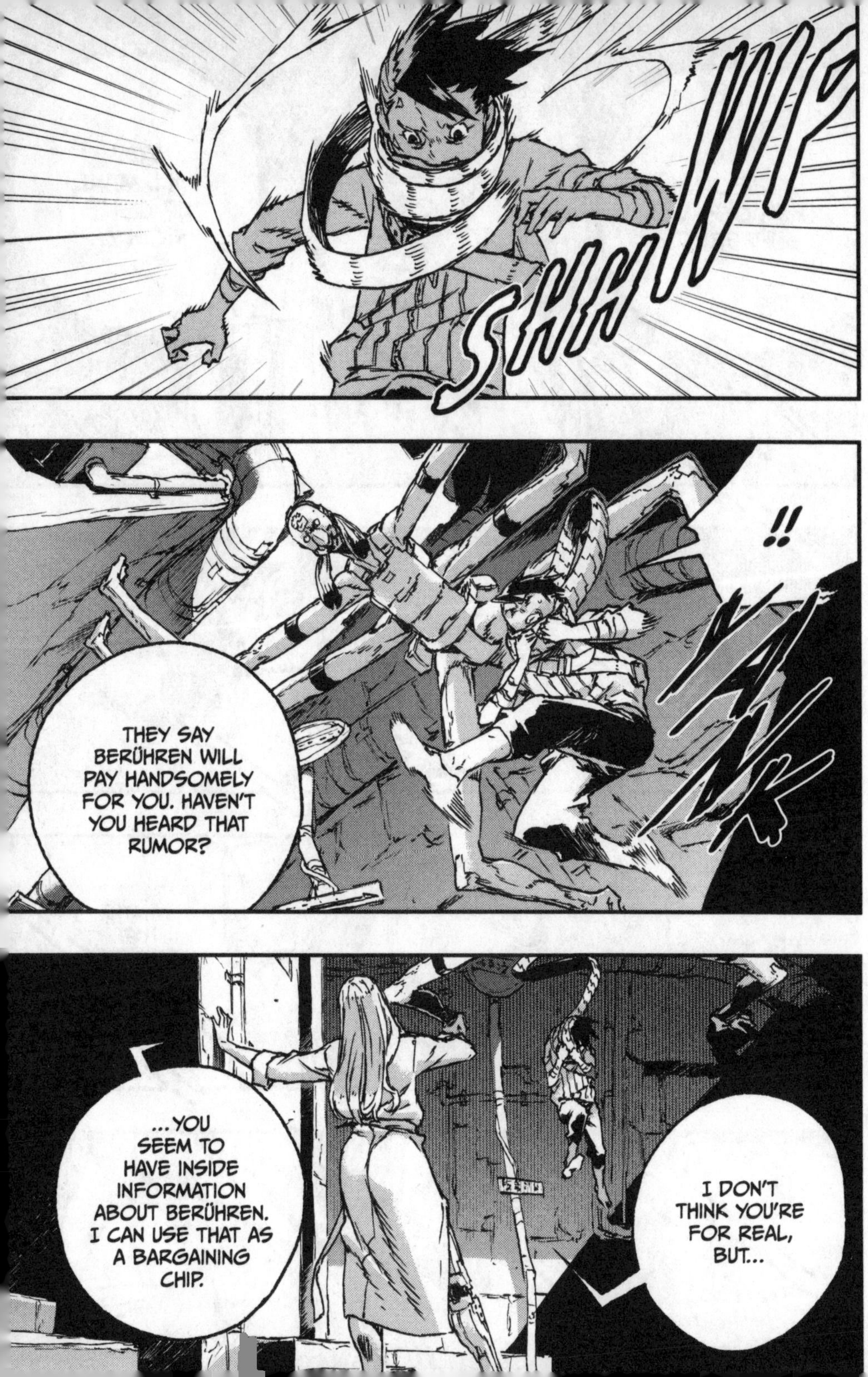
SHHWP
!!
YANK
THEY SAY BERÜHREN WILL PAY HANDSOMELY FOR YOU. HAVEN'T YOU HEARD THAT RUMOR?
I DON'T THINK YOU'RE FOR REAL, BUT...
...YOU SEEM TO HAVE INSIDE INFORMATION ABOUT BERÜHREN. I CAN USE THAT AS A BARGAINING CHIP.

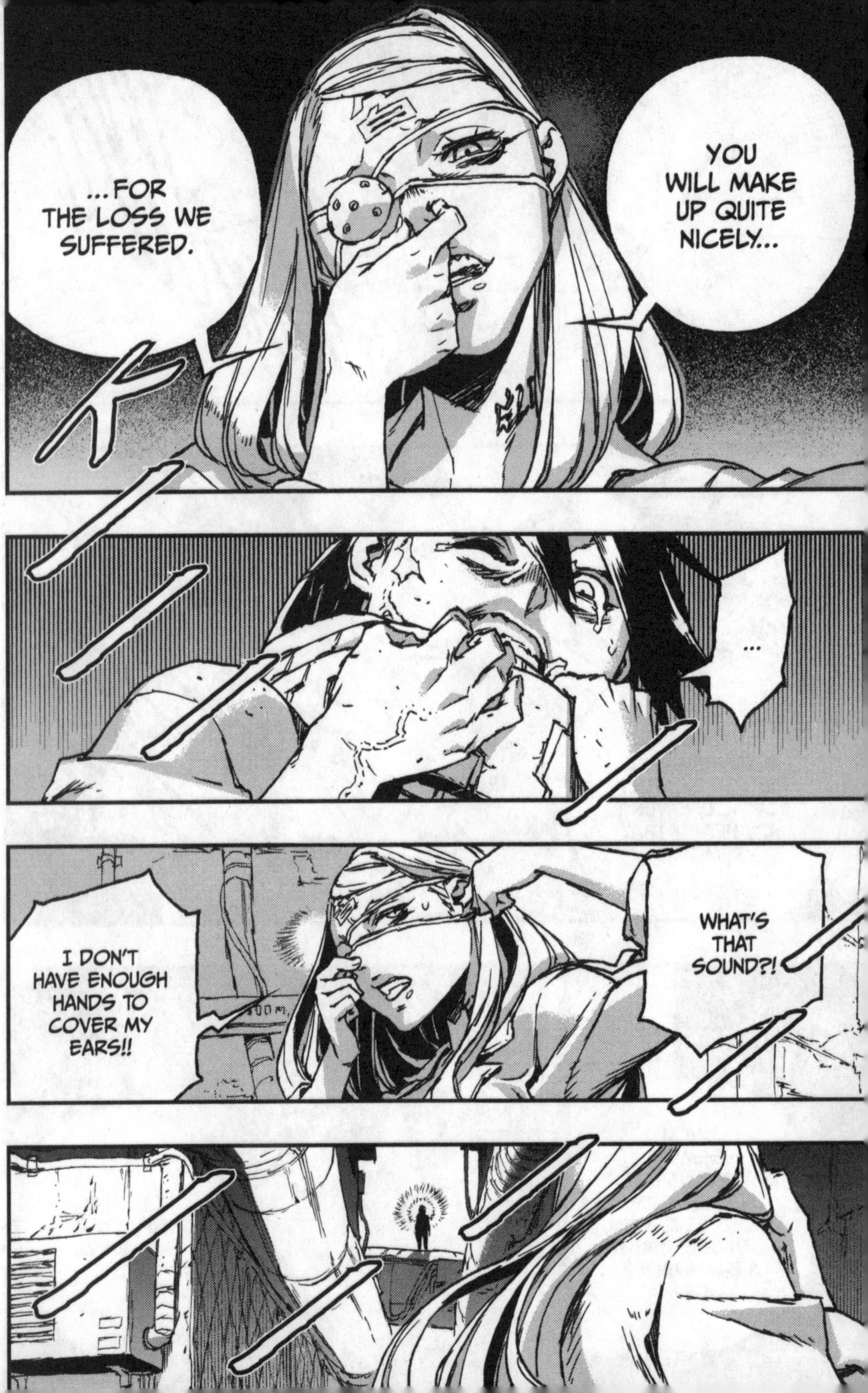
YOU WILL MAKE UP QUITE NICELY...
...FOR THE LOSS WE SUFFERED.
...
WHAT'S THAT SOUND?!
I DON'T HAVE ENOUGH HANDS TO COVER MY EARS!!

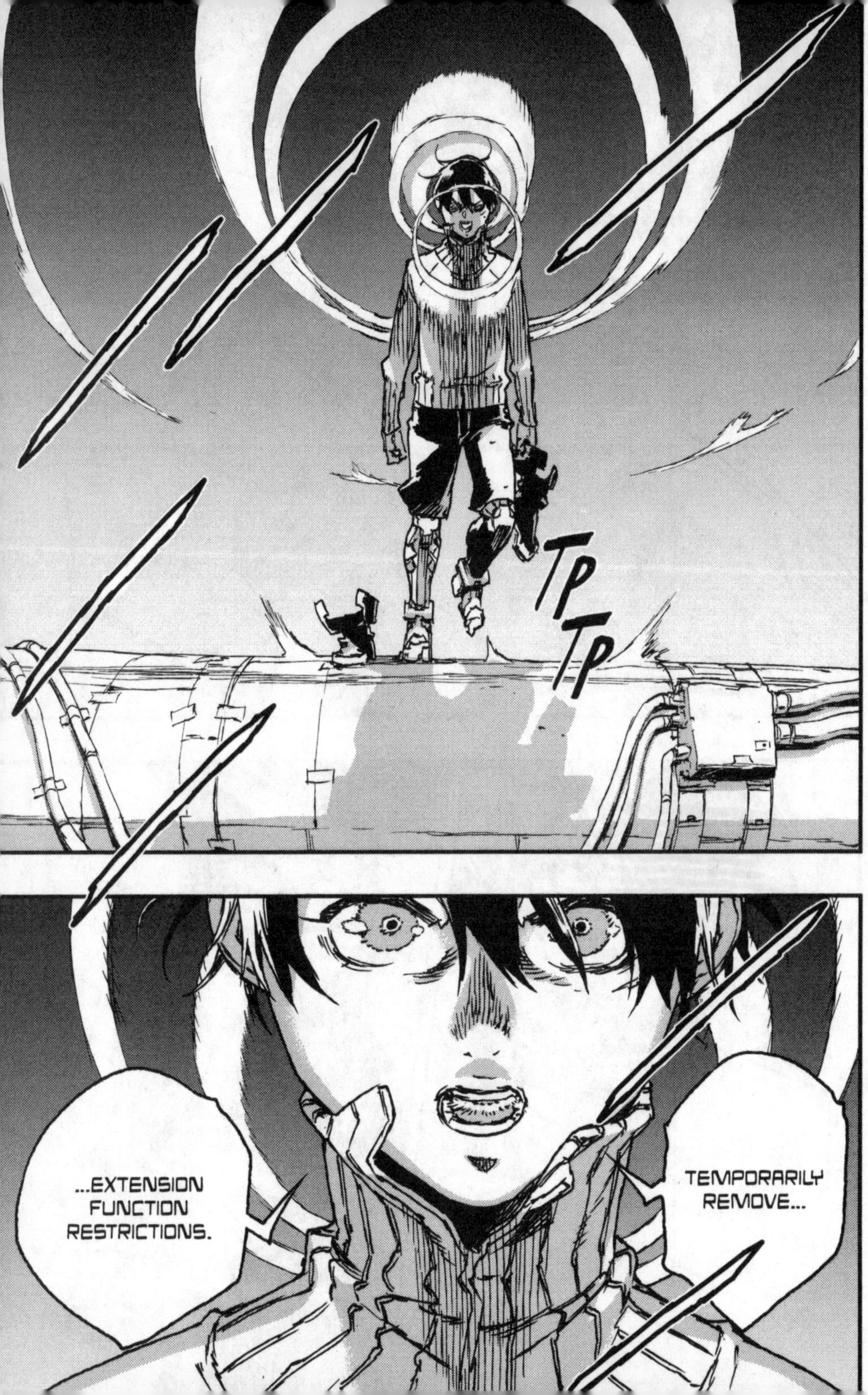
TPTP
TEMPORARILY REMOVE...
...EXTENSION FUNCTION RESTRICTIONS.

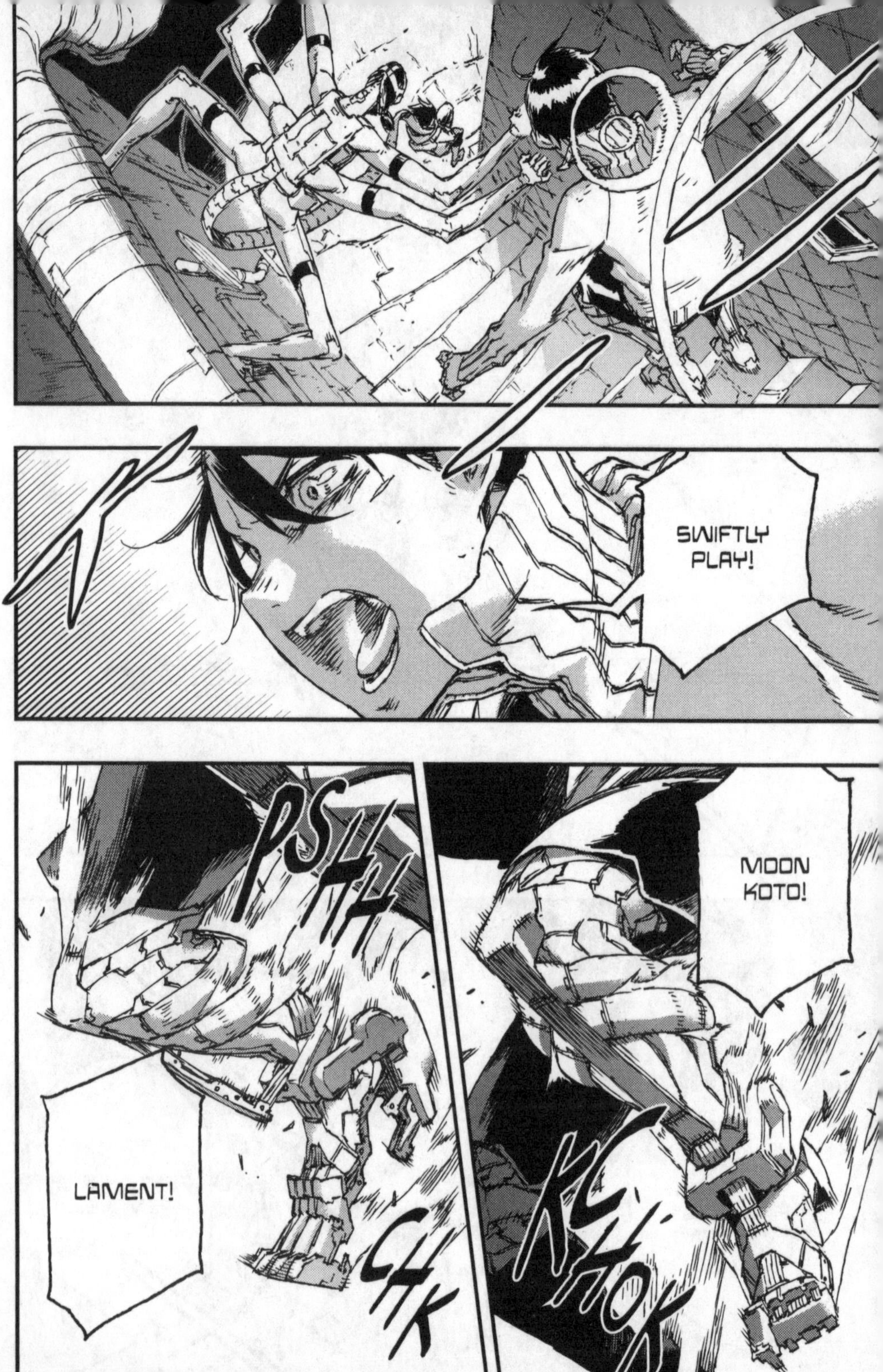
SWIFTLY PLAY!
MOON KOTO!
KCHOK
PSHH
LAMENT!
CHK

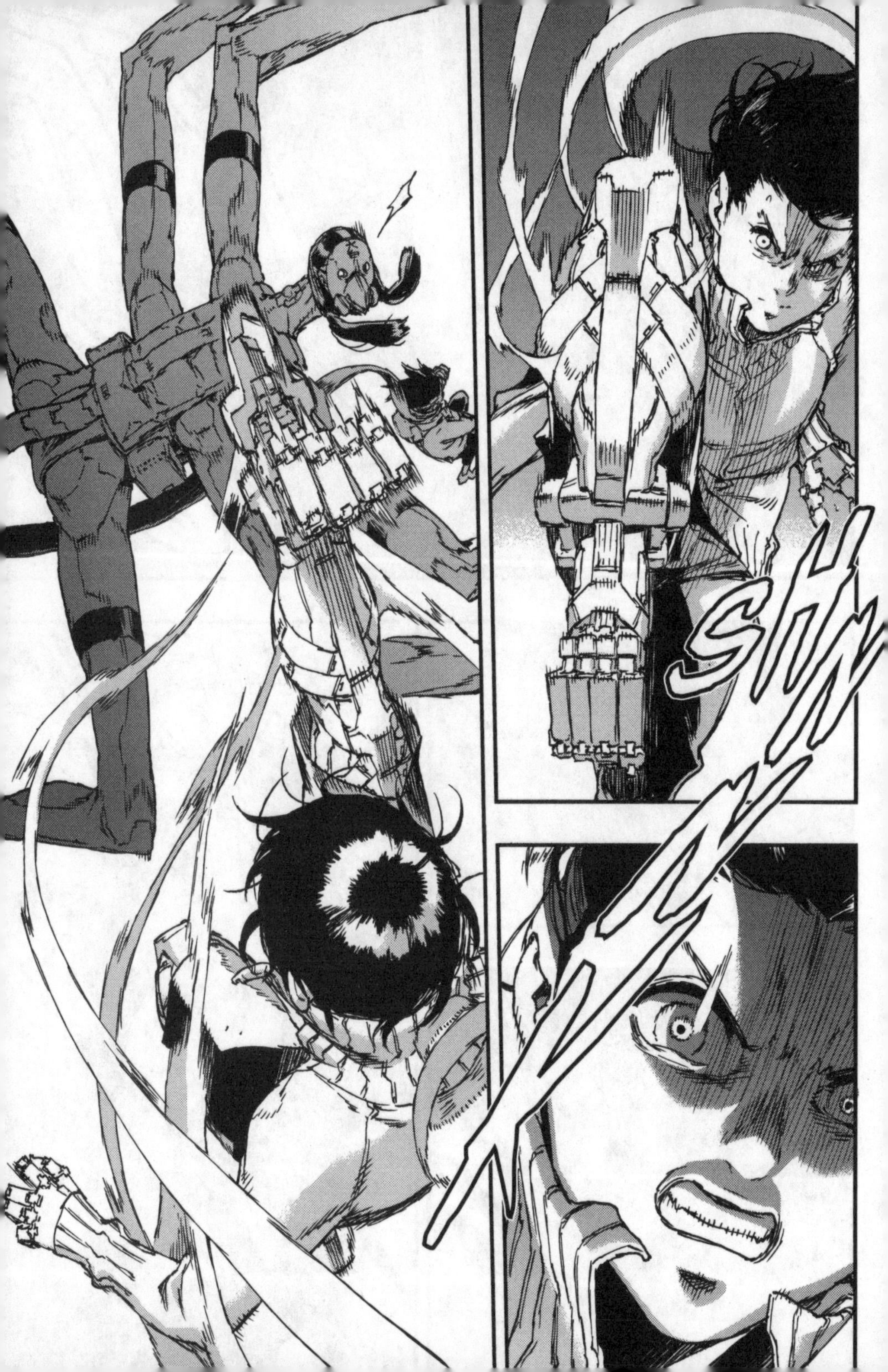
SHHN

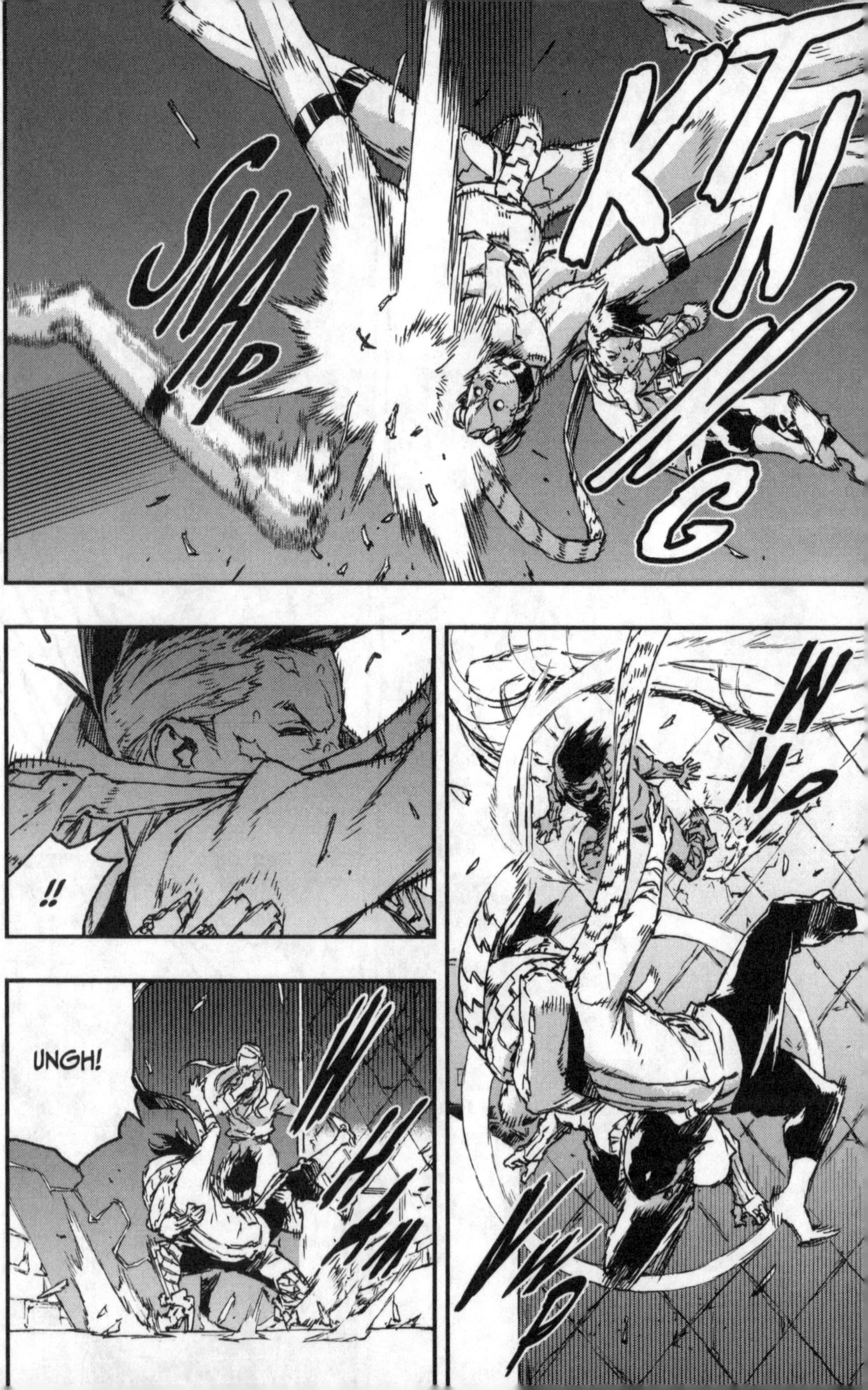
SNAP
WMP
!!
WMP
UNGH!
WHAM

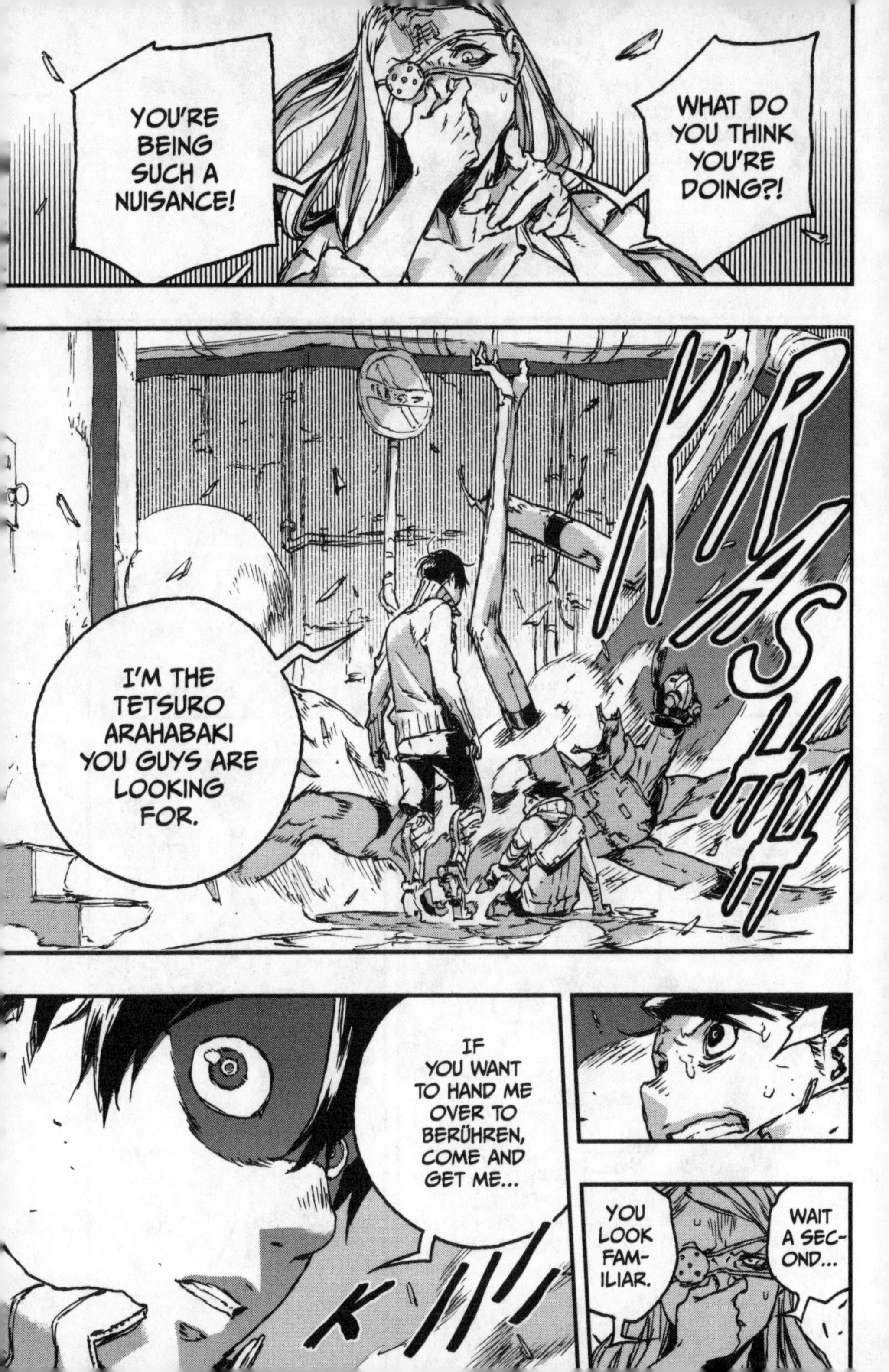
WHAT DO YOU THINK YOU'RE DOING?!
YOU'RE BEING SUCH A NUISANCE!
KRASHHH
I'M THE TETSURO ARAHABAKI YOU GUYS ARE LOOKING FOR.
WAIT A SEC-OND...
YOU LOOK FAM-ILIAR.
IF YOU WANT TO HAND ME OVER TO BERÜHREN, COME AND GET ME...
K

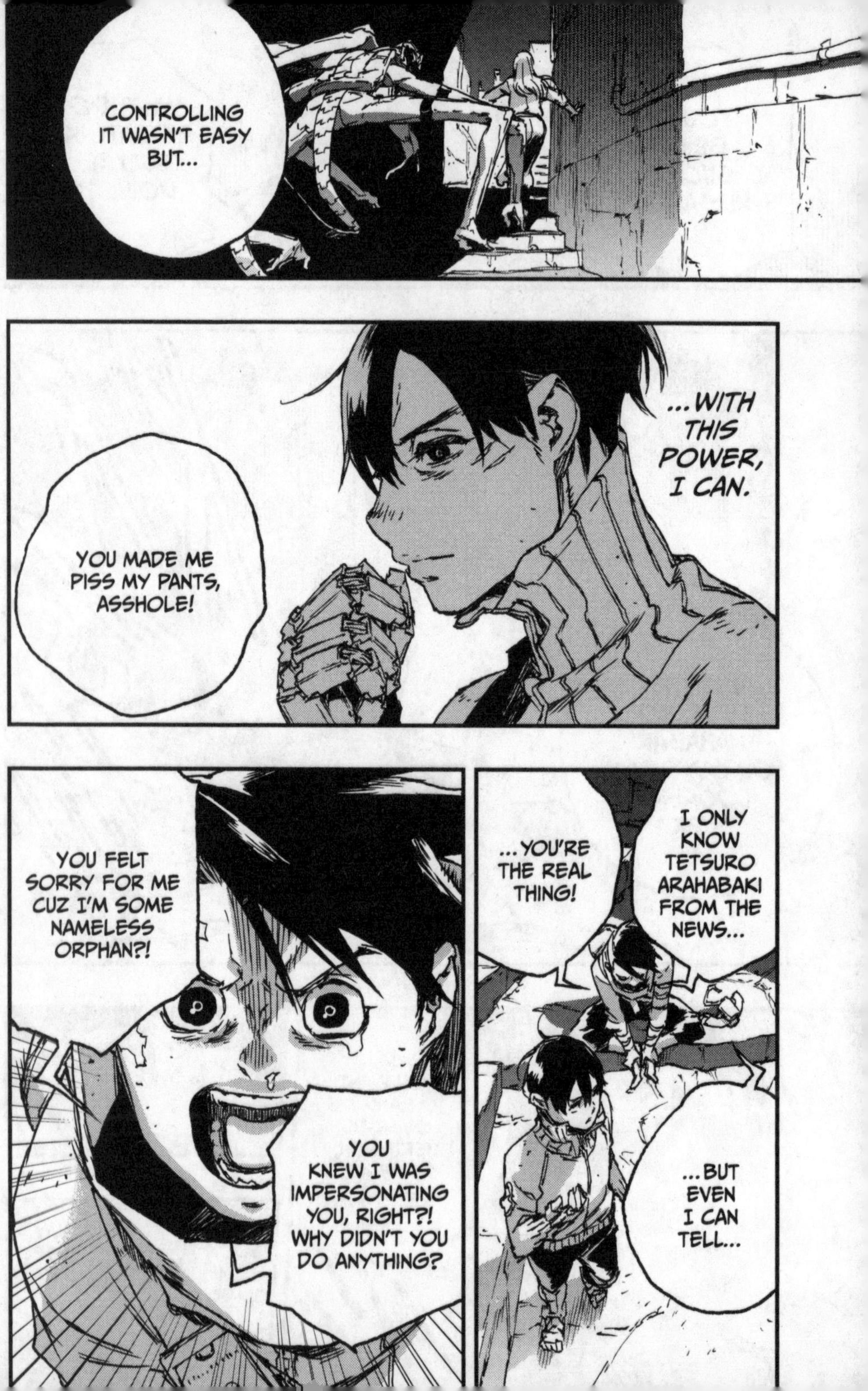
CONTROLLING IT WASN'T EASY BUT...
...WITH THIS POWER, I CAN.
YOU MADE ME PISS MY PANTS, ASSHOLE!
I ONLY KNOW TETSURO ARAHABAKI FROM THE NEWS...
...BUT EVEN I CAN TELL...
...YOU'RE THE REAL THING!
YOU FELT SORRY FOR ME CUZ I'M SOME NAMELESS ORPHAN?!
YOU KNEW I WAS IMPERSONATING YOU, RIGHT?! WHY DIDN'T YOU DO ANYTHING?

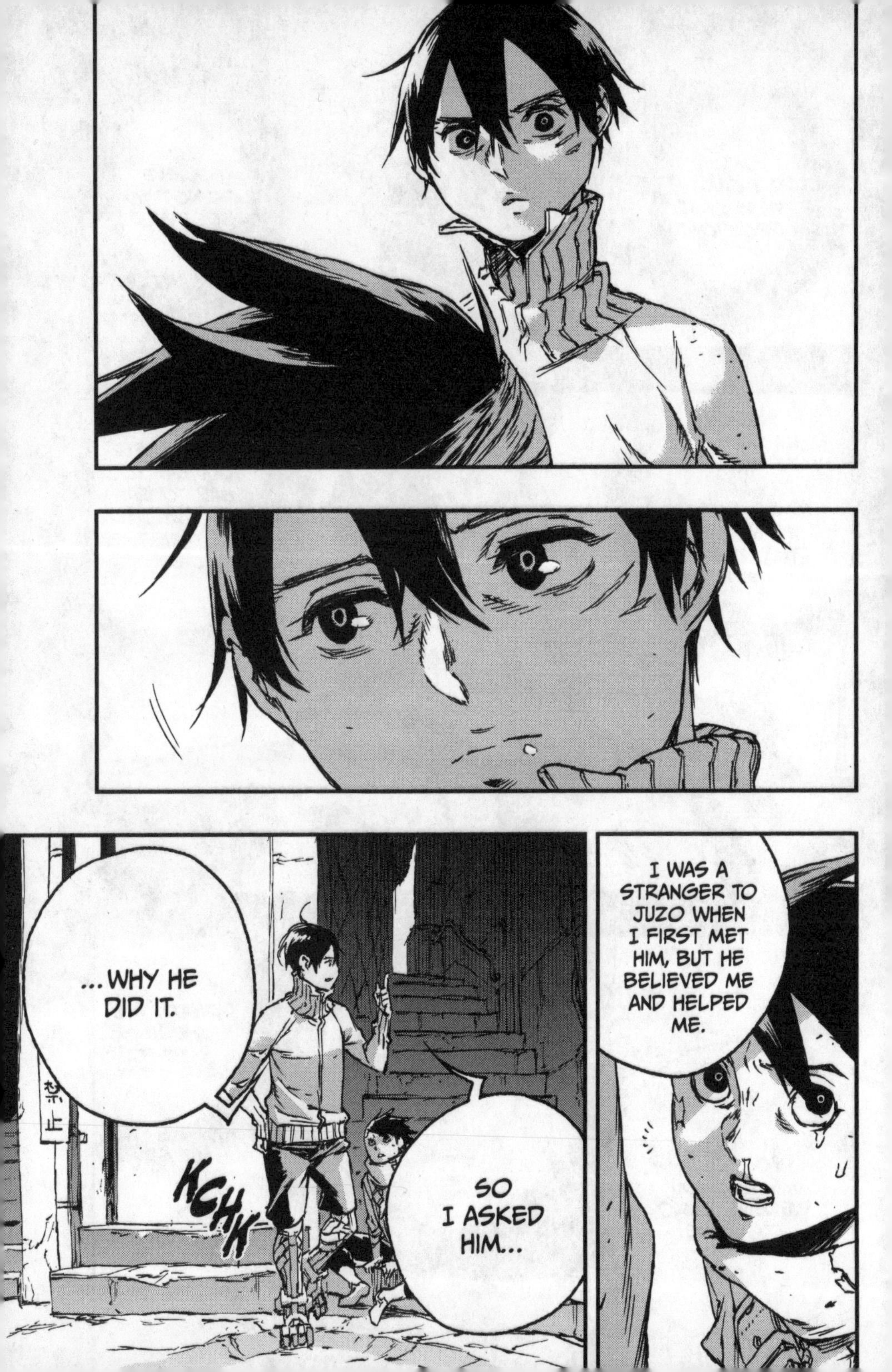
I WAS A STRANGER TO JUZO WHEN I FIRST MET HIM, BUT HE BELIEVED ME AND HELPED ME.
SO I ASKED HIM...
...WHY HE DID IT.
KCHK
禁止

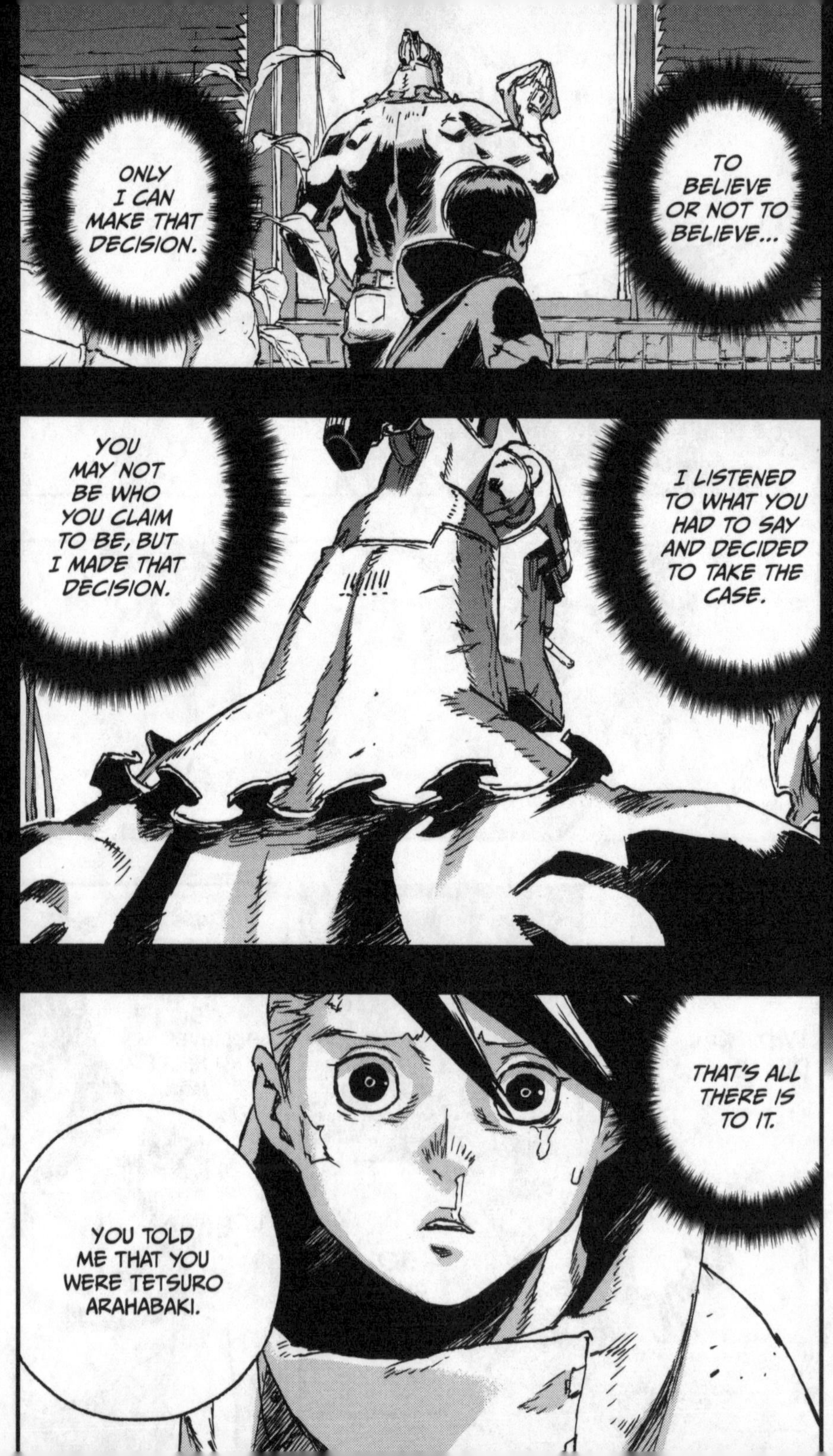
TO BELIEVE OR NOT TO BELIEVE...
ONLY I CAN MAKE THAT DECISION.
I LISTENED TO WHAT YOU HAD TO SAY AND DECIDED TO TAKE THE CASE.
YOU MAY NOT BE WHO YOU CLAIM TO BE, BUT I MADE THAT DECISION.
THAT'S ALL THERE IS TO IT.
YOU TOLD ME THAT YOU WERE TETSURO ARAHABAKI.

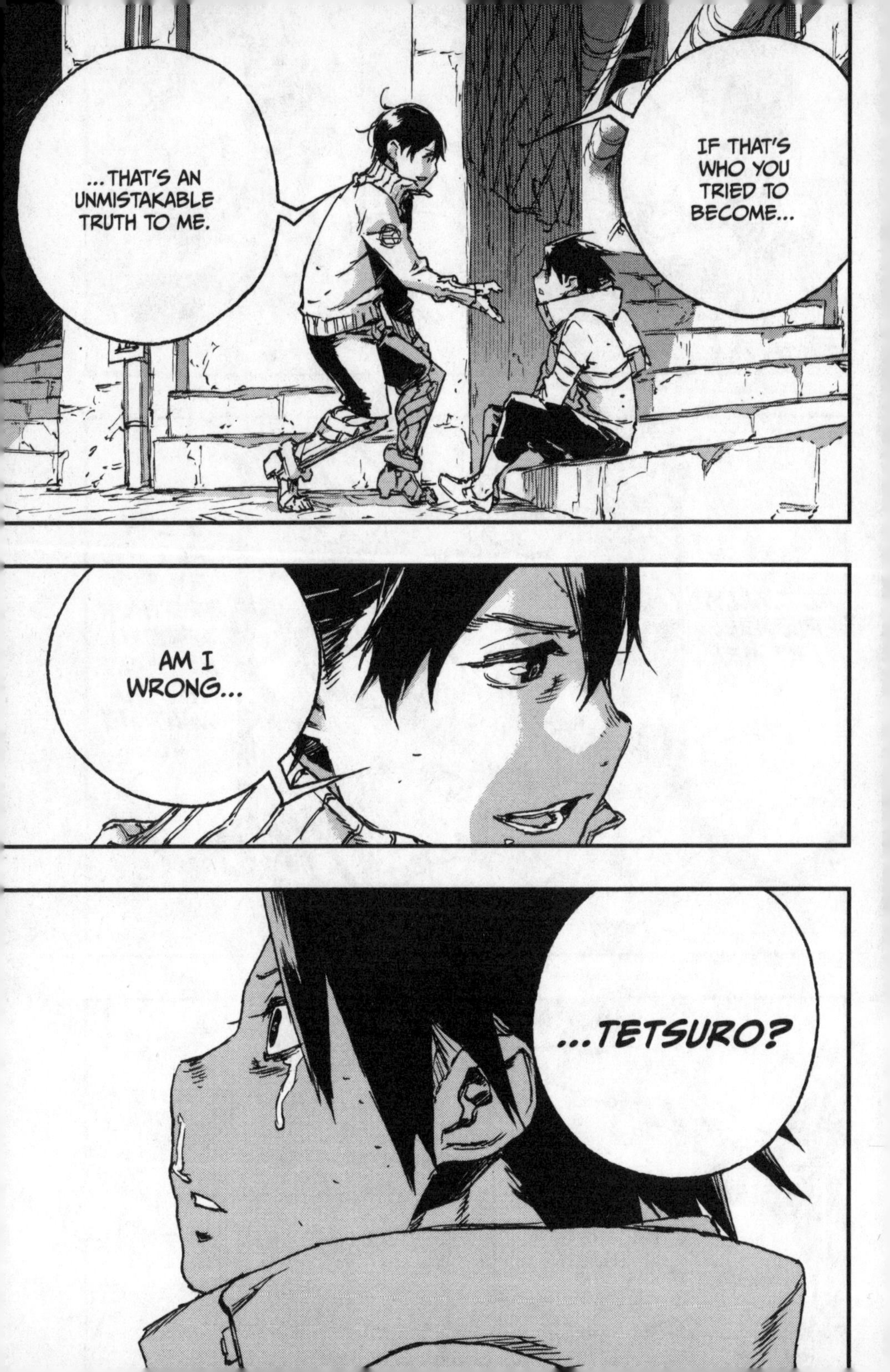
IF THAT'S WHO YOU TRIED TO BECOME...
...THAT'S AN UNMISTAKABLE TRUTH TO ME.
AM I WRONG...
...TETSURO?

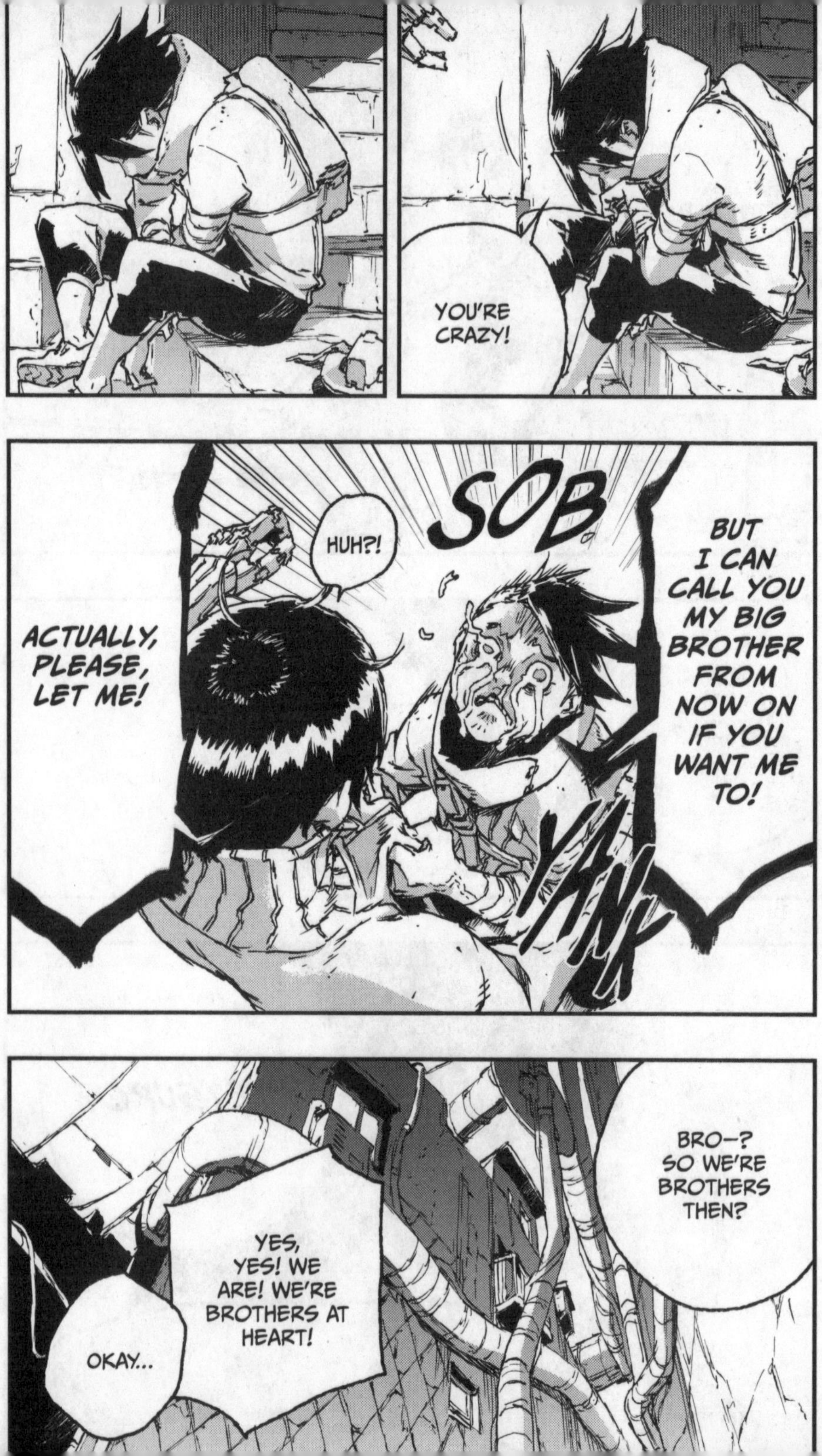
YOU'RE CRAZY!
BUT I CAN CALL YOU MY BIG BROTHER FROM NOW ON IF YOU WANT ME TO!
SOB
HUH?!
ACTUALLY, PLEASE, LET ME!
YANK
BRO—? SO WE'RE BROTHERS THEN?
YES, YES! WE ARE! WE'RE BROTHERS AT HEART!
OKAY...

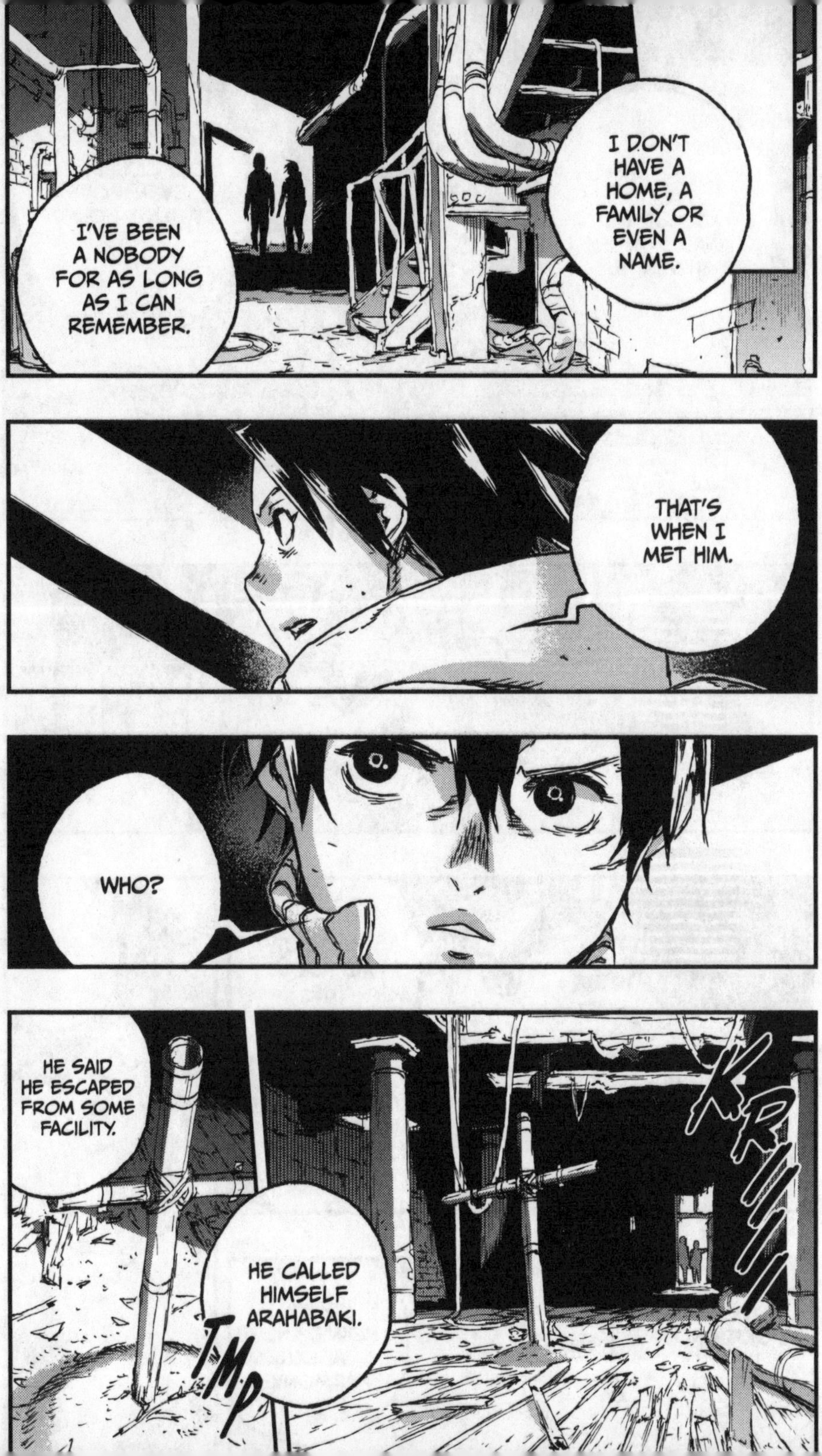
I DON'T HAVE A HOME, A FAMILY OR EVEN A NAME.
I'VE BEEN A NOBODY FOR AS LONG AS I CAN REMEMBER.
THAT'S WHEN I MET HIM.
WHO?
KRIIII
HE SAID HE ESCAPED FROM SOME FACILITY.
HE CALLED HIMSELF ARAHABAKI.
TMP

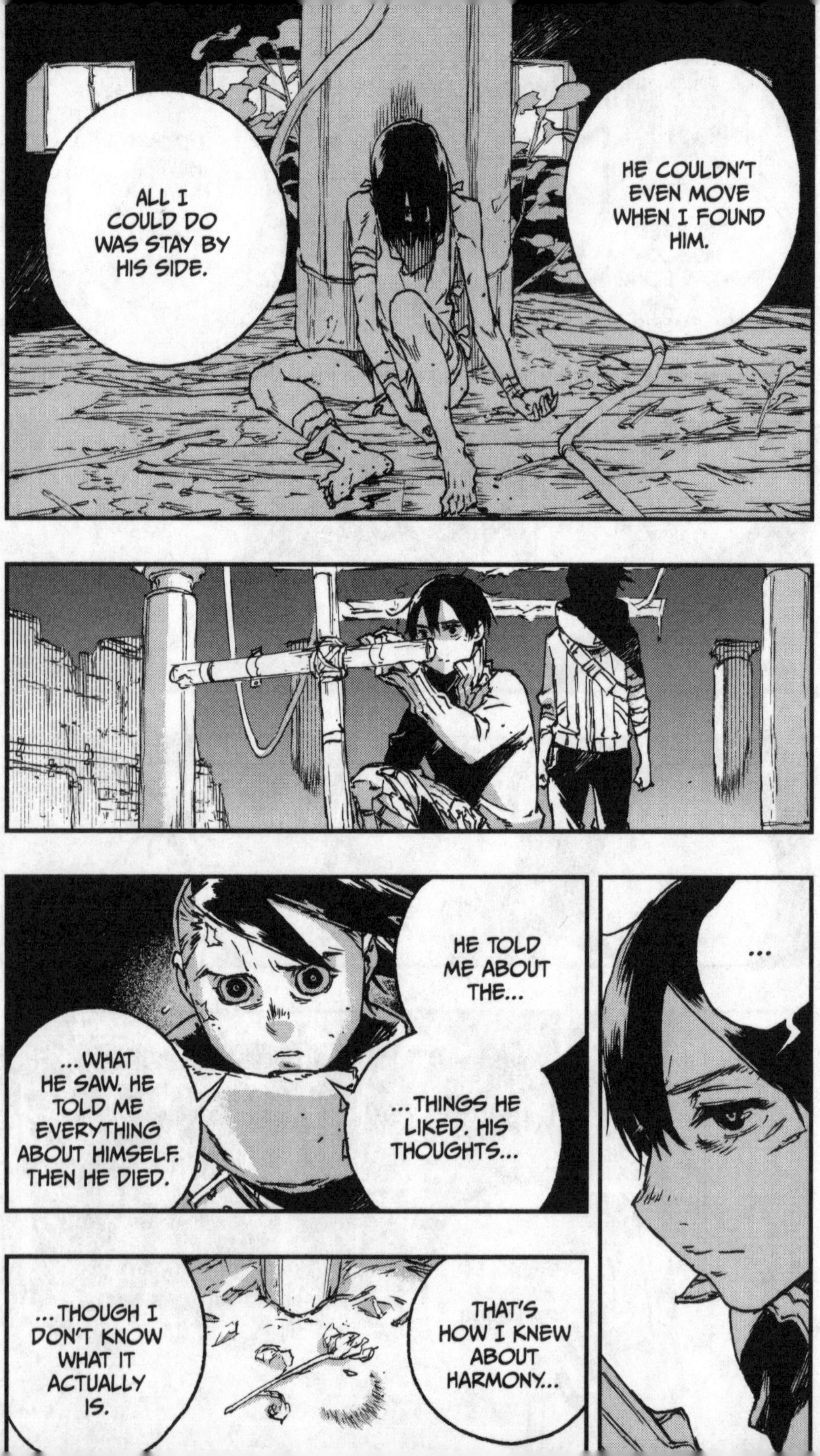
HE COULDN'T EVEN MOVE WHEN I FOUND HIM.
ALL I COULD DO WAS STAY BY HIS SIDE.
...
HE TOLD ME ABOUT THE...
...THINGS HE LIKED. HIS THOUGHTS...
...WHAT HE SAW. HE TOLD ME EVERYTHING ABOUT HIMSELF. THEN HE DIED.
THAT'S HOW I KNEW ABOUT HARMONY...
...THOUGH I DON'T KNOW WHAT IT ACTUALLY IS.

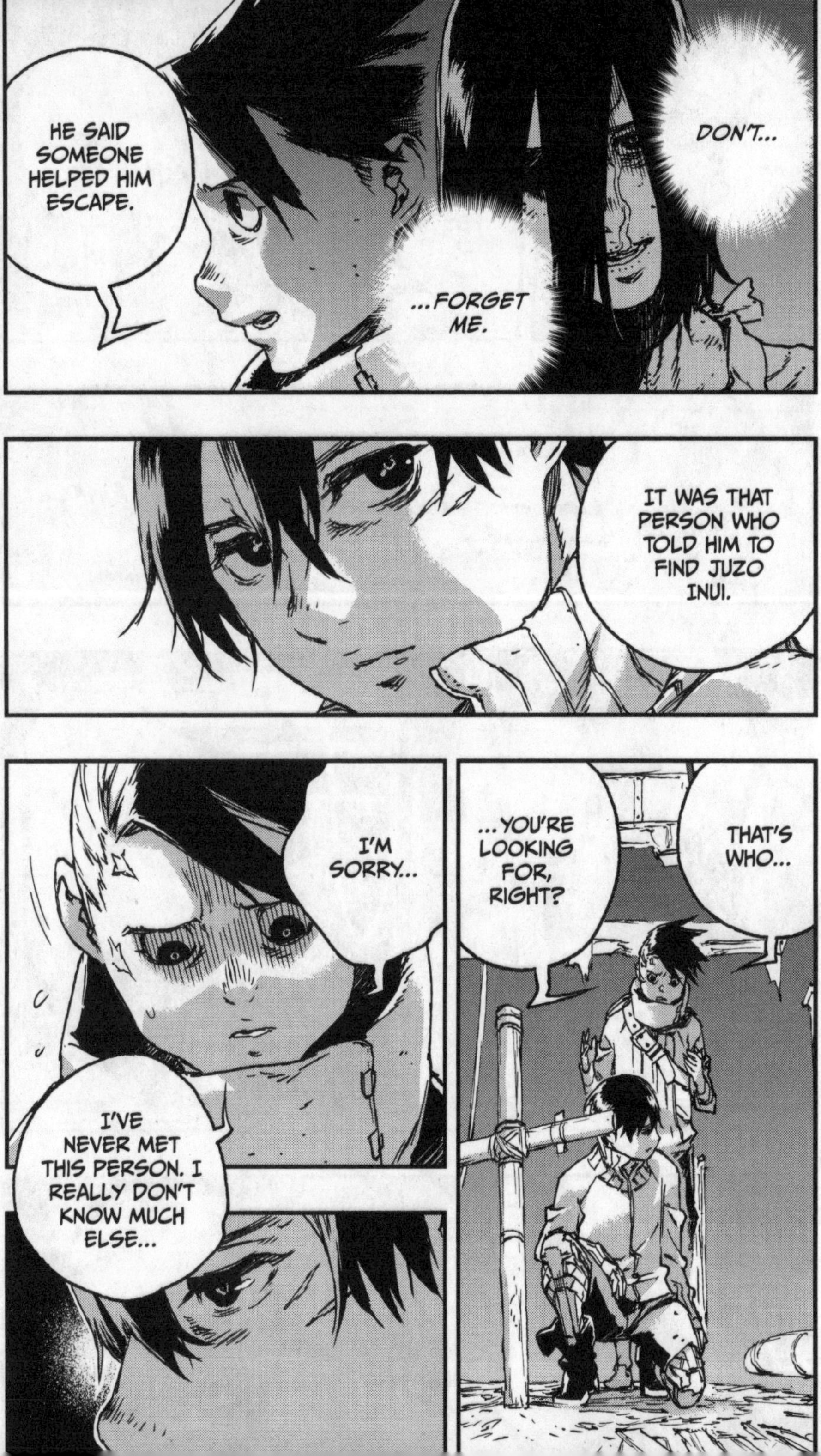

DON'T...
...FORGET ME.
HE SAID SOMEONE HELPED HIM ESCAPE.
IT WAS THAT PERSON WHO TOLD HIM TO FIND JUZO INUI.
THAT'S WHO...
...YOU'RE LOOKING FOR, RIGHT?
I'M SORRY...
I'VE NEVER MET THIS PERSON. I REALLY DON'T KNOW MUCH ELSE...

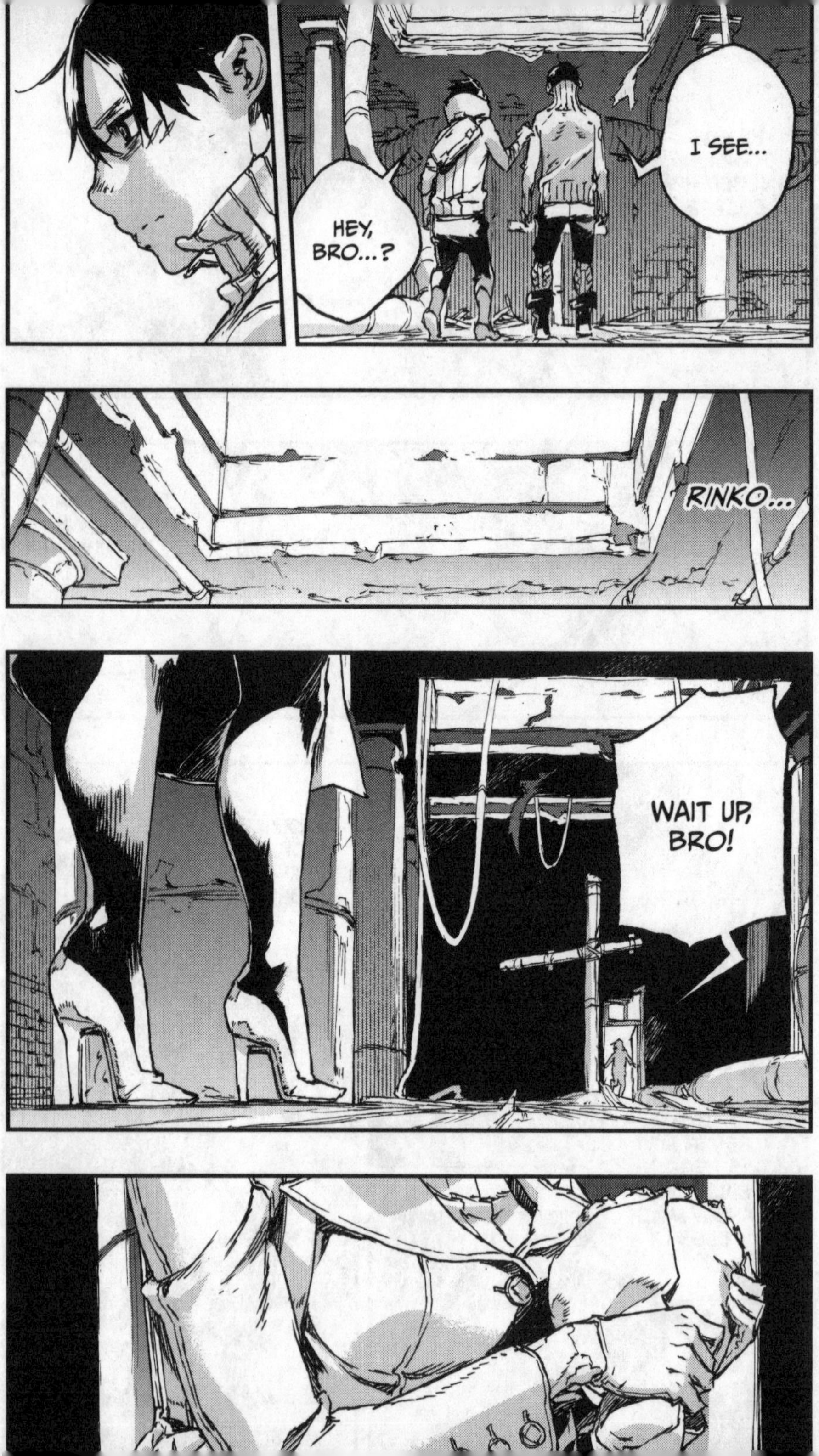
I SEE...
HEY, BRO...?
RINKO...
WAIT UP, BRO!

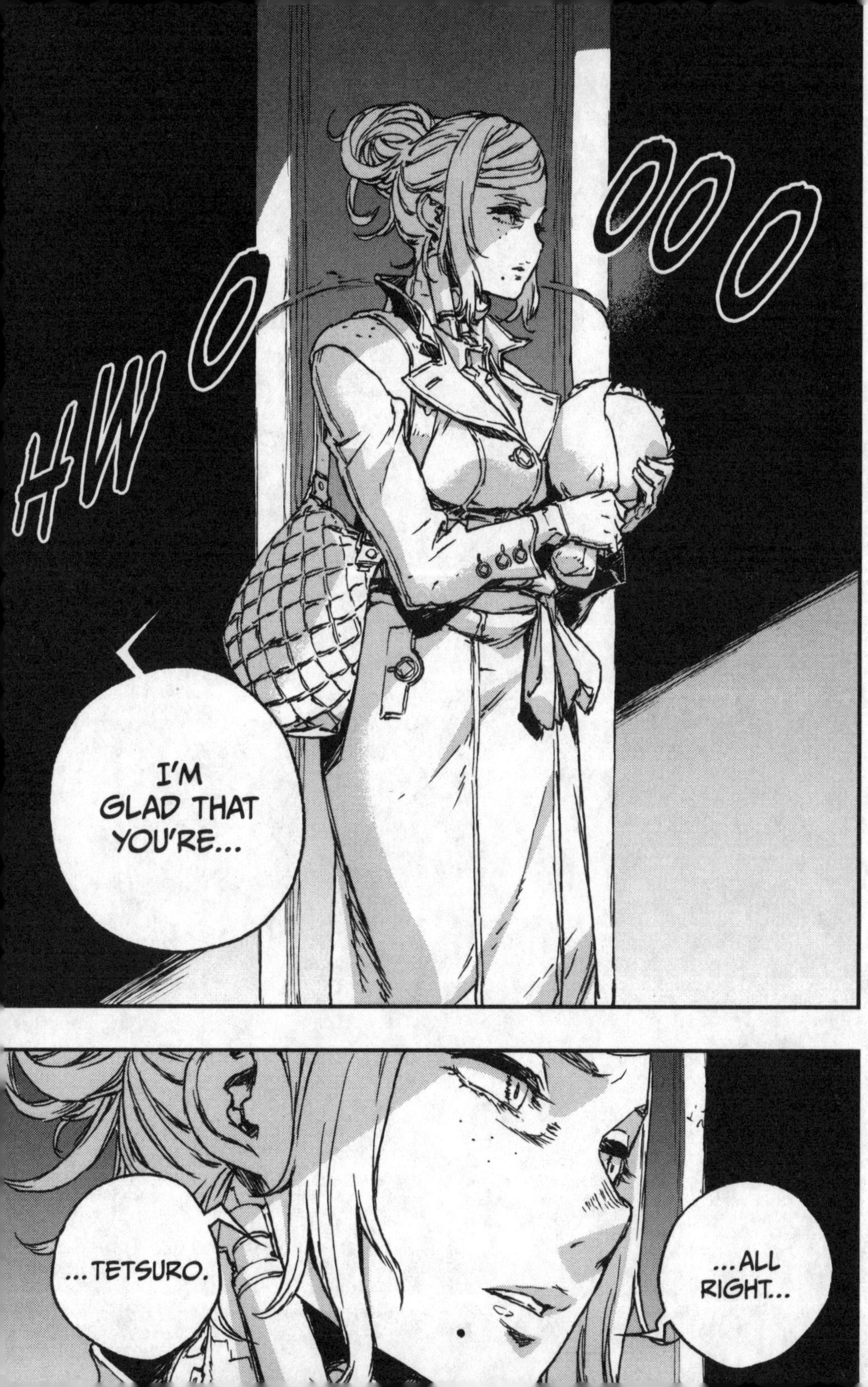
HWOOOOO
I'M GLAD THAT YOU'RE...
...ALL RIGHT...
...TETSURO.

NO GUNS LIFE

The gunsmoke drifts, the muzzle talks

Chapter 61

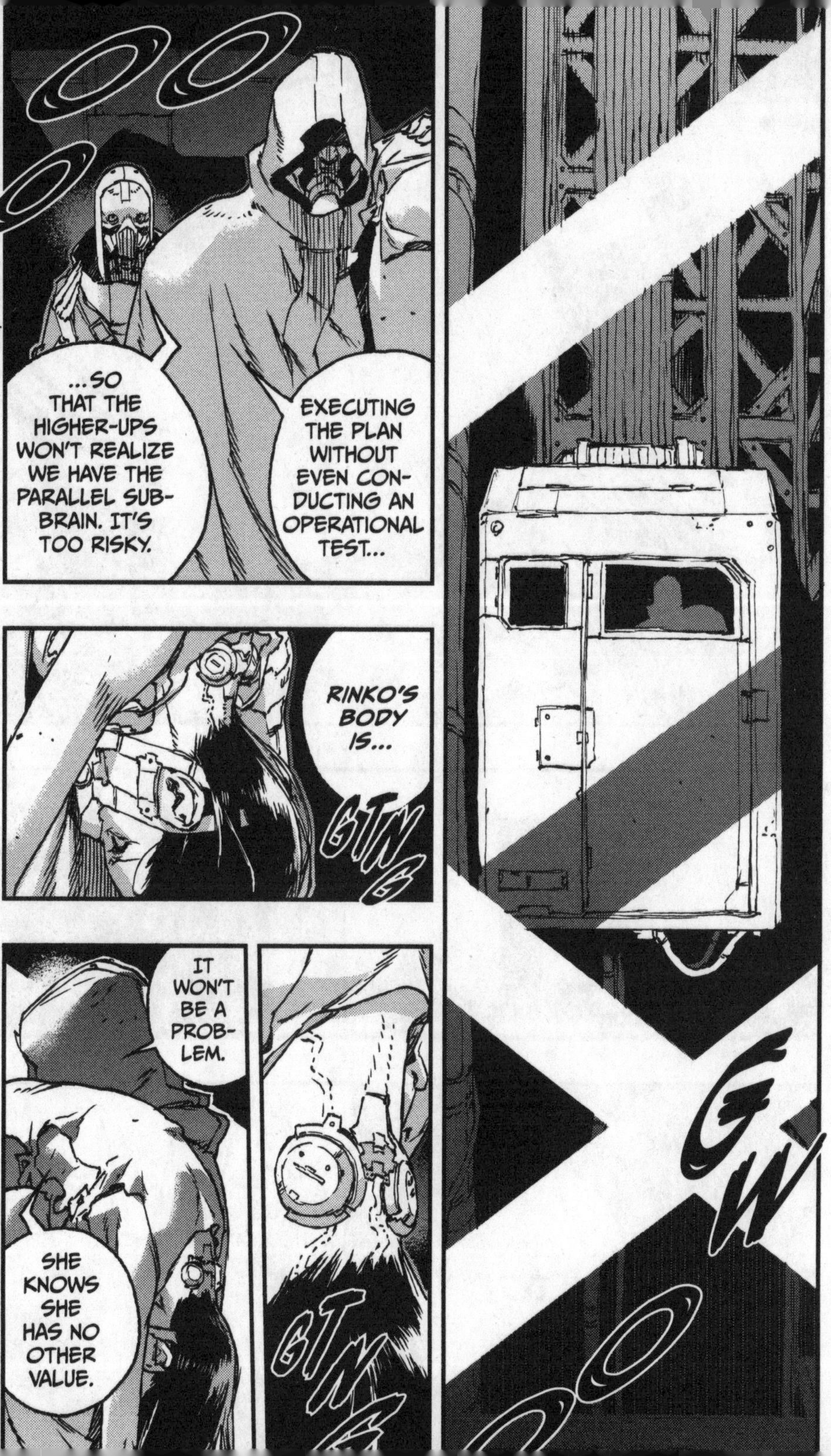

GW
EXECUTING THE PLAN WITHOUT EVEN CONDUCTING AN OPERATIONAL TEST...
...SO THAT THE HIGHER-UPS WON'T REALIZE WE HAVE THE PARALLEL SUB-BRAIN. IT'S TOO RISKY.
RINKO'S BODY IS...
GTNG
GTNG
IT WON'T BE A PROBLEM.
SHE KNOWS SHE HAS NO OTHER VALUE.

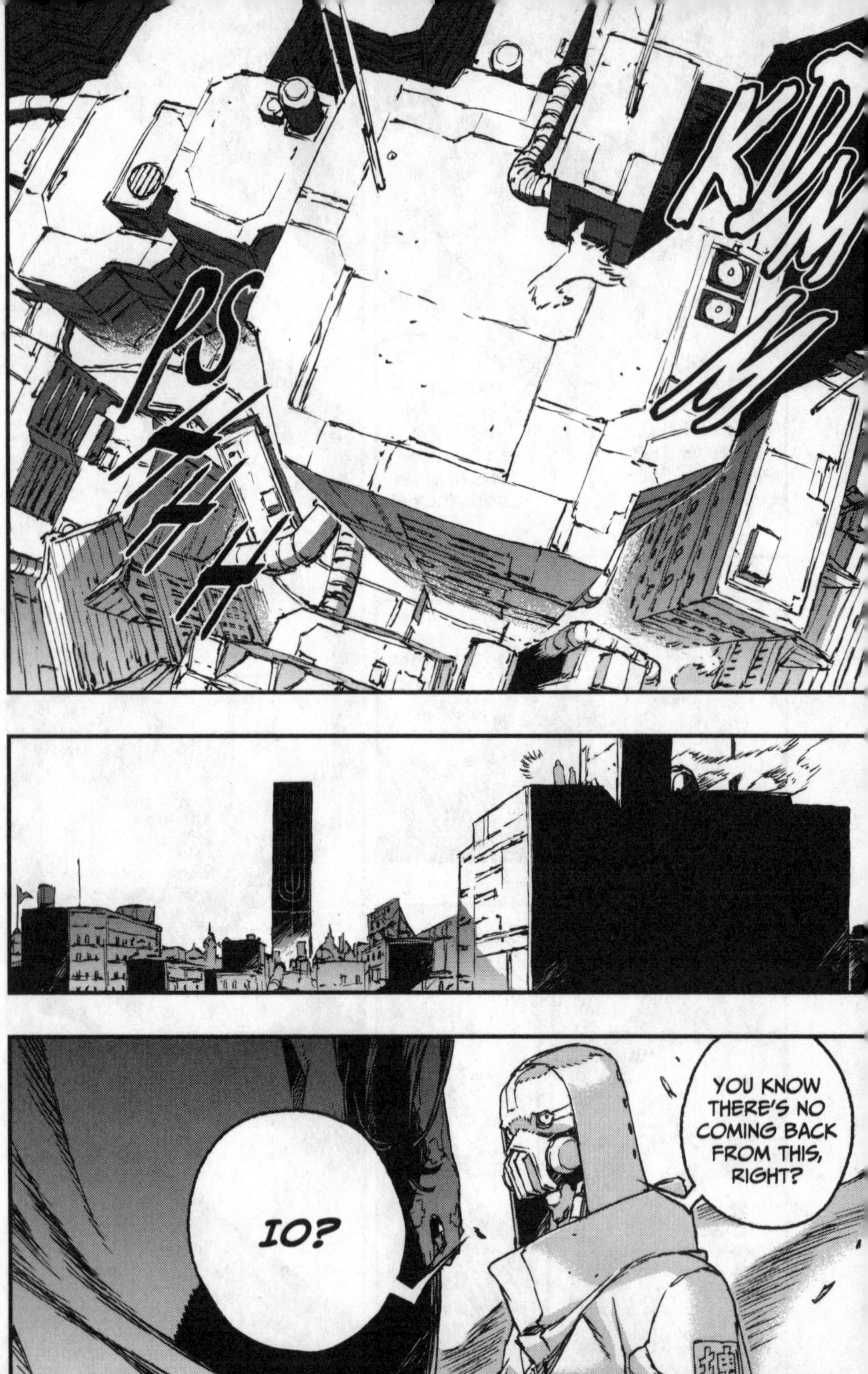
PSHHH
YOU KNOW THERE'S NO COMING BACK FROM THIS, RIGHT?
IO?

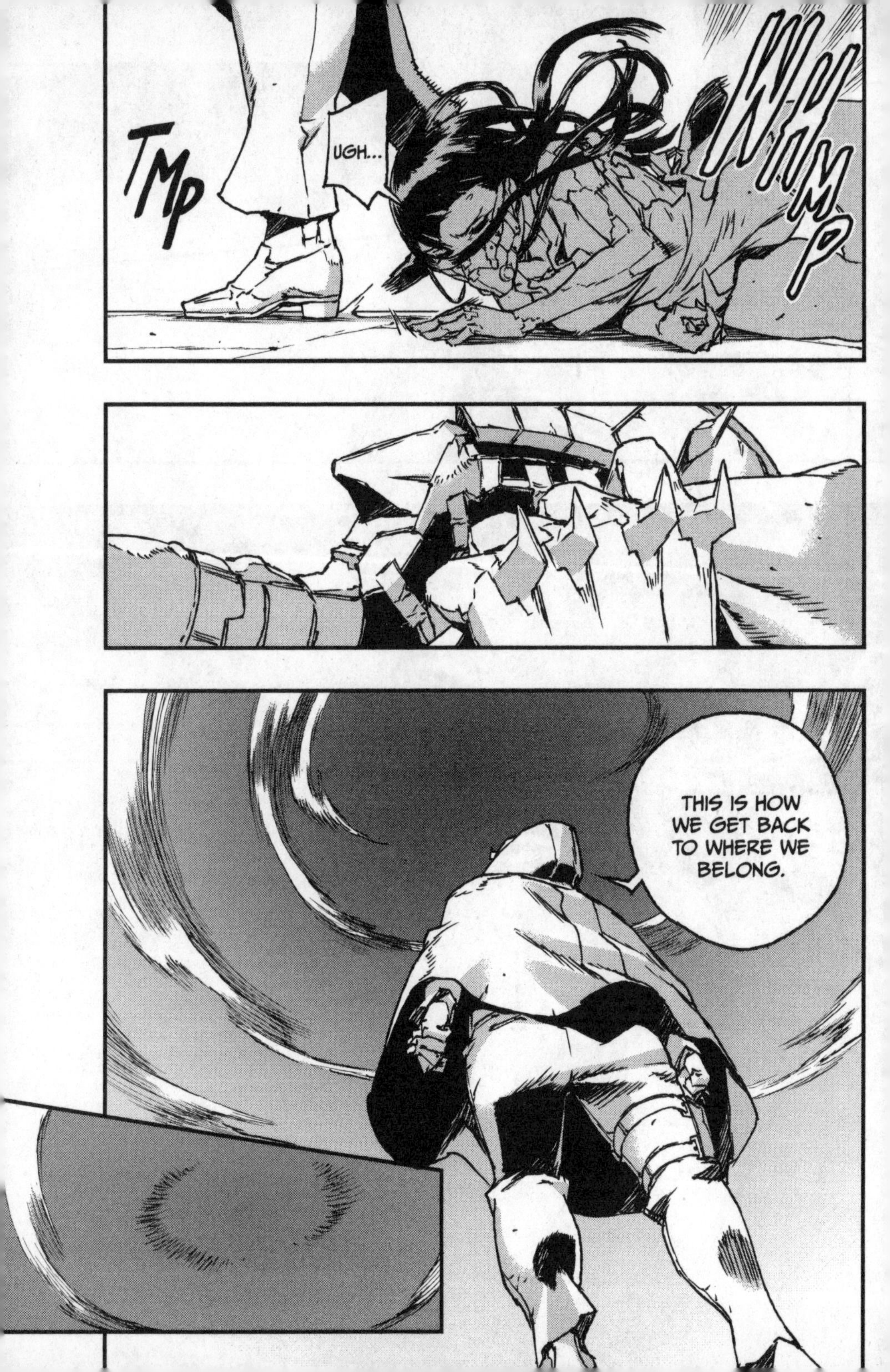
WHUMP
UGH...
TMP
THIS IS HOW WE GET BACK TO WHERE WE BELONG.

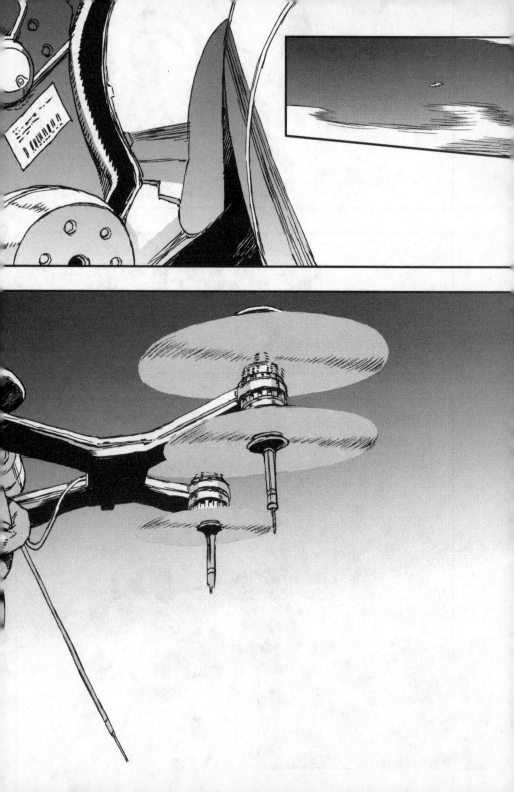

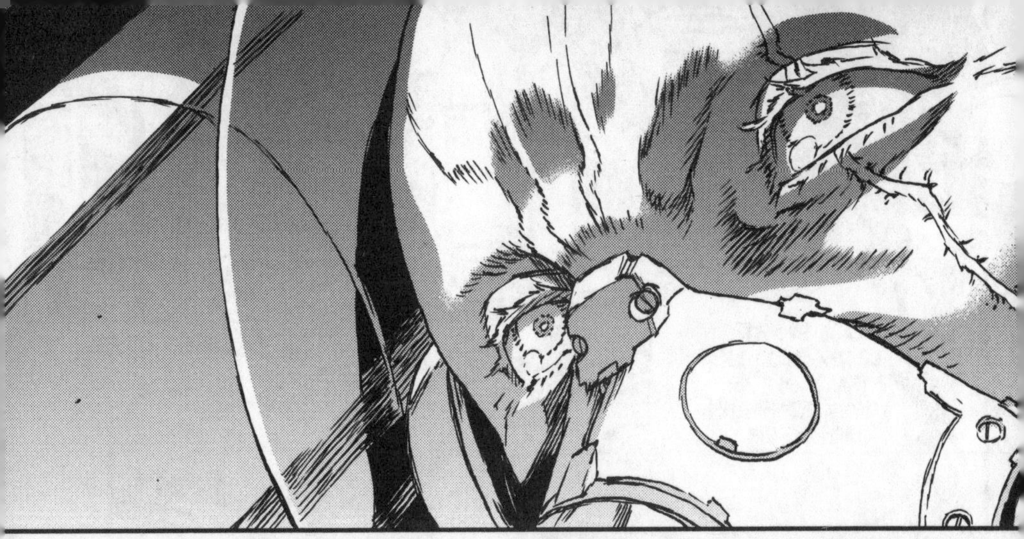

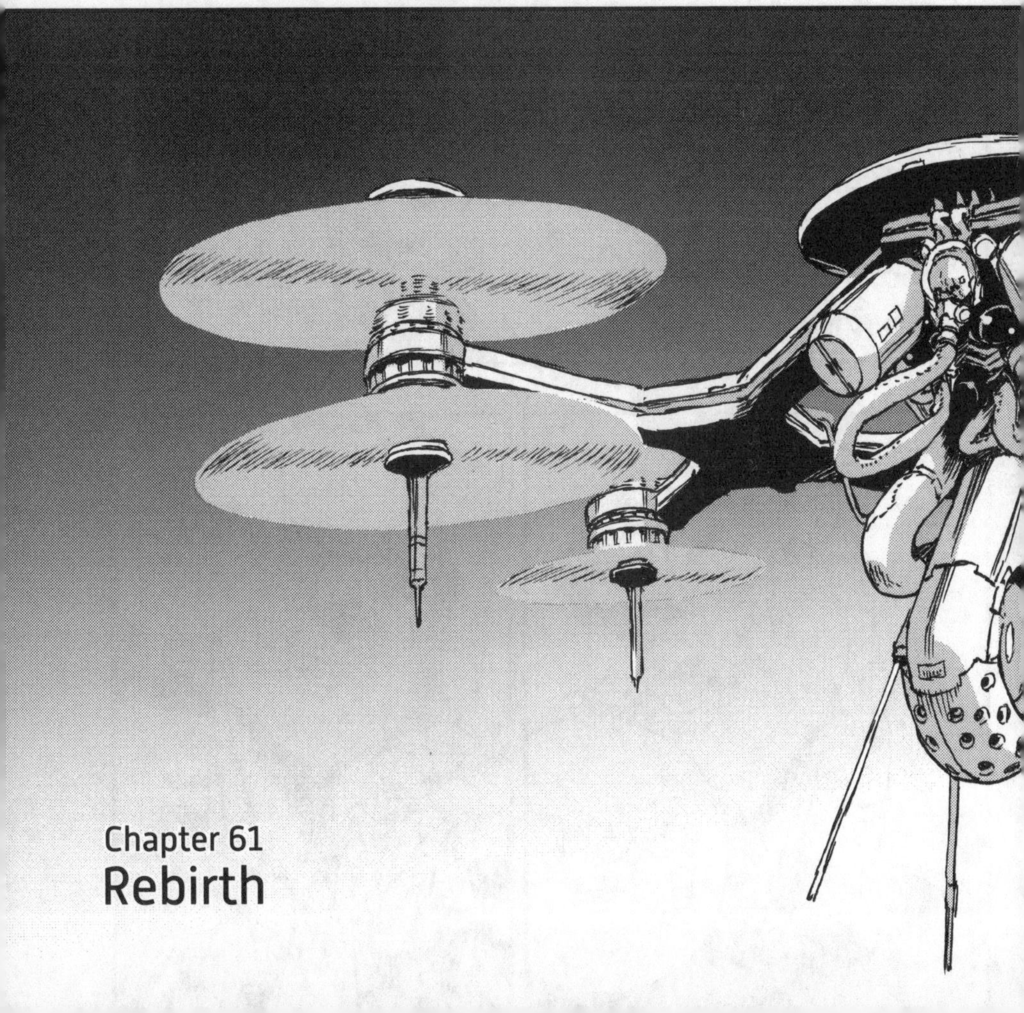
Chapter 61
Rebirth

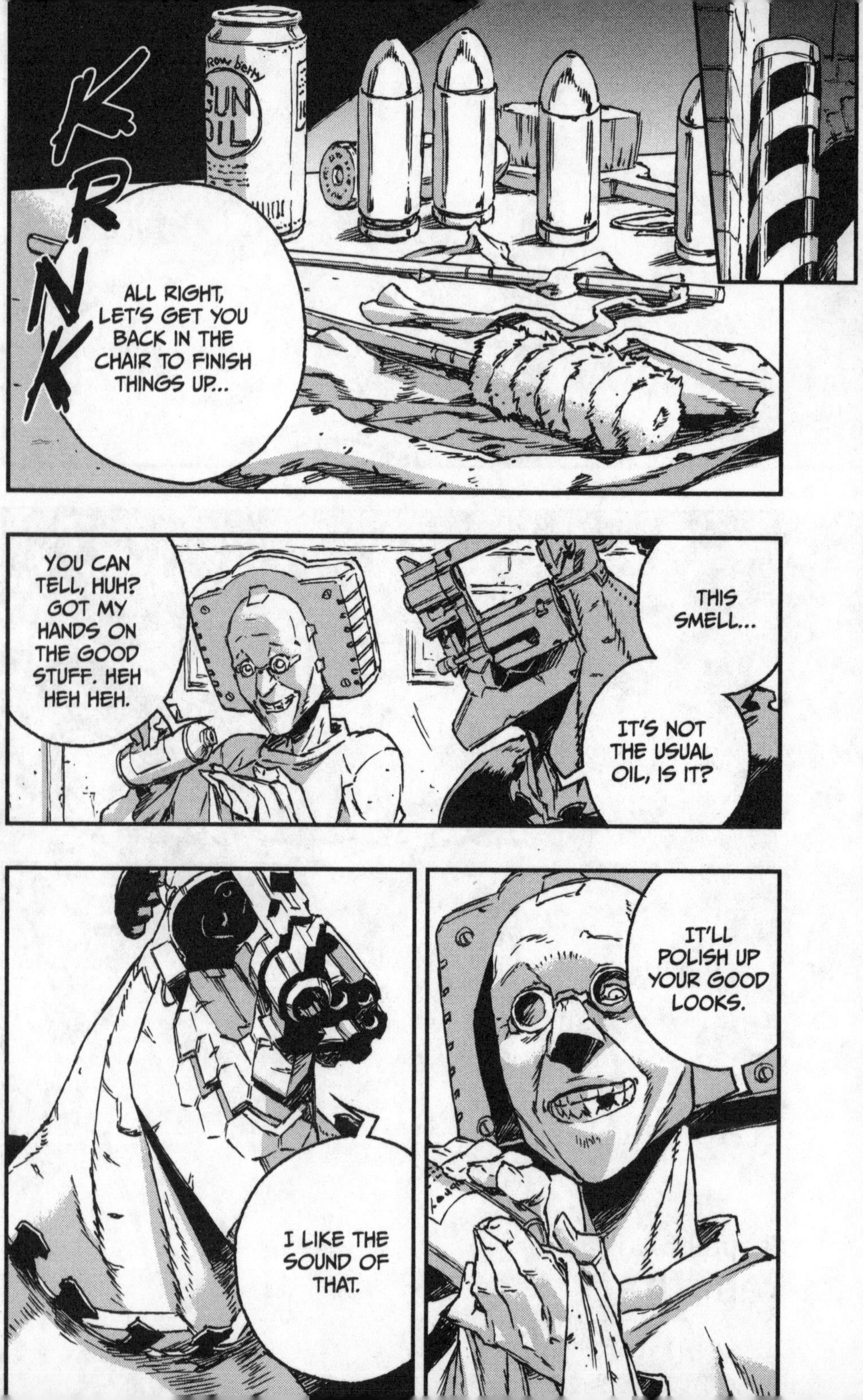
GUN OIL
KRNK
ALL RIGHT, LET'S GET YOU BACK IN THE CHAIR TO FINISH THINGS UP...
THIS SMELL...
IT'S NOT THE USUAL OIL, IS IT?
YOU CAN TELL, HUH? GOT MY HANDS ON THE GOOD STUFF. HEH HEH HEH.
IT'LL POLISH UP YOUR GOOD LOOKS.
I LIKE THE SOUND OF THAT.

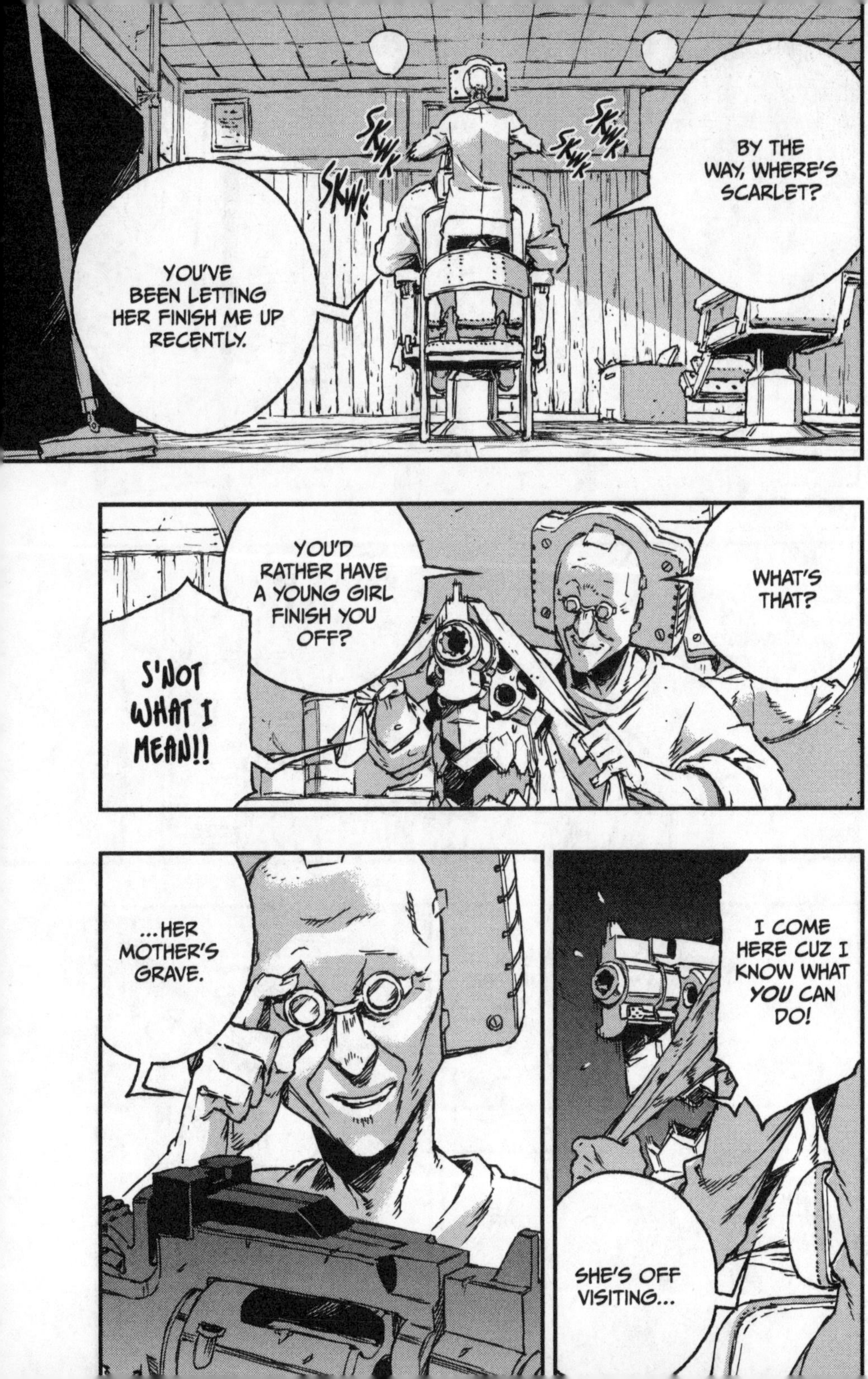
SKWK
SKWK
SKWK
SKWK
BY THE WAY, WHERE'S SCARLET?
YOU'VE BEEN LETTING HER FINISH ME UP RECENTLY.
WHAT'S THAT?
YOU'D RATHER HAVE A YOUNG GIRL FINISH YOU OFF?
S'NOT WHAT I MEAN!!
I COME HERE CUZ I KNOW WHAT *YOU* CAN DO!
SHE'S OFF VISITING...
...HER MOTHER'S GRAVE.

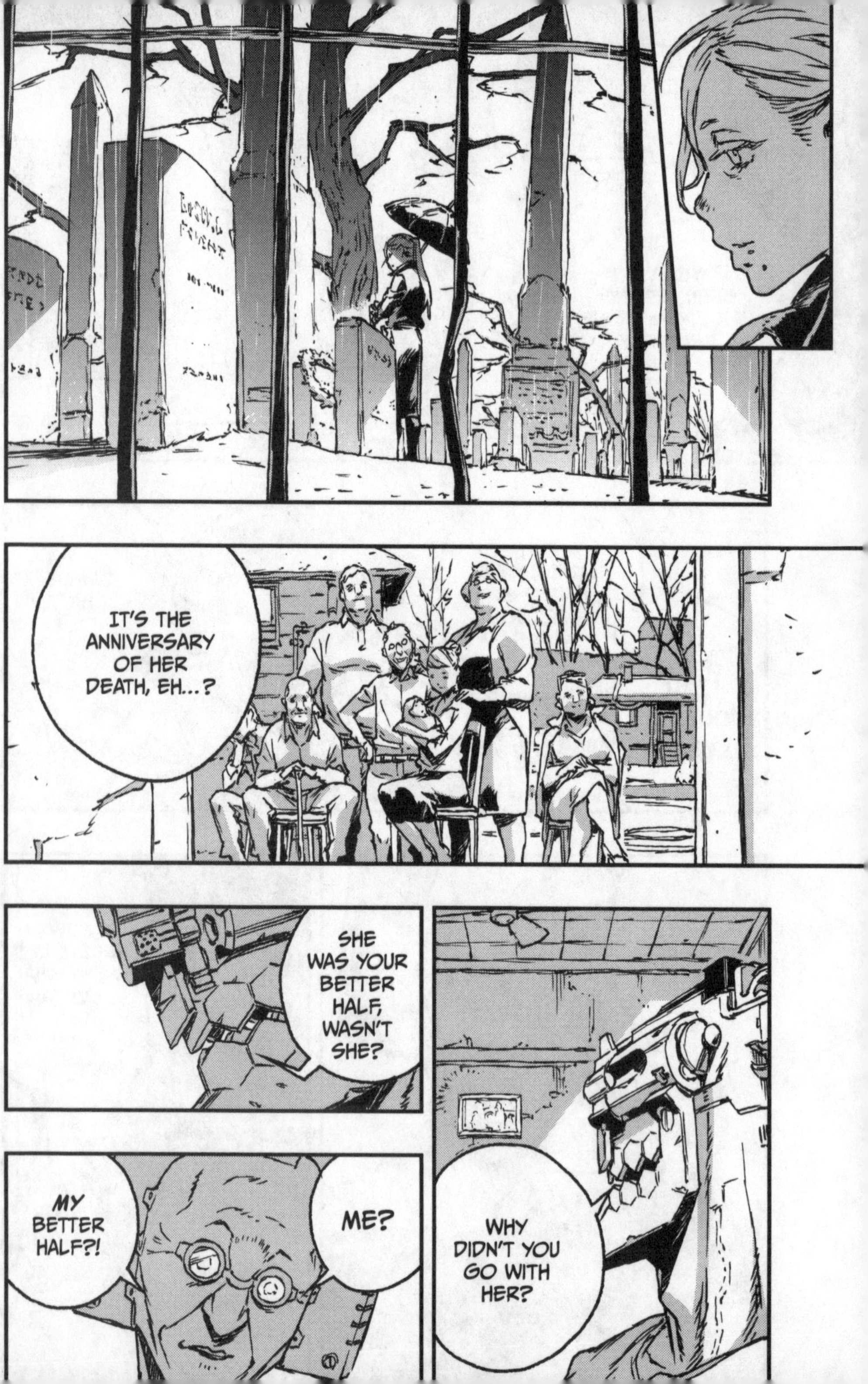
IT'S THE ANNIVERSARY OF HER DEATH, EH...?
WHY DIDN'T YOU GO WITH HER?
SHE WAS YOUR BETTER HALF, WASN'T SHE?
ME?
MY BETTER HALF?!

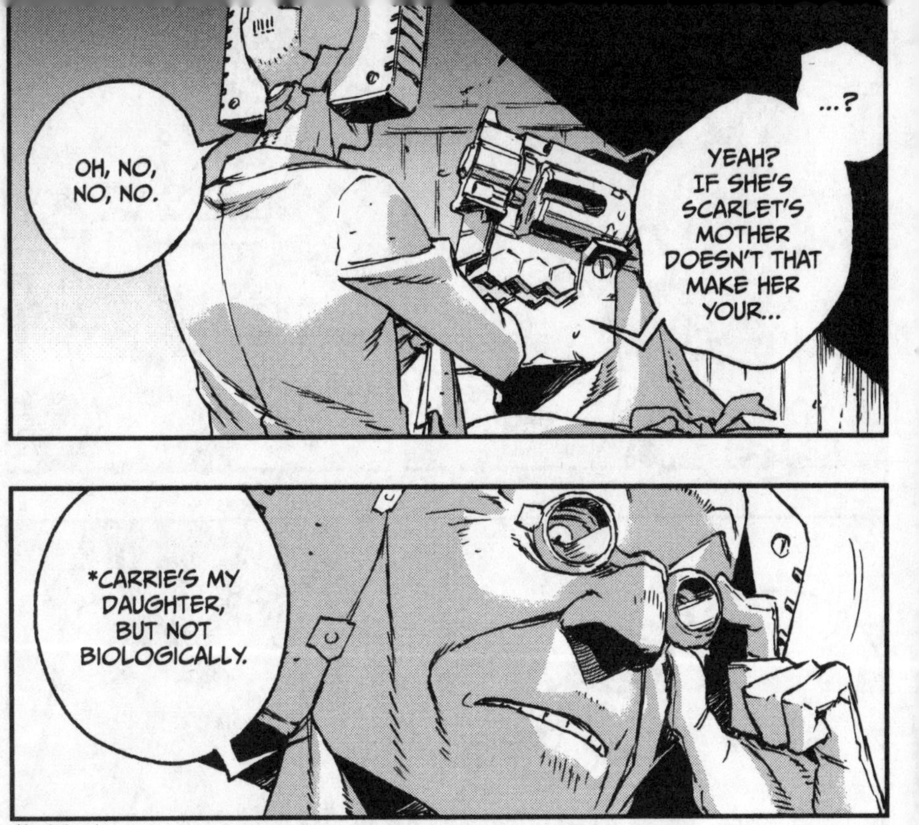

...?
YEAH? IF SHE'S SCARLET'S MOTHER DOESN'T THAT MAKE HER YOUR...
OH, NO, NO, NO.
*CARRIE'S MY DAUGHTER, BUT NOT BIOLOGICALLY.

*Scarlet's nickname.

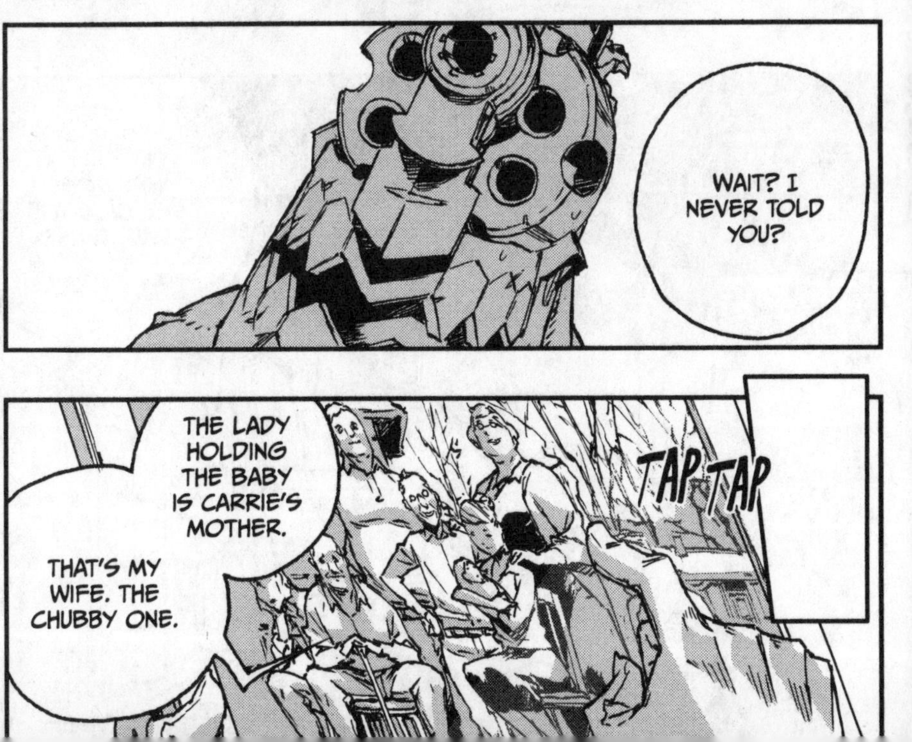

WAIT? I NEVER TOLD YOU?
TAP TAP
THE LADY HOLDING THE BABY IS CARRIE'S MOTHER.
THAT'S MY WIFE. THE CHUBBY ONE.

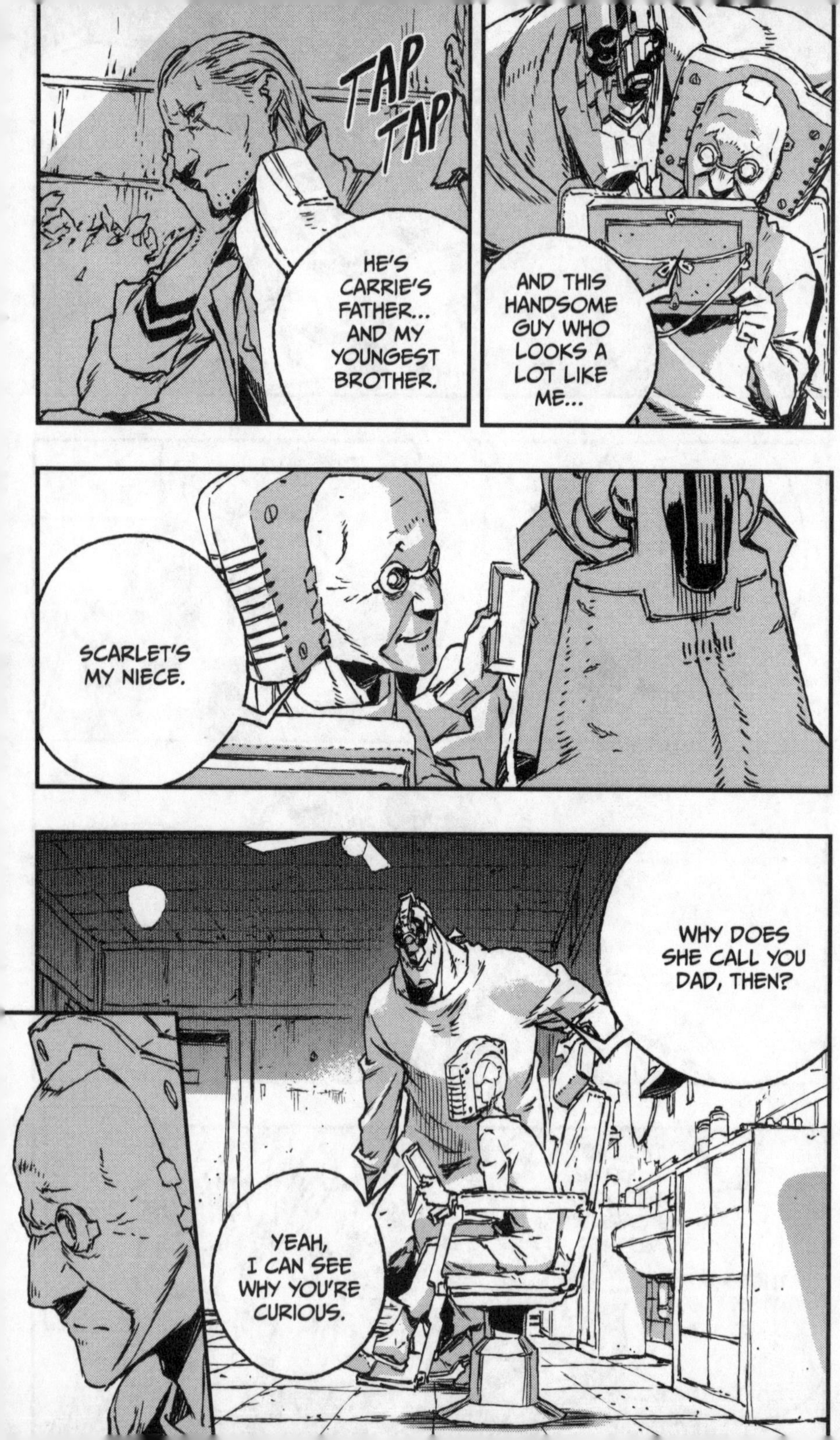
AND THIS HANDSOME GUY WHO LOOKS A LOT LIKE ME...
TAP TAP
HE'S CARRIE'S FATHER... AND MY YOUNGEST BROTHER.
SCARLET'S MY NIECE.
WHY DOES SHE CALL YOU DAD, THEN?
YEAH, I CAN SEE WHY YOU'RE CURIOUS.

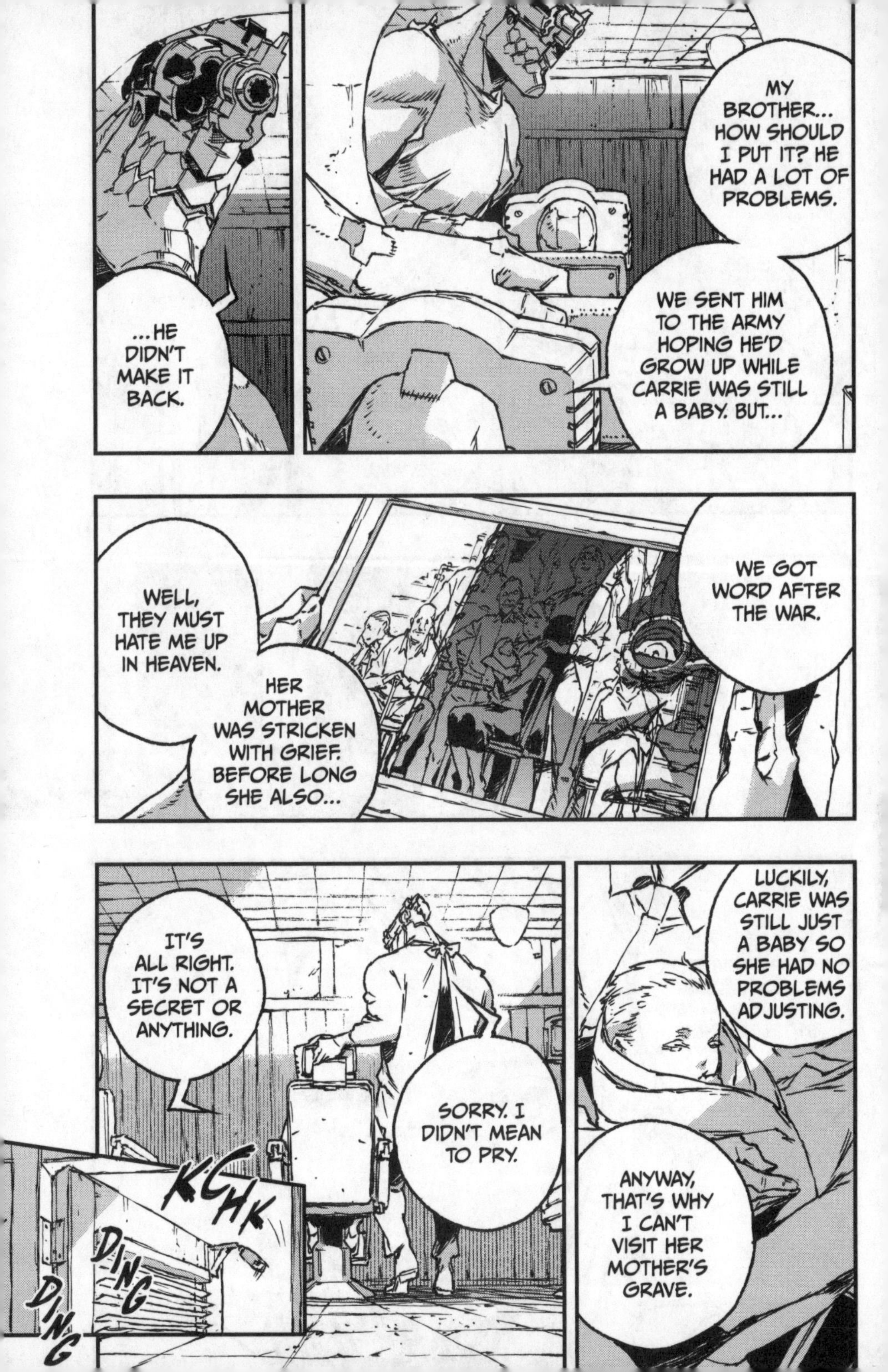
MY BROTHER... HOW SHOULD I PUT IT? HE HAD A LOT OF PROBLEMS.
WE SENT HIM TO THE ARMY HOPING HE'D GROW UP WHILE CARRIE WAS STILL A BABY. BUT...
...HE DIDN'T MAKE IT BACK.
WE GOT WORD AFTER THE WAR.
HER MOTHER WAS STRICKEN WITH GRIEF. BEFORE LONG SHE ALSO...
WELL, THEY MUST HATE ME UP IN HEAVEN.
LUCKILY, CARRIE WAS STILL JUST A BABY SO SHE HAD NO PROBLEMS ADJUSTING.
ANYWAY, THAT'S WHY I CAN'T VISIT HER MOTHER'S GRAVE.
SORRY. I DIDN'T MEAN TO PRY.
IT'S ALL RIGHT. IT'S NOT A SECRET OR ANYTHING.
KCHK
DING
DING

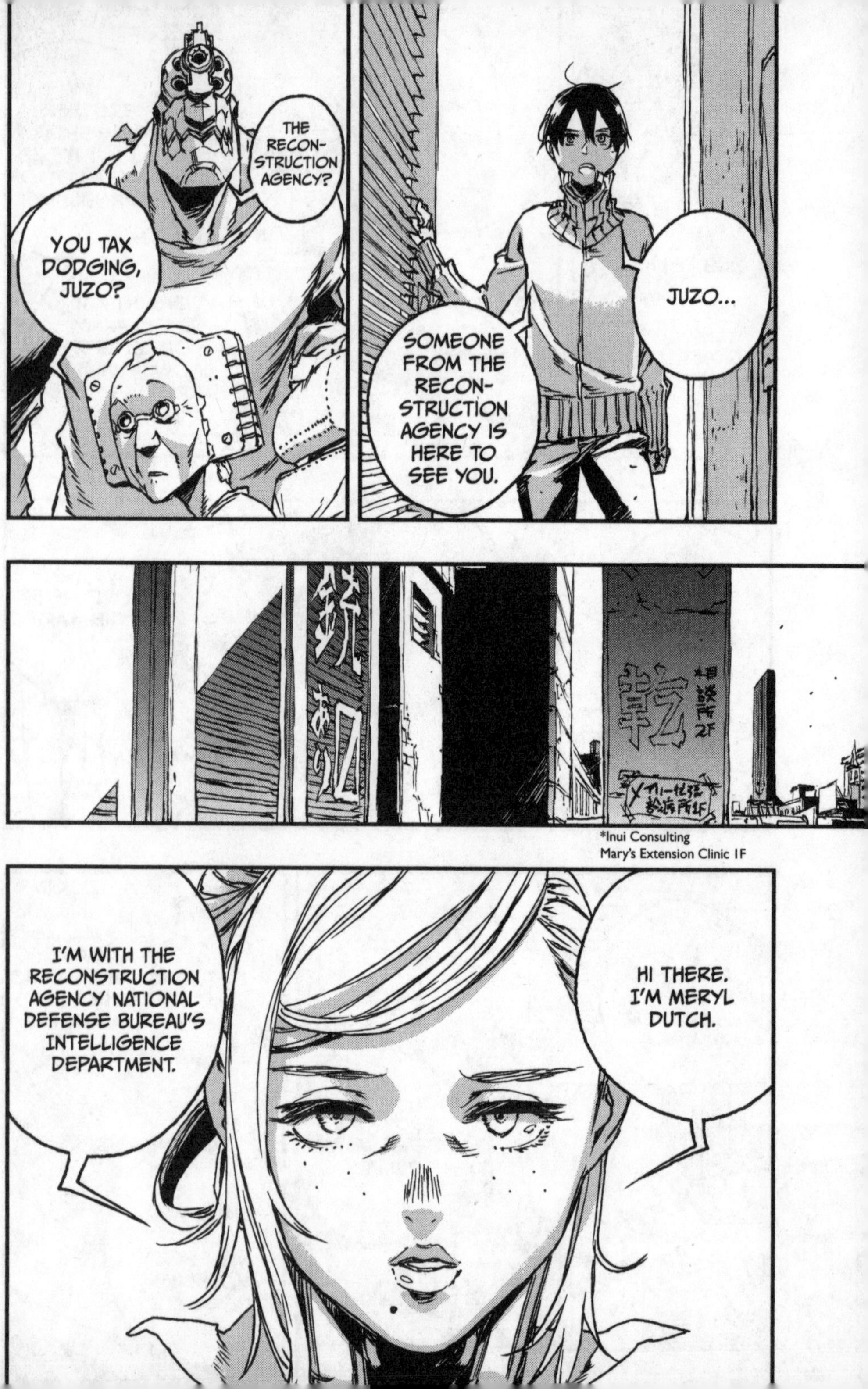
JUZO...
SOMEONE FROM THE RECON-STRUCTION AGENCY IS HERE TO SEE YOU.
THE RECON-STRUCTION AGENCY?
YOU TAX DODGING, JUZO?
*Inui Consulting
Mary's Extension Clinic 1F
HI THERE. I'M MERYL DUTCH.
I'M WITH THE RECONSTRUCTION AGENCY NATIONAL DEFENSE BUREAU'S INTELLIGENCE DEPARTMENT.

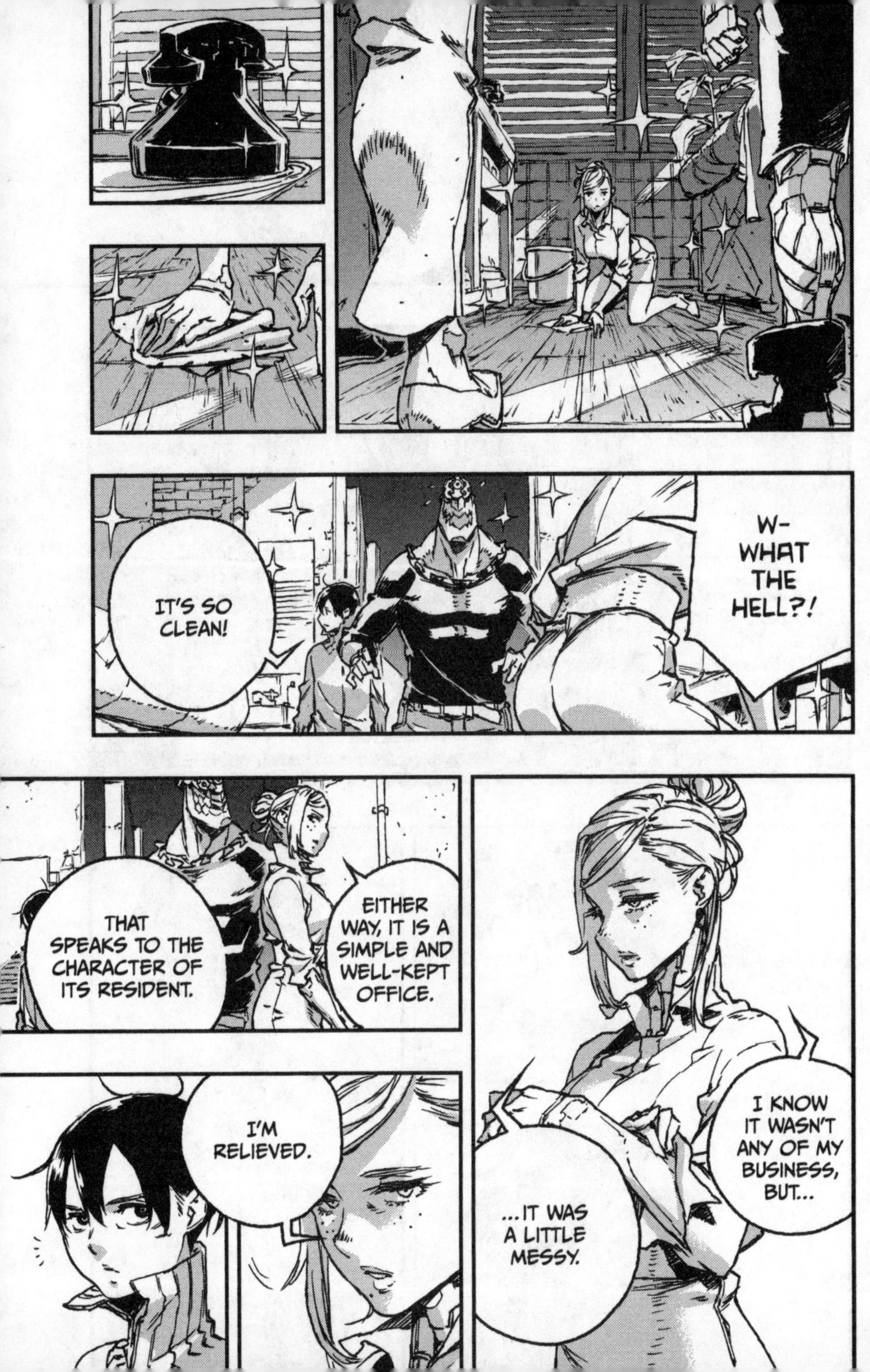
W- WHAT THE HELL?!
IT'S SO CLEAN!
I KNOW IT WASN'T ANY OF MY BUSINESS, BUT...
...IT WAS A LITTLE MESSY.
EITHER WAY, IT IS A SIMPLE AND WELL-KEPT OFFICE.
THAT SPEAKS TO THE CHARACTER OF ITS RESIDENT.
I'M RELIEVED.

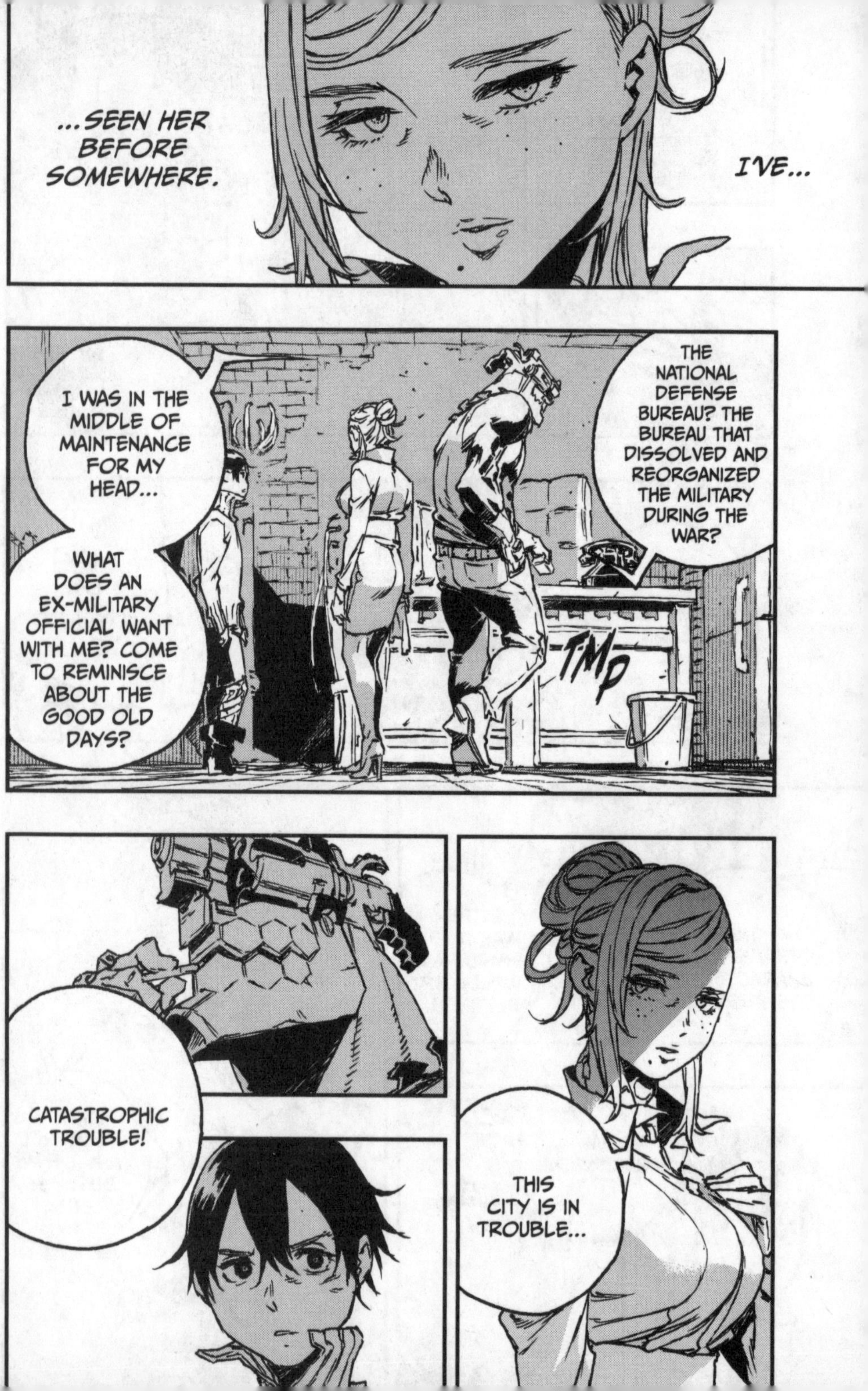
I'VE...
...SEEN HER BEFORE SOMEWHERE.
THE NATIONAL DEFENSE BUREAU? THE BUREAU THAT DISSOLVED AND REORGANIZED THE MILITARY DURING THE WAR?
TMP
I WAS IN THE MIDDLE OF MAINTENANCE FOR MY HEAD...
WHAT DOES AN EX-MILITARY OFFICIAL WANT WITH ME? COME TO REMINISCE ABOUT THE GOOD OLD DAYS?
THIS CITY IS IN TROUBLE...
CATASTROPHIC TROUBLE!

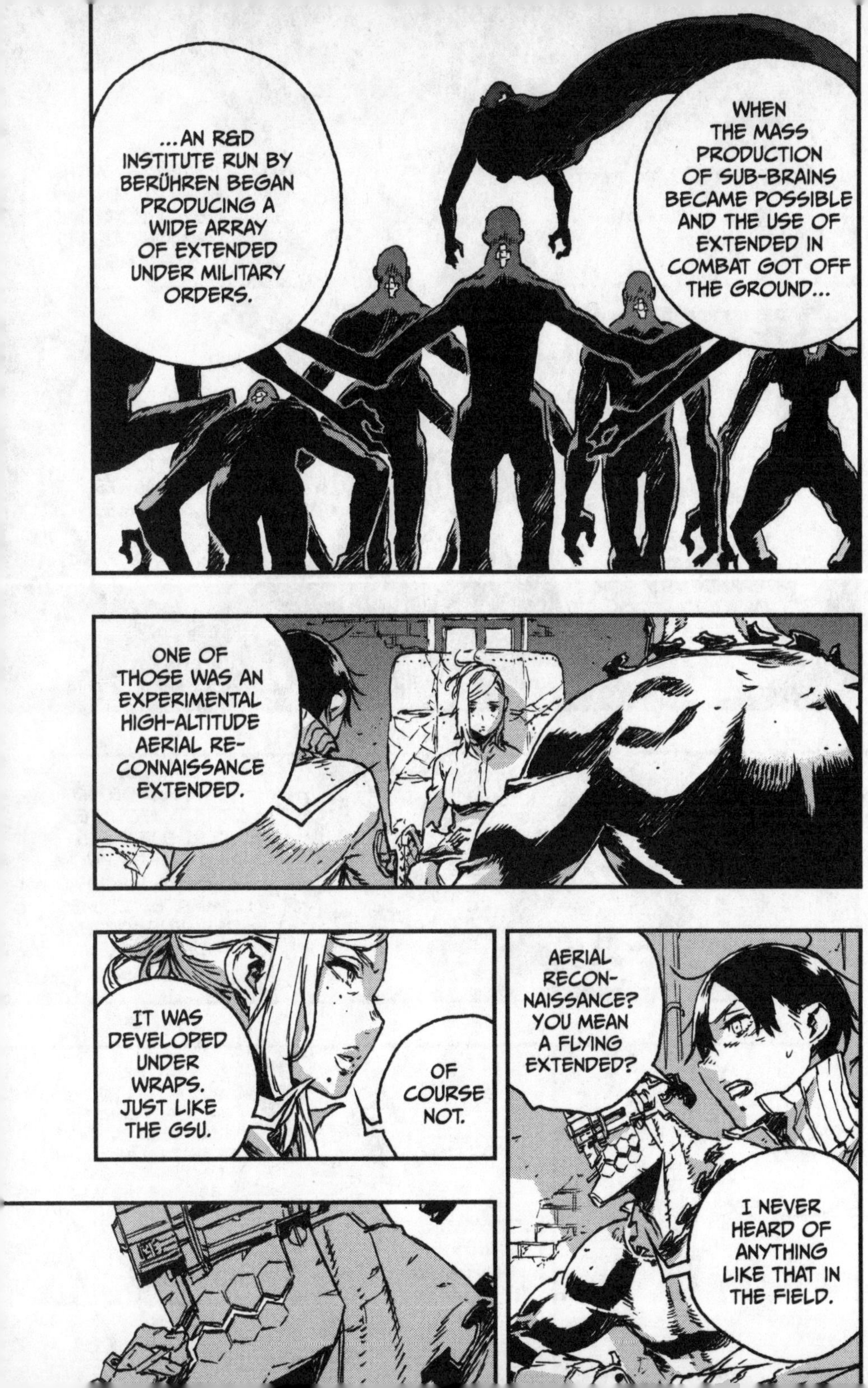
WHEN THE MASS PRODUCTION OF SUB-BRAINS BECAME POSSIBLE AND THE USE OF EXTENDED IN COMBAT GOT OFF THE GROUND...
...AN R&D INSTITUTE RUN BY BERÜHREN BEGAN PRODUCING A WIDE ARRAY OF EXTENDED UNDER MILITARY ORDERS.
ONE OF THOSE WAS AN EXPERIMENTAL HIGH-ALTITUDE AERIAL RE-CONNAISSANCE EXTENDED.
AERIAL RECON-NAISSANCE? YOU MEAN A FLYING EXTENDED?
I NEVER HEARD OF ANYTHING LIKE THAT IN THE FIELD.
OF COURSE NOT.
IT WAS DEVELOPED UNDER WRAPS. JUST LIKE THE GSU.

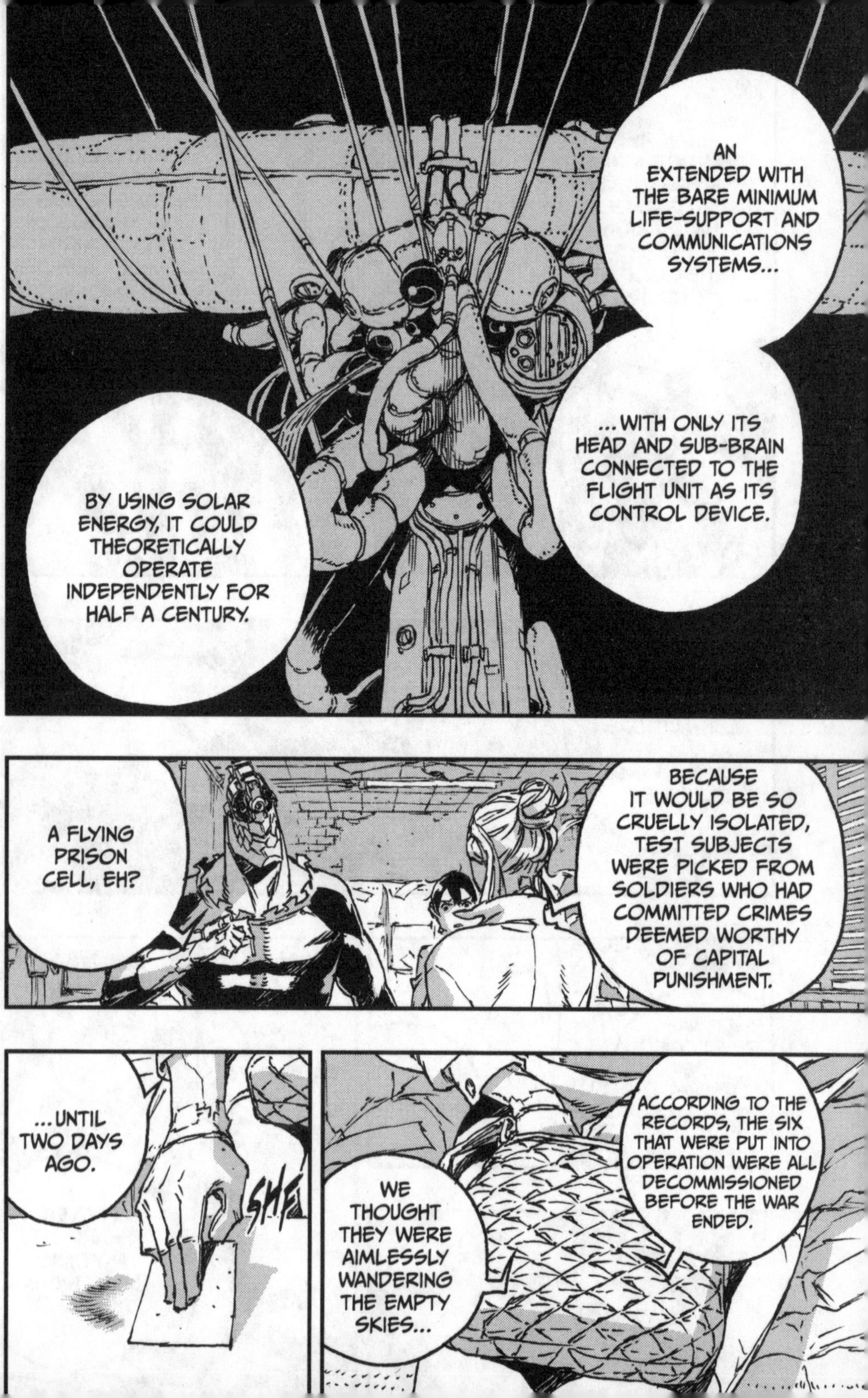
AN EXTENDED WITH THE BARE MINIMUM LIFE-SUPPORT AND COMMUNICATIONS SYSTEMS...
...WITH ONLY ITS HEAD AND SUB-BRAIN CONNECTED TO THE FLIGHT UNIT AS ITS CONTROL DEVICE.
BY USING SOLAR ENERGY, IT COULD THEORETICALLY OPERATE INDEPENDENTLY FOR HALF A CENTURY.
BECAUSE IT WOULD BE SO CRUELLY ISOLATED, TEST SUBJECTS WERE PICKED FROM SOLDIERS WHO HAD COMMITTED CRIMES DEEMED WORTHY OF CAPITAL PUNISHMENT.
A FLYING PRISON CELL, EH?
ACCORDING TO THE RECORDS, THE SIX THAT WERE PUT INTO OPERATION WERE ALL DECOMMISSIONED BEFORE THE WAR ENDED.
WE THOUGHT THEY WERE AIMLESSLY WANDERING THE EMPTY SKIES...
...UNTIL TWO DAYS AGO.
SHF

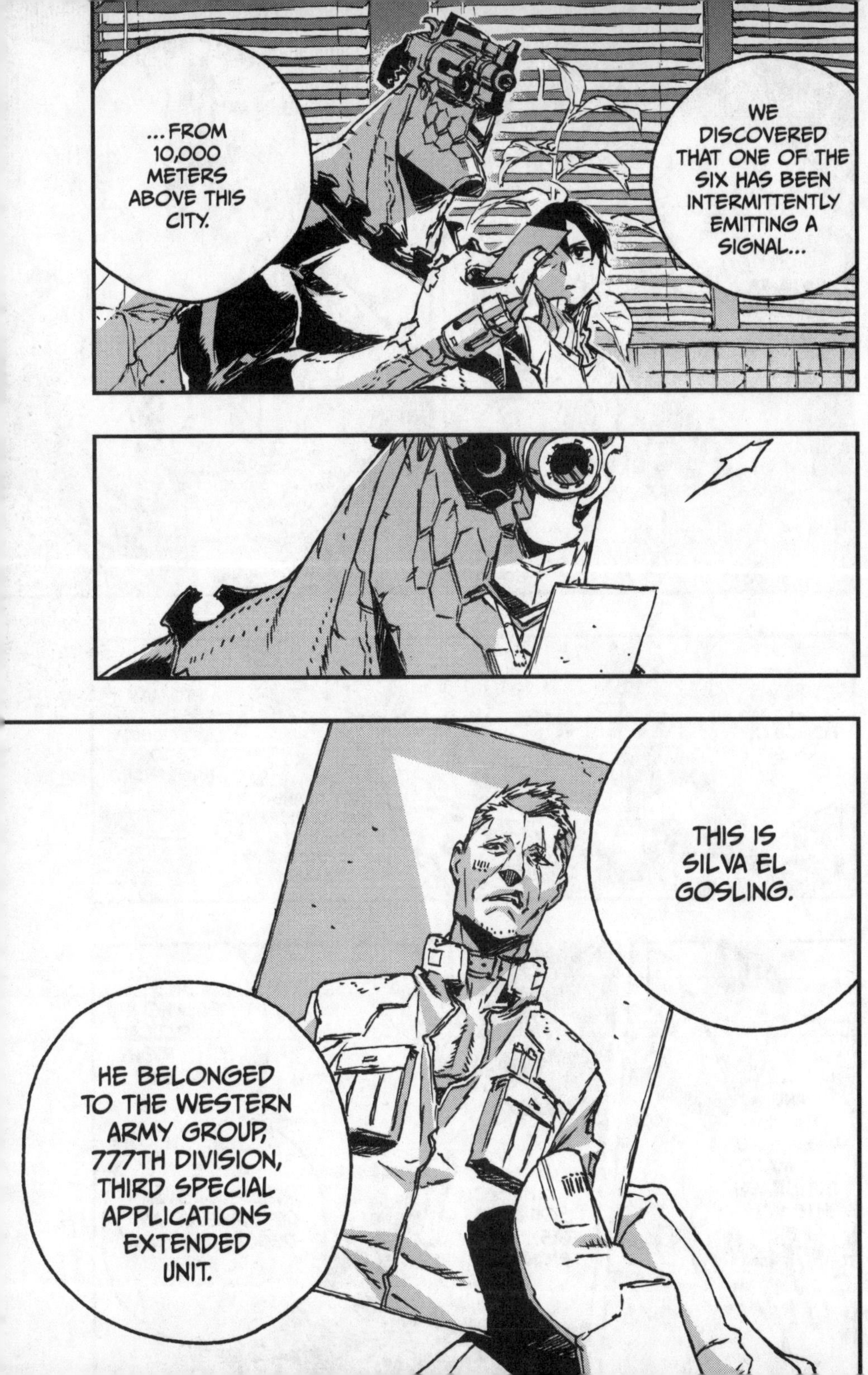
WE DISCOVERED THAT ONE OF THE SIX HAS BEEN INTERMITTENTLY EMITTING A SIGNAL...
...FROM 10,000 METERS ABOVE THIS CITY.
THIS IS SILVA EL GOSLING.
HE BELONGED TO THE WESTERN ARMY GROUP, 777TH DIVISION, THIRD SPECIAL APPLICATIONS EXTENDED UNIT.

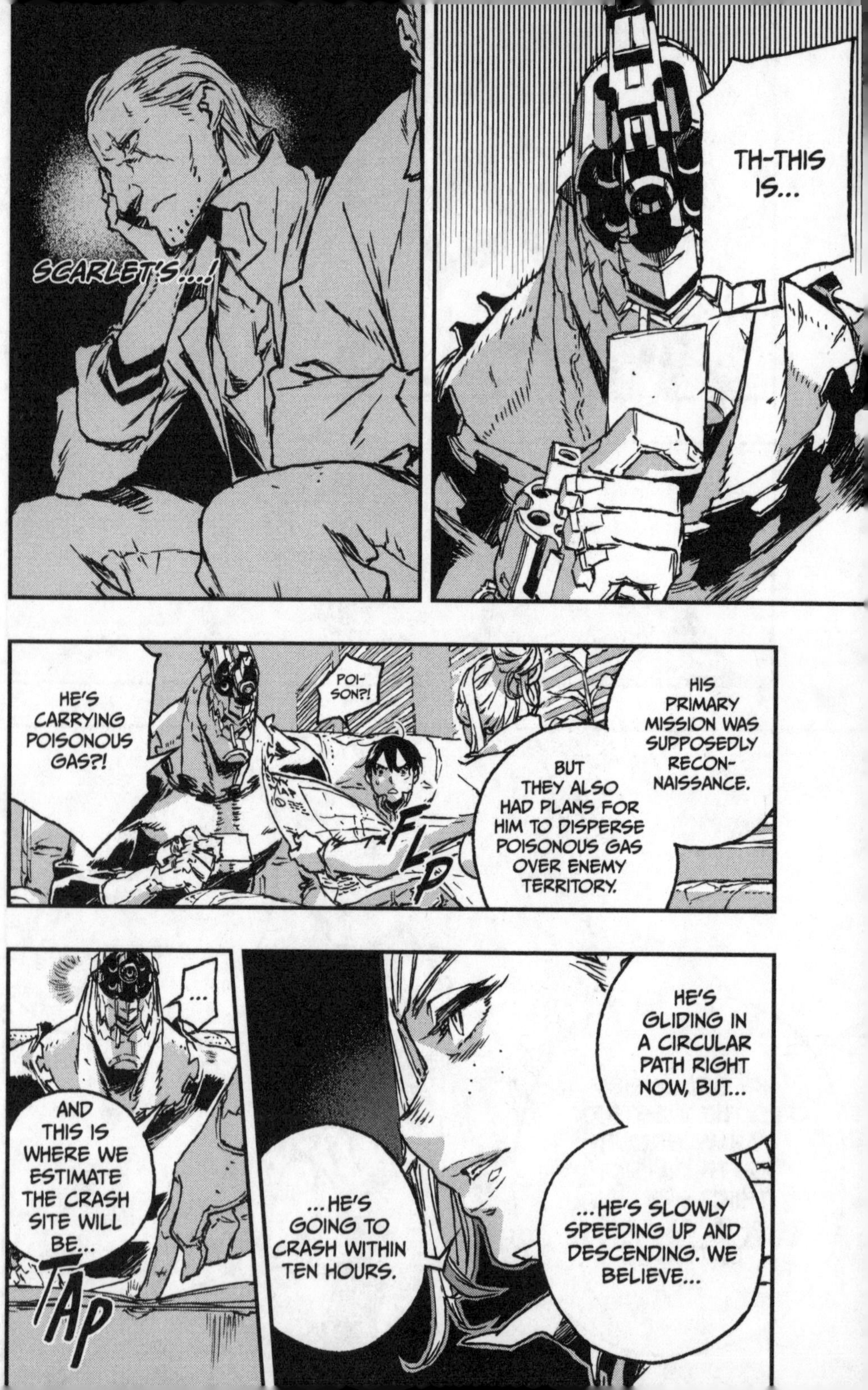

TH-THIS IS...
SCARLET'S...!
HIS PRIMARY MISSION WAS SUPPOSEDLY RECON-NAISSANCE.
BUT THEY ALSO HAD PLANS FOR HIM TO DISPERSE POISONOUS GAS OVER ENEMY TERRITORY.
POI-SON?!
HE'S CARRYING POISONOUS GAS?!
FLP
HE'S GLIDING IN A CIRCULAR PATH RIGHT NOW, BUT...
...HE'S SLOWLY SPEEDING UP AND DESCENDING. WE BELIEVE...
...HE'S GOING TO CRASH WITHIN TEN HOURS.
...
AND THIS IS WHERE WE ESTIMATE THE CRASH SITE WILL BE...
TAP

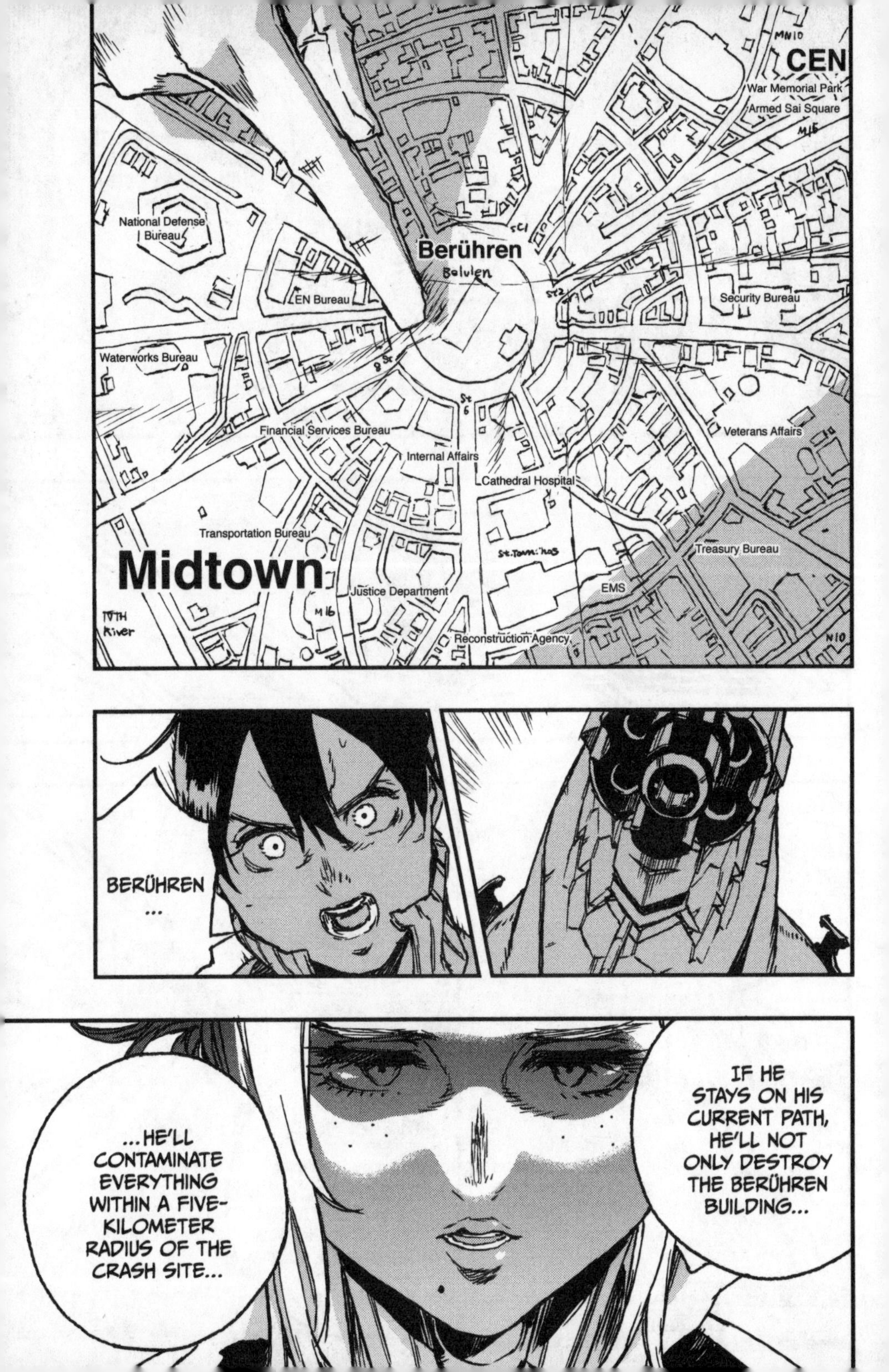
CEN
War Memorial Park
Armed Sai Square
Berühren
National Defense Bureau
Security Bureau
EN Bureau
Waterworks Bureau
Veterans Affairs
Financial Services Bureau
Internal Affairs
Cathedral Hospital
Treasury Bureau
Transportation Bureau
Midtown
EMS
Justice Department
Reconstruction Agency
BERÜHREN ...
IF HE STAYS ON HIS CURRENT PATH, HE'LL NOT ONLY DESTROY THE BERÜHREN BUILDING...
...HE'LL CONTAMINATE EVERYTHING WITHIN A FIVE-KILOMETER RADIUS OF THE CRASH SITE...

IF WE TAKE HIM OUT IN THE AIR, THE GAS WILL SPREAD OVER AN EVEN WIDER AREA.
WE ESTIMATE 20,000 PEOPLE WILL BE AFFECTED, NOT COUNTING EXTENDED THAT HAVE RESPIRATORY EXTENSIONS.
BUT IT WON'T BE THAT DIFFICULT FOR BERÜHREN TO COUNTERACT THE POISON, SINCE THEY CREATED THE EXTENSION PROCEDURES SILVA AND OTHERS RECEIVED.
THEY'LL MOST LIKELY CASH IN ON THIS OPPORTUNITY BY SELLING THE ANTIDOTE.
SHHHH

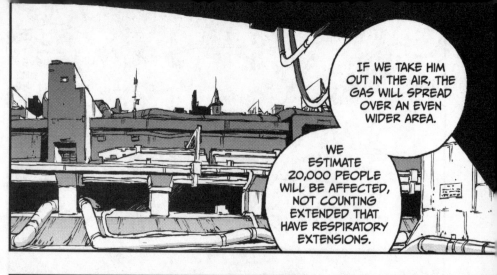

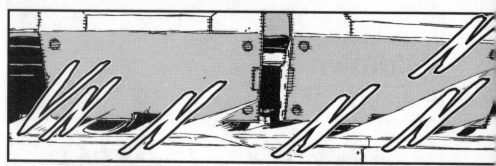

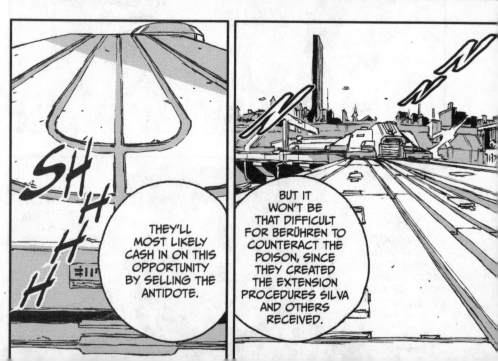

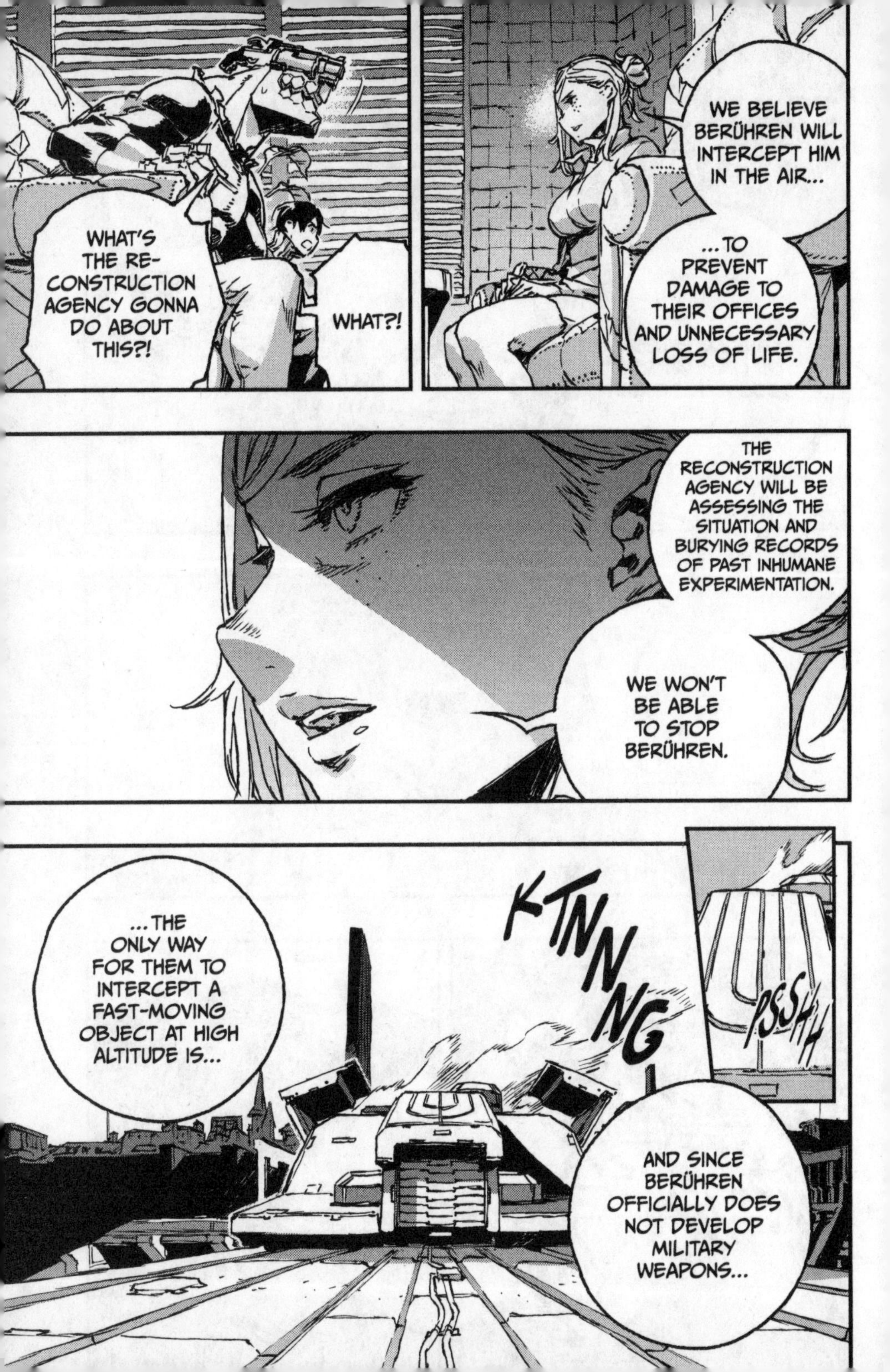
WE BELIEVE BERÜHREN WILL INTERCEPT HIM IN THE AIR...
...TO PREVENT DAMAGE TO THEIR OFFICES AND UNNECESSARY LOSS OF LIFE.
WHAT?!
WHAT'S THE RE-CONSTRUCTION AGENCY GONNA DO ABOUT THIS?!
THE RECONSTRUCTION AGENCY WILL BE ASSESSING THE SITUATION AND BURYING RECORDS OF PAST INHUMANE EXPERIMENTATION.
WE WON'T BE ABLE TO STOP BERÜHREN.
PSSHH
AND SINCE BERÜHREN OFFICIALLY DOES NOT DEVELOP MILITARY WEAPONS...
KTNNNG
...THE ONLY WAY FOR THEM TO INTERCEPT A FAST-MOVING OBJECT AT HIGH ALTITUDE IS...

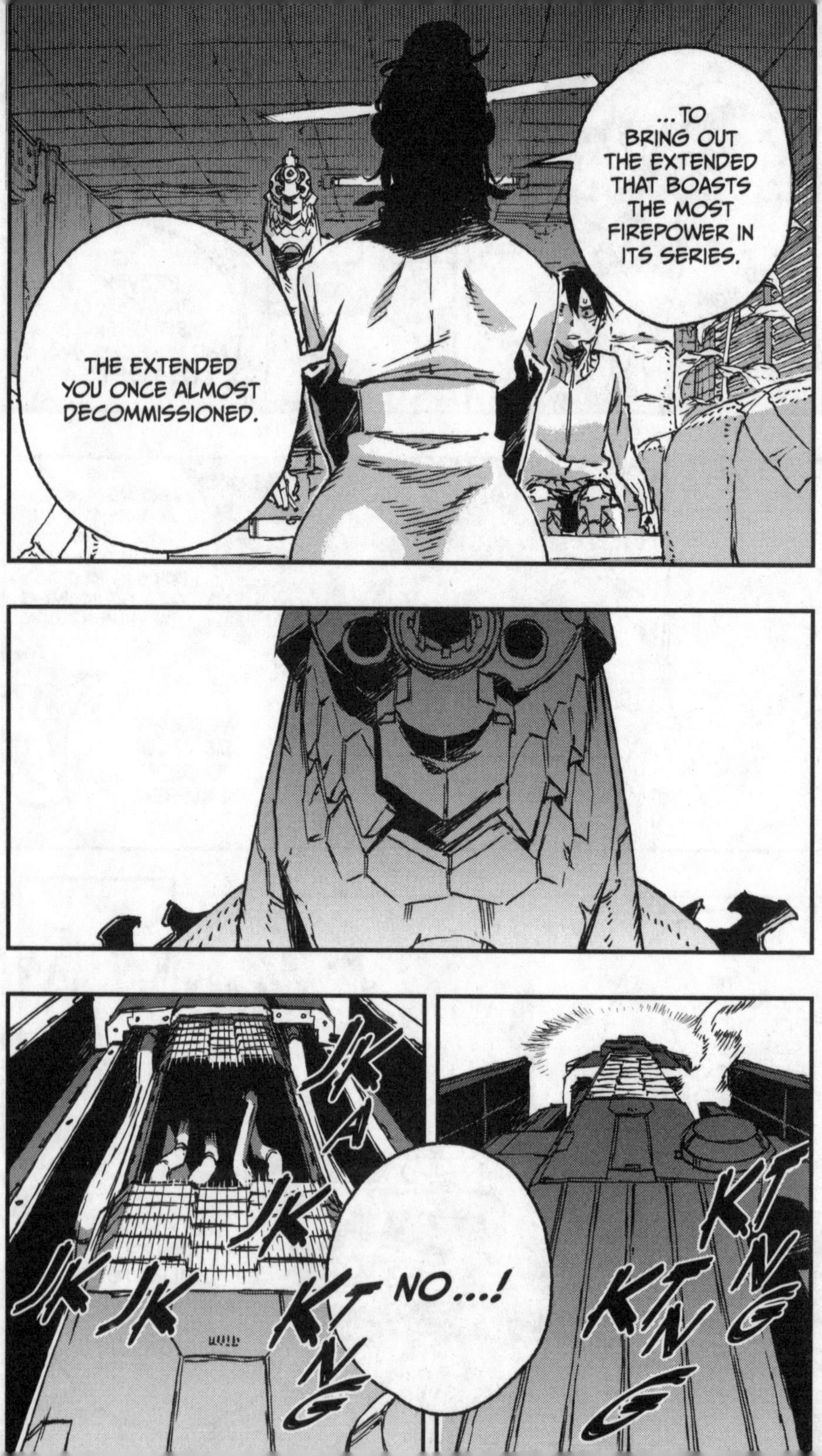
...TO BRING OUT THE EXTENDED THAT BOASTS THE MOST FIREPOWER IN ITS SERIES.
THE EXTENDED YOU ONCE ALMOST DECOMMISSIONED.
KTNG
KTNG
NO...!
JKA
JK
JK
JK
KTNG

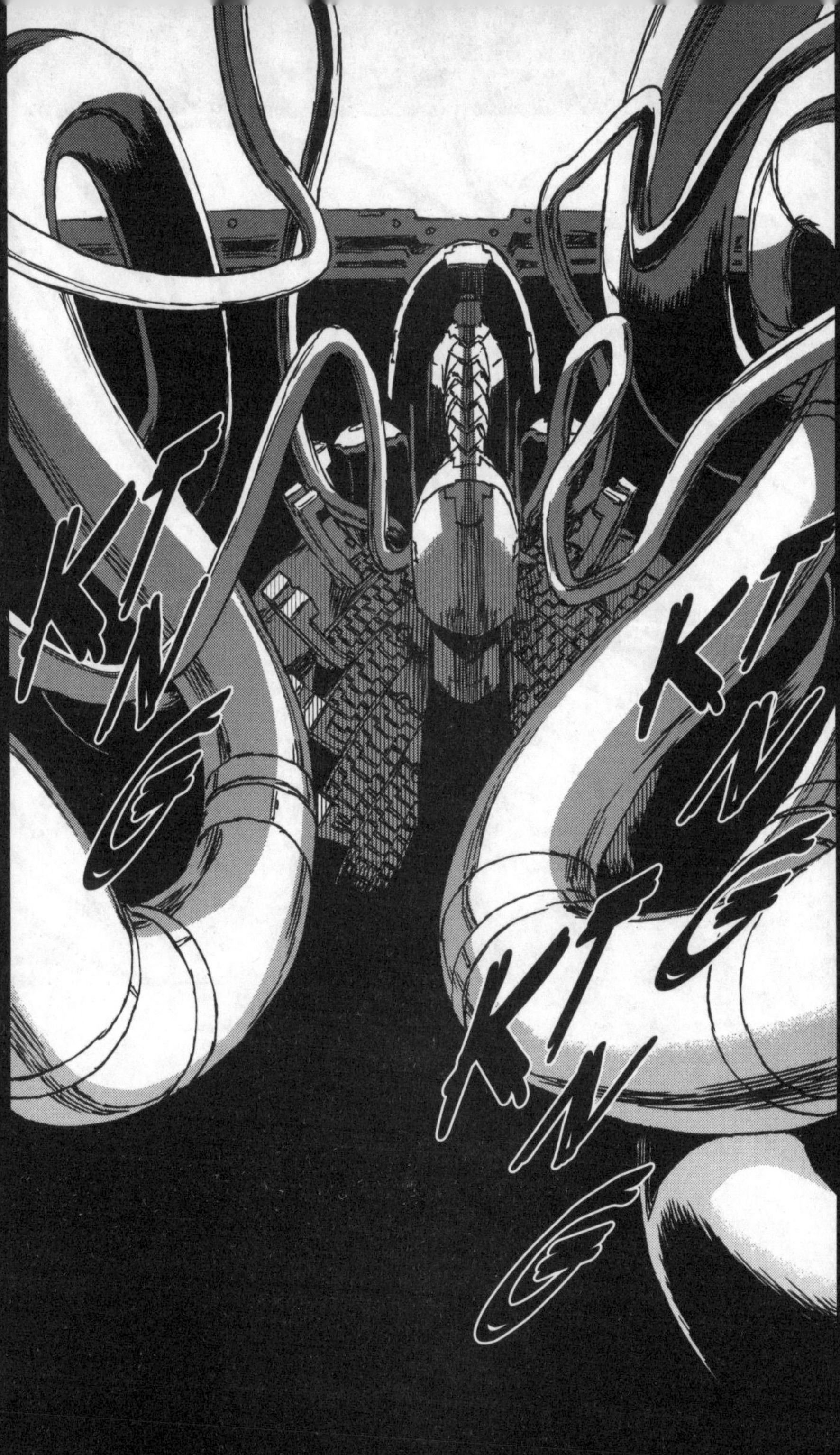
KING
KING
KING

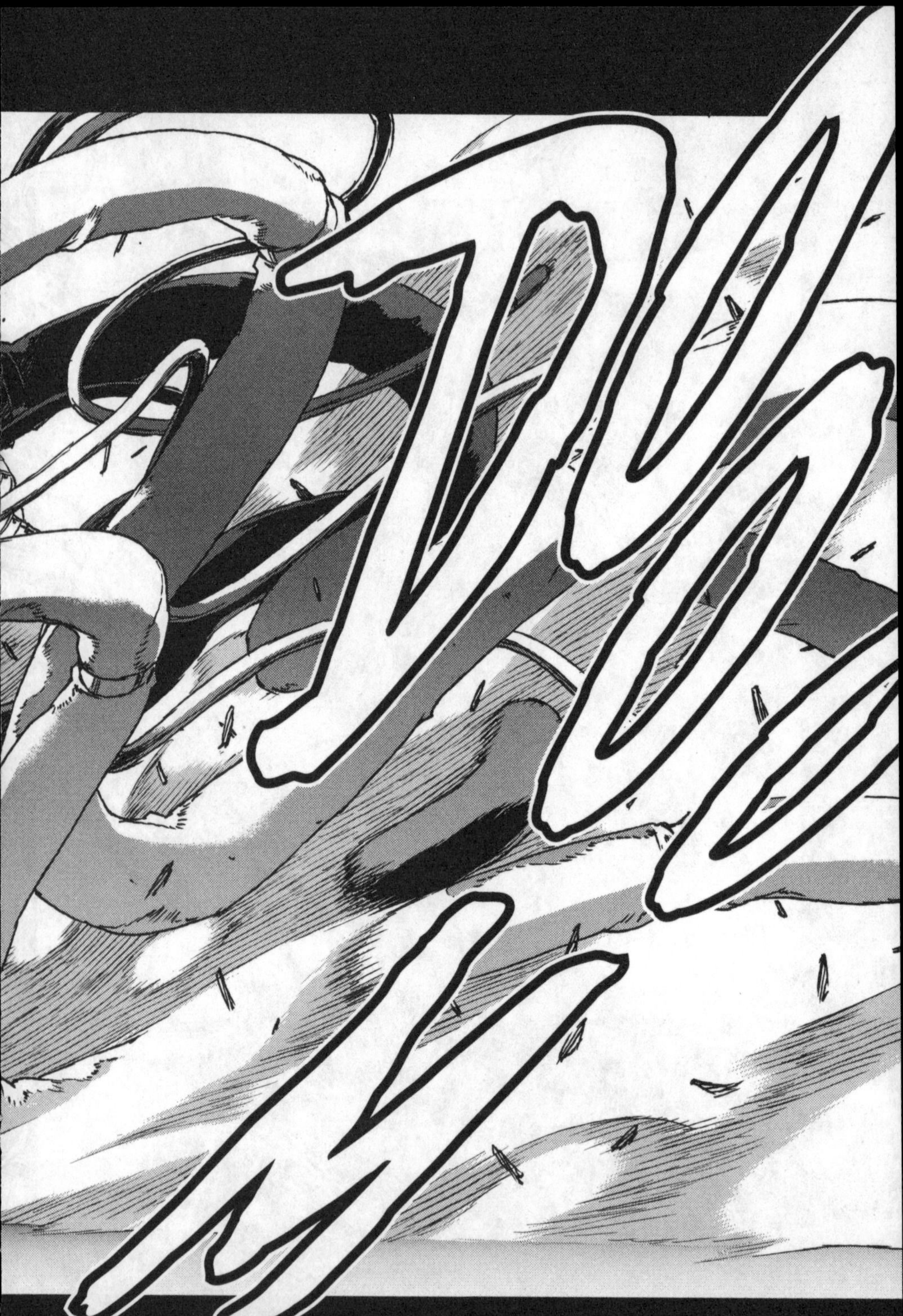

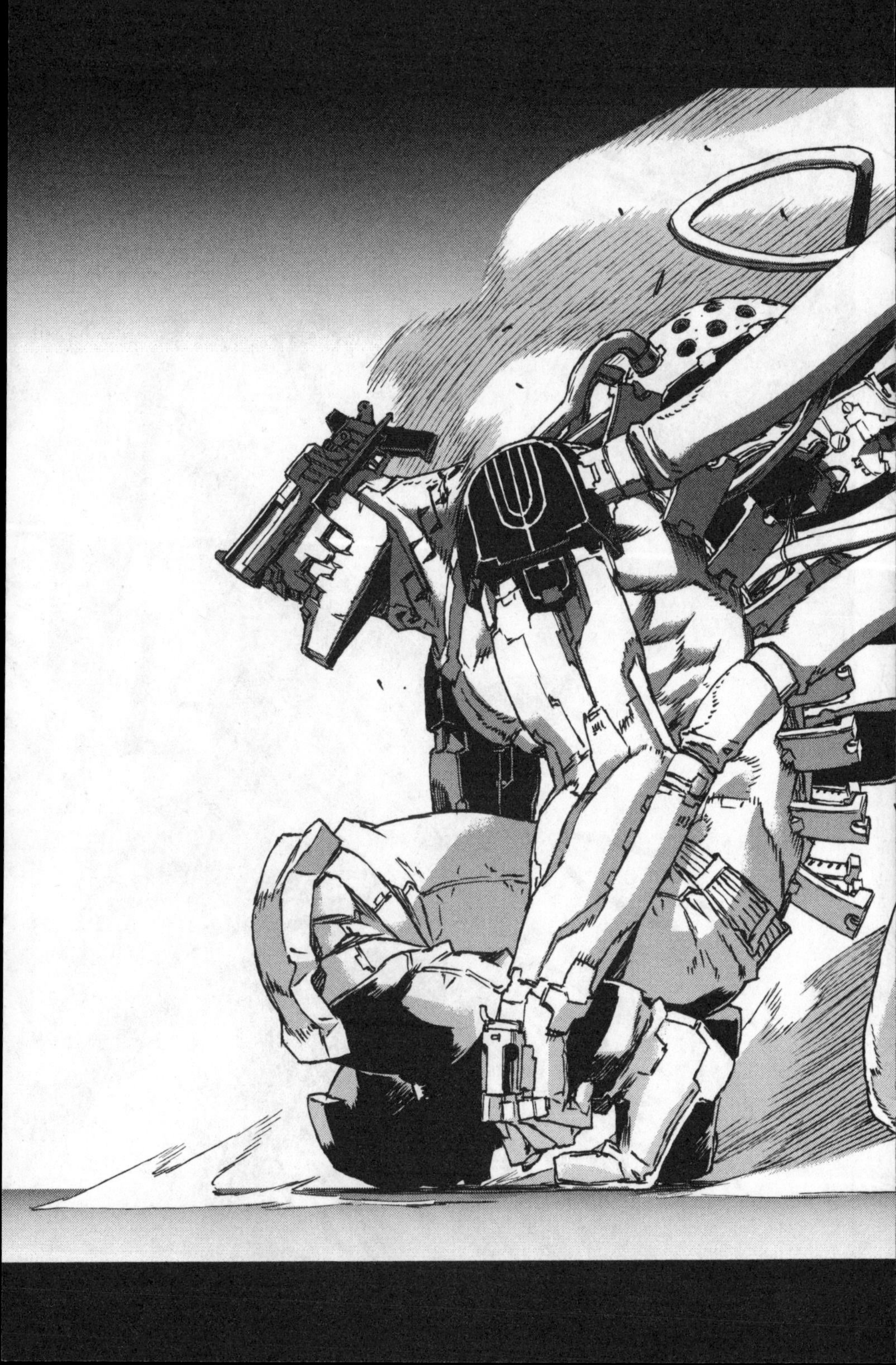

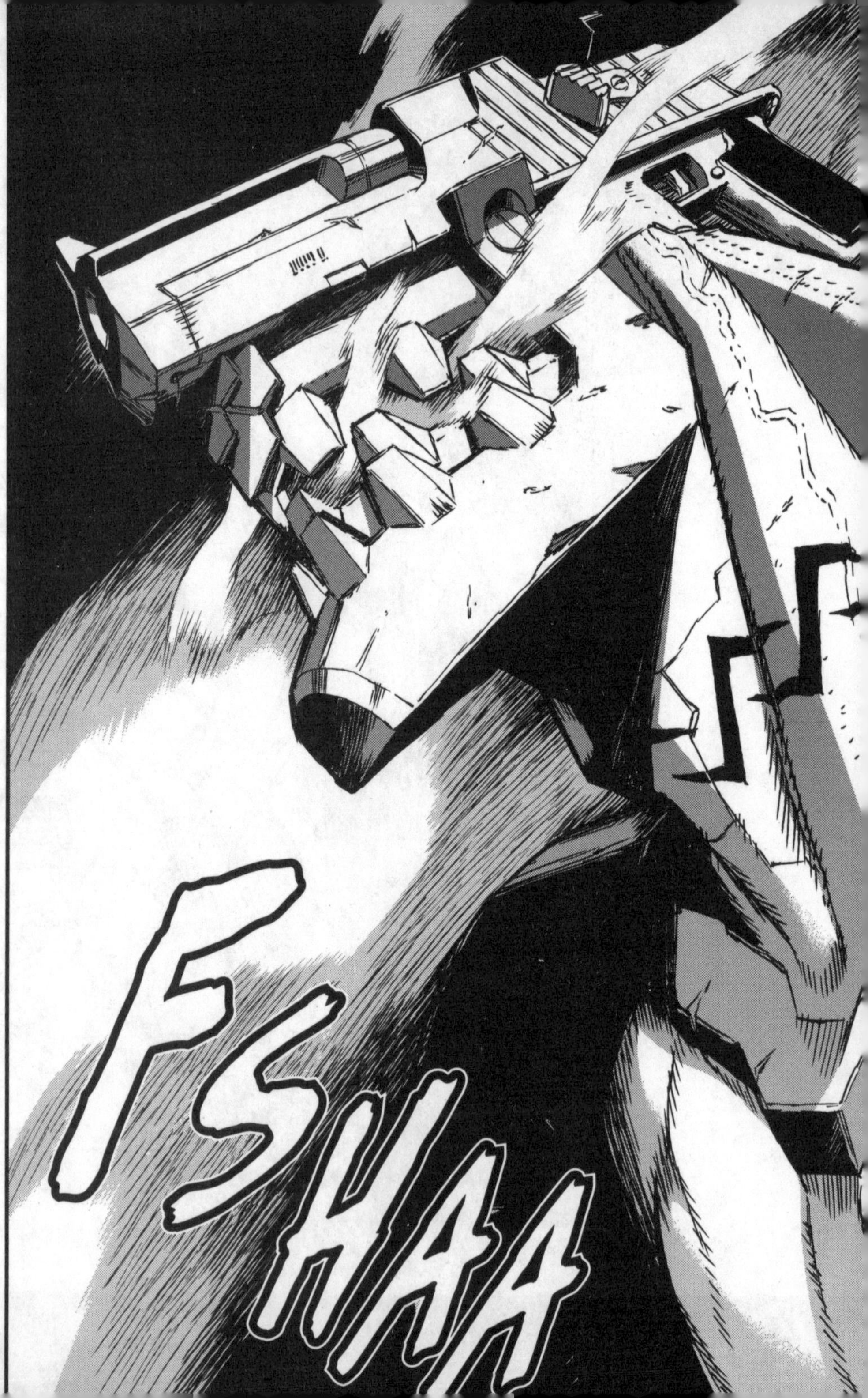
FSHAA

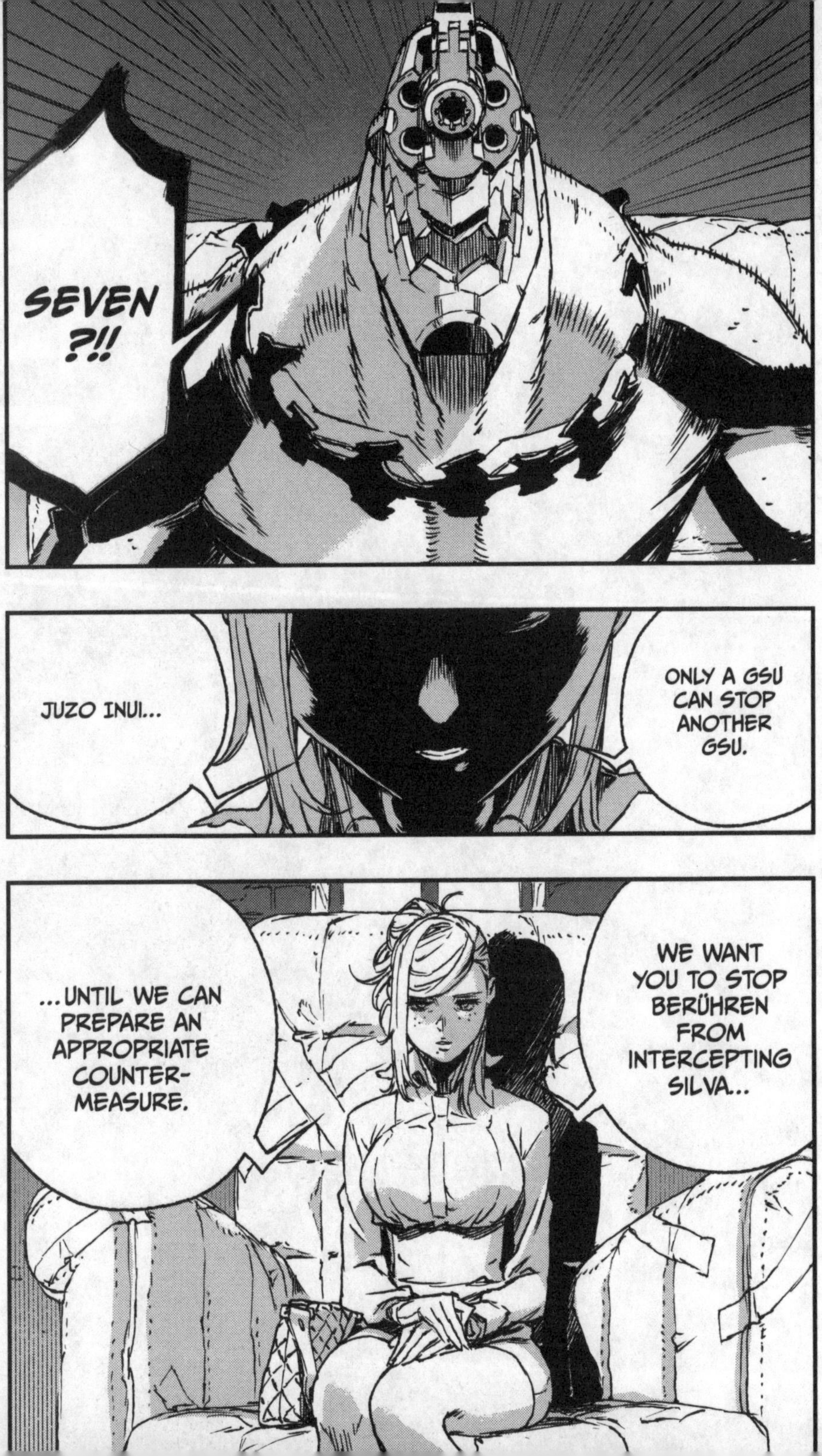
SEVEN ?!!
ONLY A GSU CAN STOP ANOTHER GSU.
JUZO INUI...
WE WANT YOU TO STOP BERÜHREN FROM INTERCEPTING SILVA...
...UNTIL WE CAN PREPARE AN APPROPRIATE COUNTER-MEASURE.

NO GUNS LIFE

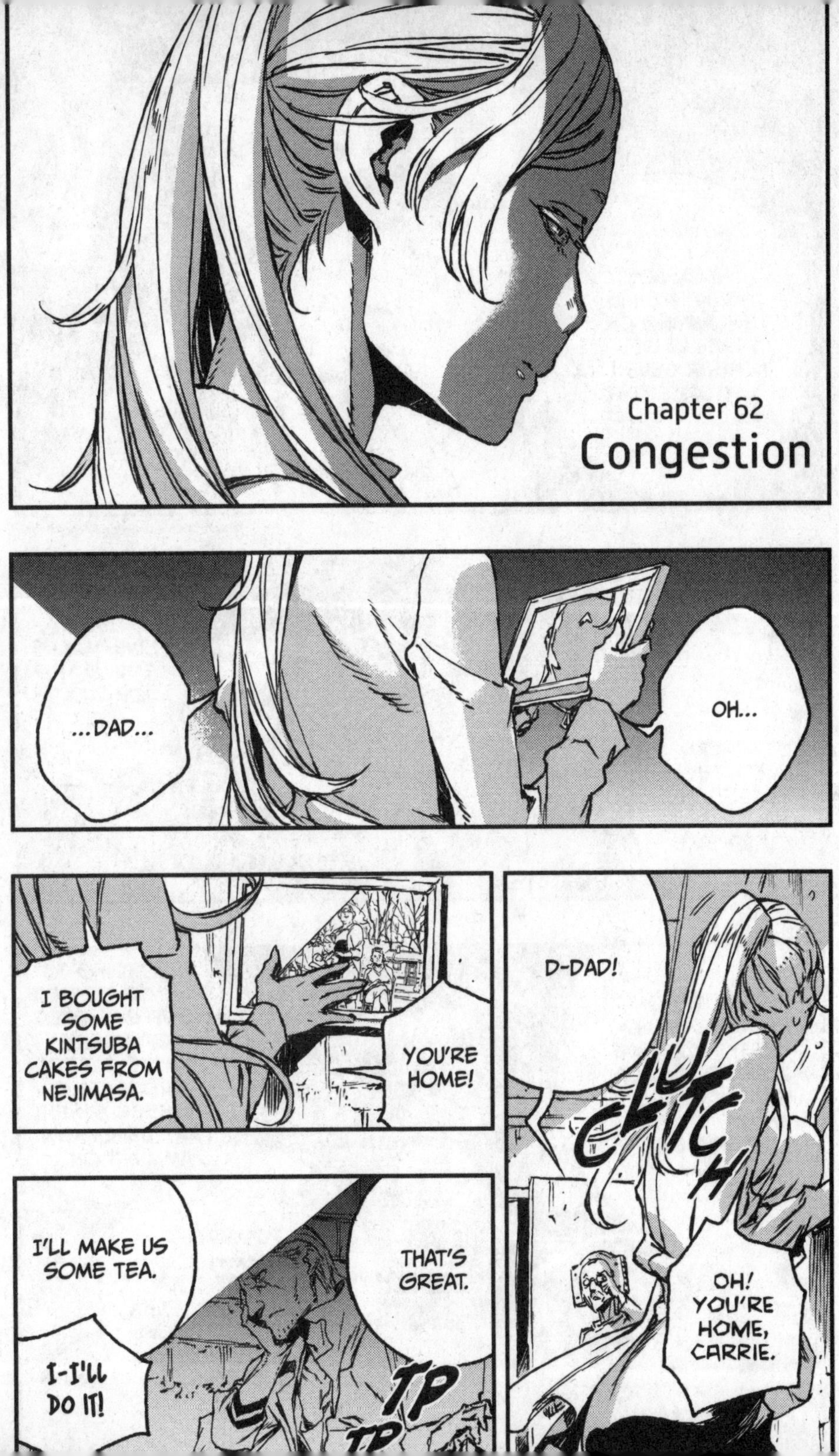

Chapter 62
Congestion
OH...
...DAD...
D-DAD!
CLUTCH
OH! YOU'RE HOME, CARRIE.
YOU'RE HOME!
I BOUGHT SOME KINTSUBA CAKES FROM NEJIMASA.
THAT'S GREAT.
I'LL MAKE US SOME TEA.
TP TP
I-I'LL DO IT!

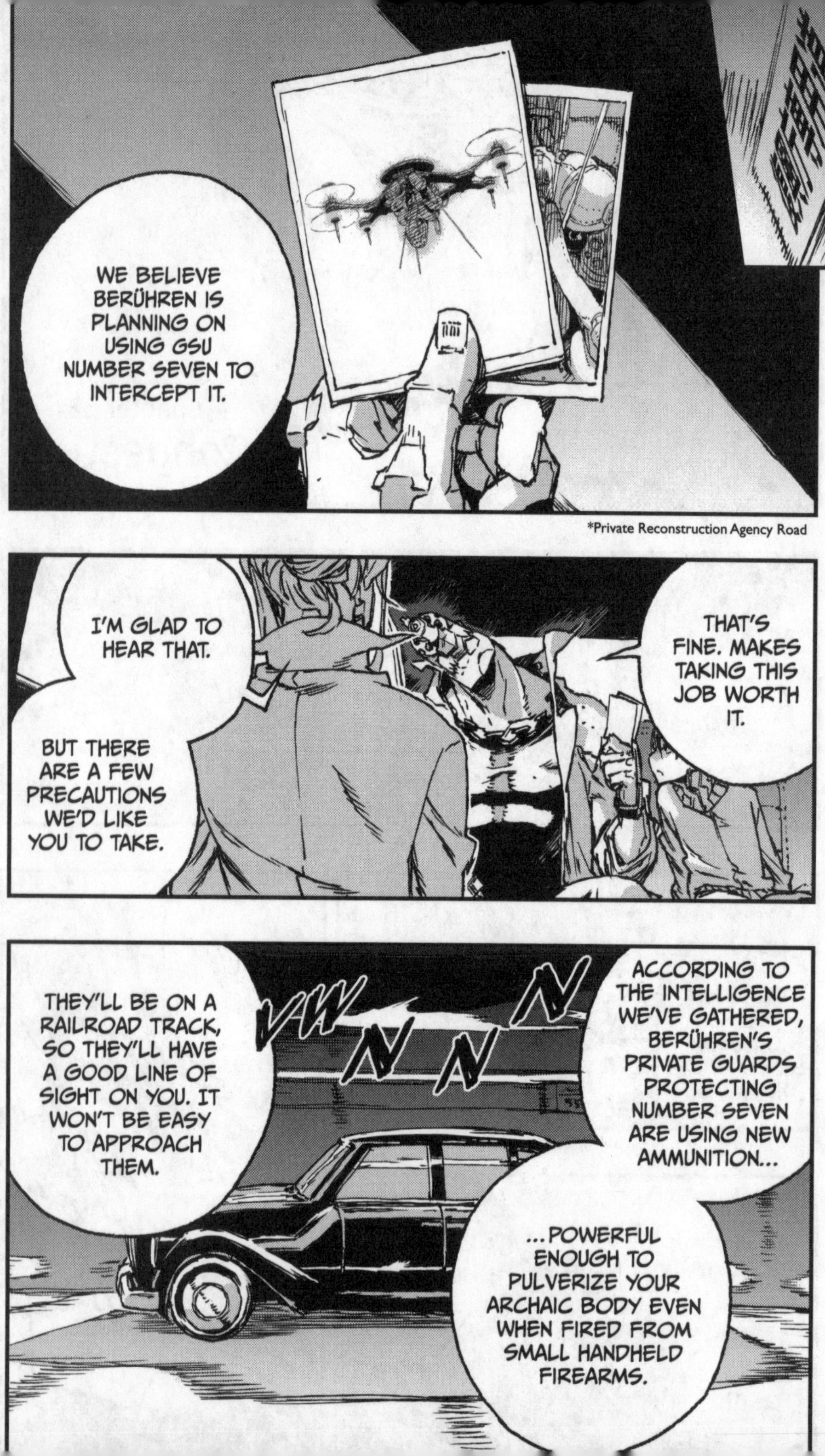
WE BELIEVE BERÜHREN IS PLANNING ON USING GSU NUMBER SEVEN TO INTERCEPT IT.
*Private Reconstruction Agency Road
THAT'S FINE. MAKES TAKING THIS JOB WORTH IT.
I'M GLAD TO HEAR THAT.
BUT THERE ARE A FEW PRECAUTIONS WE'D LIKE YOU TO TAKE.
ACCORDING TO THE INTELLIGENCE WE'VE GATHERED, BERÜHREN'S PRIVATE GUARDS PROTECTING NUMBER SEVEN ARE USING NEW AMMUNITION...
VWNNNN
...POWERFUL ENOUGH TO PULVERIZE YOUR ARCHAIC BODY EVEN WHEN FIRED FROM SMALL HANDHELD FIREARMS.
THEY'LL BE ON A RAILROAD TRACK, SO THEY'LL HAVE A GOOD LINE OF SIGHT ON YOU. IT WON'T BE EASY TO APPROACH THEM.

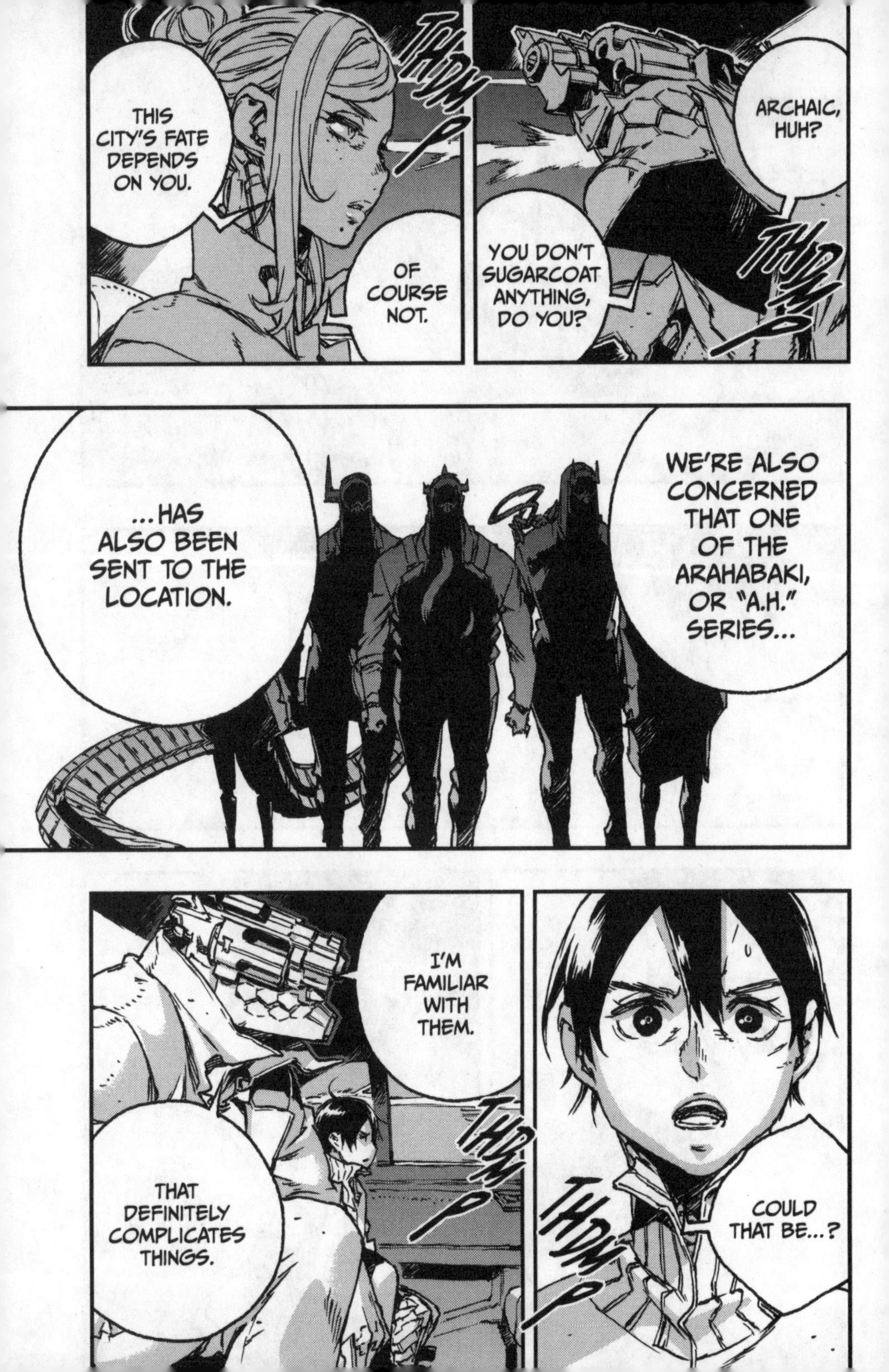
ARCHAIC, HUH?
THOMP
YOU DON'T SUGARCOAT ANYTHING, DO YOU?
THOMP
THIS CITY'S FATE DEPENDS ON YOU.
OF COURSE NOT.
WE'RE ALSO CONCERNED THAT ONE OF THE ARAHABAKI, OR "A.H." SERIES...
...HAS ALSO BEEN SENT TO THE LOCATION.
COULD THAT BE...?
THOMP
I'M FAMILIAR WITH THEM.
THOMP
THAT DEFINITELY COMPLICATES THINGS.

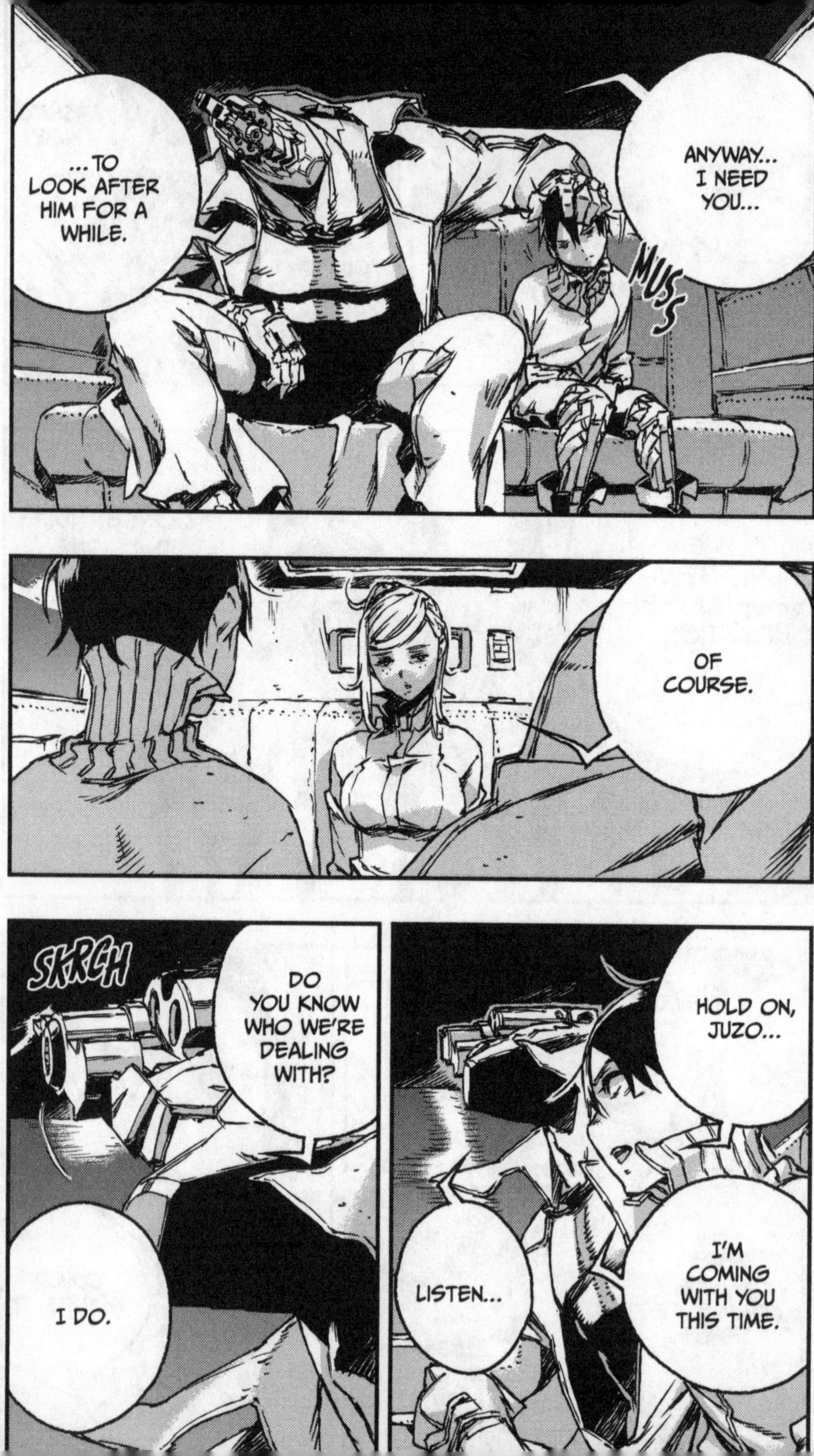
ANYWAY... I NEED YOU...
MUSS
...TO LOOK AFTER HIM FOR A WHILE.
OF COURSE.
HOLD ON, JUZO...
I'M COMING WITH YOU THIS TIME.
LISTEN...
SKRCH
DO YOU KNOW WHO WE'RE DEALING WITH?
I DO.

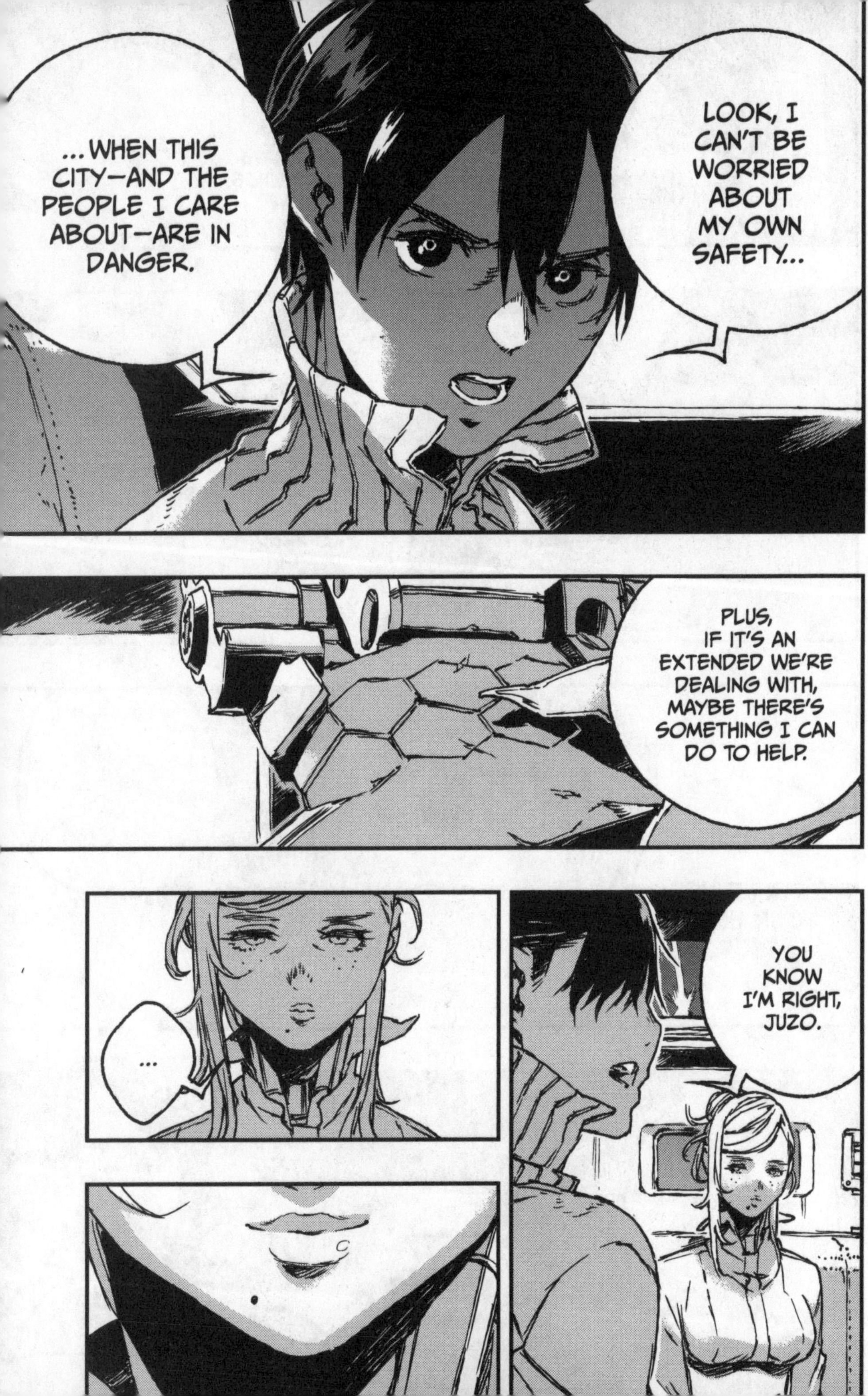
LOOK, I CAN'T BE WORRIED ABOUT MY OWN SAFETY...
...WHEN THIS CITY—AND THE PEOPLE I CARE ABOUT—ARE IN DANGER.
PLUS, IF IT'S AN EXTENDED WE'RE DEALING WITH, MAYBE THERE'S SOMETHING I CAN DO TO HELP.
YOU KNOW I'M RIGHT, JUZO.
...

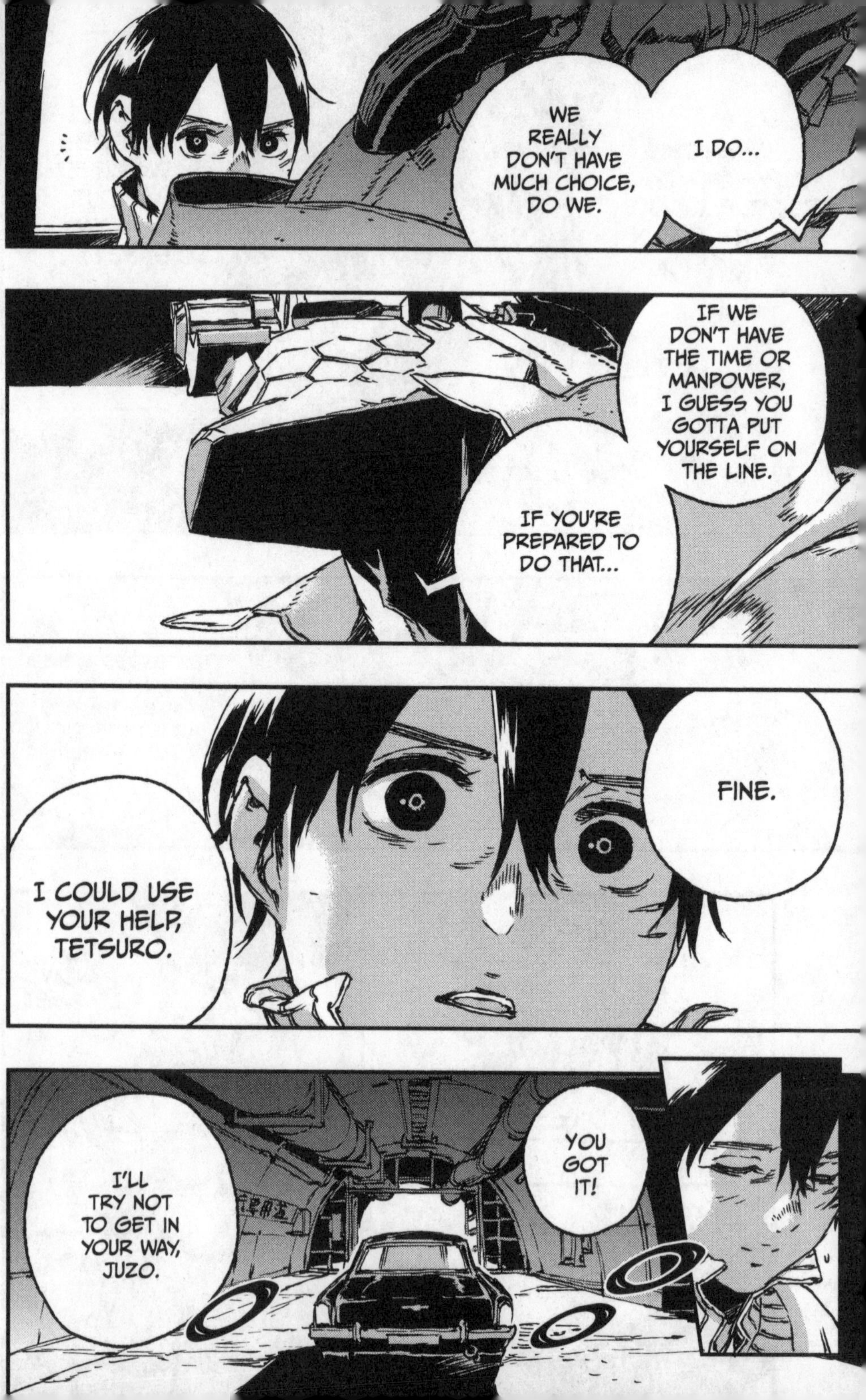

I DO...
WE REALLY DON'T HAVE MUCH CHOICE, DO WE.
IF WE DON'T HAVE THE TIME OR MANPOWER, I GUESS YOU GOTTA PUT YOURSELF ON THE LINE.
IF YOU'RE PREPARED TO DO THAT...
FINE.
I COULD USE YOUR HELP, TETSURO.
YOU GOT IT!
I'LL TRY NOT TO GET IN YOUR WAY, JUZO.

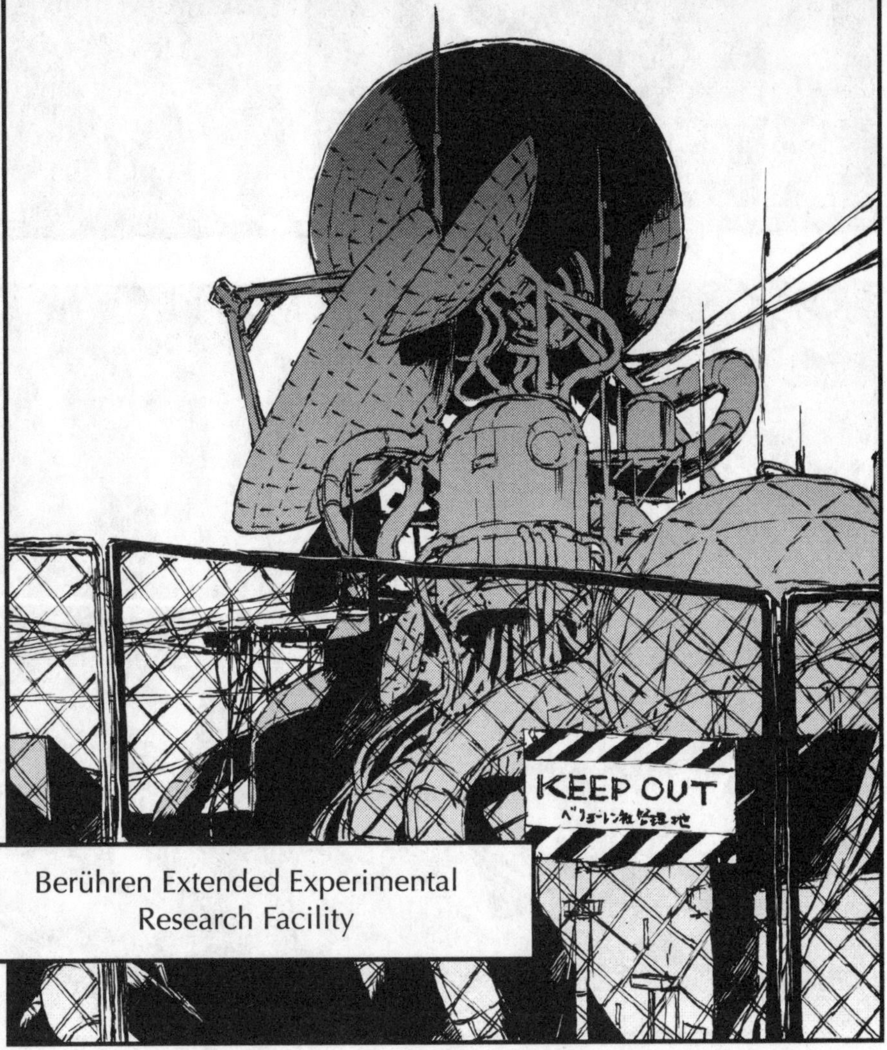
KEEP OUT
Berühren Extended Experimental Research Facility
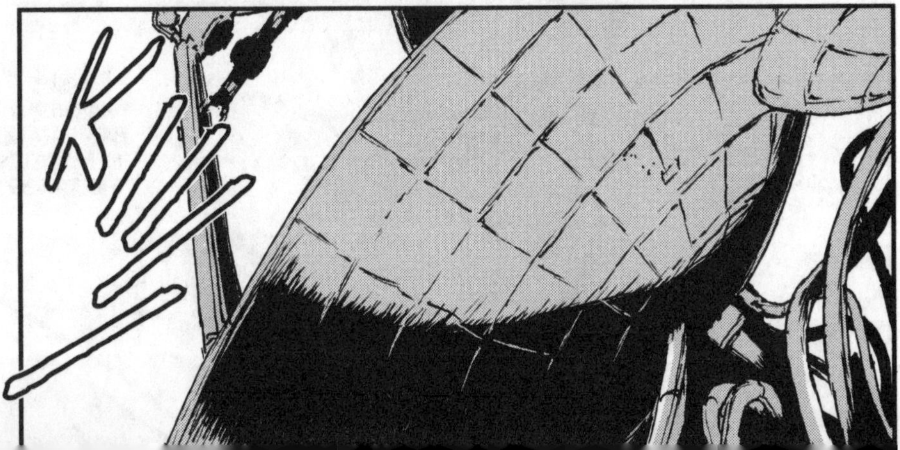
KII

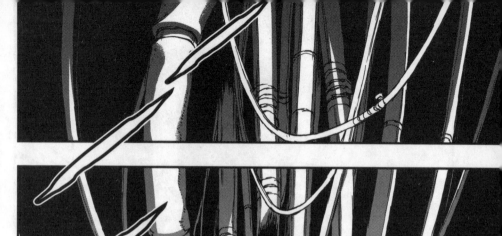

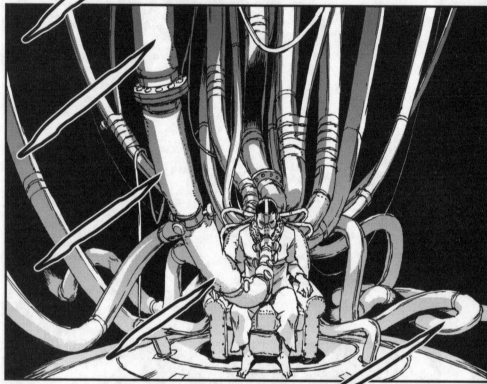

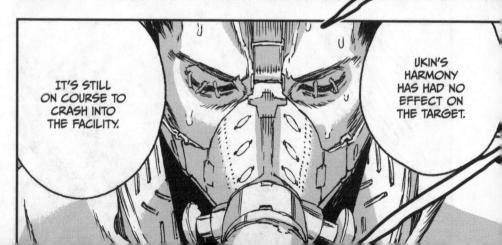

UKIN'S HARMONY HAS HAD NO EFFECT ON THE TARGET.
IT'S STILL ON COURSE TO CRASH INTO THE FACILITY.

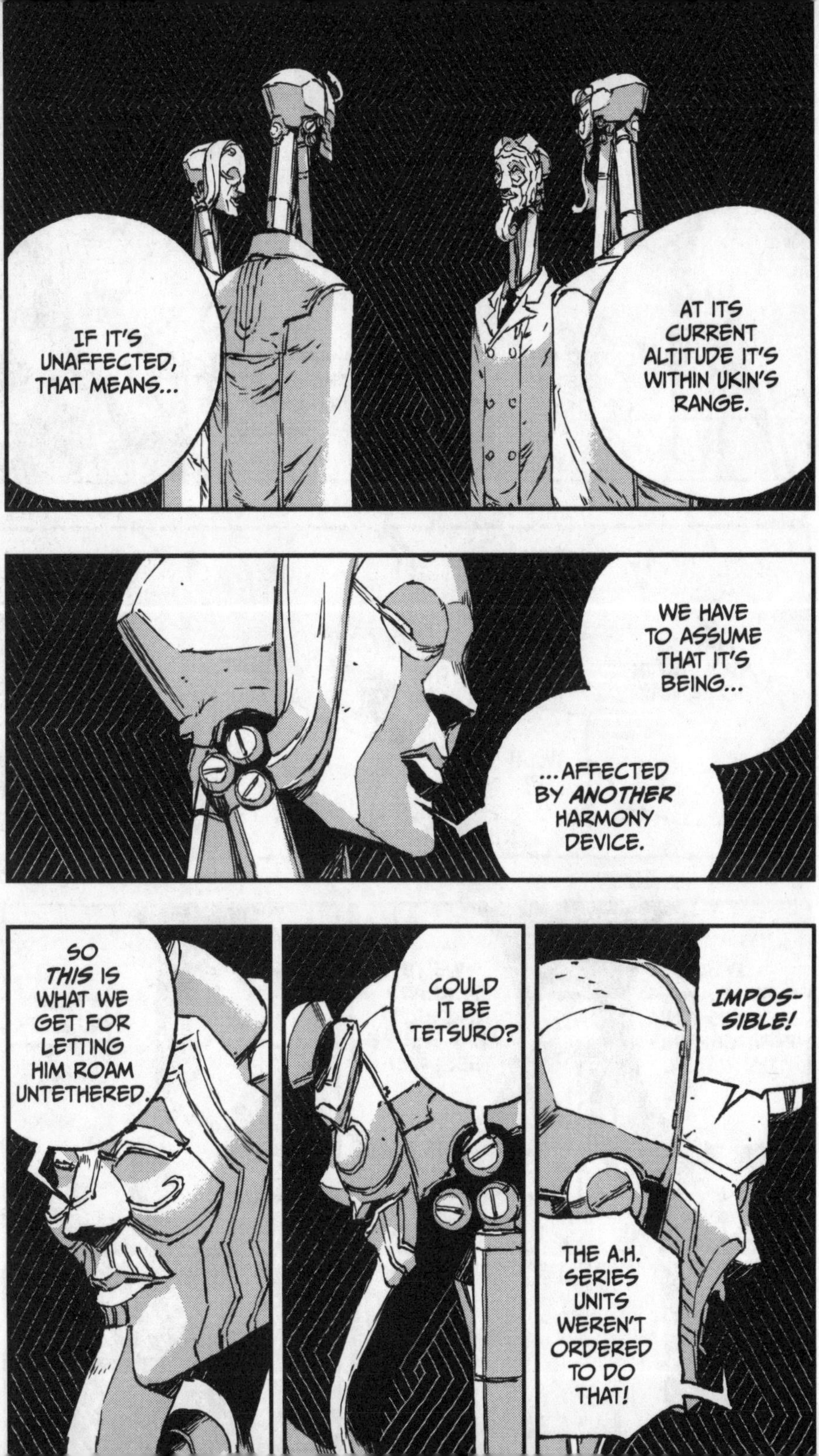
AT ITS CURRENT ALTITUDE IT'S WITHIN UKIN'S RANGE.
IF IT'S UNAFFECTED, THAT MEANS...
WE HAVE TO ASSUME THAT IT'S BEING...
...AFFECTED BY *ANOTHER* HARMONY DEVICE.
IMPOS-SIBLE!
THE A.H. SERIES UNITS WEREN'T ORDERED TO DO THAT!
COULD IT BE TETSURO?
SO *THIS* IS WHAT WE GET FOR LETTING HIM ROAM UNTETHERED.

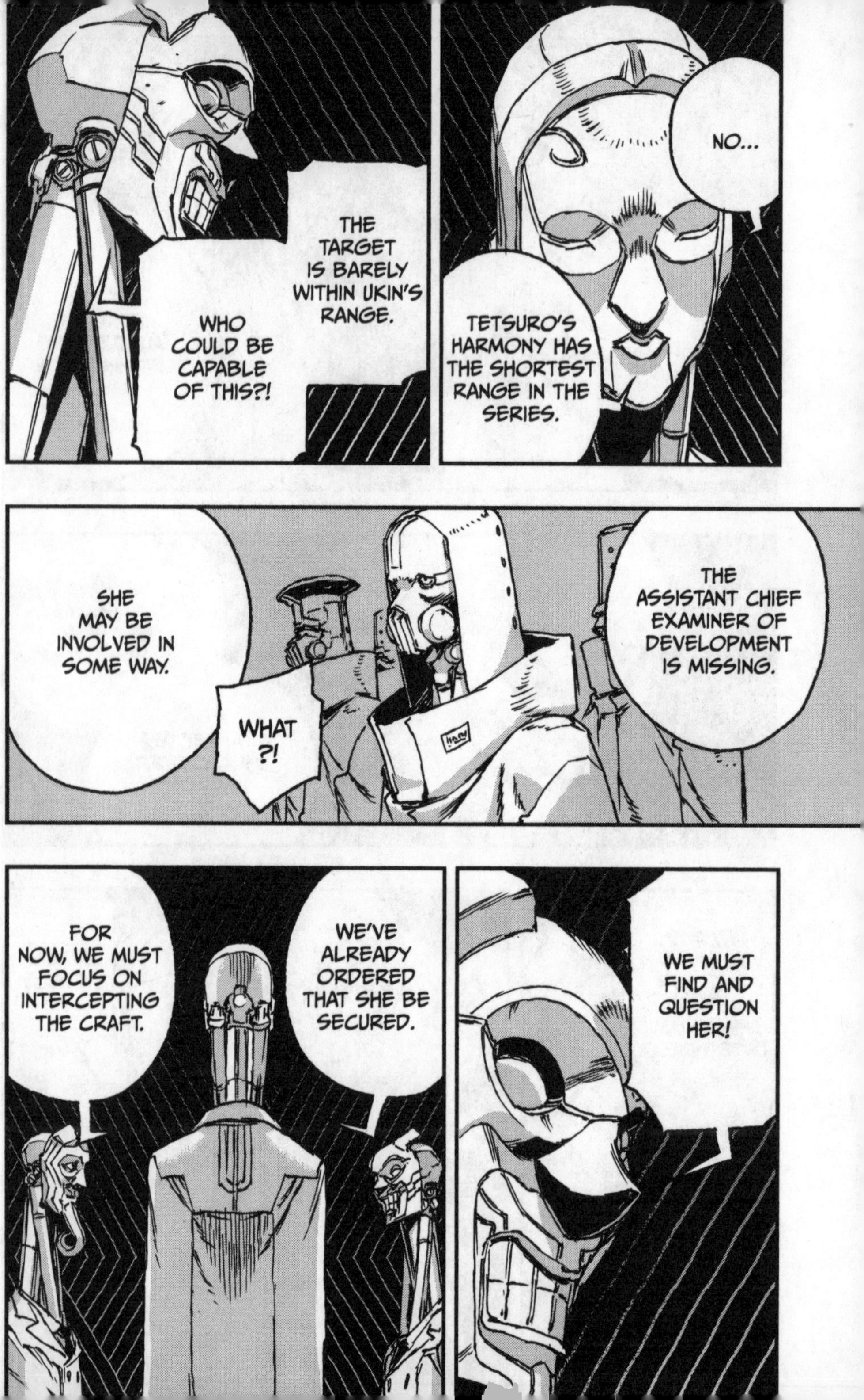
NO...
TETSURO'S HARMONY HAS THE SHORTEST RANGE IN THE SERIES.
THE TARGET IS BARELY WITHIN UKIN'S RANGE.
WHO COULD BE CAPABLE OF THIS?!
THE ASSISTANT CHIEF EXAMINER OF DEVELOPMENT IS MISSING.
WHAT?!
SHE MAY BE INVOLVED IN SOME WAY.
WE MUST FIND AND QUESTION HER!
WE'VE ALREADY ORDERED THAT SHE BE SECURED.
FOR NOW, WE MUST FOCUS ON INTERCEPTING THE CRAFT.

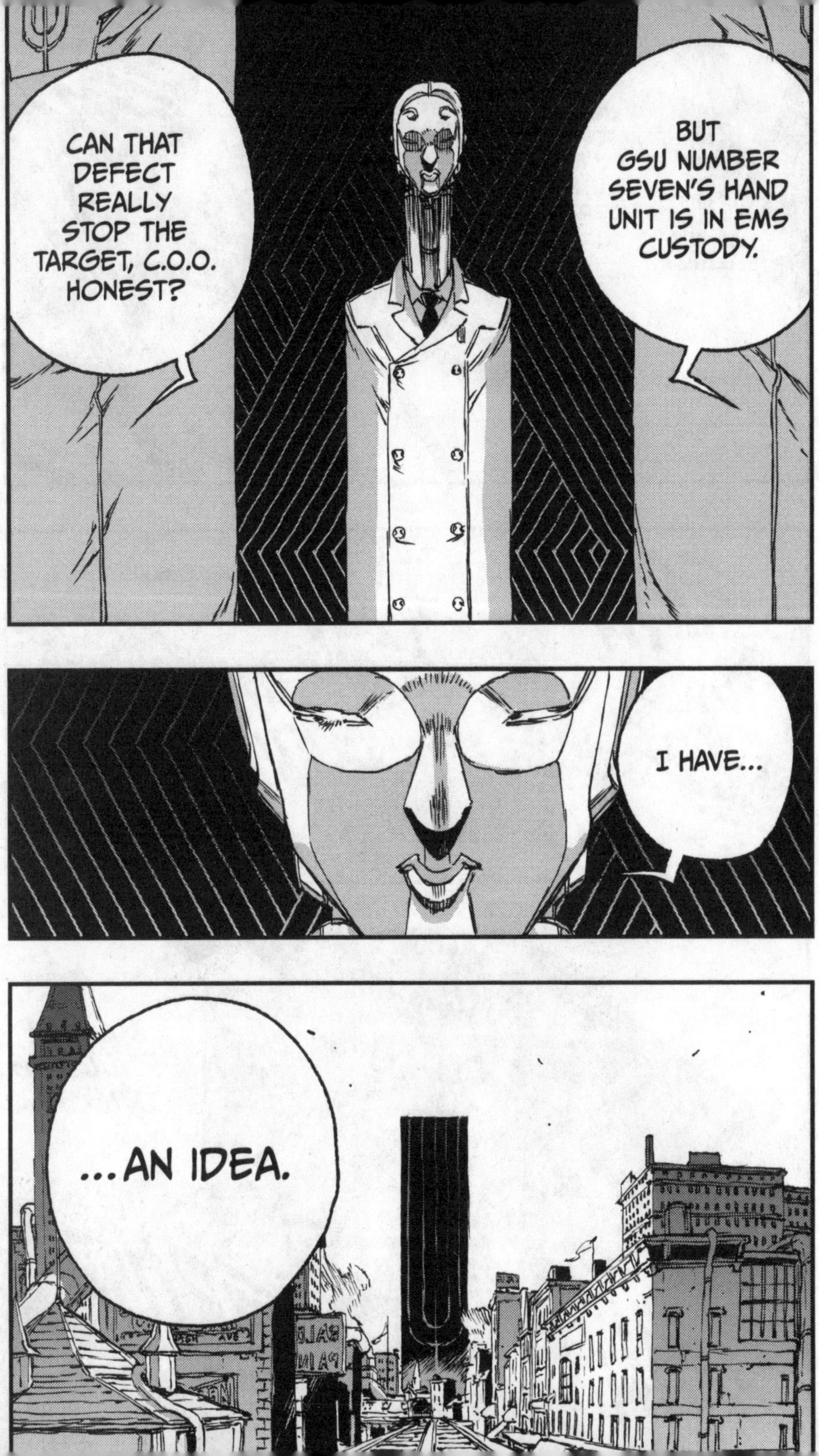
BUT GSU NUMBER SEVEN'S HAND UNIT IS IN EMS CUSTODY.
CAN THAT DEFECT REALLY STOP THE TARGET, C.O.O. HONEST?
I HAVE...
...AN IDEA.

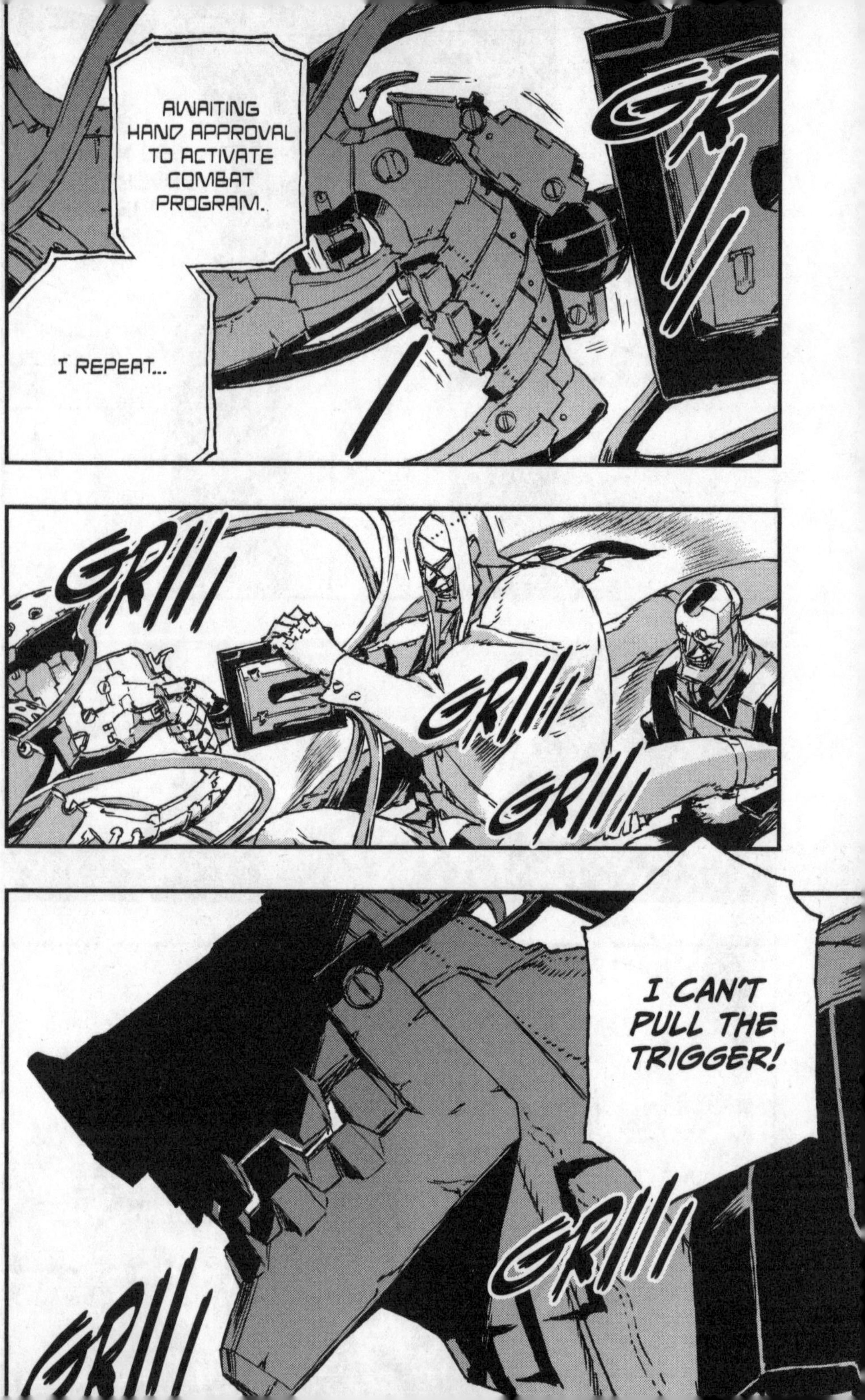
GRIII
AWAITING HAND APPROVAL TO ACTIVATE COMBAT PROGRAM..
I REPEAT...
GRIII
GRIII
GRIII
I CAN'T PULL THE TRIGGER!
GRIII
GRIII

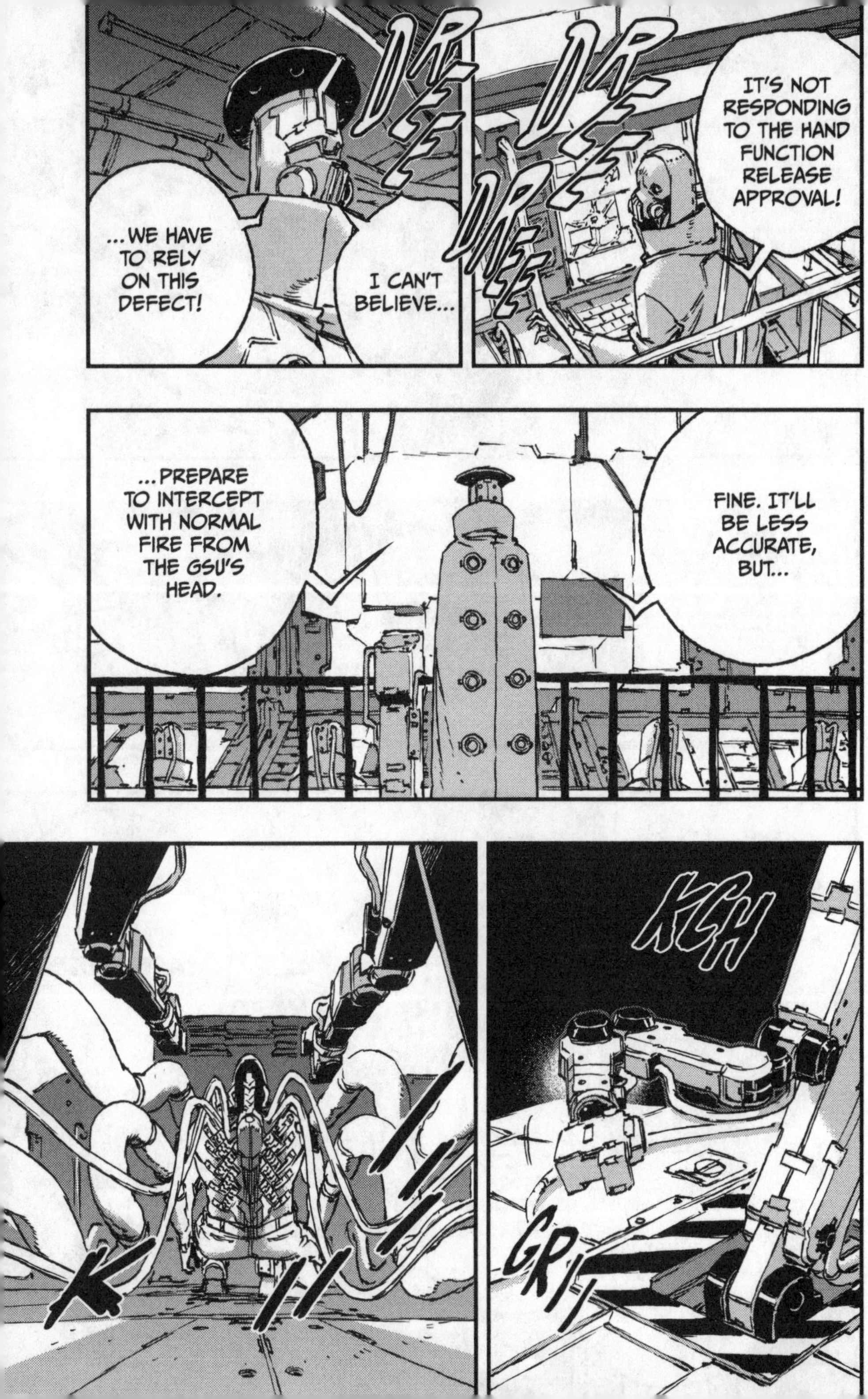

DREE
DREE
DREE
IT'S NOT RESPONDING TO THE HAND FUNCTION RELEASE APPROVAL!
I CAN'T BELIEVE...
...WE HAVE TO RELY ON THIS DEFECT!
FINE. IT'LL BE LESS ACCURATE, BUT...
...PREPARE TO INTERCEPT WITH NORMAL FIRE FROM THE GSU'S HEAD.
KCH
GRI
K

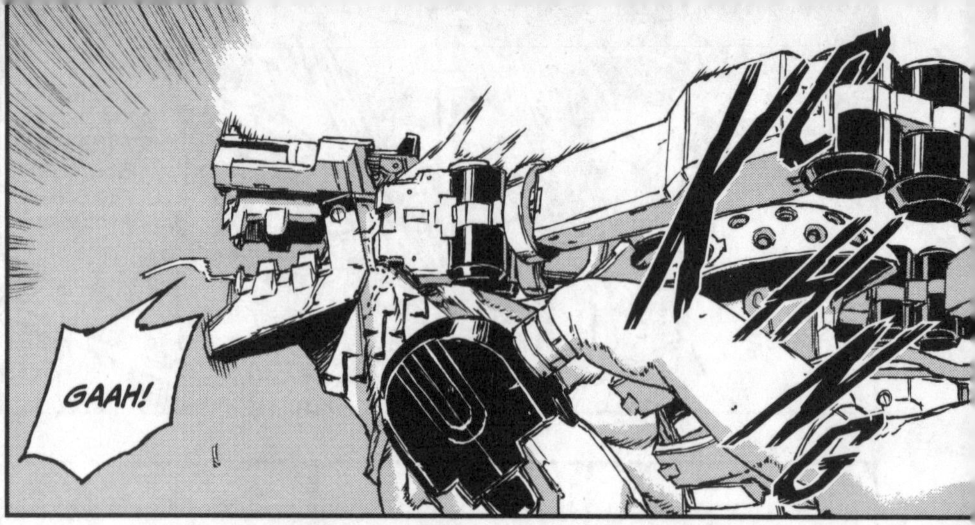
KCHHNG
GAAH!
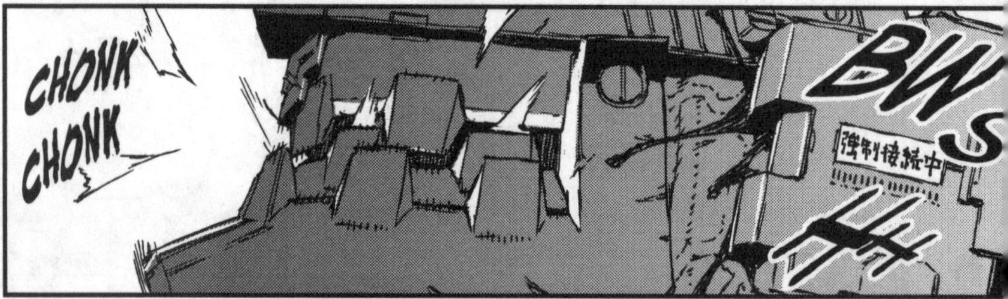
BWSHH
強制接続中
CHONK
CHONK
*Forced Connection
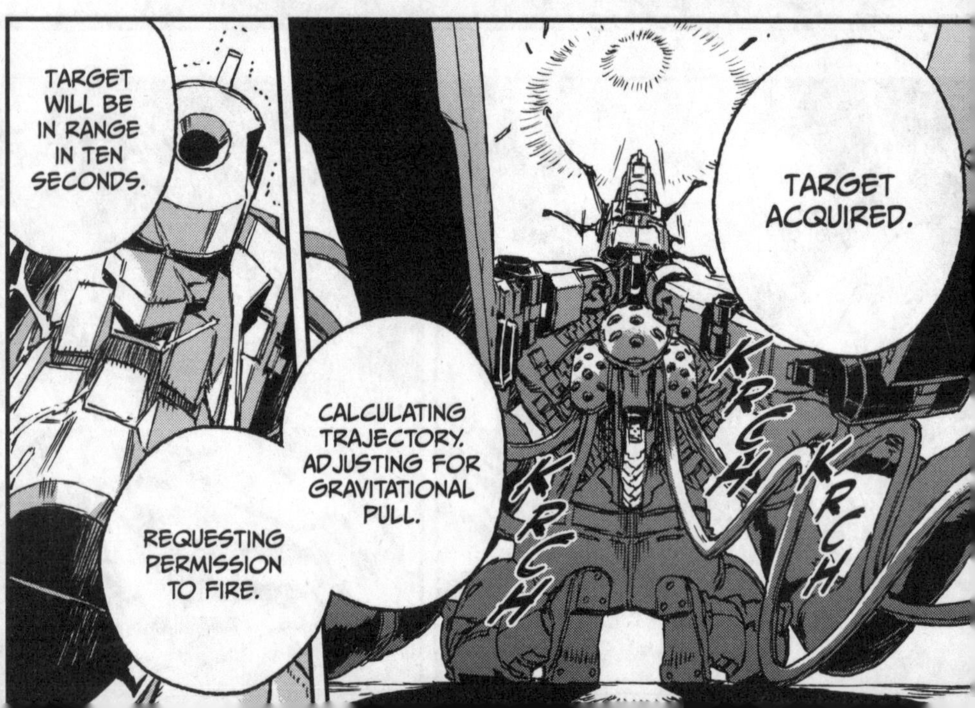
TARGET ACQUIRED.
KRCH
KRCH
KRCH
TARGET WILL BE IN RANGE IN TEN SECONDS.
CALCULATING TRAJECTORY. ADJUSTING FOR GRAVITATIONAL PULL.
REQUESTING PERMISSION TO FIRE.

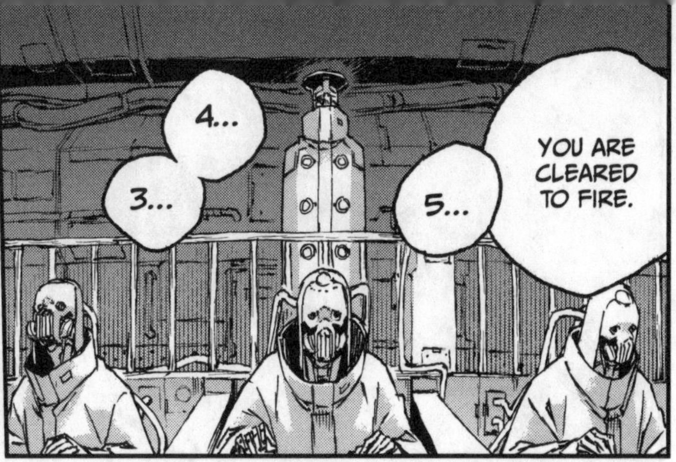
YOU ARE CLEARED TO FIRE.
5...
4...
3...
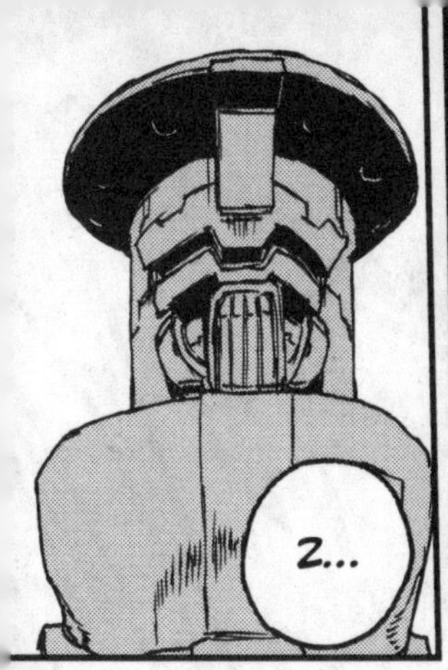
2...
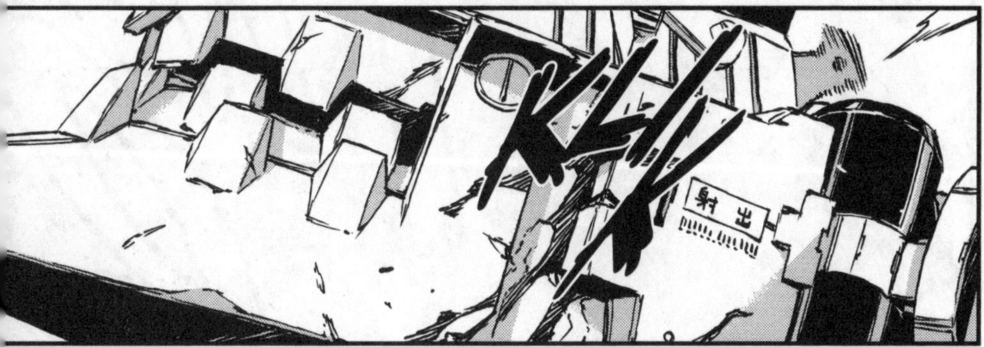
射出

*Firing

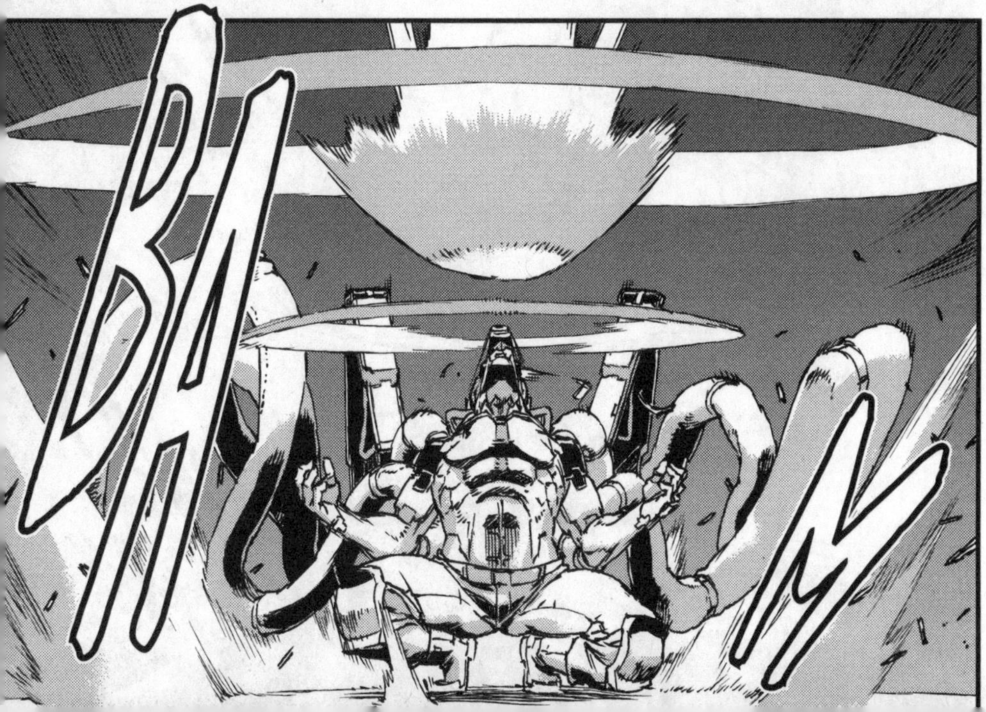
BAM

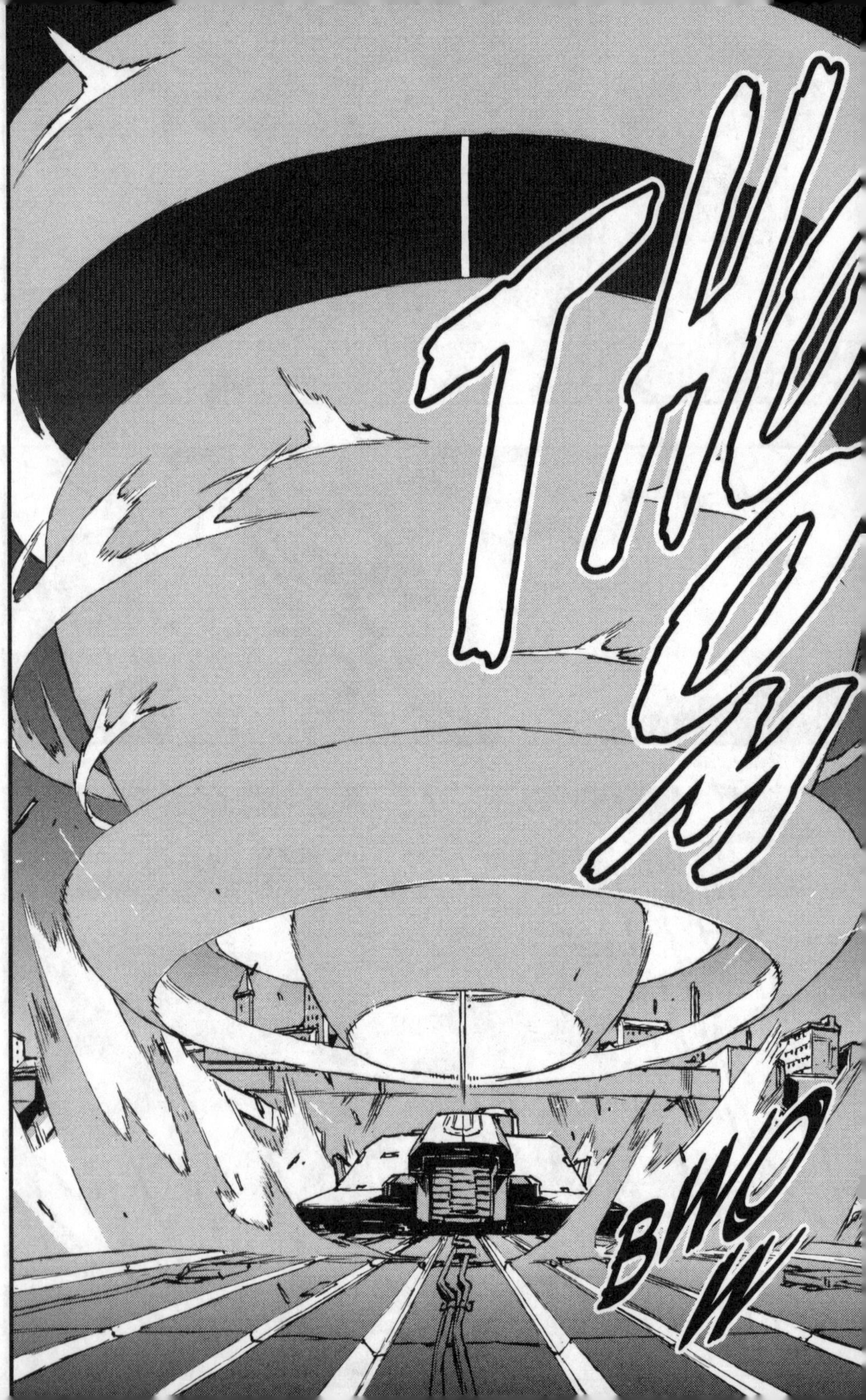
BWOOW

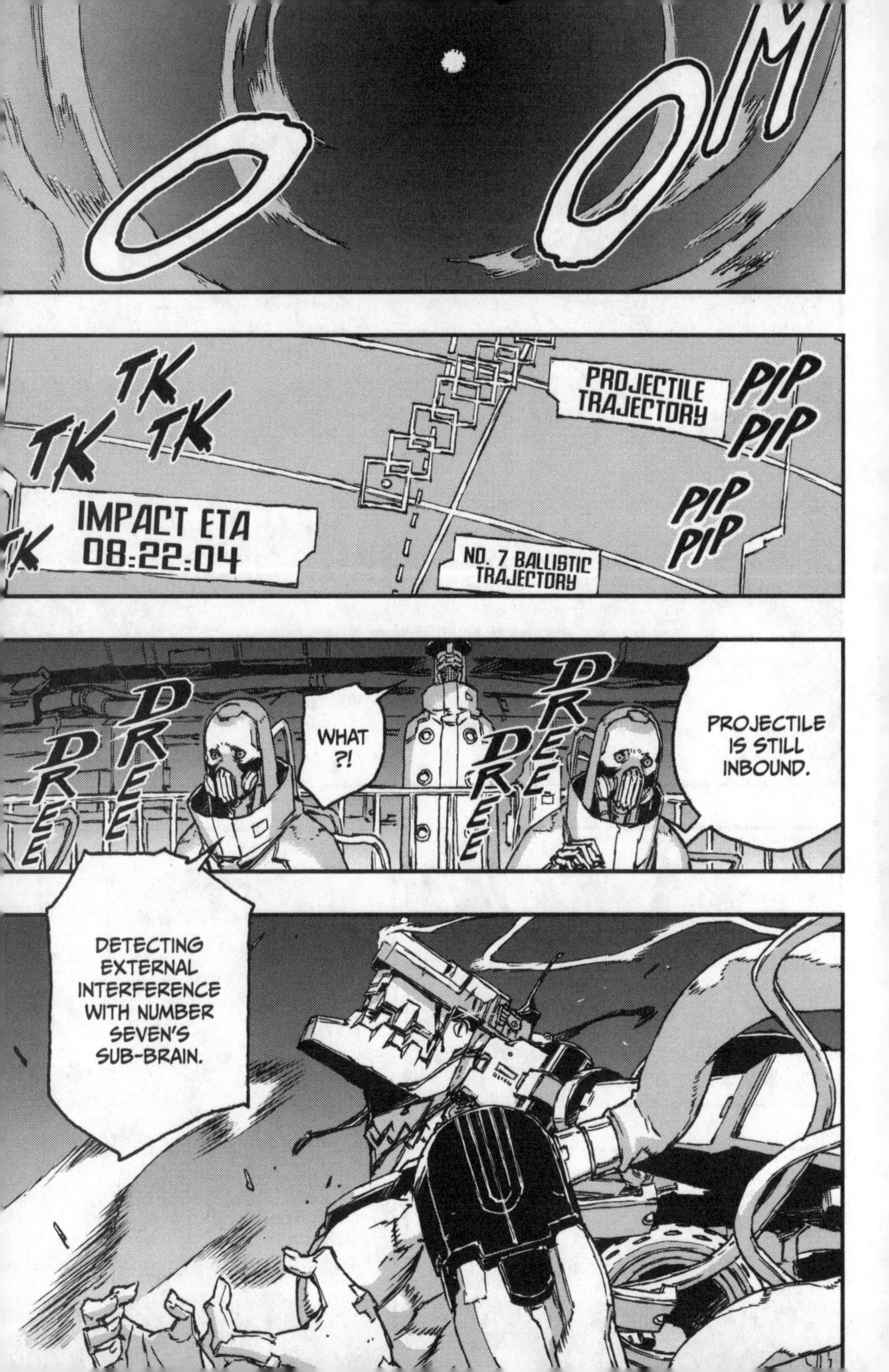
OOM
PROJECTILE TRAJECTORY
PIP PIP
PIP PIP
TK TK TK
TK
NO. 7 BALLISTIC TRAJECTORY
IMPACT ETA 08:22:04
PROJECTILE IS STILL INBOUND.
DREEE
DREEE
WHAT ?!
DREEE
DREEE
DETECTING EXTERNAL INTERFERENCE WITH NUMBER SEVEN'S SUB-BRAIN.

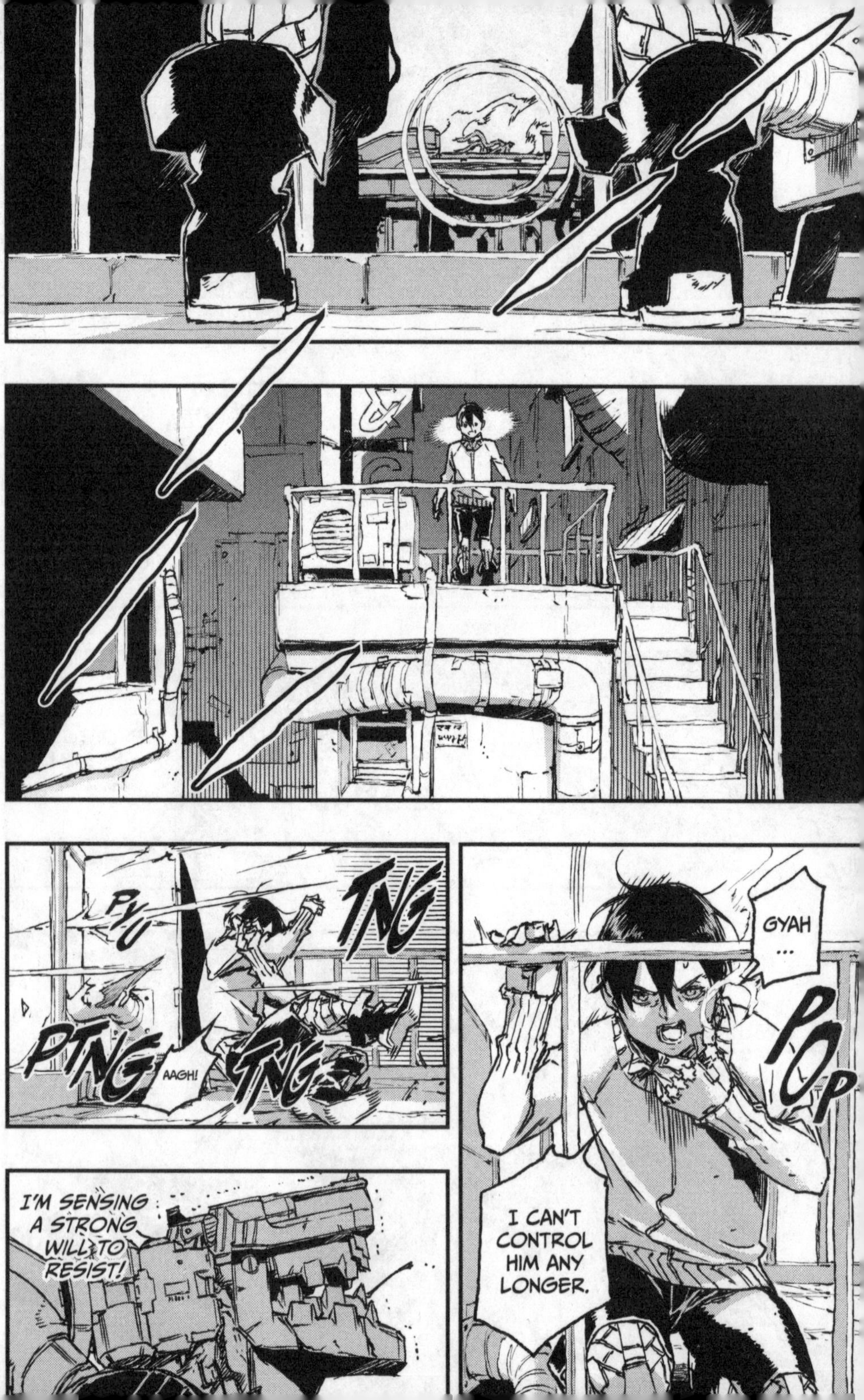
GYAH ...
POP
I CAN'T CONTROL HIM ANY LONGER.
PYU
TNG
PTNG
AAGH!
TNG
I'M SENSING A STRONG WILL TO RESIST!

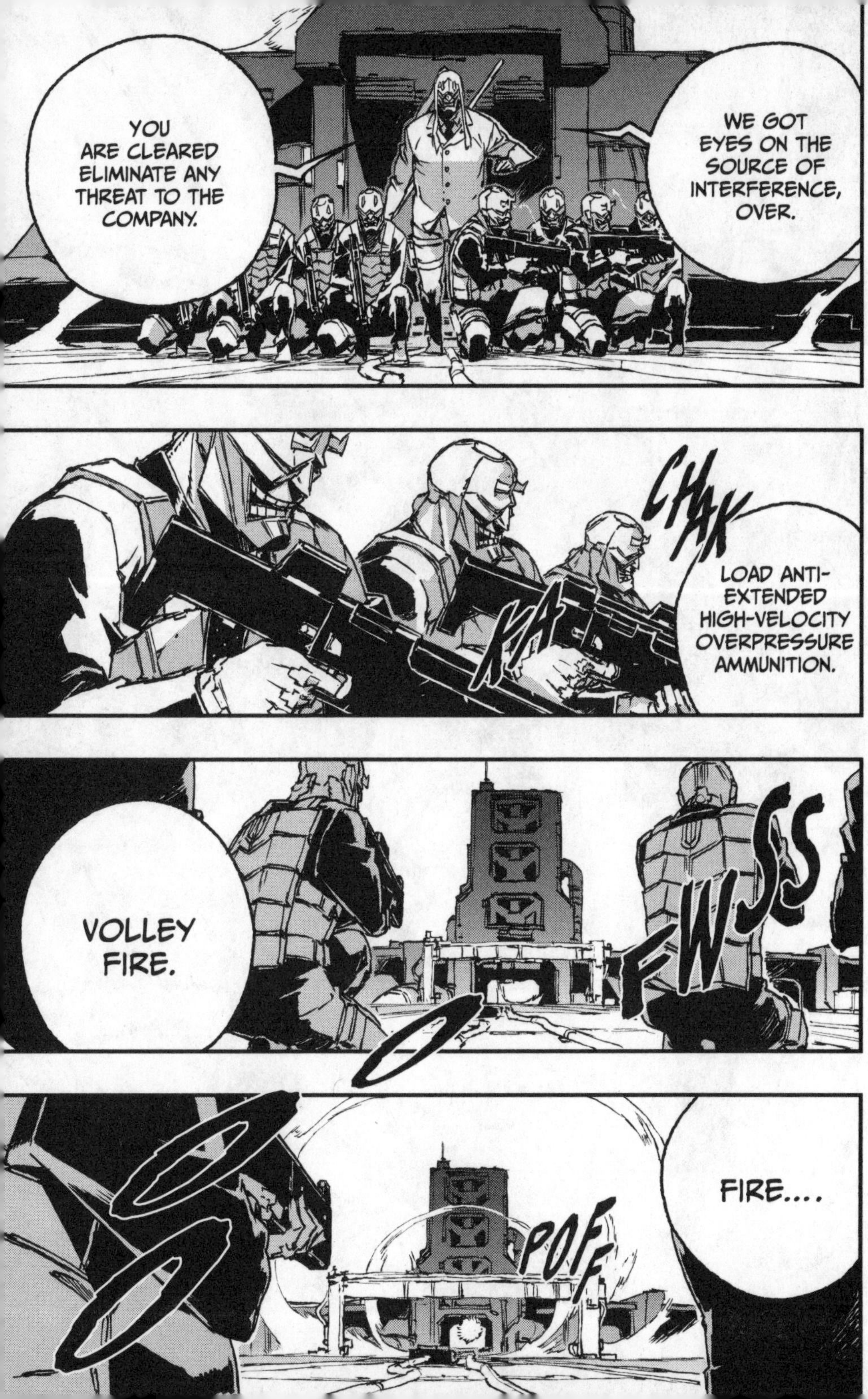
WE GOT EYES ON THE SOURCE OF INTERFERENCE, OVER.
YOU ARE CLEARED ELIMINATE ANY THREAT TO THE COMPANY.
CHAK
LOAD ANTI-EXTENDED HIGH-VELOCITY OVERPRESSURE AMMUNITION.
KA
FWSS
VOLLEY FIRE.
FIRE....
POFF

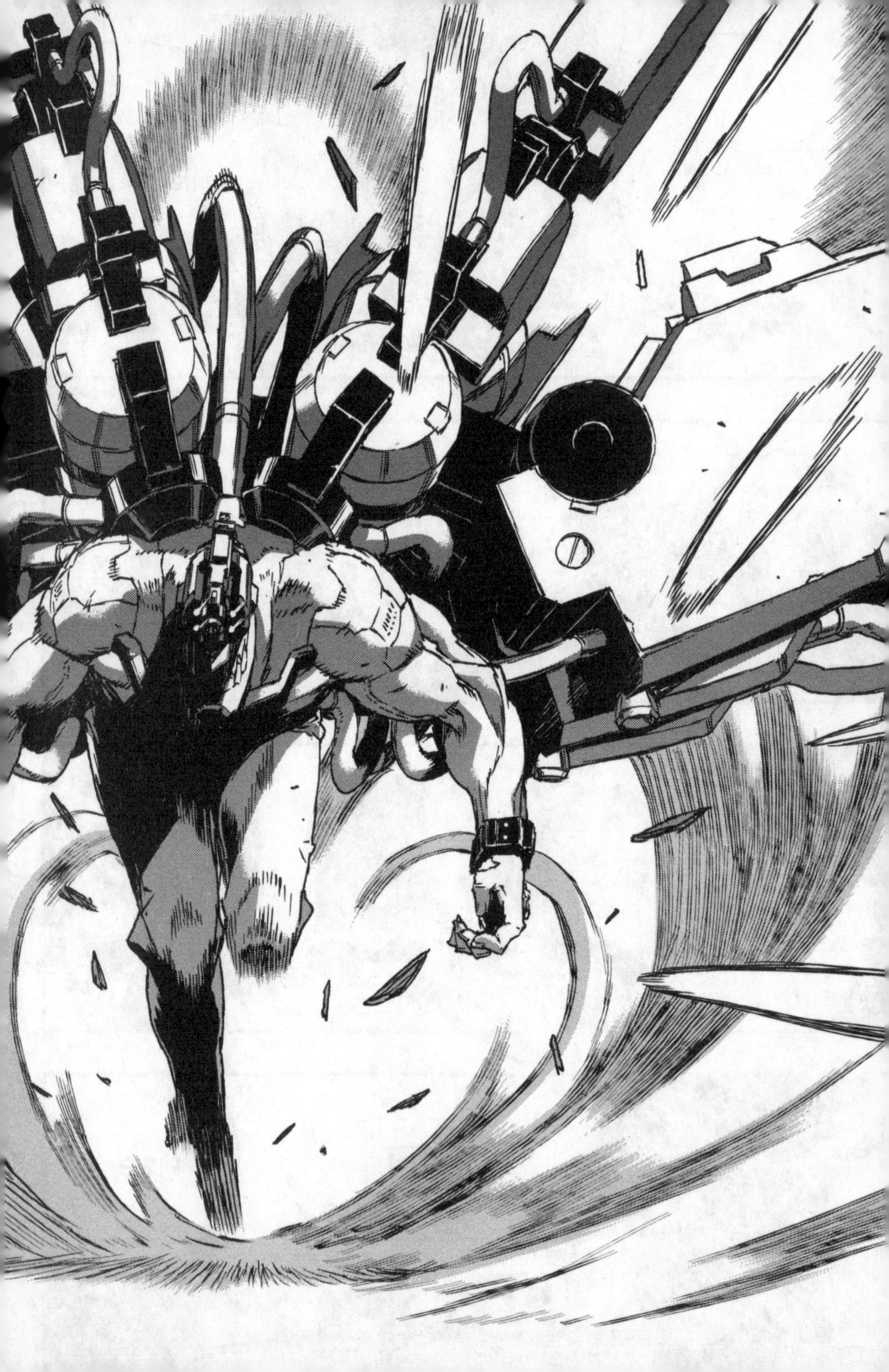

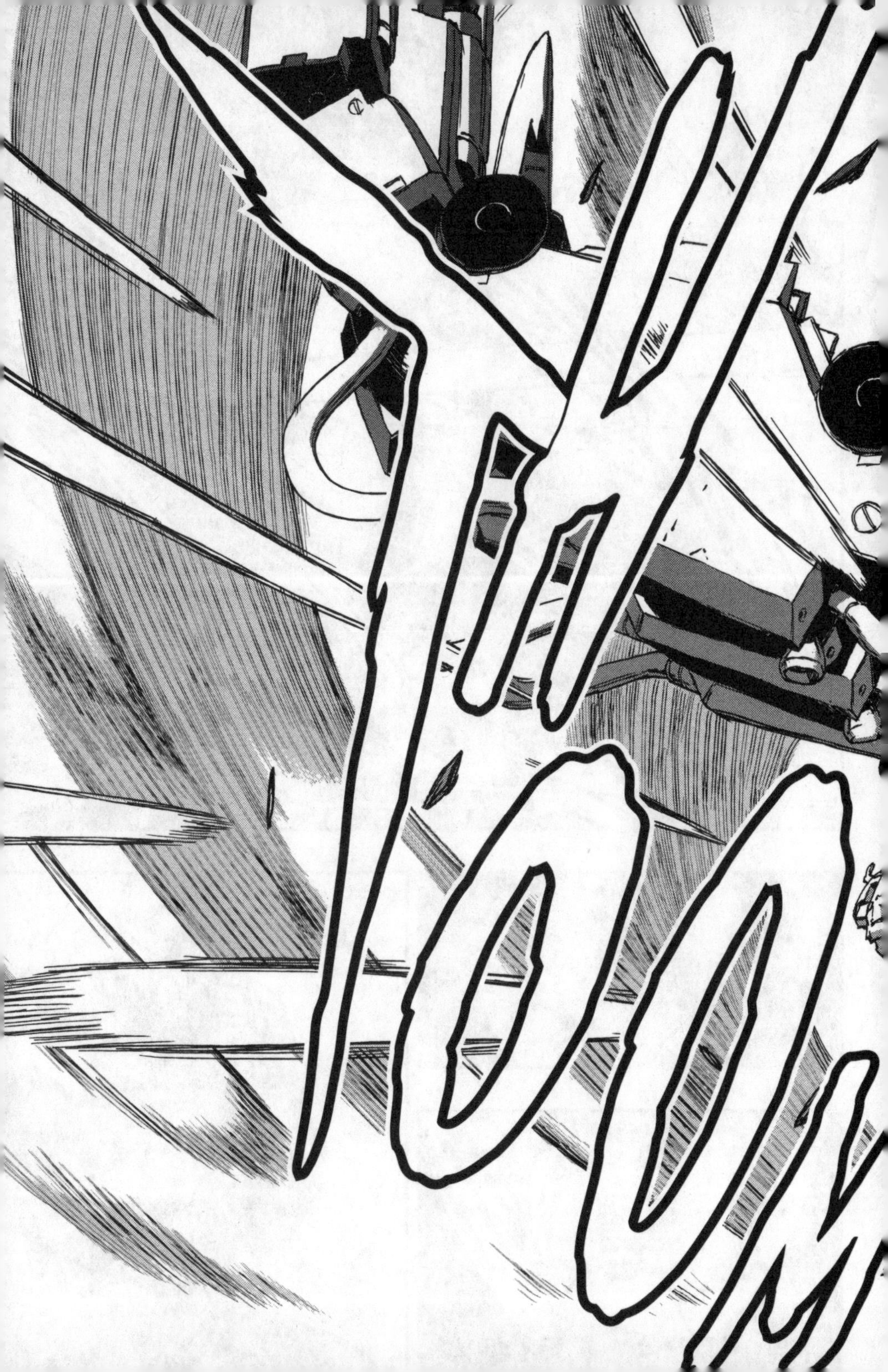

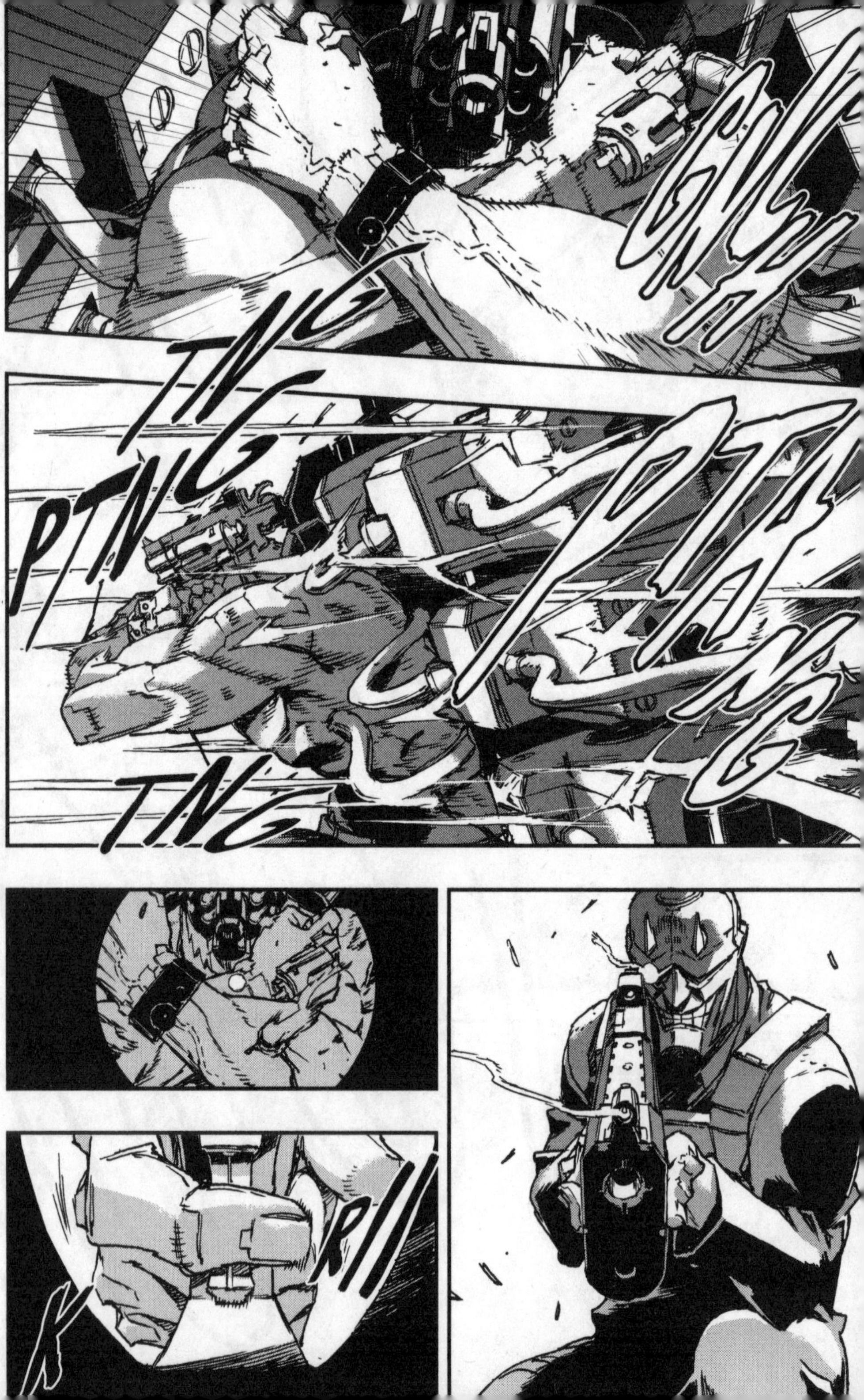
TING
PTING
TING

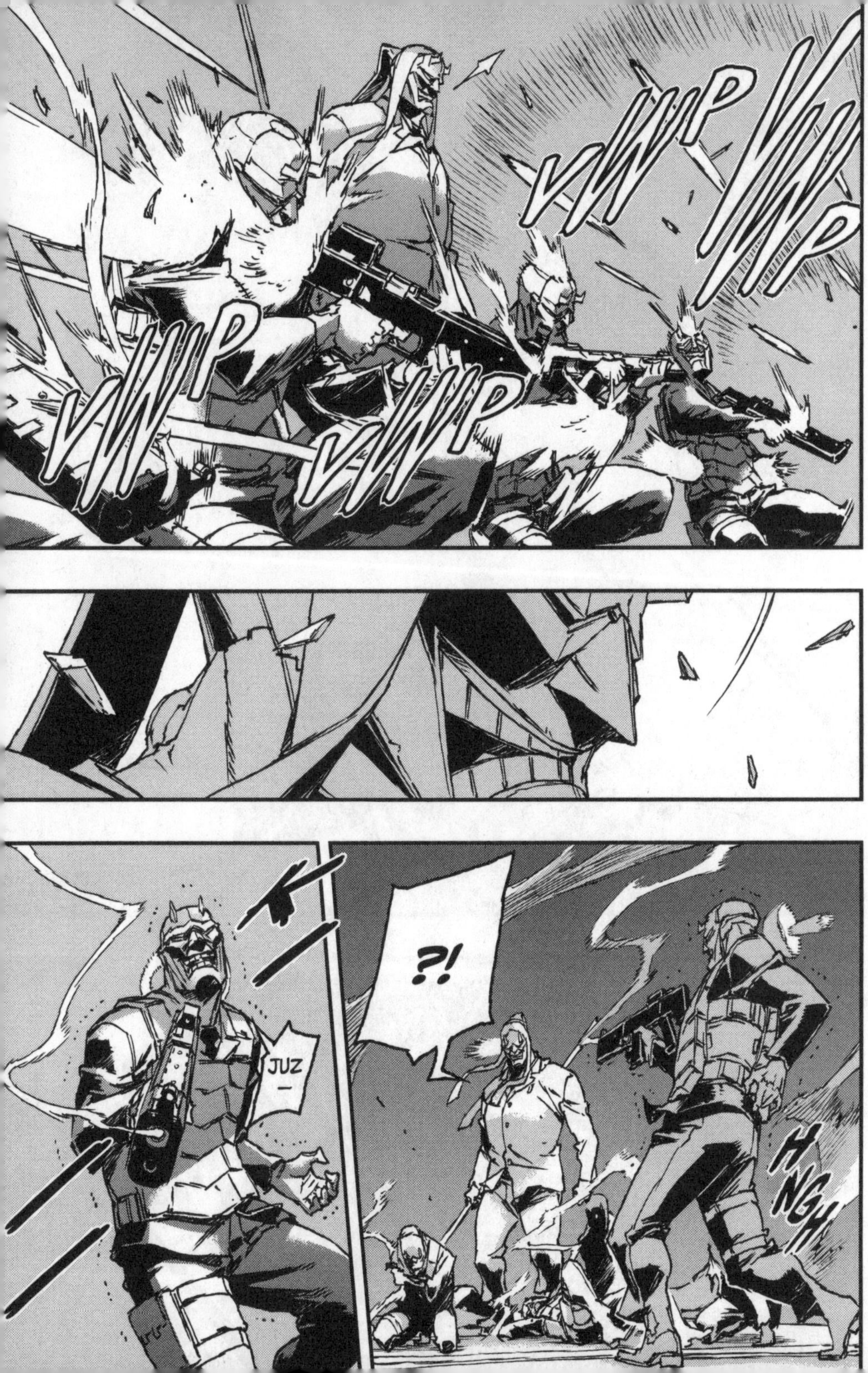
VWHIP
VWHIP
VWHIP
VWHIP
?!
HNGH
JUZ—

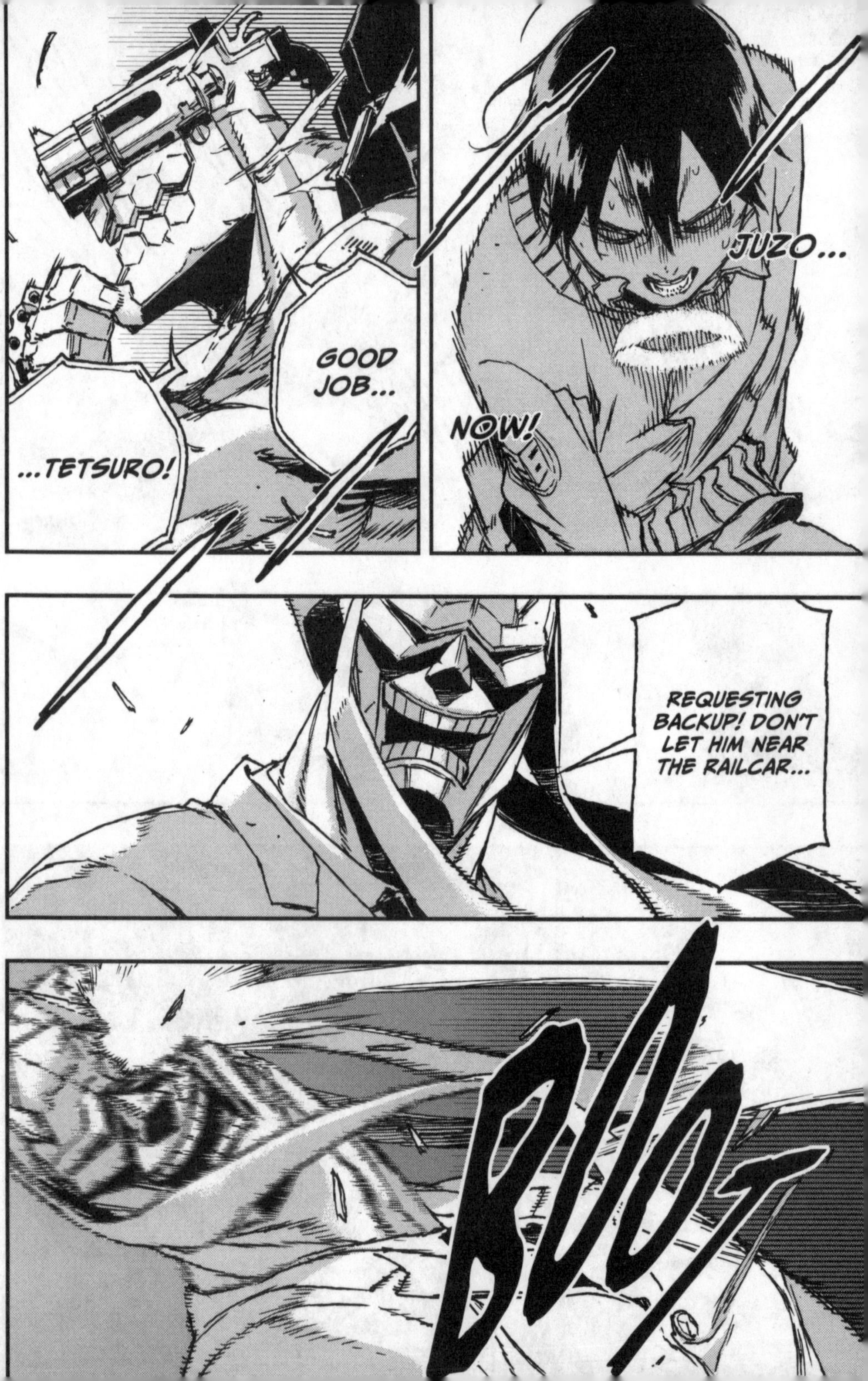
JUZO...
NOW!
GOOD JOB...
...TETSURO!
REQUESTING BACKUP! DON'T LET HIM NEAR THE RAILCAR...

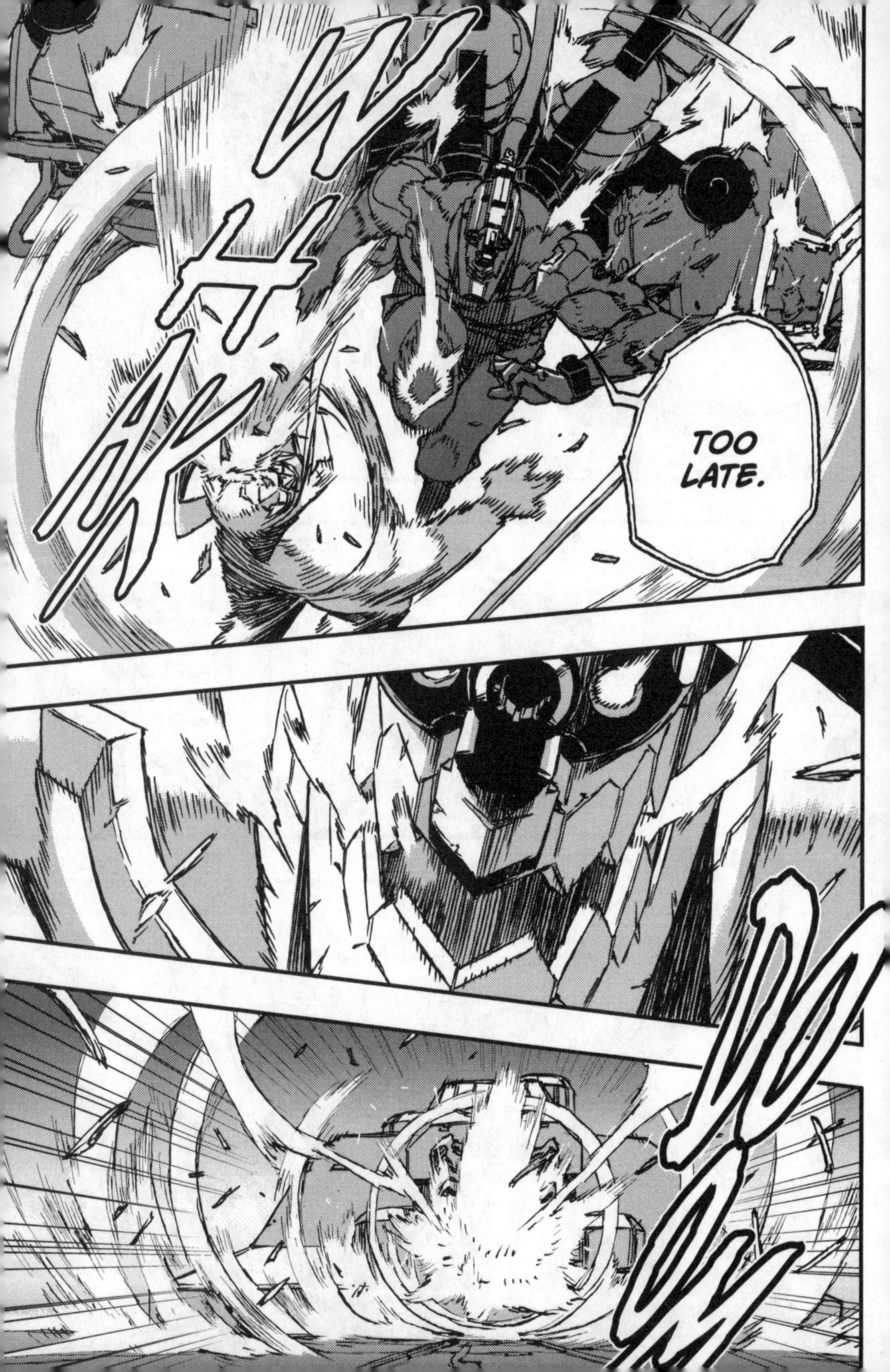
TOO LATE.

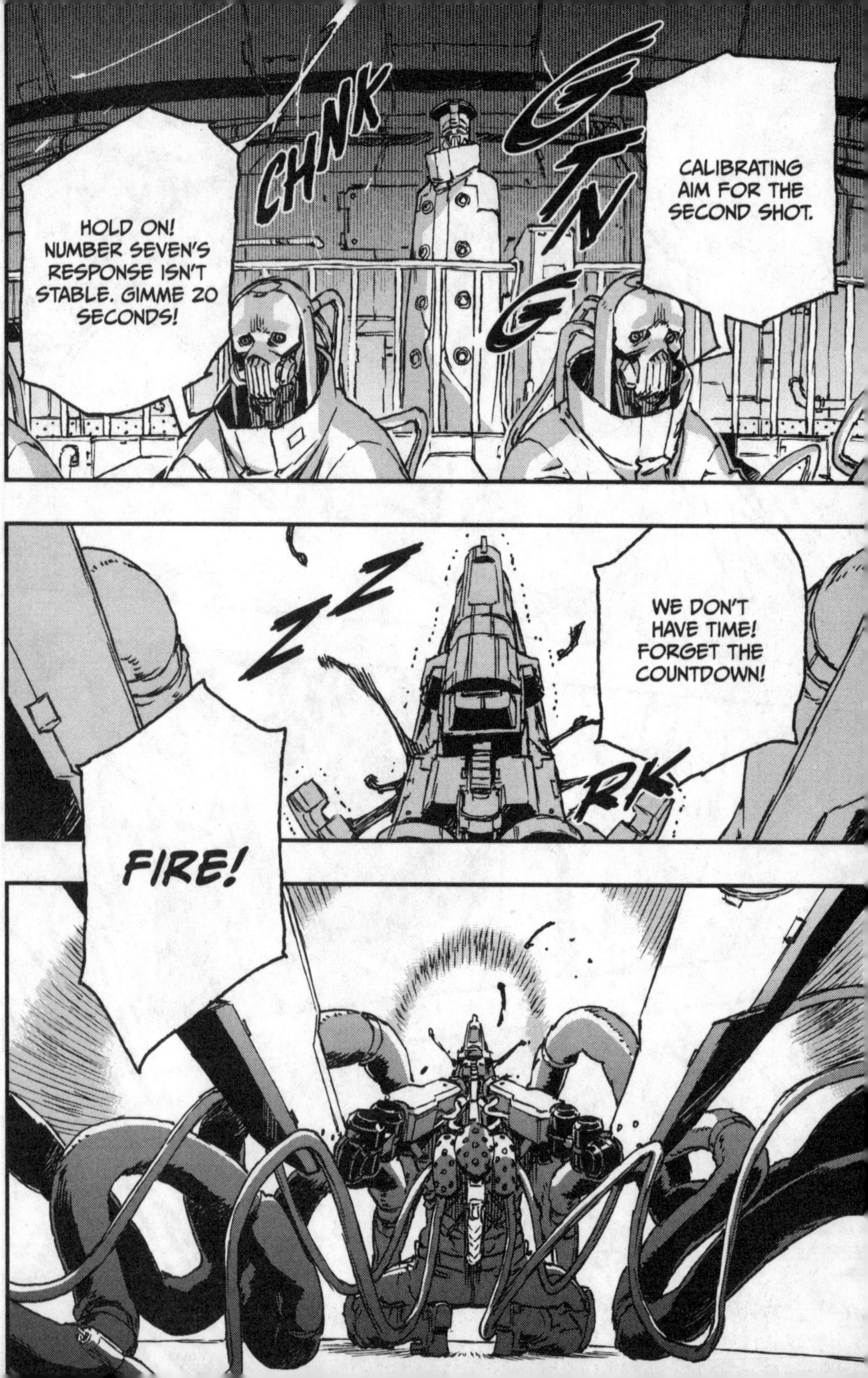

CALIBRATING AIM FOR THE SECOND SHOT.
GTNG
CHNK
HOLD ON! NUMBER SEVEN'S RESPONSE ISN'T STABLE. GIMME 20 SECONDS!
WE DON'T HAVE TIME! FORGET THE COUNTDOWN!
RK
ZZ
FIRE!

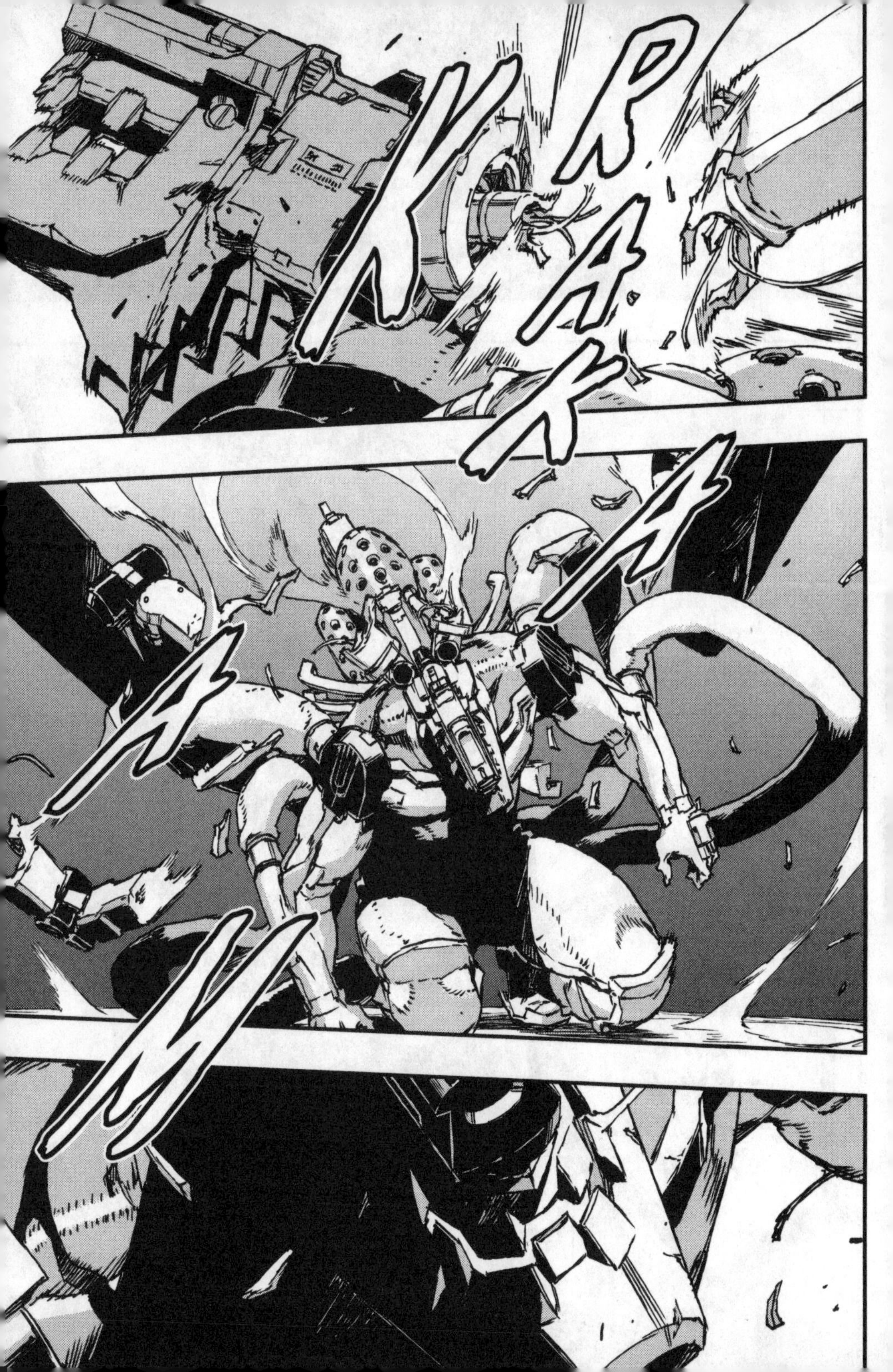

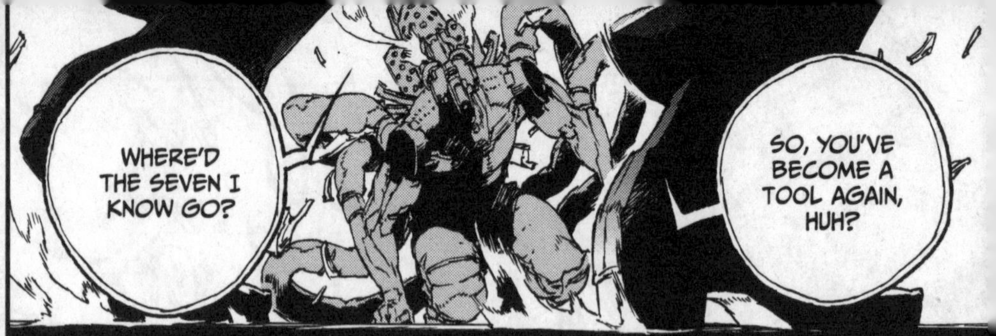
SO, YOU'VE BECOME A TOOL AGAIN, HUH?
WHERE'D THE SEVEN I KNOW GO?

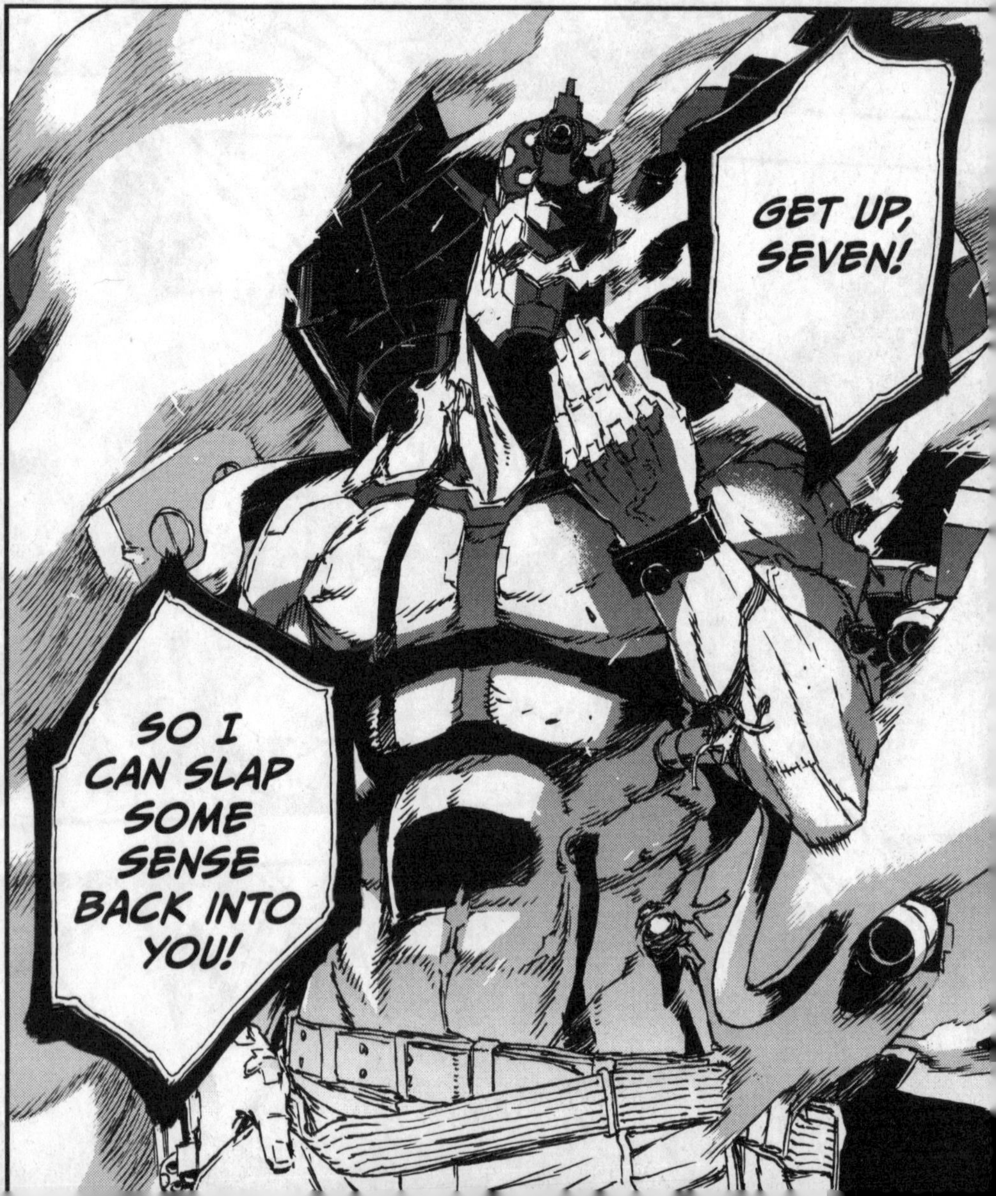
GET UP, SEVEN!
SO I CAN SLAP SOME SENSE BACK INTO YOU!

NO
GUNS
LIFE

The gunsmoke drifts, the muzzle talks

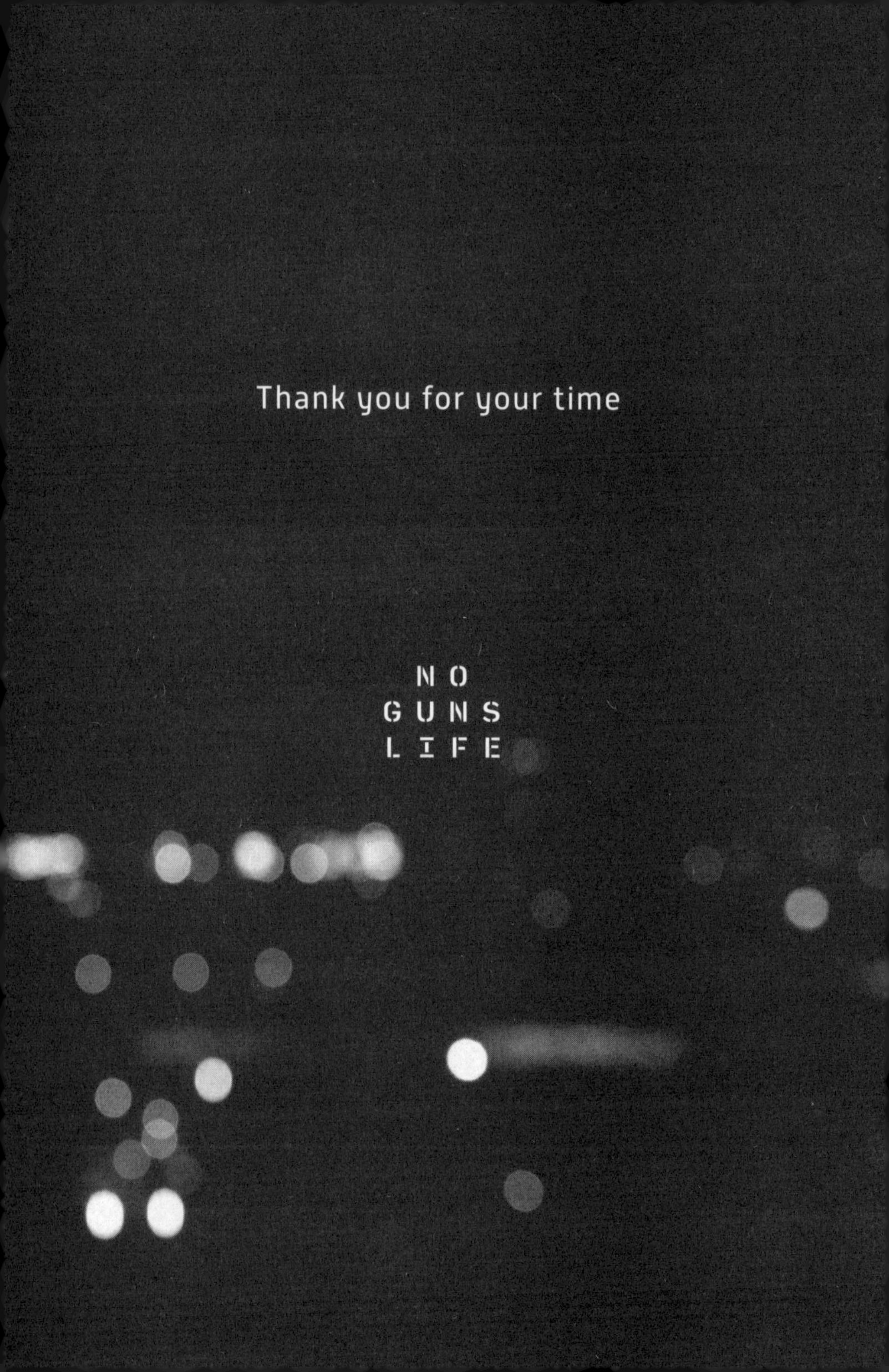
Thank you for your time
NO GUNS LIFE

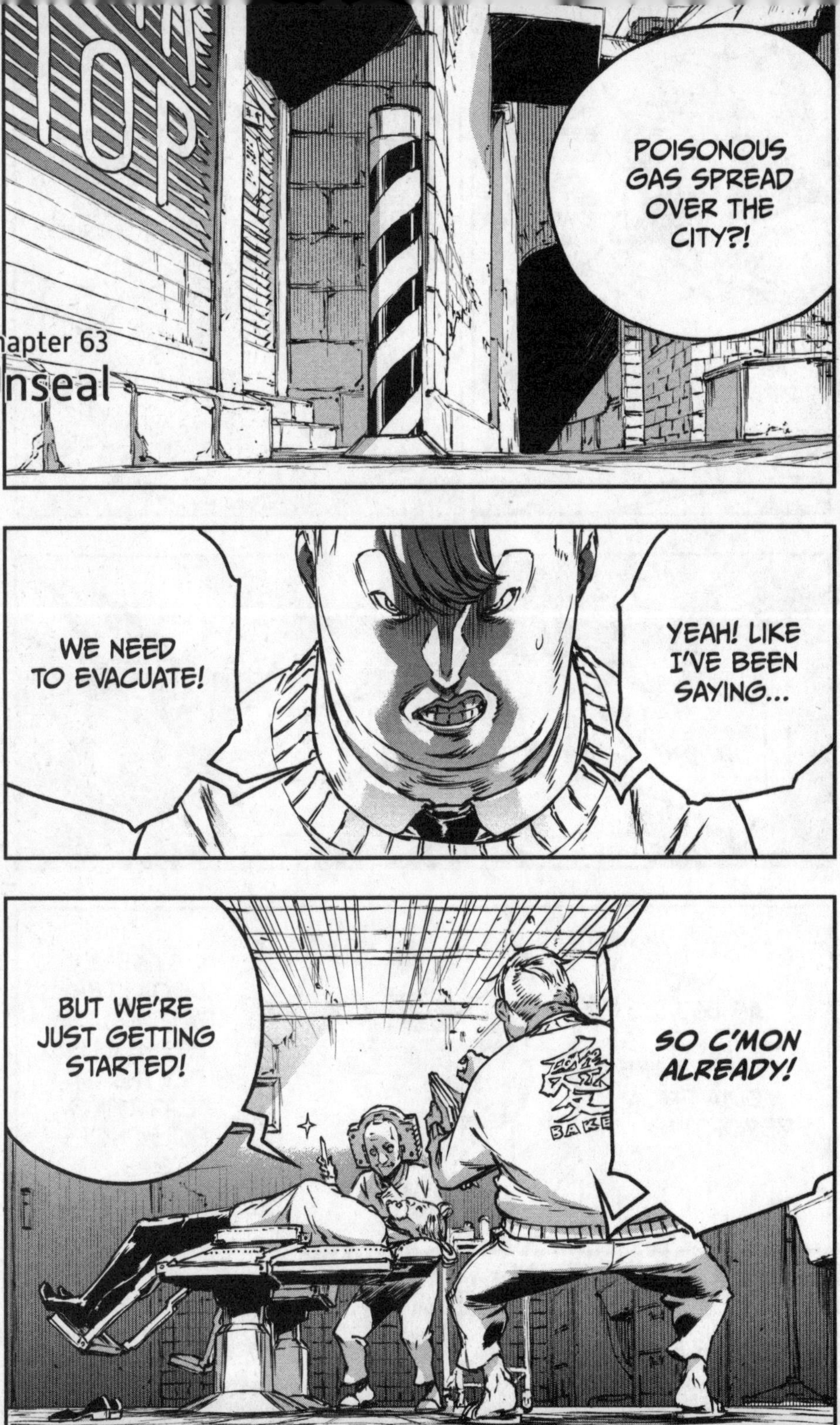
POISONOUS GAS SPREAD OVER THE CITY?!
Chapter 63
Unseal
YEAH! LIKE I'VE BEEN SAYING...
WE NEED TO EVACUATE!
SO C'MON ALREADY!
BUT WE'RE JUST GETTING STARTED!

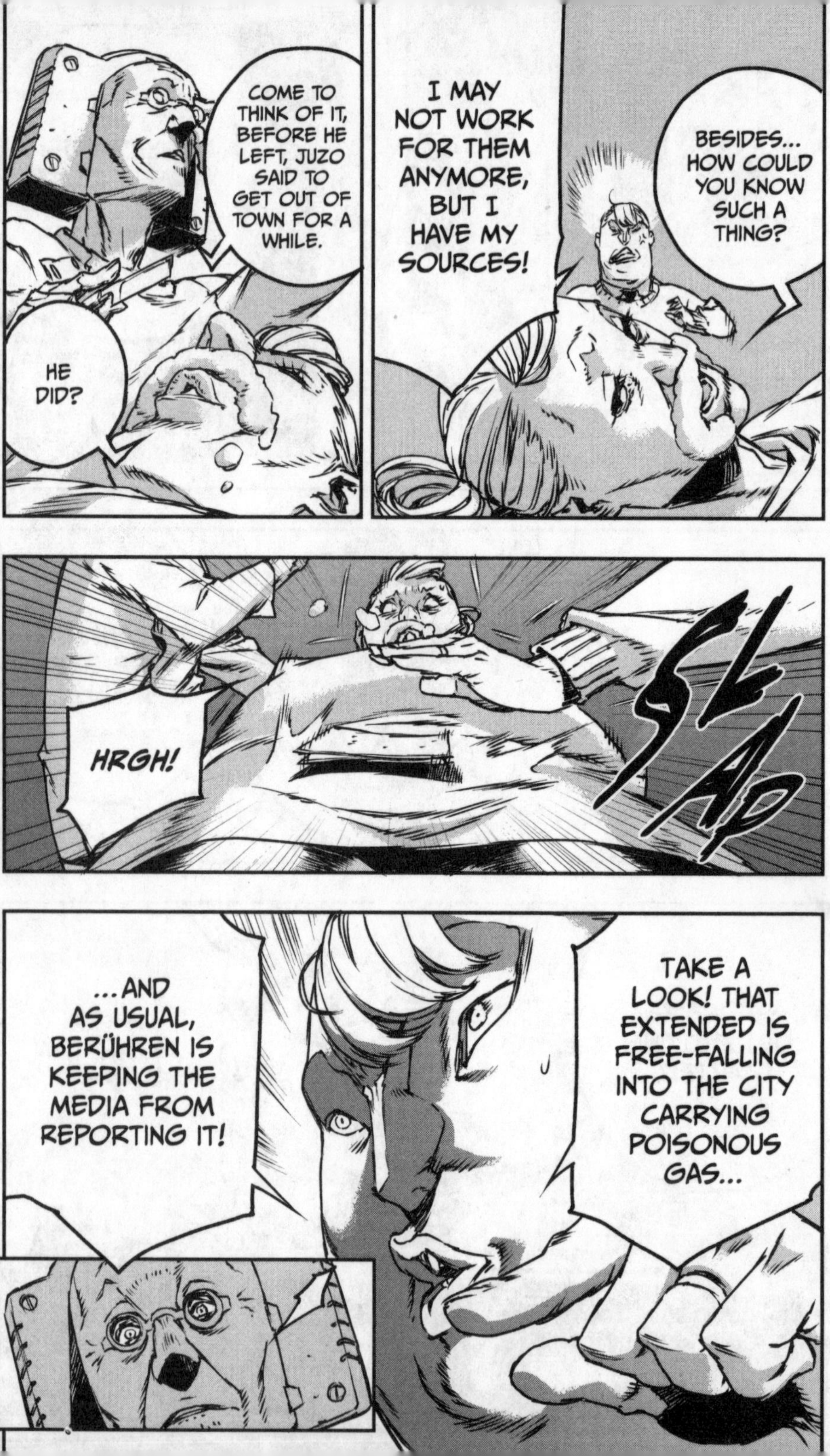

BESIDES... HOW COULD YOU KNOW SUCH A THING?
I MAY NOT WORK FOR THEM ANYMORE, BUT I HAVE MY SOURCES!
COME TO THINK OF IT, BEFORE HE LEFT, JUZO SAID TO GET OUT OF TOWN FOR A WHILE.
HE DID?
SLAP
HRGH!
TAKE A LOOK! THAT EXTENDED IS FREE-FALLING INTO THE CITY CARRYING POISONOUS GAS...
...AND AS USUAL, BERÜHREN IS KEEPING THE MEDIA FROM REPORTING IT!

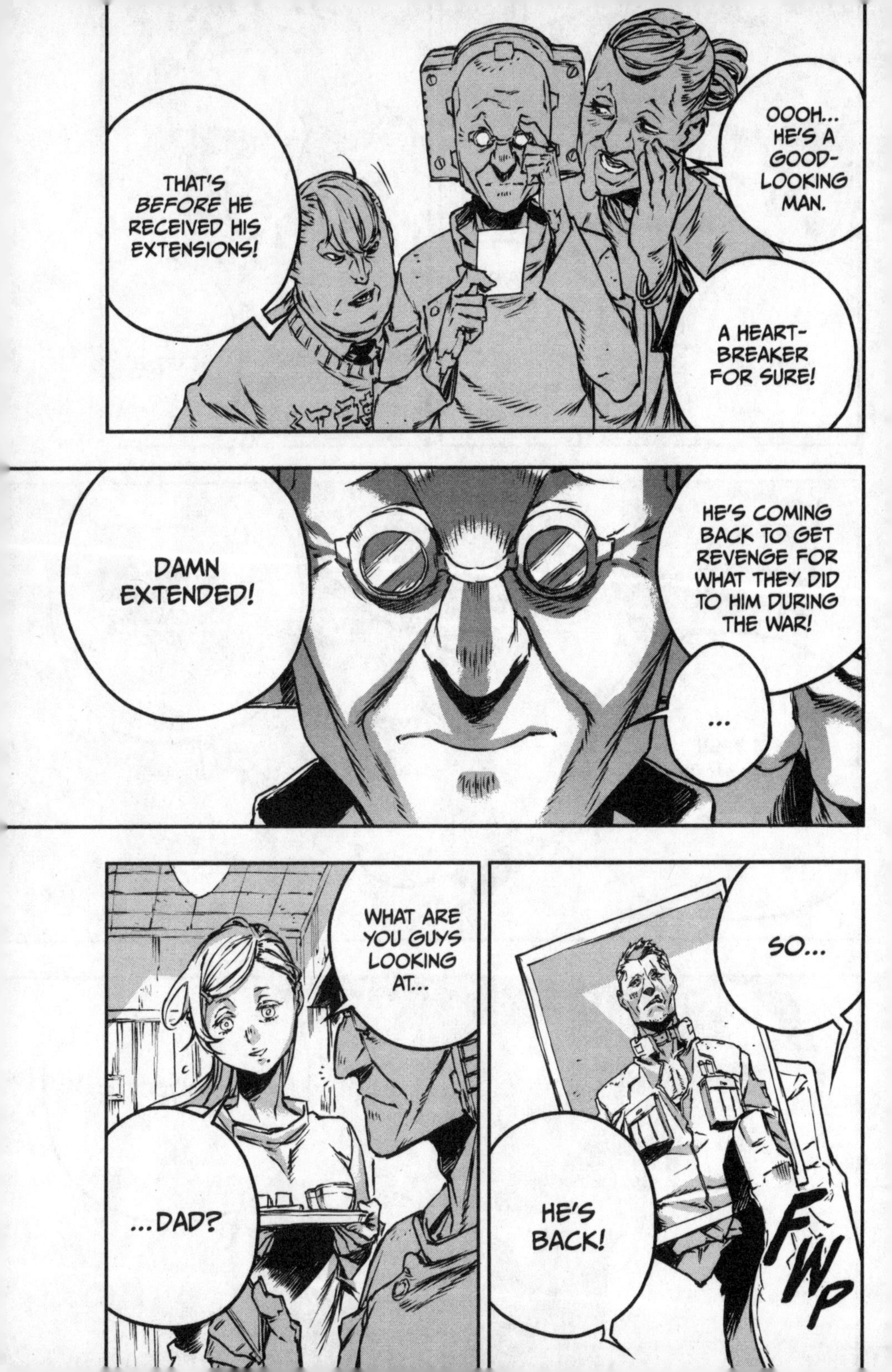
OOOH... HE'S A GOOD-LOOKING MAN.
A HEART-BREAKER FOR SURE!
THAT'S *BEFORE* HE RECEIVED HIS EXTENSIONS!
HE'S COMING BACK TO GET REVENGE FOR WHAT THEY DID TO HIM DURING THE WAR!
DAMN EXTENDED!
...
SO...
HE'S BACK!
FWP
WHAT ARE YOU GUYS LOOKING AT...
...DAD?

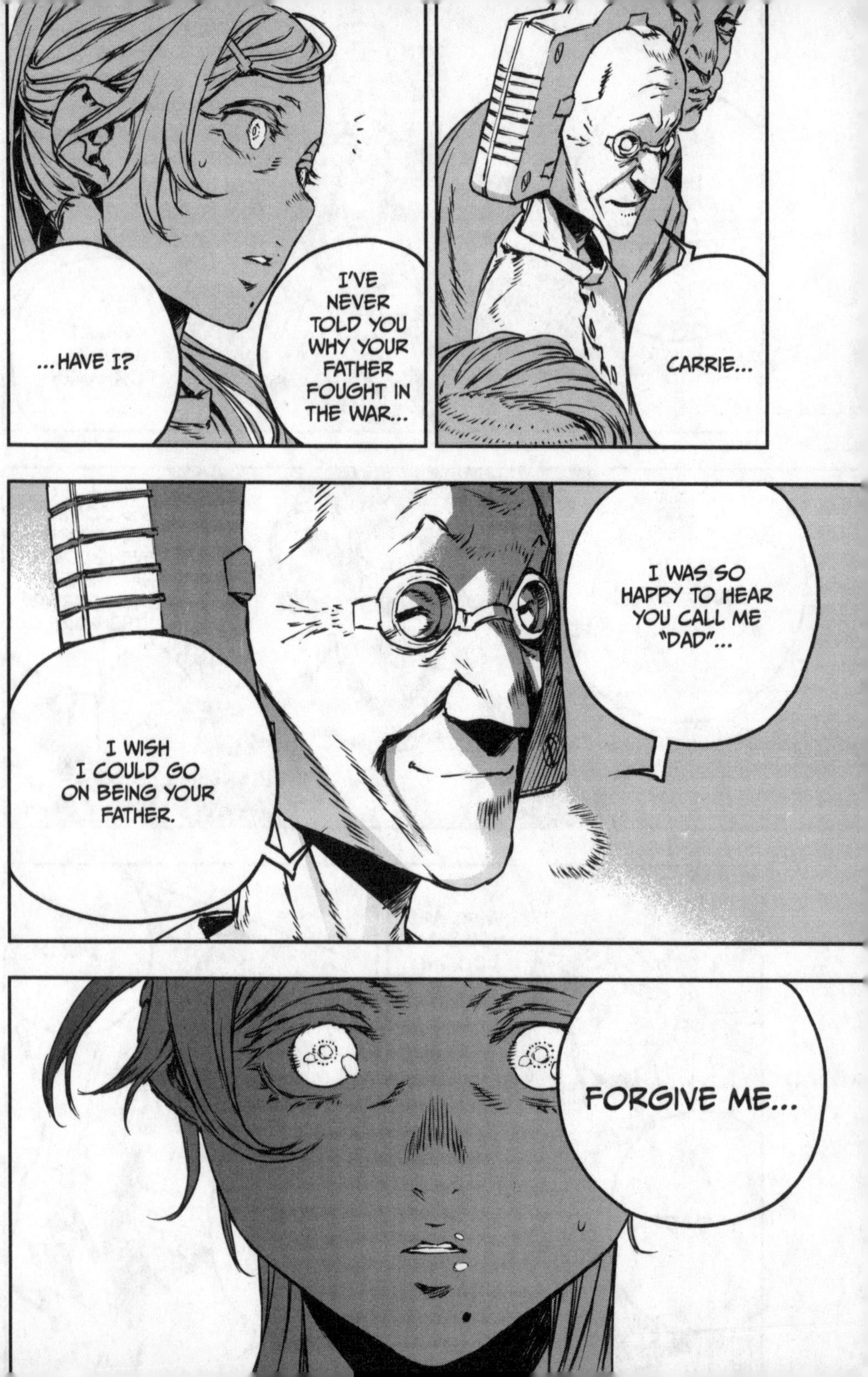
CARRIE...
I'VE NEVER TOLD YOU WHY YOUR FATHER FOUGHT IN THE WAR...
...HAVE I?
I WAS SO HAPPY TO HEAR YOU CALL ME "DAD"...
I WISH I COULD GO ON BEING YOUR FATHER.
FORGIVE ME...

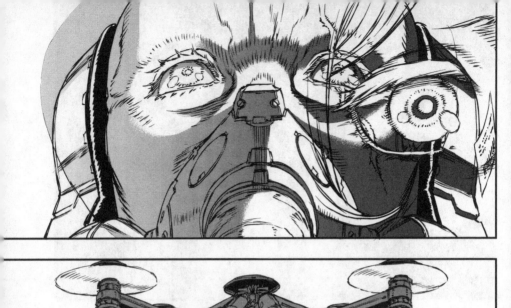

IT SEEMS NUMBER SEVEN IS BEYOND OUR CONTROL!

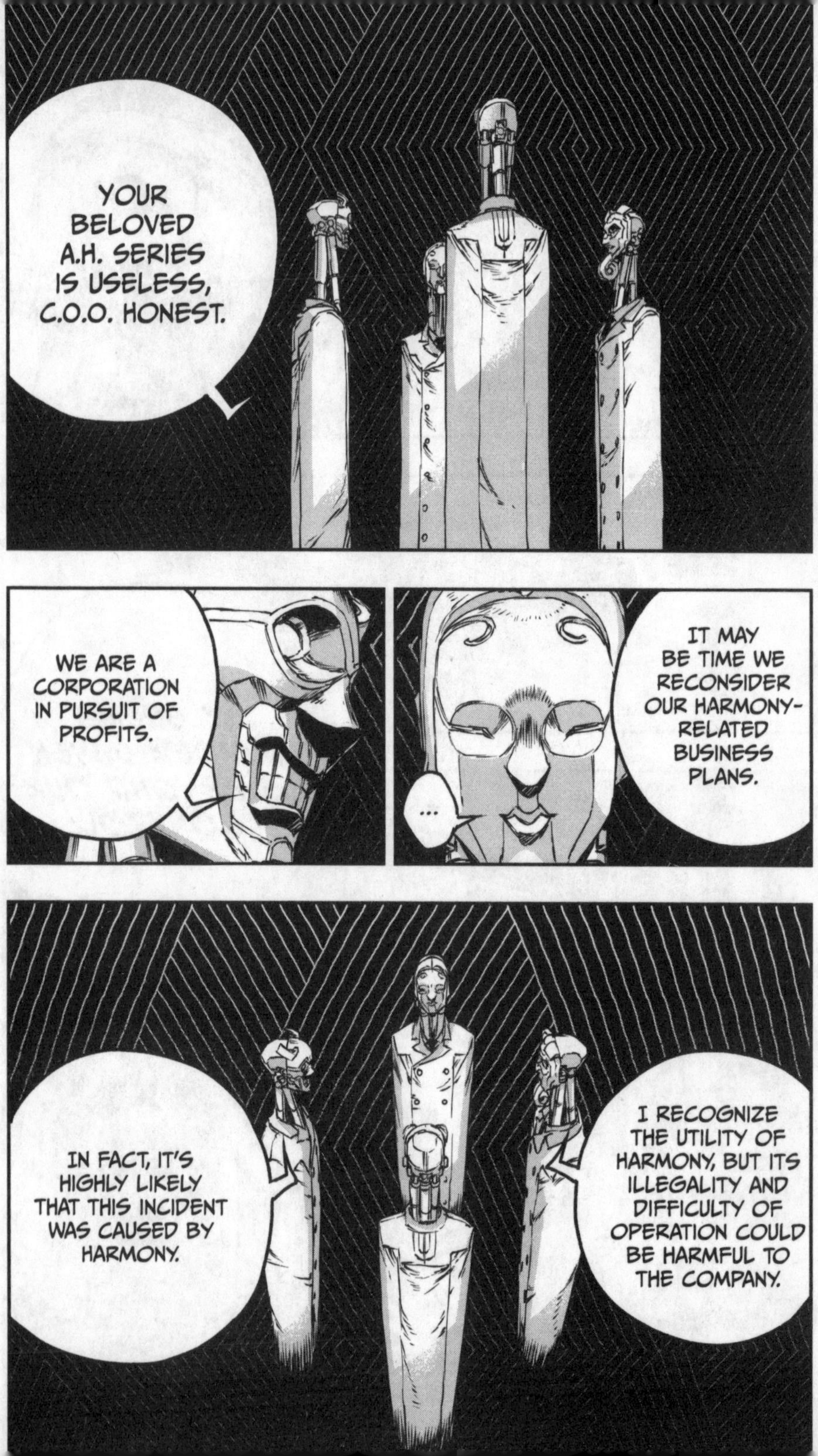
YOUR BELOVED A.H. SERIES IS USELESS, C.O.O. HONEST.
IT MAY BE TIME WE RECONSIDER OUR HARMONY-RELATED BUSINESS PLANS.
...
WE ARE A CORPORATION IN PURSUIT OF PROFITS.
I RECOGNIZE THE UTILITY OF HARMONY, BUT ITS ILLEGALITY AND DIFFICULTY OF OPERATION COULD BE HARMFUL TO THE COMPANY.
IN FACT, IT'S HIGHLY LIKELY THAT THIS INCIDENT WAS CAUSED BY HARMONY.

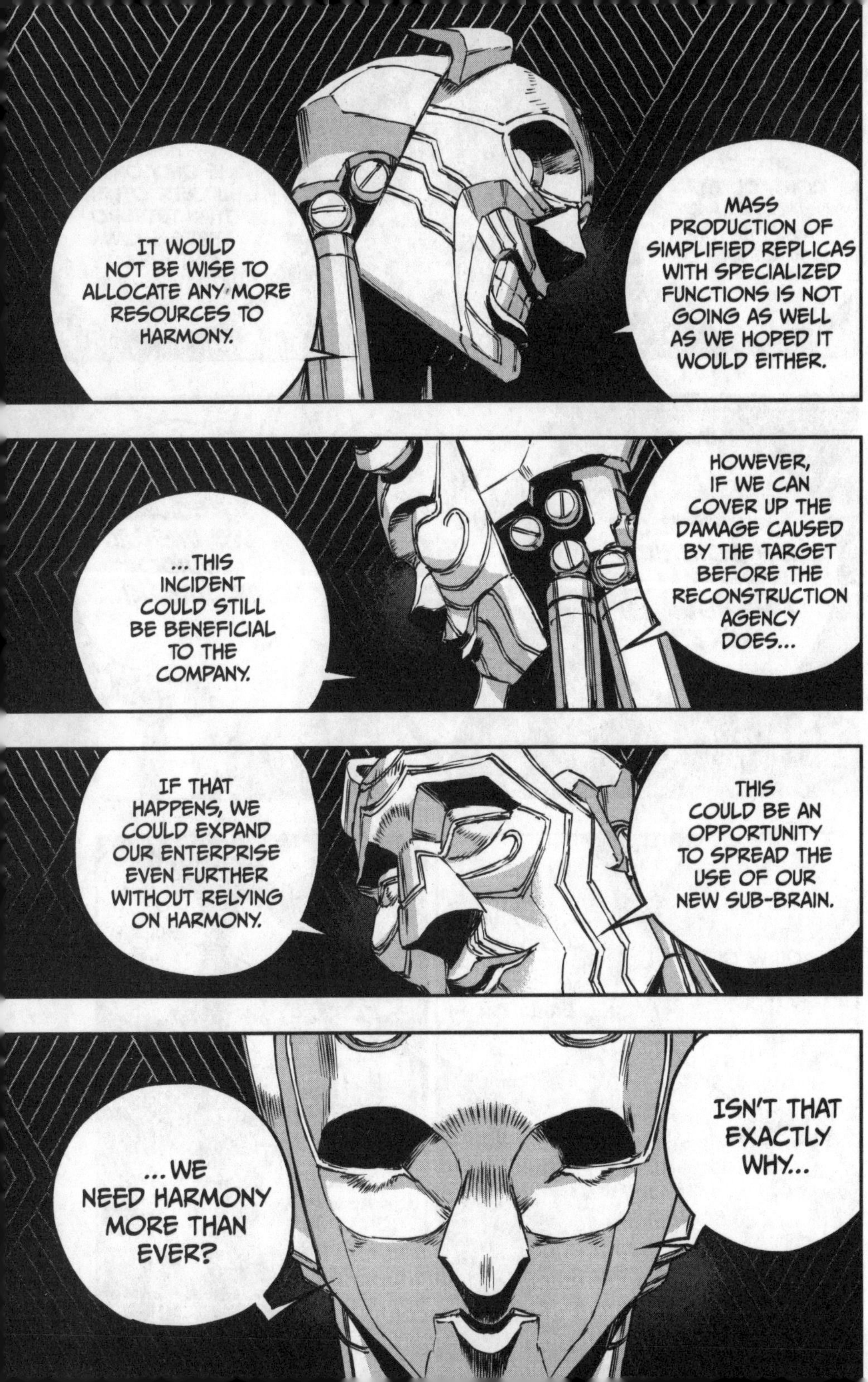
MASS PRODUCTION OF SIMPLIFIED REPLICAS WITH SPECIALIZED FUNCTIONS IS NOT GOING AS WELL AS WE HOPED IT WOULD EITHER.
IT WOULD NOT BE WISE TO ALLOCATE ANY MORE RESOURCES TO HARMONY.
HOWEVER, IF WE CAN COVER UP THE DAMAGE CAUSED BY THE TARGET BEFORE THE RECONSTRUCTION AGENCY DOES...
...THIS INCIDENT COULD STILL BE BENEFICIAL TO THE COMPANY.
THIS COULD BE AN OPPORTUNITY TO SPREAD THE USE OF OUR NEW SUB-BRAIN.
IF THAT HAPPENS, WE COULD EXPAND OUR ENTERPRISE EVEN FURTHER WITHOUT RELYING ON HARMONY.
ISN'T THAT EXACTLY WHY...
...WE NEED HARMONY MORE THAN EVER?

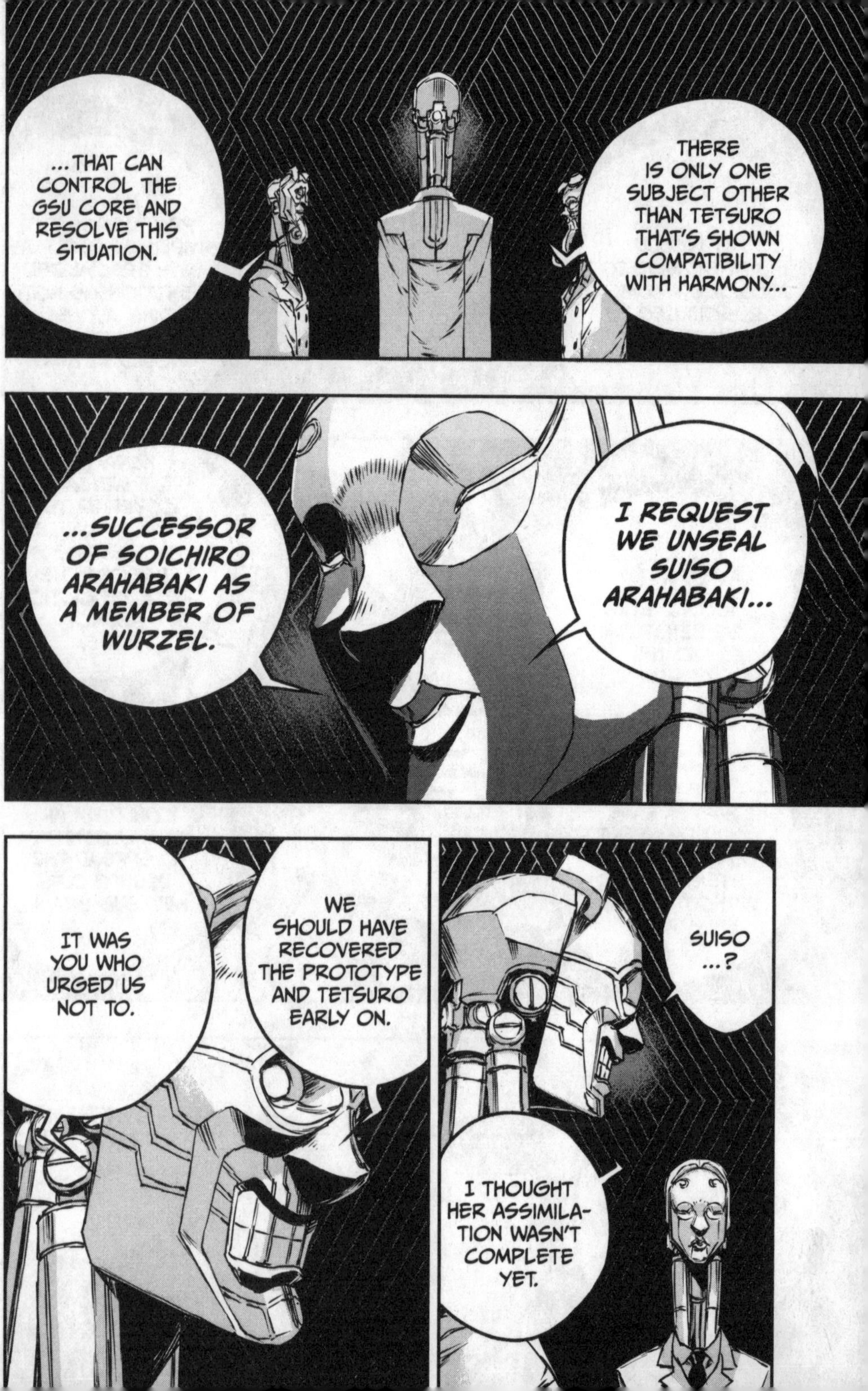
THERE IS ONLY ONE SUBJECT OTHER THAN TETSURO THAT'S SHOWN COMPATIBILITY WITH HARMONY...
...THAT CAN CONTROL THE GSU CORE AND RESOLVE THIS SITUATION.
I REQUEST WE UNSEAL SUISO ARAHABAKI...
...SUCCESSOR OF SOICHIRO ARAHABAKI AS A MEMBER OF WURZEL.
SUISO ...?
I THOUGHT HER ASSIMILATION WASN'T COMPLETE YET.
WE SHOULD HAVE RECOVERED THE PROTOTYPE AND TETSURO EARLY ON.
IT WAS YOU WHO URGED US NOT TO.

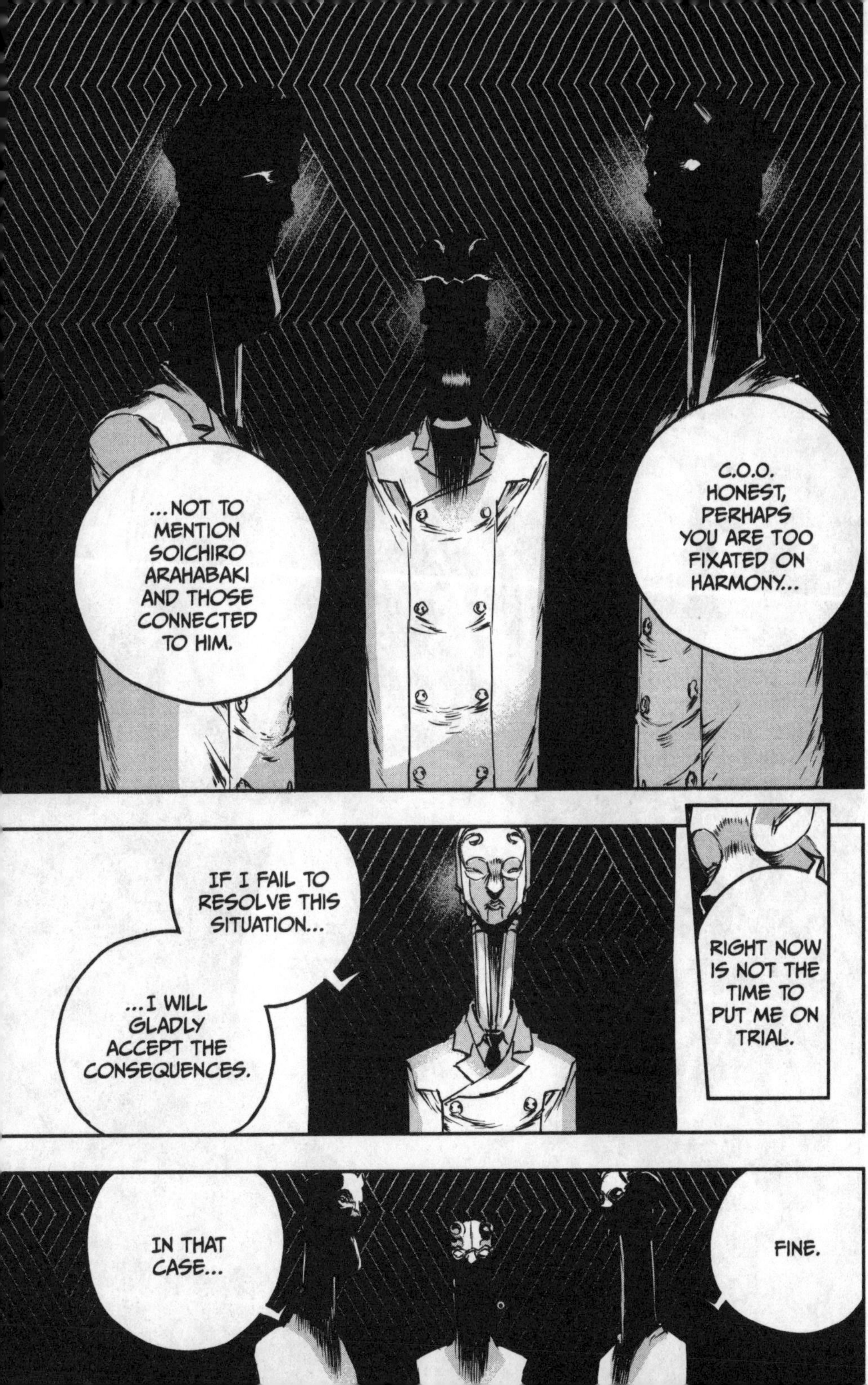
C.O.O. HONEST, PERHAPS YOU ARE TOO FIXATED ON HARMONY...
...NOT TO MENTION SOICHIRO ARAHABAKI AND THOSE CONNECTED TO HIM.
RIGHT NOW IS NOT THE TIME TO PUT ME ON TRIAL.
IF I FAIL TO RESOLVE THIS SITUATION...
...I WILL GLADLY ACCEPT THE CONSEQUENCES.
FINE.
IN THAT CASE...

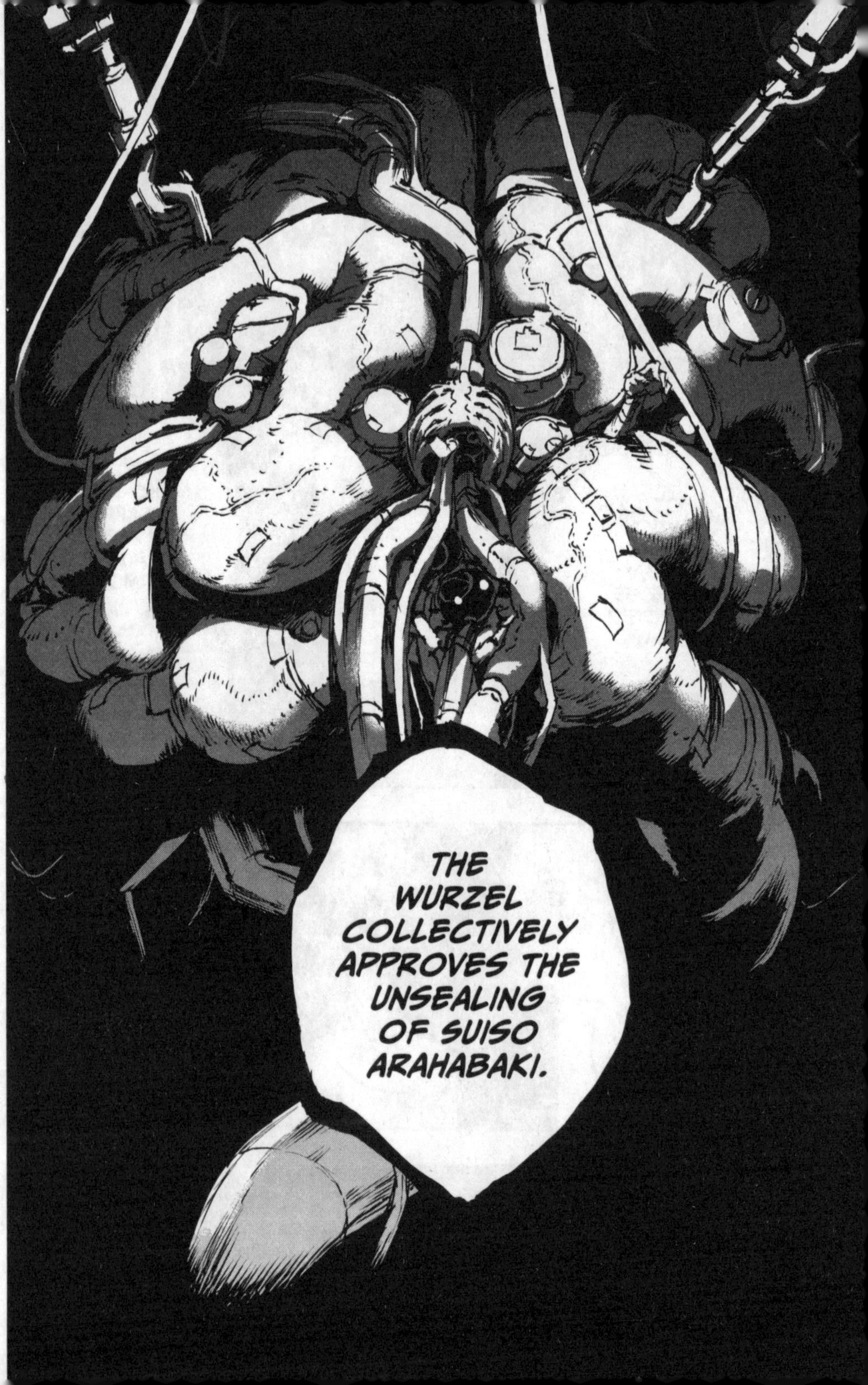
THE WURZEL COLLECTIVELY APPROVES THE UNSEALING OF SUISO ARAHABAKI.

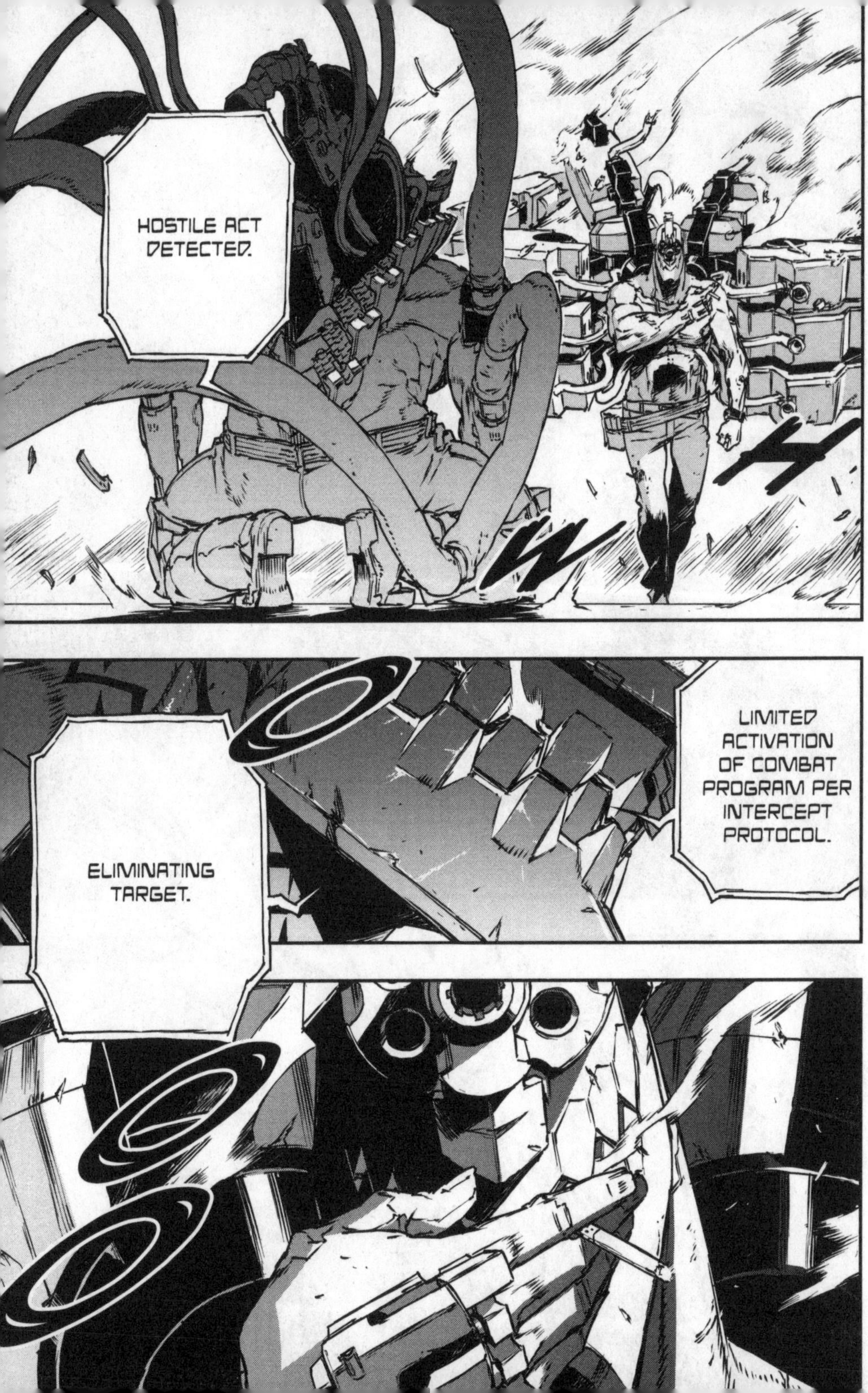
HOSTILE ACT DETECTED.
LIMITED ACTIVATION OF COMBAT PROGRAM PER INTERCEPT PROTOCOL.
ELIMINATING TARGET.

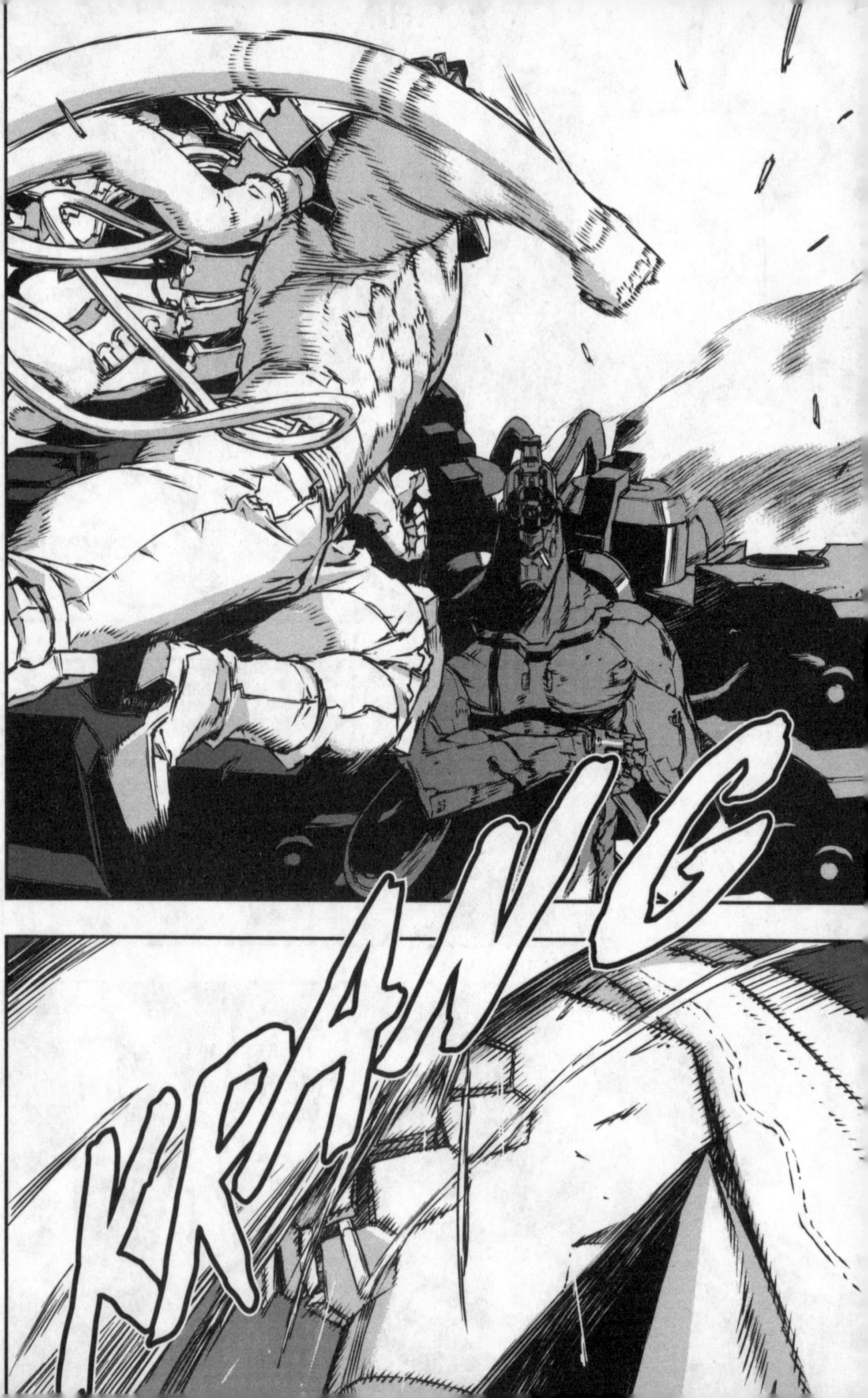
KRANG

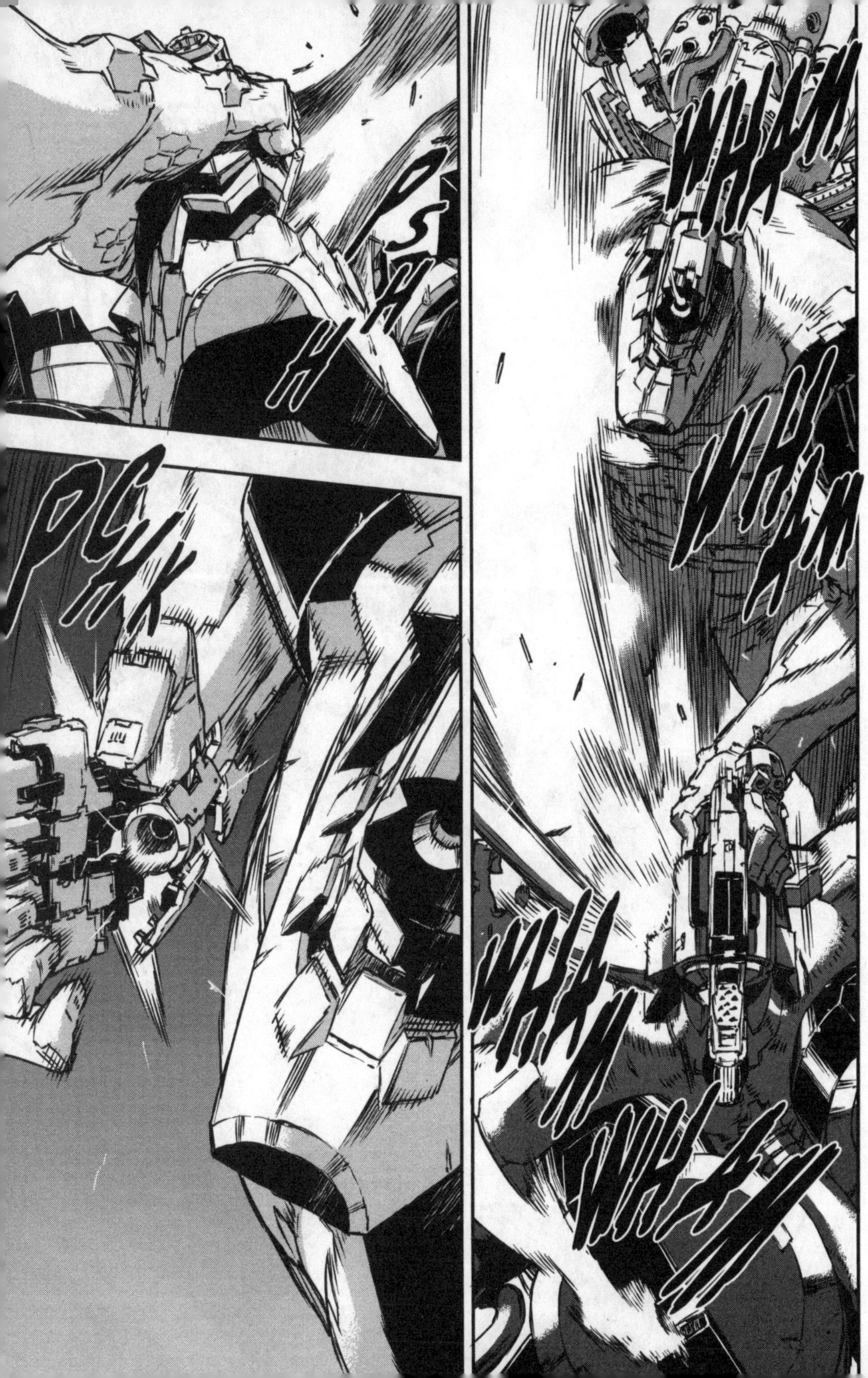
WHHUM
WHHUM
WHHUM
WHHUM
PSHHH
PCHK

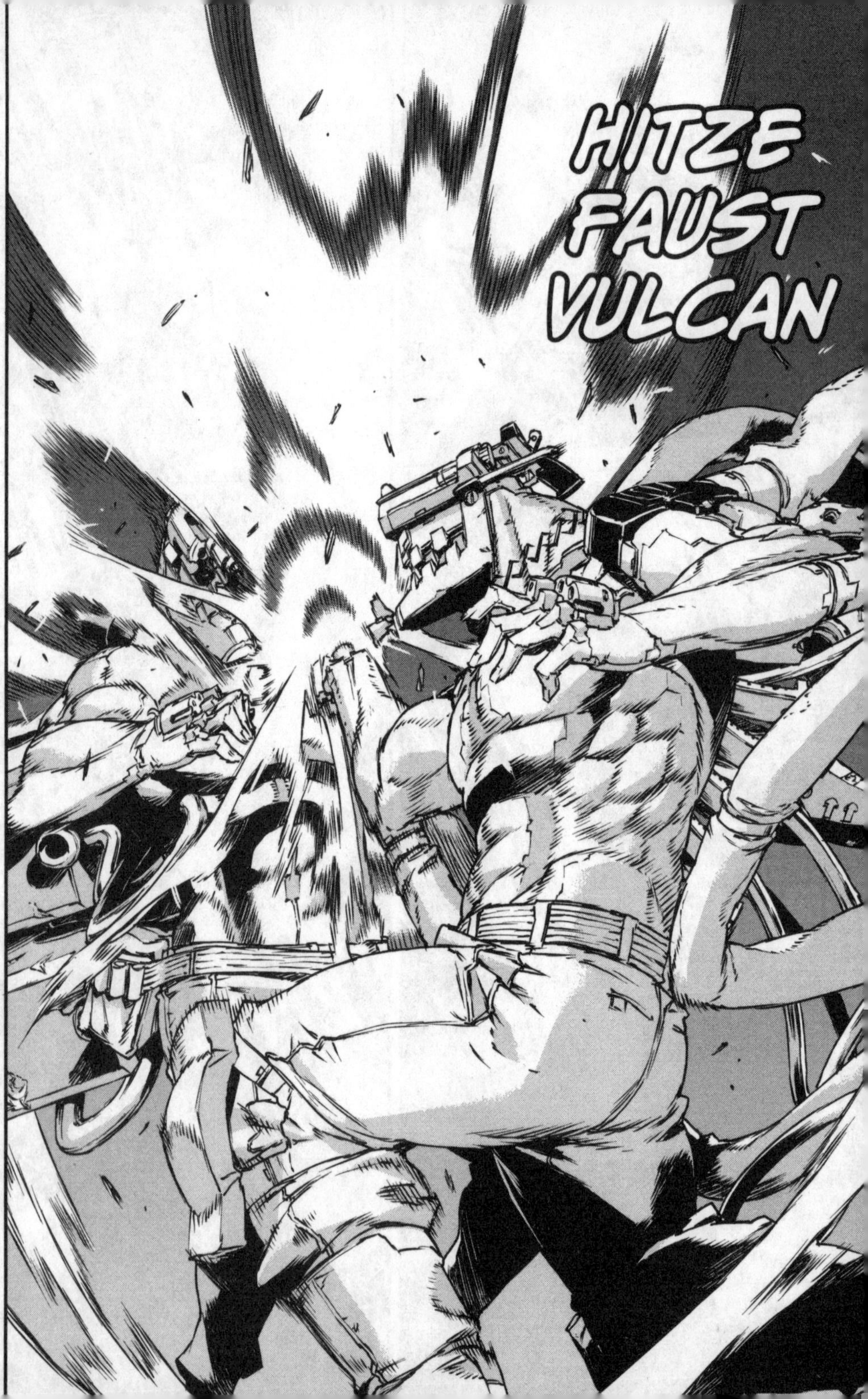
HITZE
FAUST
VULCAN

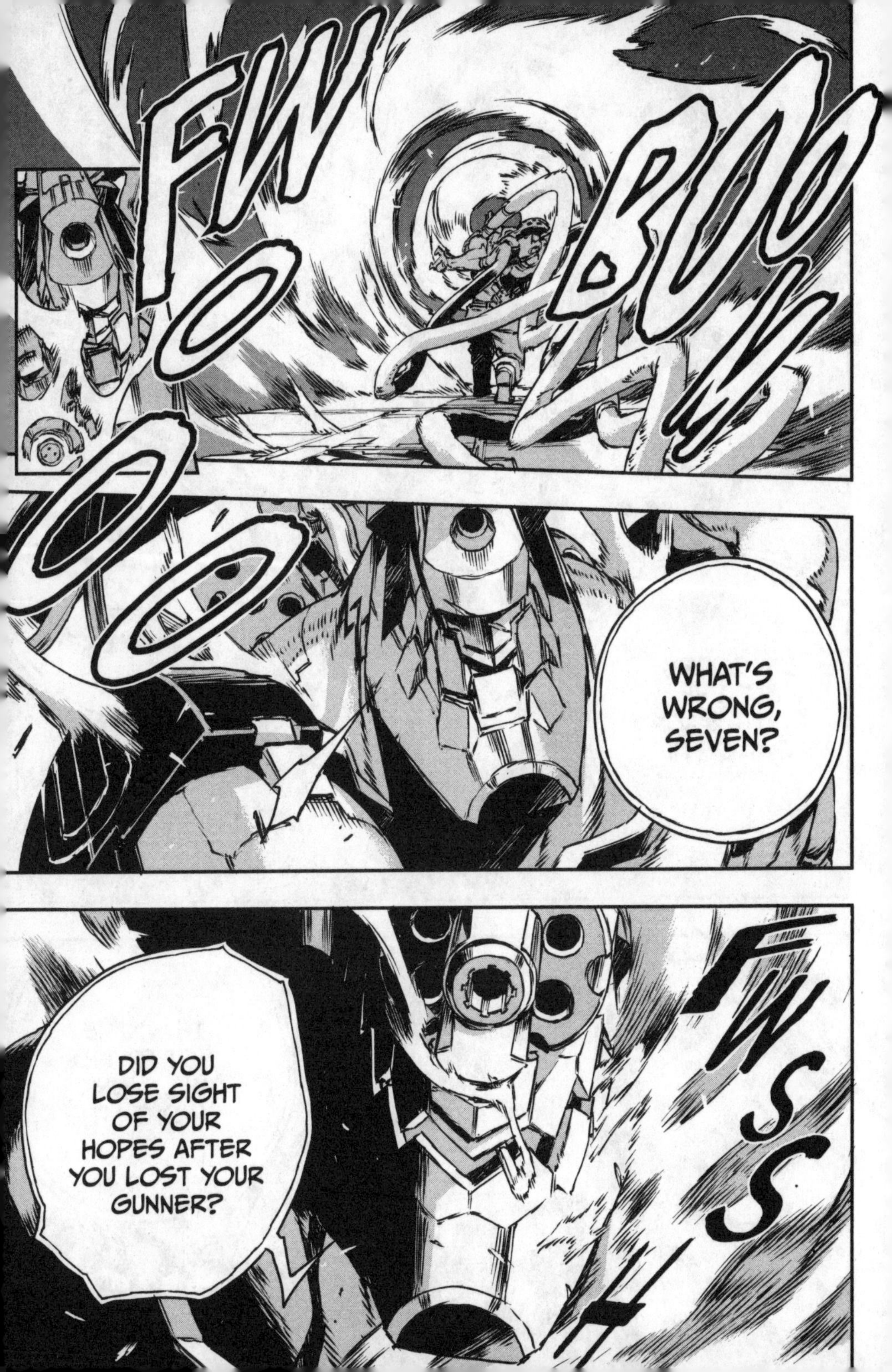
WHAT'S WRONG, SEVEN?
FWSSH
DID YOU LOSE SIGHT OF YOUR HOPES AFTER YOU LOST YOUR GUNNER?

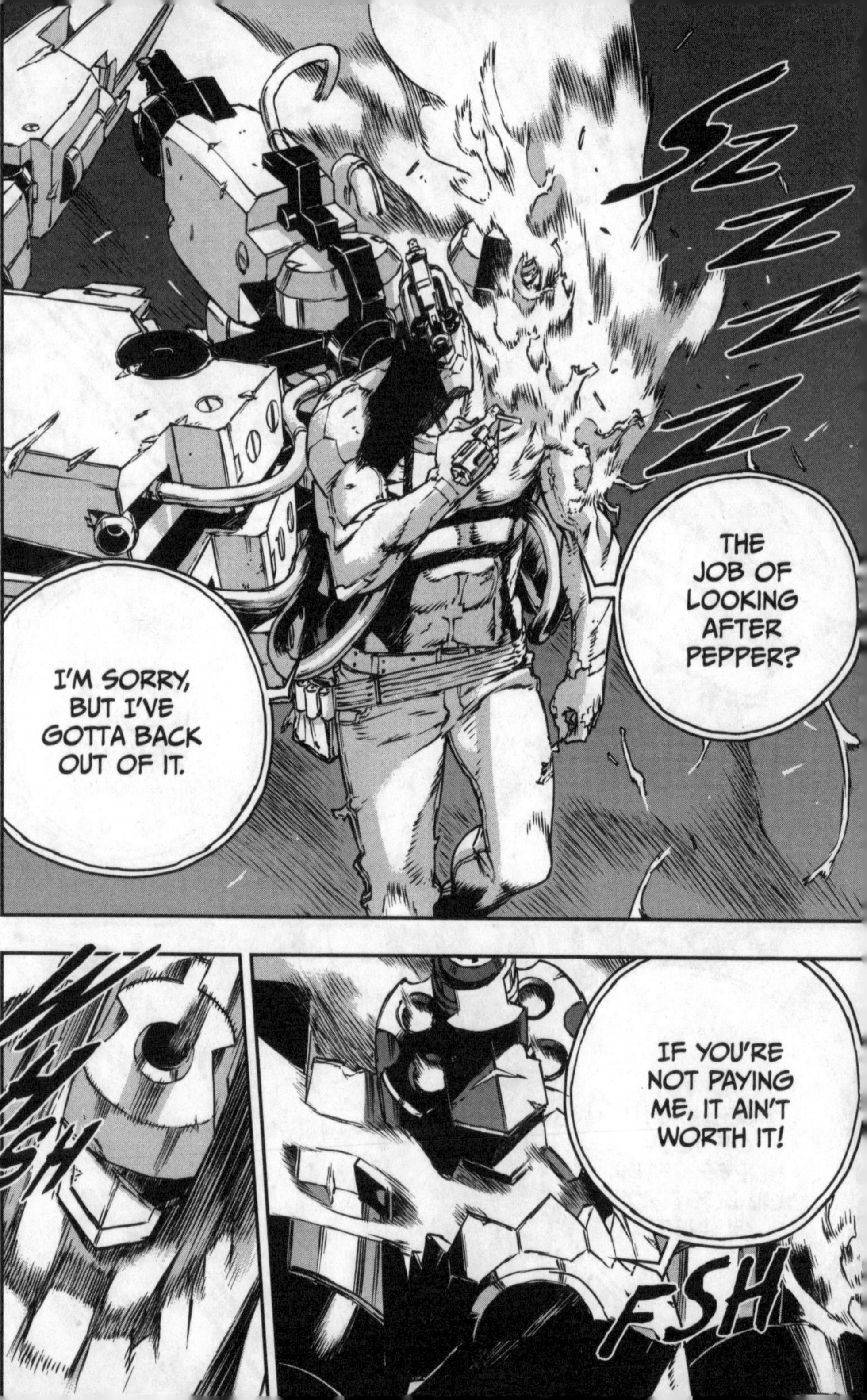
SZZZZZ
THE JOB OF LOOKING AFTER PEPPER?
I'M SORRY, BUT I'VE GOTTA BACK OUT OF IT.
IF YOU'RE NOT PAYING ME, IT AIN'T WORTH IT!
FSH
WHSH

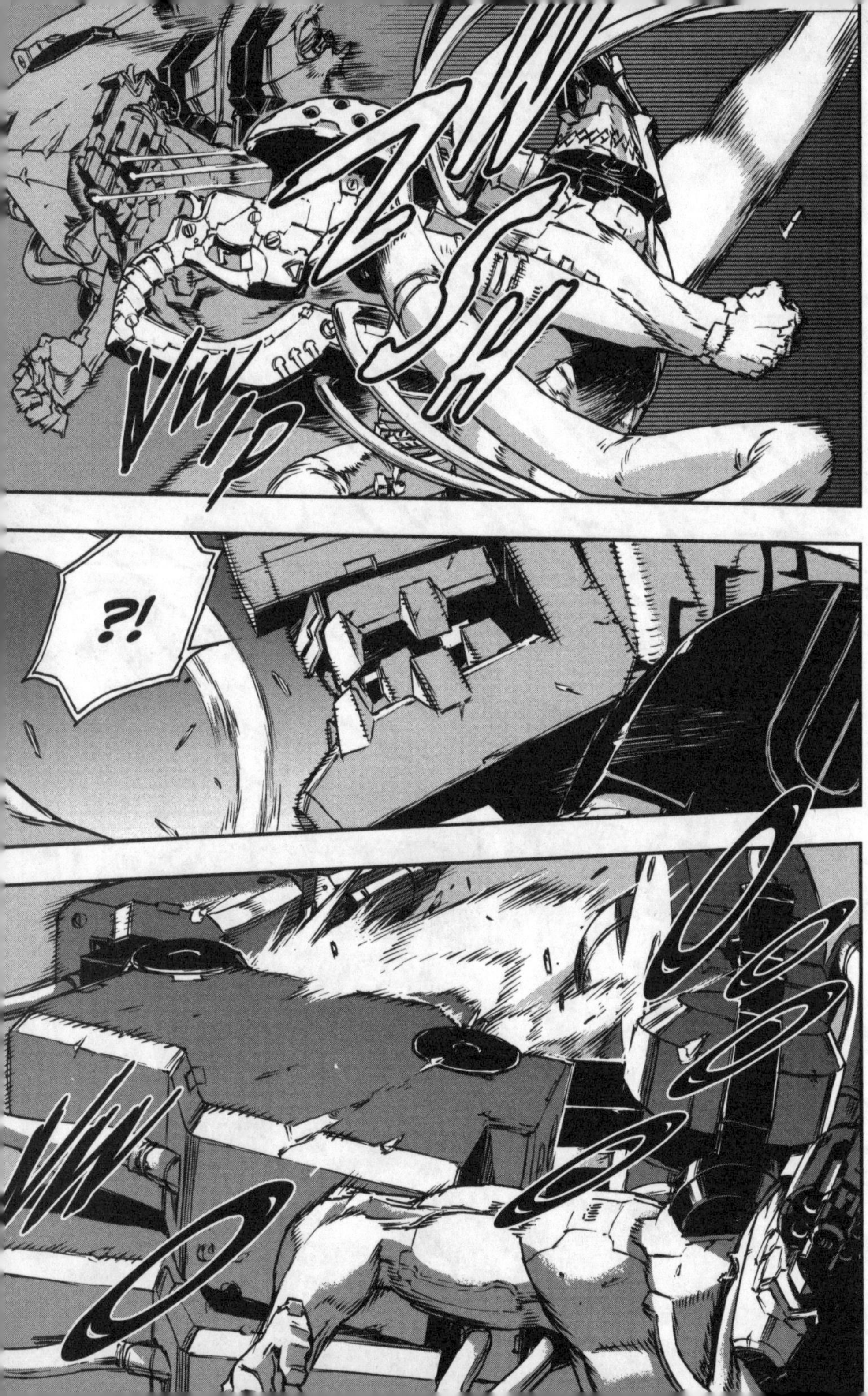
ZWSH
VWIP
?!

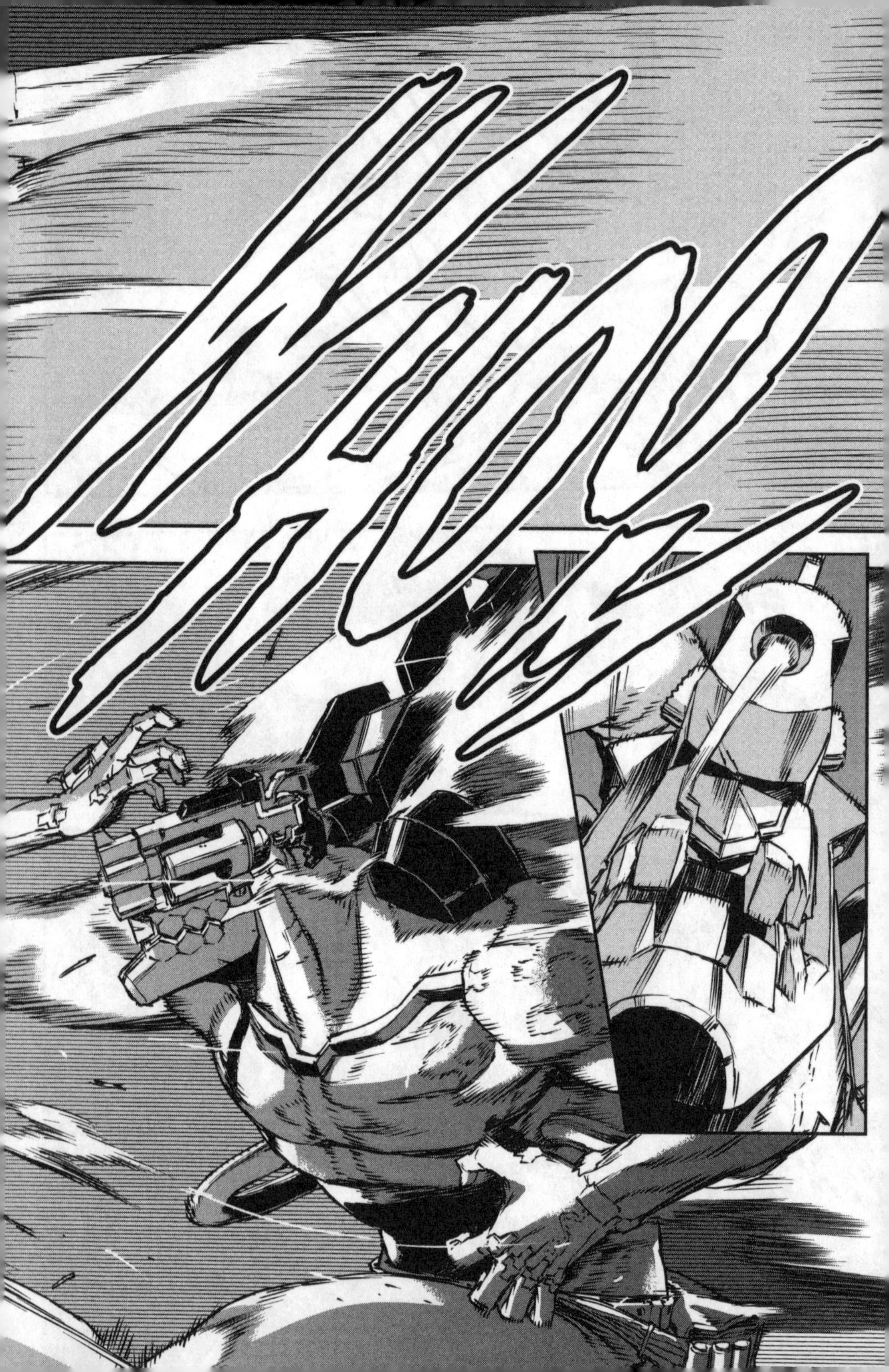

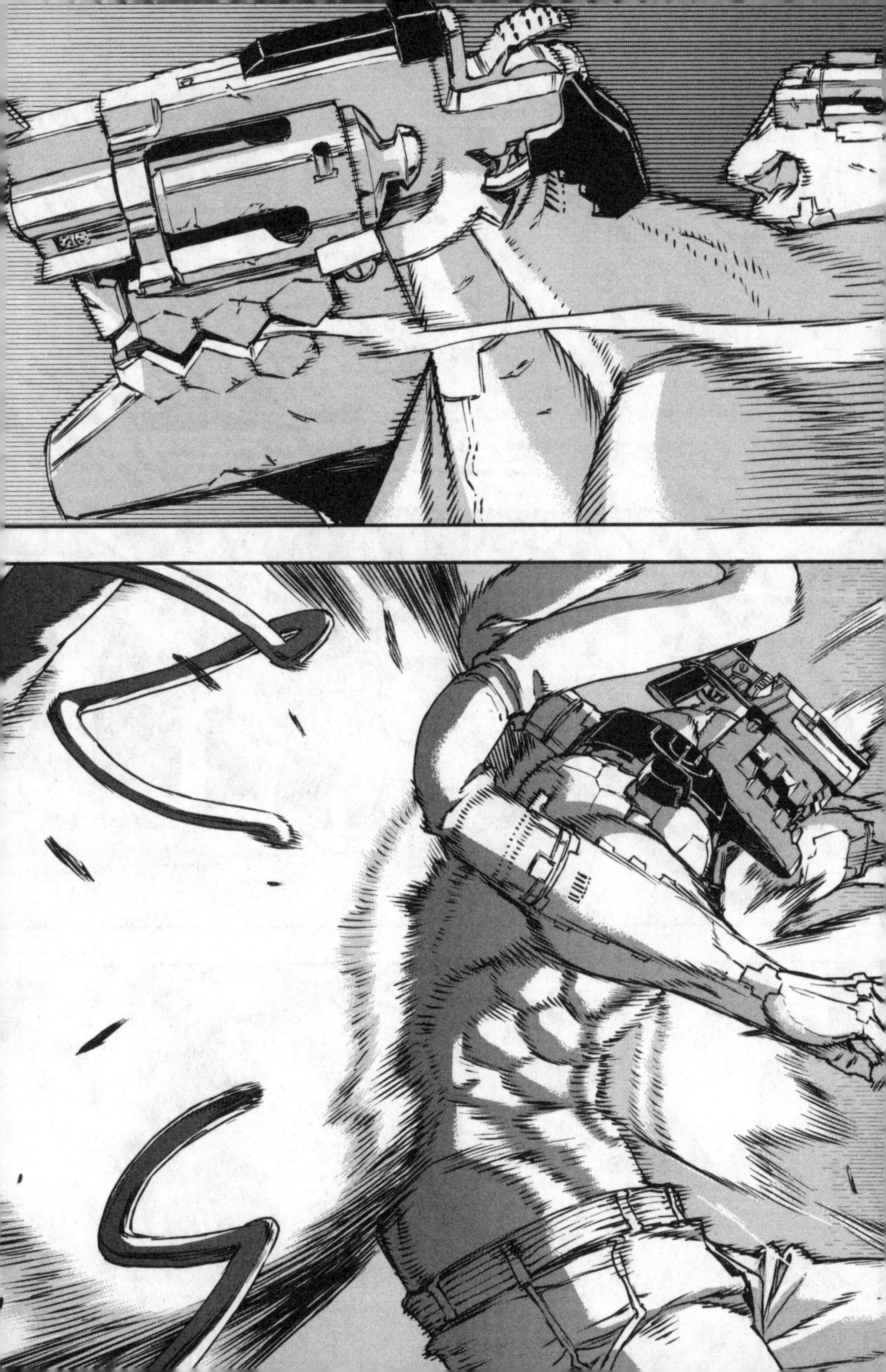

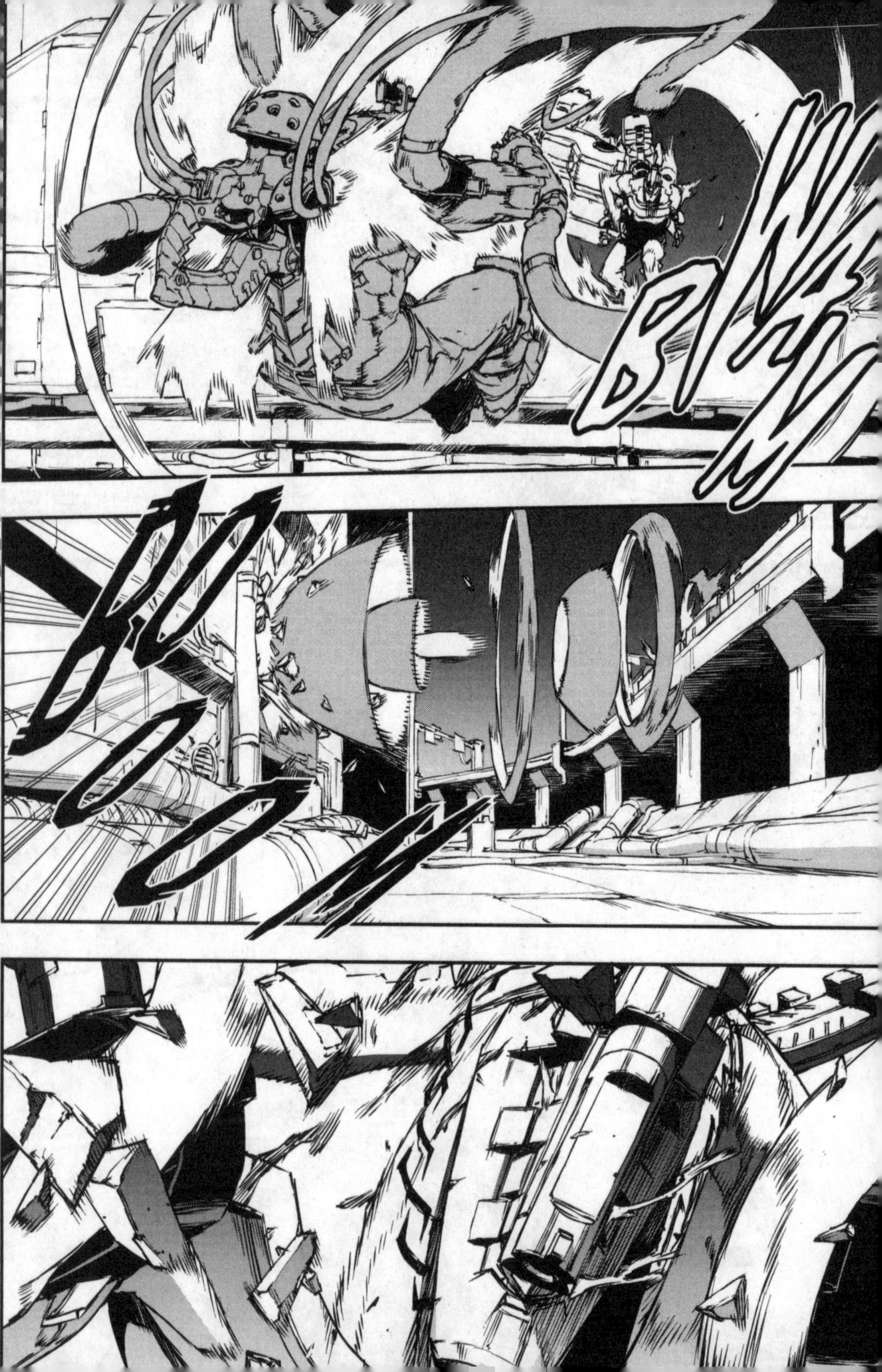
BOOM

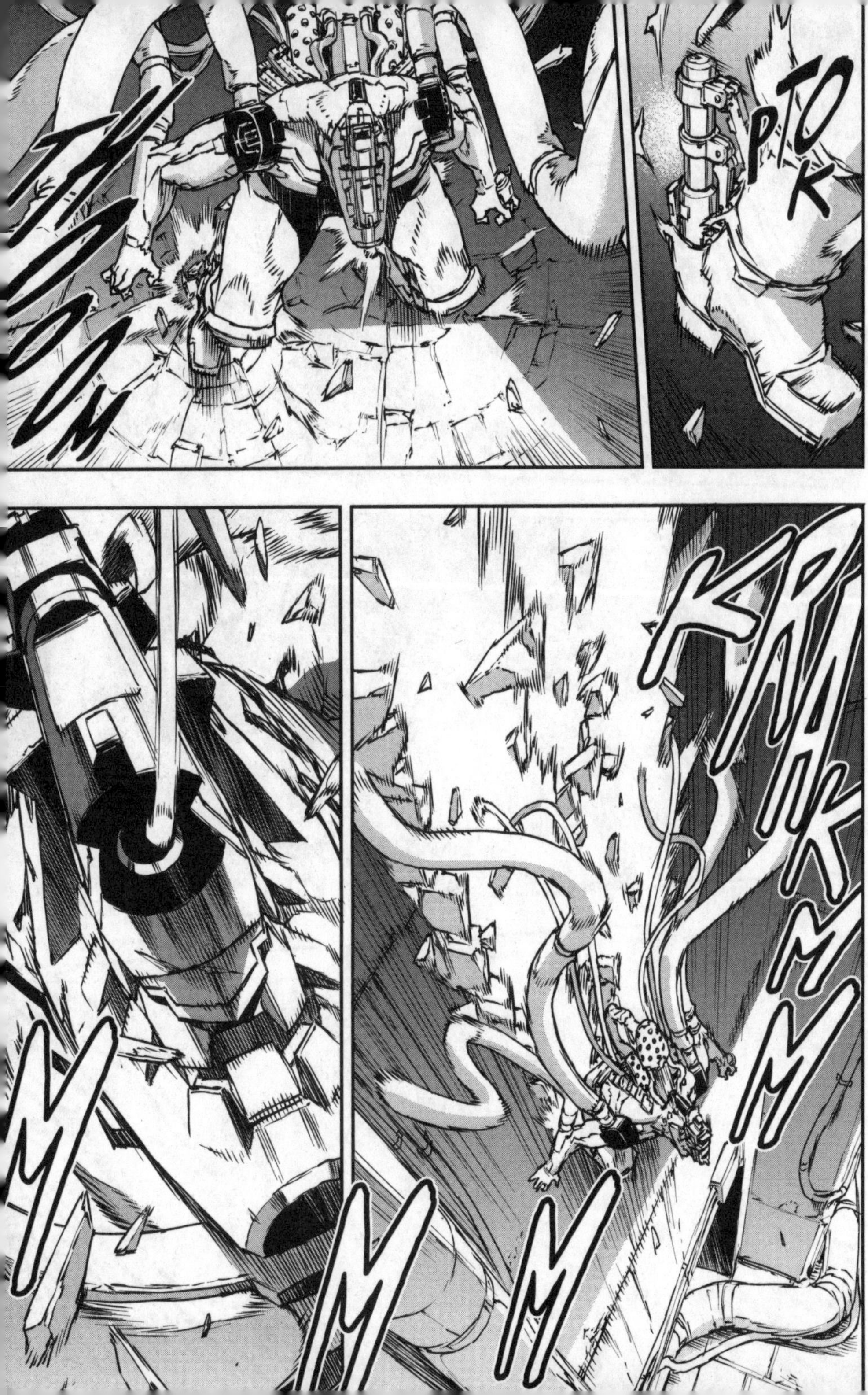
PTOK
THOOOM
KRAKKMMMMMM
MMM

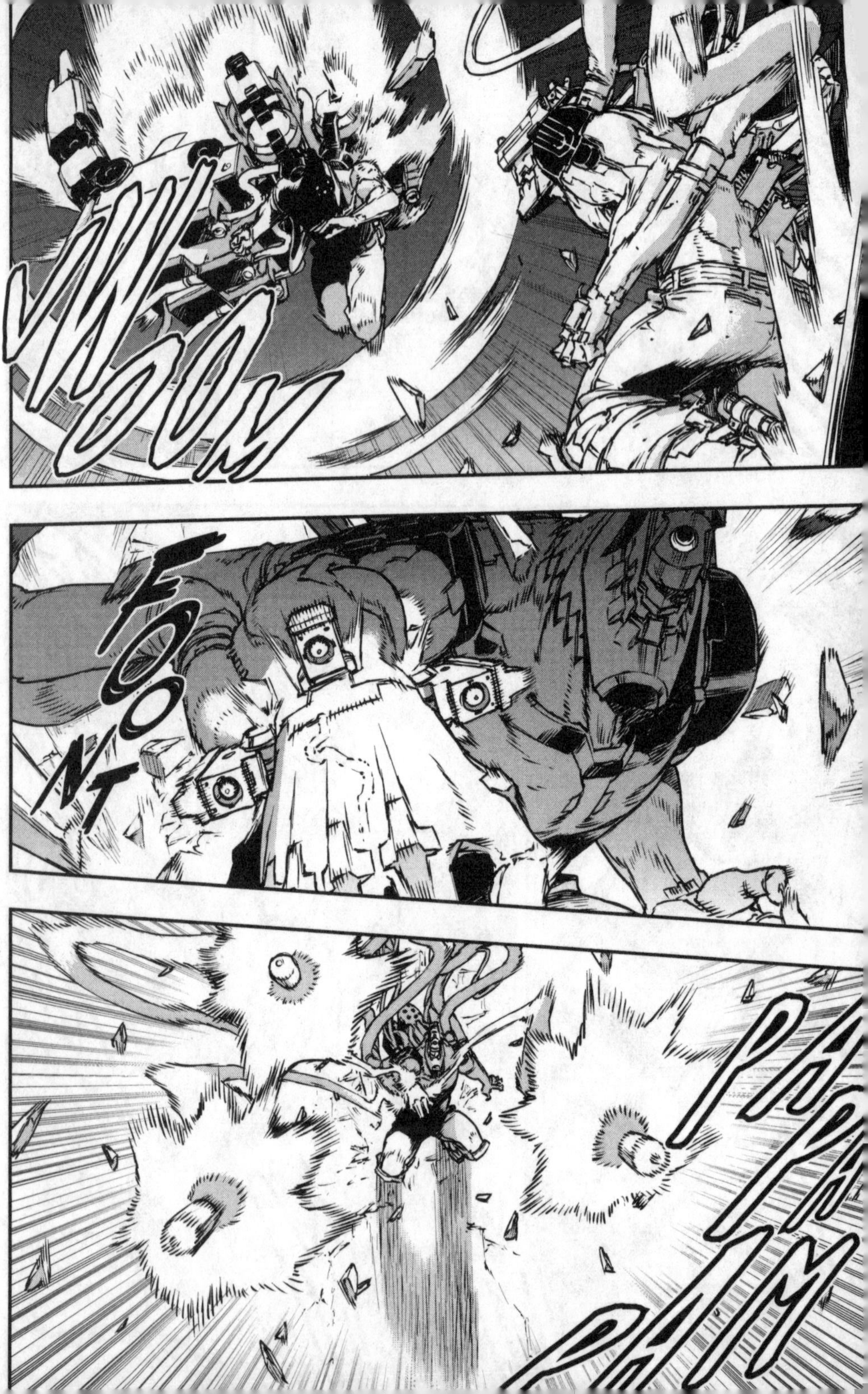
VWOOM
FOONT

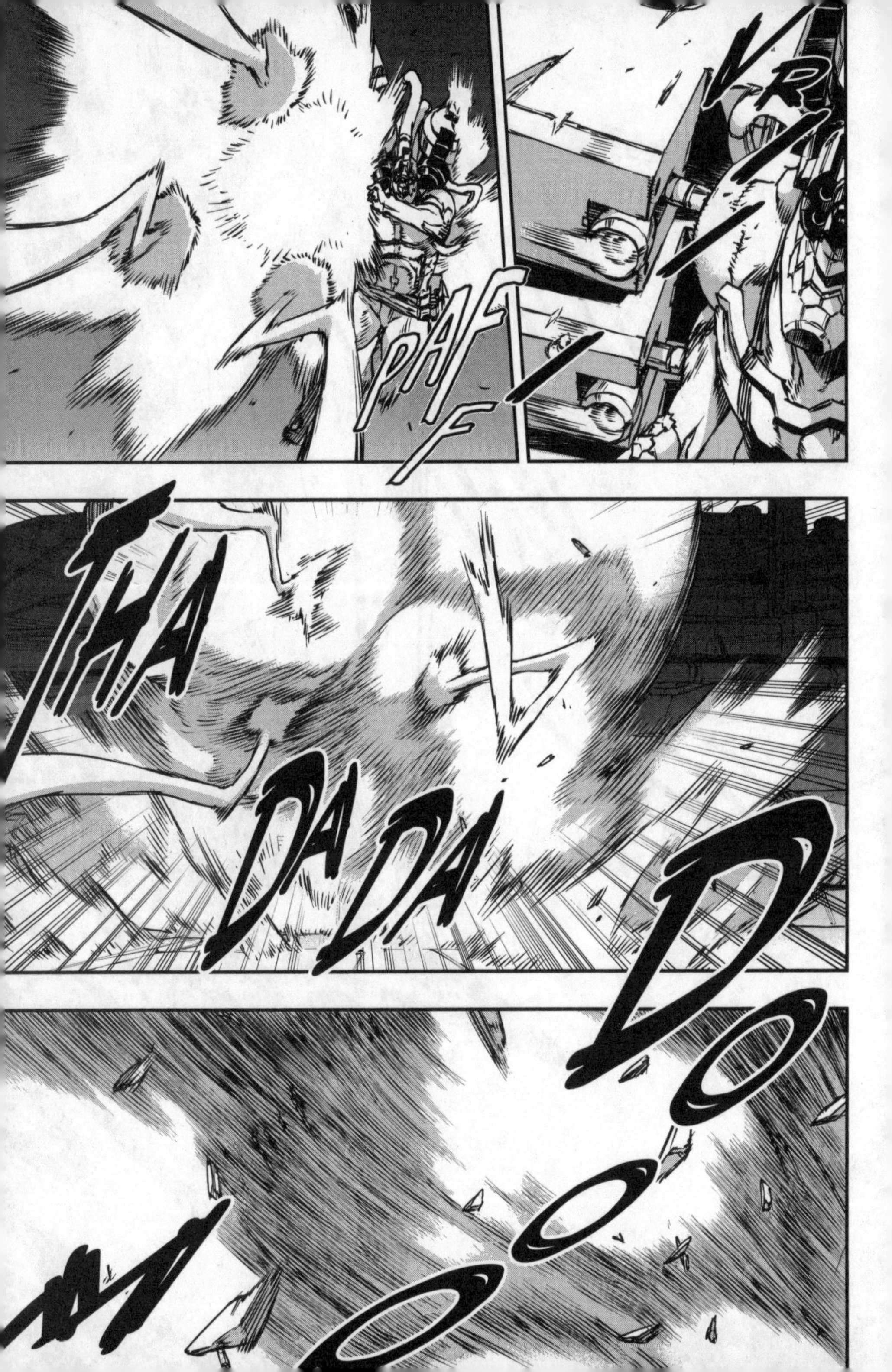
VR
PAFF
THA
DADA
DOOOO

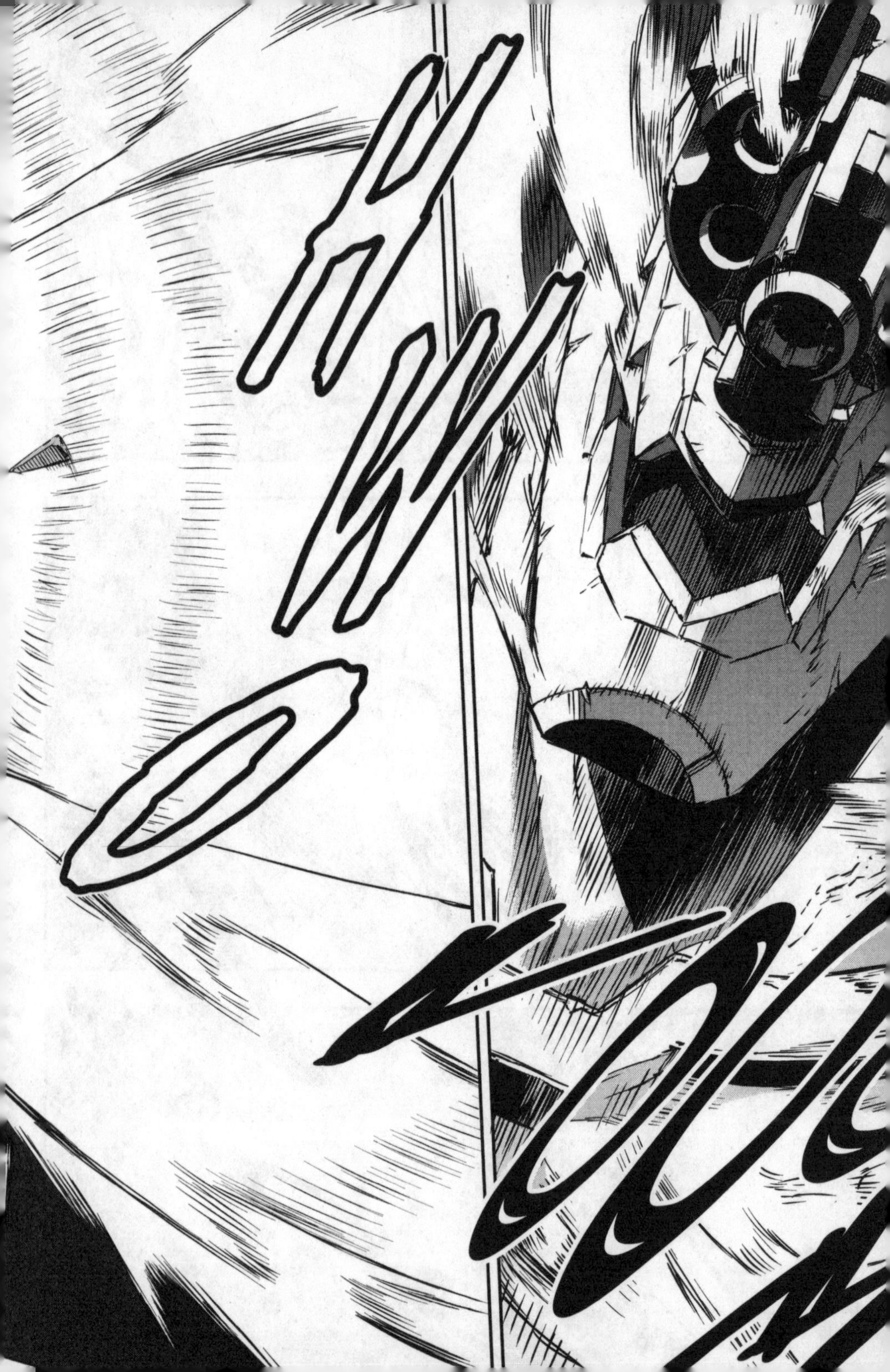

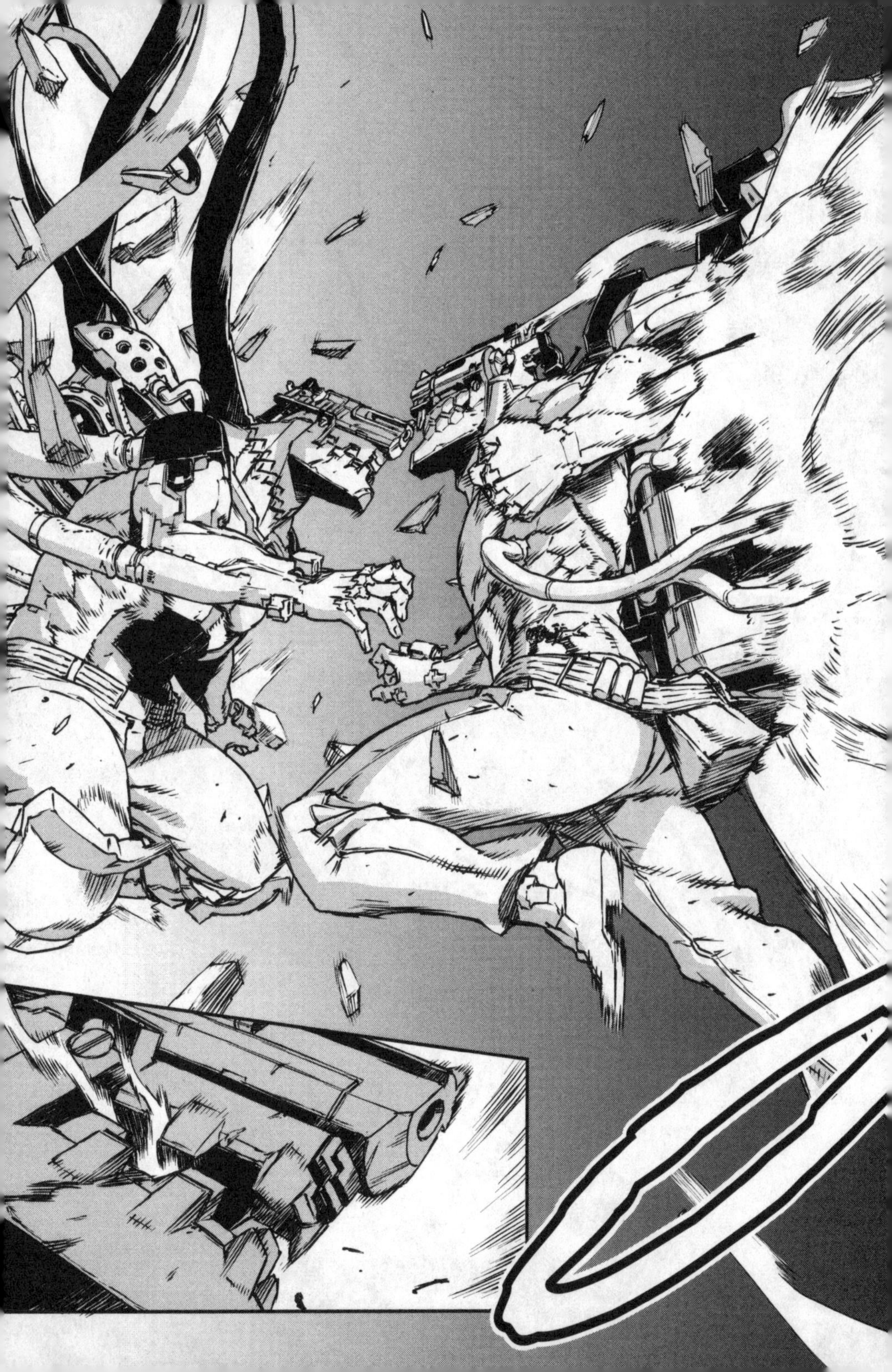

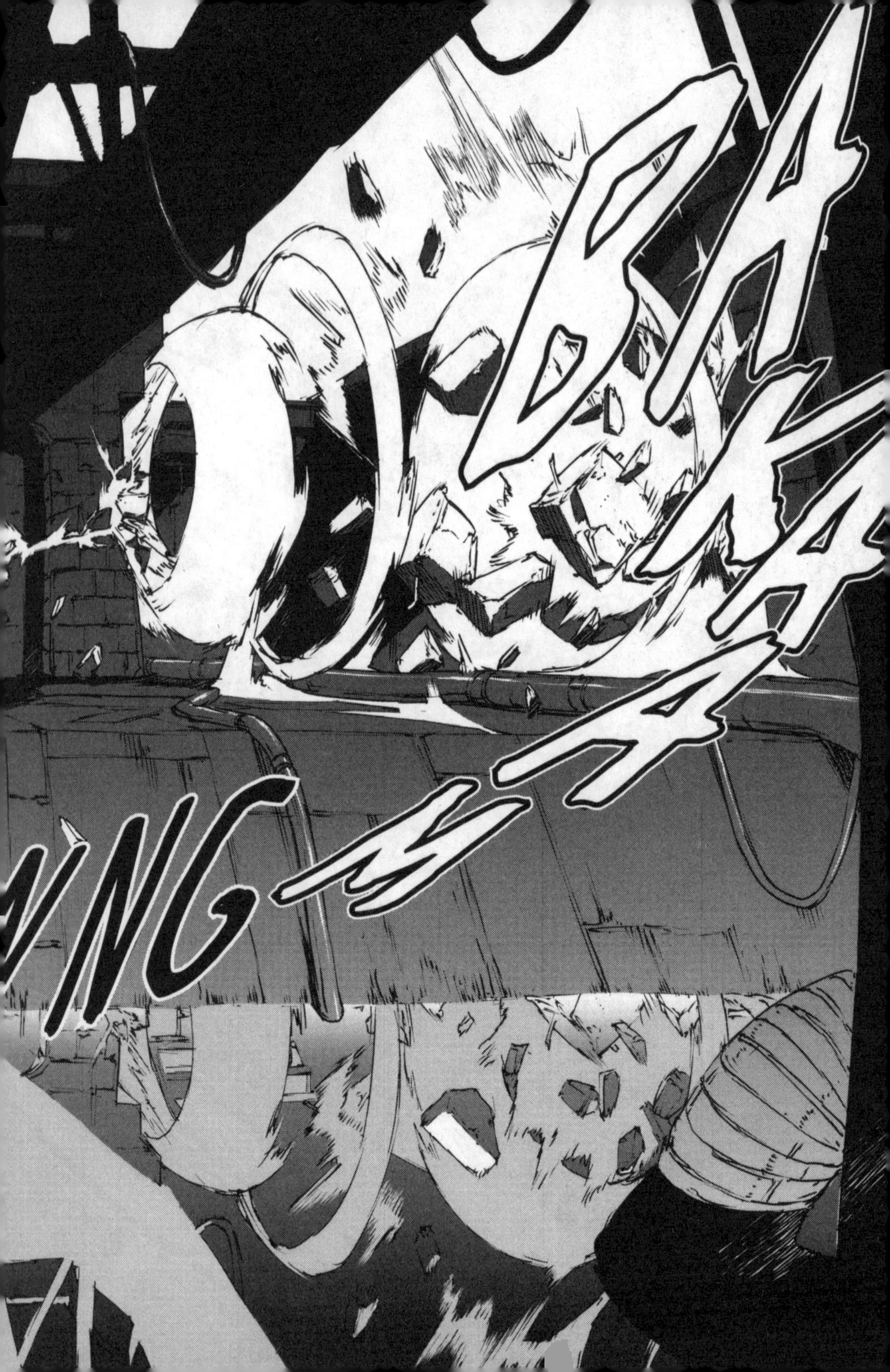

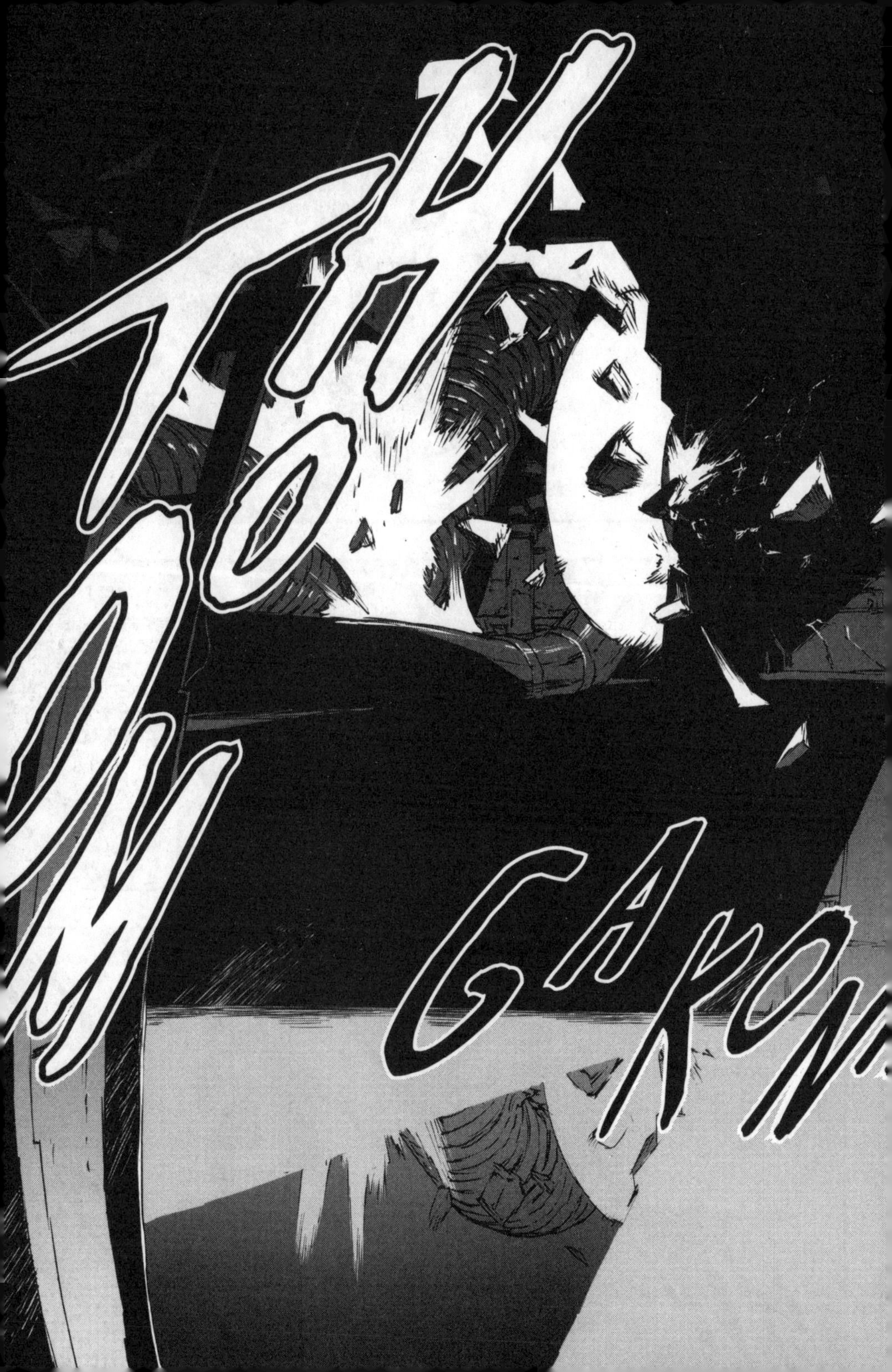
GAKON

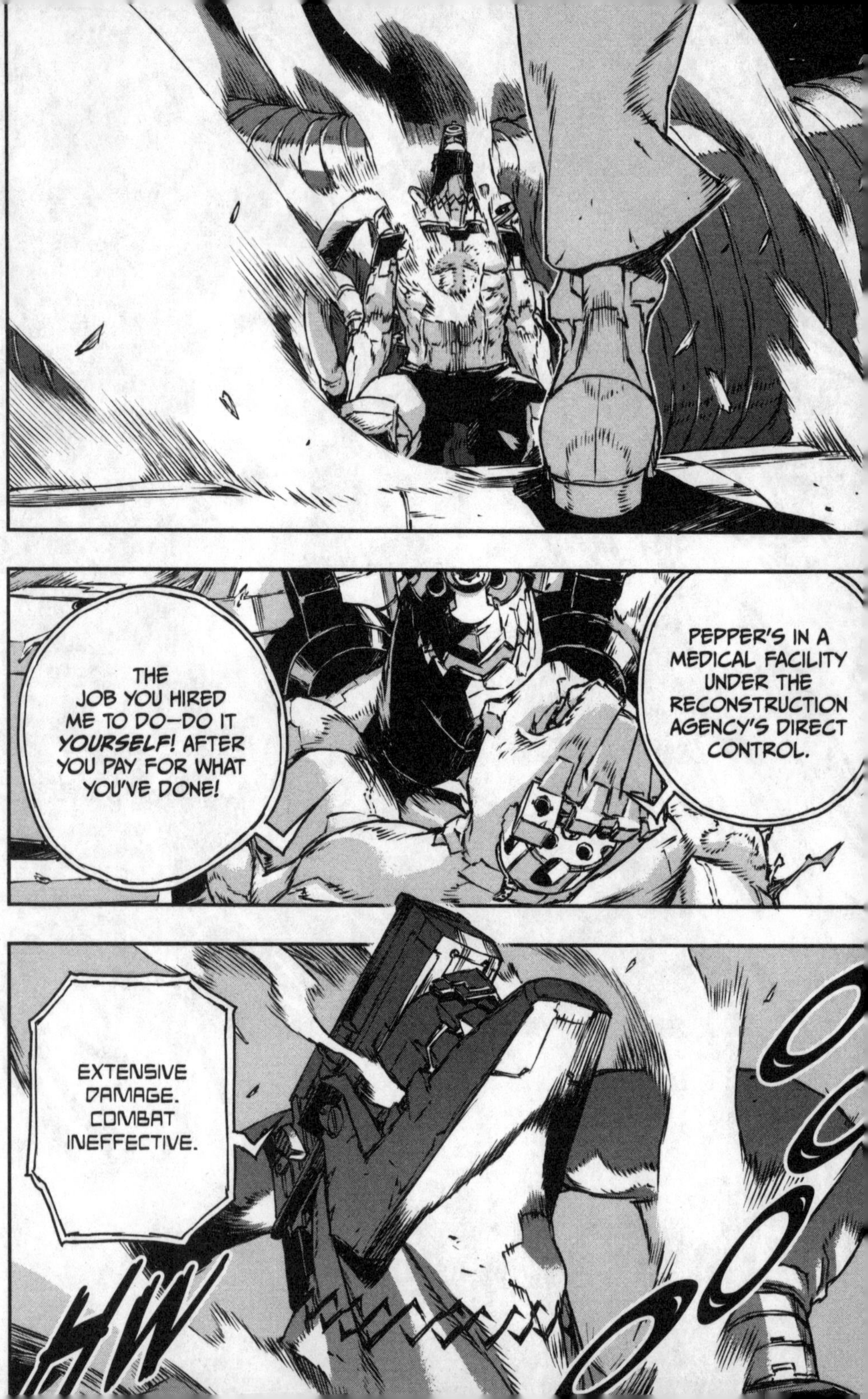
PEPPER'S IN A MEDICAL FACILITY UNDER THE RECONSTRUCTION AGENCY'S DIRECT CONTROL.
THE JOB YOU HIRED ME TO DO—DO IT *YOURSELF*! AFTER YOU PAY FOR WHAT YOU'VE DONE!
EXTENSIVE DAMAGE. COMBAT INEFFECTIVE.
KW

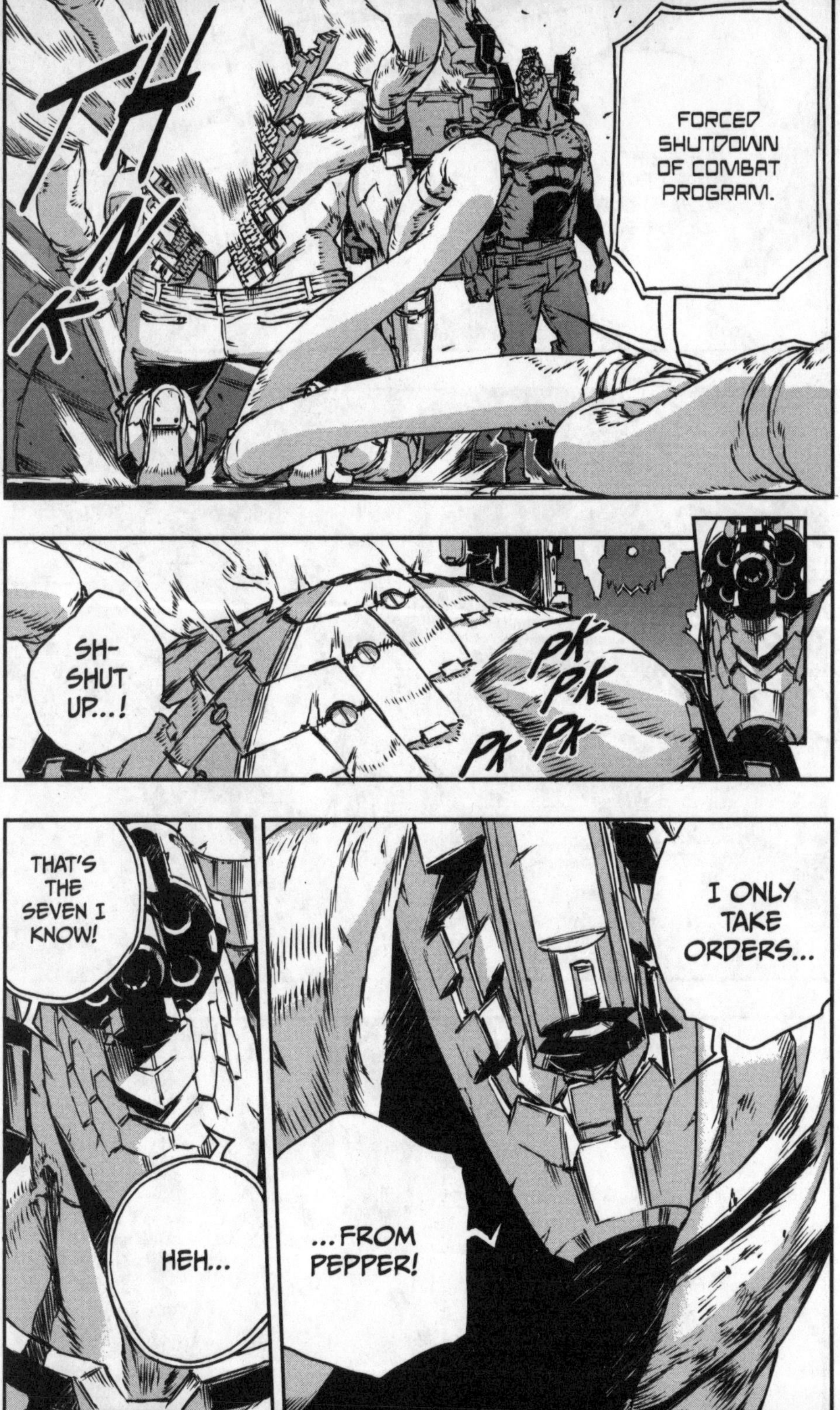
FORCED SHUTDOWN OF COMBAT PROGRAM.
THNK
PK PK PK PK
SH- SHUT UP...!
I ONLY TAKE ORDERS...
...FROM PEPPER!
THAT'S THE SEVEN I KNOW!
HEH...

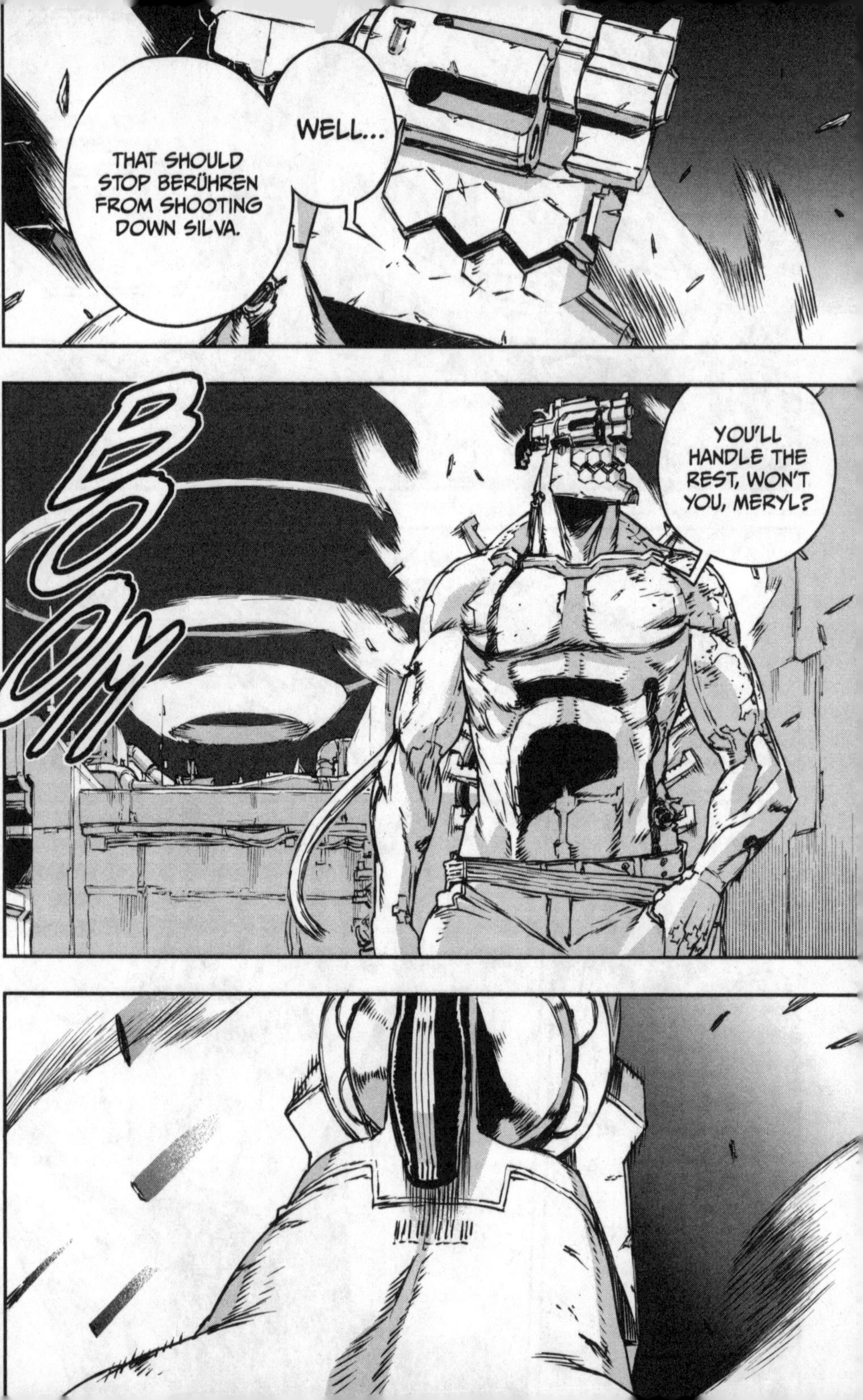
WELL...
THAT SHOULD STOP BERÜHREN FROM SHOOTING DOWN SILVA.
YOU'LL HANDLE THE REST, WON'T YOU, MERYL?
BOOM

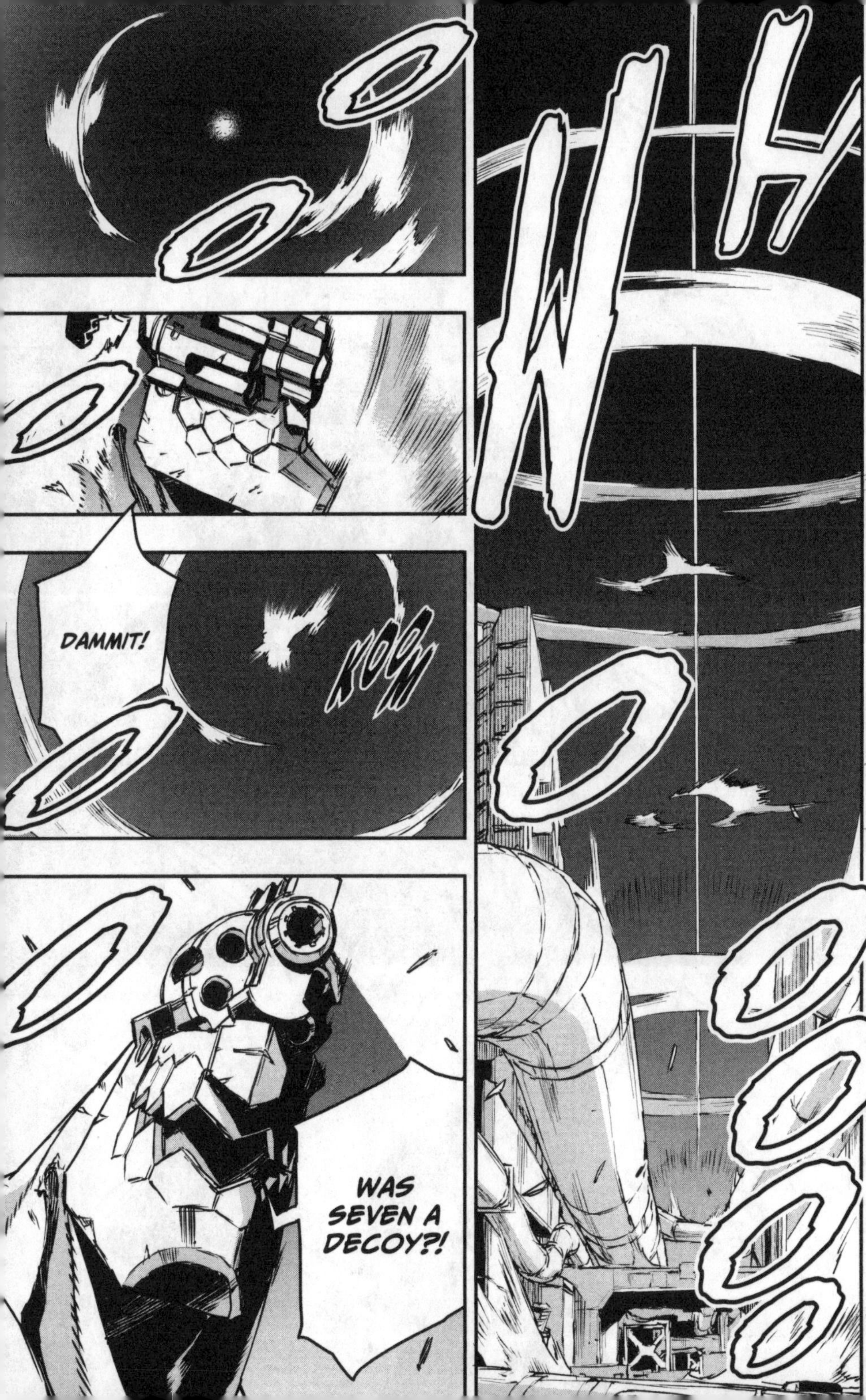
WHOOOOOO
OO
O
DAMMIT!
O
O
WAS SEVEN A DECOY?!

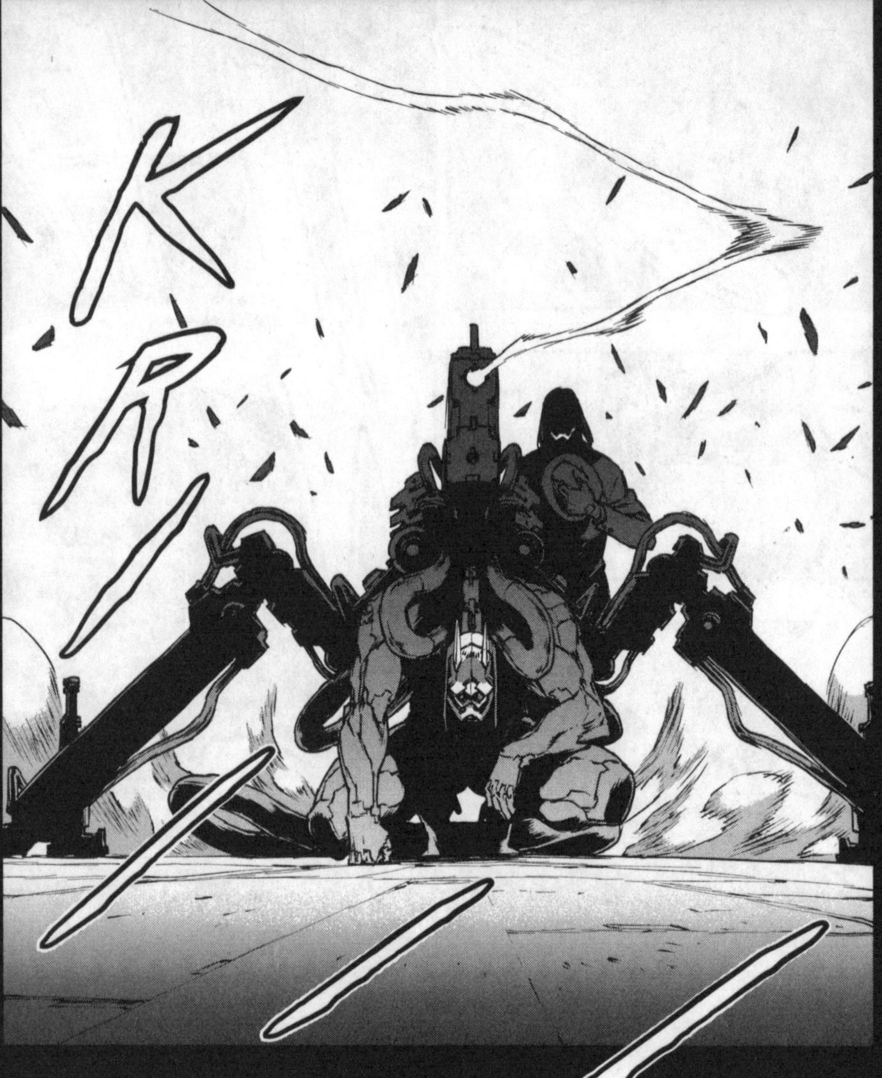
KRI

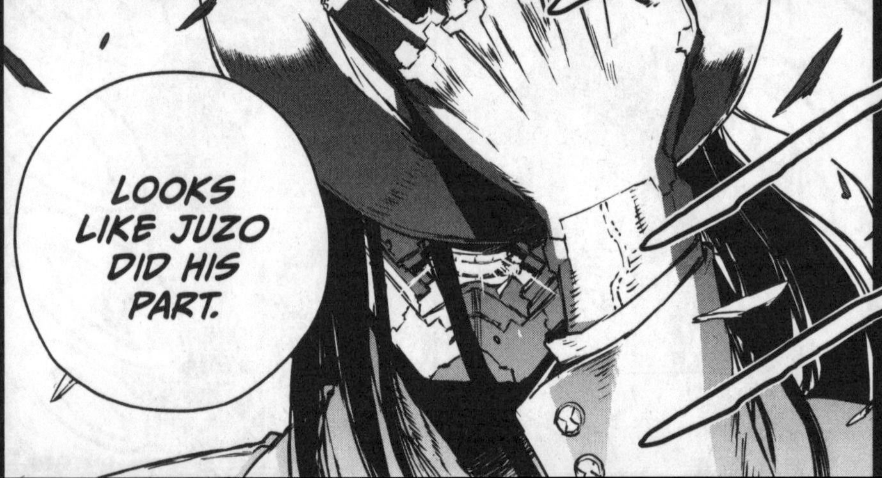
LOOKS LIKE JUZO DID HIS PART.

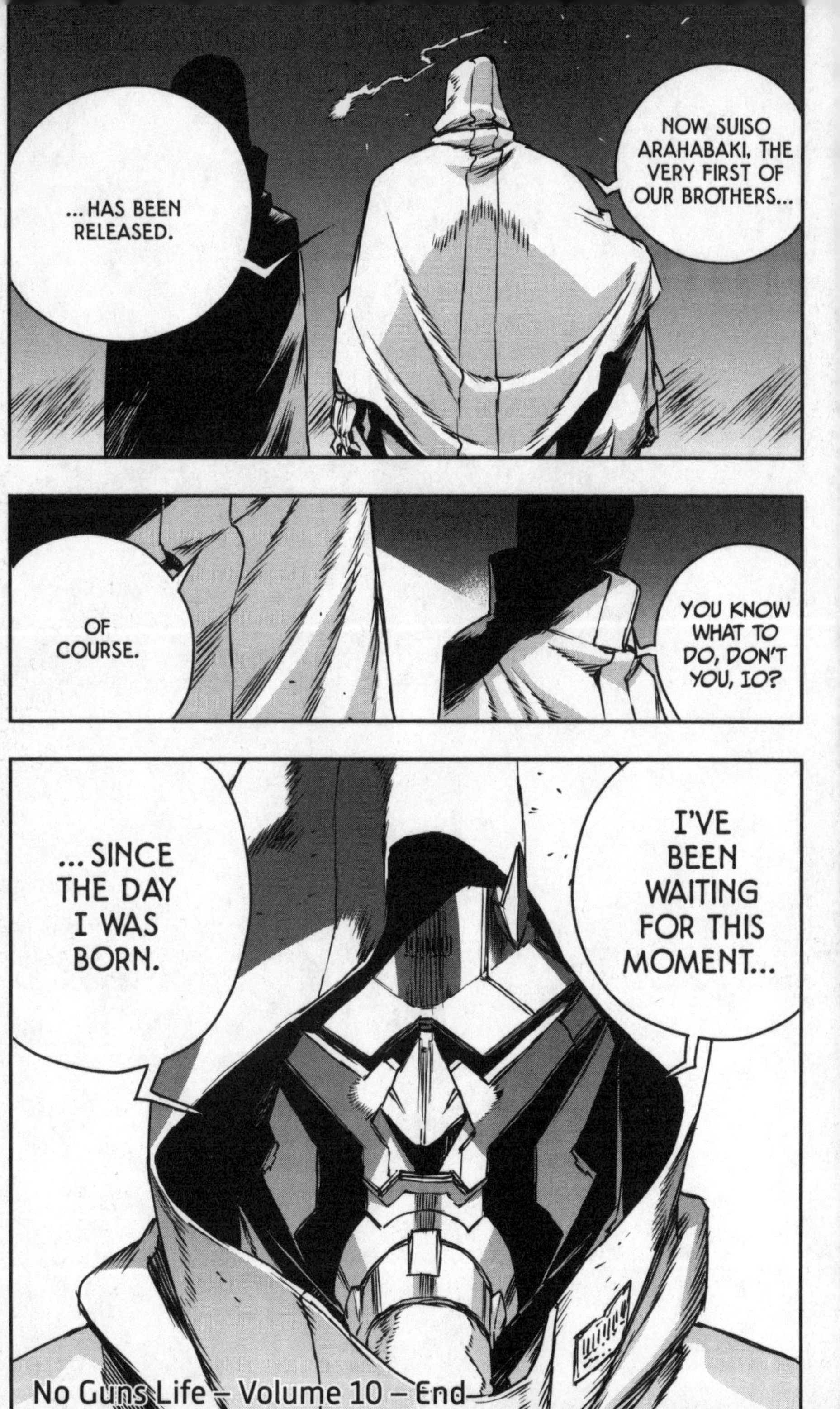
NOW SUISO ARAHABAKI, THE VERY FIRST OF OUR BROTHERS...
...HAS BEEN RELEASED.
YOU KNOW WHAT TO DO, DON'T YOU, IO?
OF COURSE.
I'VE BEEN WAITING FOR THIS MOMENT...
...SINCE THE DAY I WAS BORN.
No Guns Life – Volume 10 – End

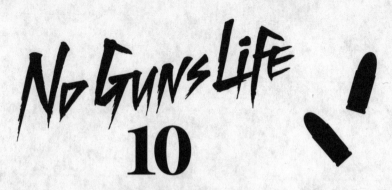

NO GUNS LIFE

10

STORY AND ART BY
TASUKU KARASUMA

VIZ SIGNATURE EDITION

TRANSLATION Joe Yamazaki
ENGLISH ADAPTATION Stan!
TOUCH-UP ART & LETTERING Evan Waldinger
DESIGN Shawn Carrico
EDITOR Mike Montesa

First published in Japan in 2014 by SHUEISHA Inc., Tokyo.
English translation rights arranged by SHUEISHA Inc.

Printed in Canada

Published by VIZ Media, LLC
P.O. Box 77010
San Francisco, CA 94107

10 9 8 7 6 5 4 3 2 1
First printing, May 2021

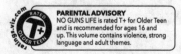

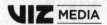

VIZ MEDIA VIZ SIGNATURE

viz.com vizsignature.com

YOU'RE
READING THE
WRONG WAY.

NO GUNS LIFE is printed from right to left
in the original Japanese format in order to
present the art as it was meant to be seen.